MASS COMMUNICATIONS RESEARCH RESOURCES

An Annotated Guide

LEA's COMMUNICATION SERIES
Jennings Bryant/Dolf Zillmann, General Editors

Selected titles in Mass Communication (Alan Rubin, Advisory Editor) include:

Harris • A Cognitive Psychology of Mass Communication, Second Edition

Moore • Mass Communication Law and Ethics

Moore/Farrar/Collins • Advertising and Public Relations Law

Sterling/Bracken/Hill • Mass Communication Research Resources: An Annotated Guide

Van Evra • Television and Children, Second Edition

Warner • Media Management Review

For a complete list of other titles in LEA's Communication Series, please contact Lawrence Erlbaum Associates, Publishers.

MASS COMMUNICATIONS RESEARCH RESOURCES

An Annotated Guide

Edited by
Christopher H. Sterling
The George Washington University

James K. Bracken
The Ohio State University

and
Susan M. Hill
National Association of Broadcasters

With contributions from:
Louise Benjamin, Pamela Czapla,
Harry Sova, and Frances G. Wilhoit

LEA LAWRENCE ERLBAUM ASSOCIATES, PUBLISHERS
1998 Mahwah, New Jersey London

The final camera copy for this work was prepared by the author, and therefore the publisher takes no responsibility for consistency or correctness of typographical style. However, this arrangement helps to make publication of this kind of scholarship possible.

Lawrence Erlbaum Associates, Inc., Publishers
10 Industrial Avenue
Mahwah, NJ 07430

Cover design by Jennifer Sterling

Library of Congress Cataloging-in-Publication Data

Mass communications research resources : an annotated guide / edited by Christopher H. Sterling, James K. Bracken, and Susan M. Hill : with contributions from Louise Benjamin . . . [et al.].
p. cm.
Includes bibliographical references and index
ISBN 0-8058-2024-8 (alk. paper)
1. Communication—Bibliography. 2. Mass media—Bibliography. I. Sterling, Christopher H., 1943- . II. Bracken, James K., 1952- . III. Hill, Susan M., IV. Series : Communications (Mahwah, N.J.)
Z7164.T28M37 1997
[HE7631]
016.384—dc21 97-28441
CIP

Books published by Lawrence Erlbaum Associates are printed on acid-free paper, and their bindings are chosen for strength and durability.

Printed in the United States of America
10 9 8 7 6 5 4 3 2 1

Contents

Introduction

In the past two decades, the amount of material published about American mass communications has expanded so dramatically that only computerized databases and online services can adequately keep up with the flow. Yet we feel a continuing need for an easily used printed guide to the massive accumulation of resources on these pervasive industries.

This book is designed as a road map for researchers who need to find specific information as expeditiously as possible. The model for this book is a volume published two decades ago—the ASPEN HANDBOOK ON THE MEDIA. In our book, however, we have taken a topical approach, integrating publications and organizations into subject-focused chapters for easier user reference. This volume parallels Bracken and Sterling's earlier TELECOMMUNICATIONS RESEARCH RESOURCES: AN ANNOTATED GUIDE (1995).

What This Book Covers...

We define mass communications to include print journalism and electronic media and the processes by which they communicate messages to their audiences. Included are newspapers, magazines, radio, television, cable, and newer electronic services. Within that definition, this volume offers an indexed inventory of over 1,400 resources on most aspects of American mass communications history, technology, economics, content, audience research, policy, and regulation. We focus primarily on the domestic American print and electronic media industries, although chapter 8 details the more important international publications.

While we make no claim to a complete census of all materials on print journalism and electronic media—what is available is now too vast for any single handy guide—the most important and useful items *are* here as a good indication of what is available. Our emphasis is on material published since 1980, although selected useful older resources are included as well, especially in chapter 2.

Each chapter is designed to stand alone, providing the most important and useful resources of a primary nature (organizations and documents) as well as secondary books and reports. Where possible, we have included online resources and Internet citations.

...and What it Does Not

In part to maintain a workable size to this volume, several important exclusions should be noted. Generally, we do not include the following *topics*—most of which fall outside a print-journalism and electronic-media definition: books, book publishing, and all forms of comics; popular culture (but see 0099) and popular music; motion pictures; public relations and advertising (although titles concerned with advertising in either print or electronic media *are* included); or nonmedia telecommunications (which are covered in a companion volume by two of the editors).

We also exclude certain *types* of publications, largely because of limited space: specific Congressional hearings (but see 0904 for one guide to the genre); foreign media systems; books not in English; "how-to" guides on media production or writing; and studies of individual actors, actresses, stations, newspapers, or magazines (although guides included here provide some access to that material).

Although our focus throughout is on primary research resources, we indicate some of the best secondary material as well. The amount of secondary material available on all aspects of mass communications is immense, however. Our chapter sections annotating secondary books can only suggest the total body of material available; they are designed to emphasize both important classic titles and the best recent work. They are by *no* means inclusive, nor could they be within the scope of a volume designed to survey research resources. Thus, although listings of bibliographies and other research references are as inclusive as possible, vast numbers of popular works are largely excluded.

Entries, Annotations, and Arrangement

In general, entries for published works cite author(s), title and subtitle, place of publication, publisher, publication year(s), edition, and inclusive pagination. Entries for organizations and other entities give the organization's name, main address, telephone and fax numbers and (where available), Internet or World Wide Web (WWW) addresses (excluding "http://" in each case to save space). Annotations generally identify former titles and organization names. In particular, entries for reference works also indicate availability and coverage of electronic versions as well as particularly relevant sections or subject headings. In general, organizational entries indicate useful journals or other publications as well as guides or finding aids for resources issued by or about the organizations. Entries for secondary works note the inclusion of bibliographies, appendices, and indexes.

Annotations are indicative of an organization's or resource's focus or content rather than an exhaustive inventory of specific details. Additionally, comments are intended to place an organization or a work in the context of American mass communications or in the context of the research literature. Annotations aim at objectivity; on the other hand, given that inclusion is limited by selectivity, we admit that we feel that everything included is at least important and in many cases essential.

As the detailed table of contents makes clear, this volume is arranged in topical order to facilitate finding sources on related subjects. Each chapter begins with the basic reference literature—book-length bibliographies, indexes and abstracting services, directories, yearbooks, dictionaries, and the like. Each chapter concludes with a brief survey of the more valuable secondary sources (chiefly books) useful for background or a broad introduction. These lists focus on titles published within the past decade, with a scattering of classic and still useful older titles.

Individual titles or organizations appear but once, although we make use of extensive cross-reference by entry number. We have provided appendices that detail the Dewey Decimal and Library of Congress classification systems for mass communications and Library of Congress subject headings related to mass communications and mass media.

We warn readers that our references to online/electronic (WWW and CD-ROM) reference works must be used with care given the rapid changes affecting electronic publishing. What was available from one vendor last year may belong to another vendor now. With many vendors establishing a presence on the web, users may be able to initially search there as opposed to subscribing to the database via the vendor.

Keeping Current

Any published bibliographic guide is dated before it is published. Given the pace of publication of new resources and revised standards, we strongly recommend the review columns of the periodicals listed in chapter 9 for descriptions of new publications on print and electronic mass communications. See especially COMMUNICATION BOOKNOTES QUARTERLY (0004).

Acknowledgements

The media industries covered in this book—and their literatures—are now so huge and varied that without the help of our board of editors we could not have undertaken the project. It is no longer possible for any one or two persons to have adequate current bibliographic grasp of such scope. We therefore were pleased when the following people, all occupying key positions at important research centers, agreed to help us identify and describe many of the resources listed here. Each of them provided at least two rounds of extensive input and helped to review the final product. The value of this book is increased by their willing (and constant) participation:

Louise Benjamin, associate director of the George Peabody Awards program at the University of Georgia at Athens. Dr. Benjamin is largely responsible for chapter 10 on video and audio resources.

Pamela Czapla, director of the library program, National Cable Television Center, Pennsylvania State University at University Park. Dr. Czapla helped to identify the many resources on cable and related services that appear throughout the book.

Harry Sova, president of Blue Ridge Interactive, Virginia Beach, VA. Dr. Sova brought his unparalleled knowledge of media periodicals to bear in chapter 9.

Frances Goins Wilhoit, librarian for the Ernie Pyle School of Journalism and Mass Communication of Indiana University at Bloomington. Ms. Wilhoit has provided many of the journalism resources included herein.

About the Editors

Christopher H. Sterling is associate dean for graduate affairs in Columbian School of Arts and Sciences at George Washington University. He is also a professor of media and public affairs, and of telecommunications, having served on the GWU faculty since 1982. Author, editor, or co-author of more than a dozen books including both references and texts on electronic media and telecommunications subjects, Sterling edited and published COMMUNICATION BOOKNOTES from 1969 though 1997 and continues to edit COMMUNICATION BOOKNOTES QUARTERLY (0004). He holds a PhD in communication from the University of Wisconsin, Madison.

James K. Bracken is an associate professor in the Ohio State University Libraries where he has been bibliographer for communication since 1988. Among other works, he has co-authored (with Eleanor Block) COMMUNICATION AND THE MASS MEDIA: A GUIDE TO THE REFERENCE LITERATURE (0002), and (with Sterling) TELECOMMUNICATIONS RESEARCH RESOURCES: AN ANNOTATED GUIDE (1995), companion to the present volume. He holds a PhD in English literature and M.L. (master of librarianship) from the University of South Carolina.

Susan M. Hill, was vice president, Library and Information Center, National Association of Broadcasters in Washington, DC during the time this volume was prepared. As NAB's librarian from 1973-1997, Ms. Hill edited a number of NAB publications, including BROADCASTING BIBILIOGRAPHY (0022). She has lectured and written about the importance and value of trade association libraries. Ms. Hill joined the staff of the Pennsylvania Association of Broadcasters in 1997. She holds an MLS (Master in Library Service) from Rutgers University and an MA in English education from Teachers College, Columbia University.

1

General Reference

This first chapter identifies major resources for research on mass communications in general. More importantly it includes selected standard general resources that place media in a larger context. Among the most useful general works is Balay's 11th ed. of the standard GUIDE TO REFERENCE BOOKS (0001). Likewise, we have identified several electronic services recently made widely available in the Online Computer Library Center (OCLC) bibliographic utility as well as by newer service providers, like GaleNet. We are also pleased to provide information about the electronic index, COMINDEX (0033), published by Communication Institute for Online Scholarship, which surely represents one of the first attempts in the United States to make the literature of mass communications more readily accessible. Likewise, COMMSEARCH95 (0034) offers an expanded CD-ROM replication of Matlon and Ortiz's 4th ed. of INDEX TO JOURNALS IN COMMUNICATION STUDIES THROUGH 1990, published by the Speech Communication Association.

In general, data about the availability of online, CD-ROM, floppy disk, and other electronic services are from the products themselves, supplemented by the standard GALE DIRECTORY OF DATABASES (0042). For more recent information, researchers should consult the web pages for particular databases and services. Although only a few of these standard printed and electronic reference resources can be regarded as specific to mass communications, each covers far more than media literature, organizations, or personalities. General resources like many of those in this chapter serve to measure inevitable integration and convergence of mass communications into many aspects of daily life.

We give particular attention in the last section of this chapter to statistical resources published by both government and industry. By far the most useful guidance to mass communications statistics is provided by STATISTICAL MASTERFILE (0109). Researchers with access to its accompanying microfiche collections should consider themselves very fortunate indeed.

1-A. Bibliographies

1-A-1. General

0001 Balay, Robert, and Vee Friesner Carrington, eds. **GUIDE TO REFERENCE BOOKS.** 11th ed. Chicago: American Library Association, 1996, 2,020 pp. This supersedes Eugene Sheehy's 1986 10th ed. and Balay's supplement of 1992. This is once again *the* authoritative guide to standard reference materials (bibliographies, indexes, dictionaries, handbooks, guides) in all subjects and fields. Particularly strong coverage of directories, catalogs, and union lists of domestic and international newspapers and serial publications (journalism is covered in "Newspapers"). Relevant classified annotated entries in chapters on mass media and radio–television. Author, title, and subject index. Particularly useful for advanced researchers attempting comprehensive literature searches.

0002 Block, Eleanor S. and James K. Bracken. **COMMUNICATION AND THE MASS MEDIA: A GUIDE TO THE REFERENCE LITERATURE.** Englewood, CO: Libraries Unlimited, 1991, 198 pp. Covers electronic mass communications as well as organizational, political, and speech commmunication and rhetoric. Some 500 entries, with many other resources cited within long annotations, arranged in 10 sections by type of information source (e.g., bibliographies, periodicals, research centers). Author/title and subject indexes.

0003 Blum, Eleanor and Frances Goins Wilhoit. **MASS MEDIA BIBLIOGRAPHY: AN ANNOTATED GUIDE TO BOOKS AND JOURNALS FOR RESEARCH AND REFERENCE.** Champaign, IL: University of Illinois Press, 1989 (3rd ed.), 344 pp. Some 2,100 indexed entries on general communications, book publishing, broadcasting, editorial journalism, film, magazines, and advertising. International in scope but limited to English-language materials. Basic source for items published before 1988 with commonsense evaluations. Author, title, and subject indexes.

0004 **COMMUNICATION BOOKNOTES QUARTERLY.** Mahwah, NJ: Lawrence Erlbaum, 1998 (Vol. 29)–date, quarterly. Brief reviews of new books, periodicals, documents and other monographs in mass communications, telecommunication and information, with contributions from an active board of contributing editors. Reviews several hundred publications each year. Continues COMMUNICATION BOOKNOTES (1980–1997), MASS MEDIA BOOKNOTES (1973–1980), and BROADCASTING BIBLIOPHILE'S BOOKNOTES (1969–1972).

0005 **DIRECTORIES IN PRINT.** Detroit: Gale, 1989–date, annual. Formerly DIRECTORY OF DIRECTORIES (1980–1988). Included in online GALE DATABASE OF PUBLICATIONS AND BROADCAST MEDIA available from Dialog and GaleNet: covers current edition, updated semiannually. Diskette version available from Gale. Volume I of 13th ed. for 1996 includes classified descriptions of professional, trade, and other listings of membership, personnel, or companies, buyer's guides to services, products, ratings and rankings lists, and other kinds of directories. Relevant entries included in chapters on publishing and broadcast media, arts and entertainment. Volume II includes title and keyword index and subject index; useful headings include radio broadcasting, television broadcasting, and video industry.

0006 Hoffman, Frank W. **AMERICAN POPULAR CULTURE: A GUIDE TO THE REFERENCE LITERATURE.** Englewood, CO: Libraries Unlimited, 1995, 286 pp. Concentrates on reference works, special collections, societies, associations, and journals. Entries are fully annotated. See also: Inge (0099).

0007 Kwiatek, Kathy Krendl, ed. **FROM PREHISTORY TO PRESENT-DAY: A BIBLIOGRAPHY OF COMMUNICATION.** Ann Arbor: University of Michigan, Howard R. Marsh Center for the Study of Journalistic Performance, Department of Communication, 1980, 20 pp. A short bibliography, with an introduction by Wilbur Schramm. Developed by members of an informal seminar led by Schramm at the University of Michigan, its value is in selectivity—57 books covering broad communication topics intelligently and accurately. Schramm's essay explains that the books chosen are useful for grasping the "broad sweep of Human communication..."

0008 Orenstein, Ruth M., ed. **FULLTEXT SOURCES ONLINE: FOR PERIODICALS, NEWSPAPERS, NEWSLETTERS, NEWSWIRES & TV/RADIO TRANSCRIPTS.** Needham Heights, MA: BiblioData, 1989–date, semiannual. Gives locations of fulltext computer files for U.S. and foreign periodicals, newspapers, newsletters, newswires and television and radio transcripts. Fulltext is defined to mean complete articles are found online, not that a publication is found cover-to-cover in the database (features like tables, charts, graphics, illustrations, and photographs are excluded). Covers major vendors.

0009 Rubin, R.B. et al. **COMMUNICATION RESEARCH: STRATEGIES AND SOURCES.** Belmont, CA: Wadsworth, 1996 (4th ed.), 353 pp. A step-by-step guide to use of many types of media reference materials, combined with solid annotated bibliography. Offers substantive advice on research methods and resources.

See 1159. Sova, COMMUNICATIONS SERIALS.

0010 Sterling, Christopher H. **TELECOMMUNICATIONS, ELECTRONIC MEDIA, AND GLOBAL COMMUNICATIONS: A SURVEY BIBLIOGRAPHY.** Annandale, VA: Communication Booknotes, 1996 (2nd ed.), 30 pp. About 500 references (mostly after 1990) in subject and format arrangement, with further topical subdivisions: dictionaries, encyclopedias, glossaries; directories and yearbooks; bibliographies; development; technology; industry, economics; content; impact, effects; policy and regulation; area studies. Concise critical annotations. Cumulates and updates Sterling's previous separate bibliographies, based on COMMUNICATION BOOKNOTES (0004), and formerly issued about every 2 years (last revised in 1991): FOREIGN AND INTERNATIONAL COMMUNICATIONS SYSTEMS: A SURVEY BIBLIOGRAPHY; BIBLIOGRAPHY OF MASS COMMUNICATION AND ELECTRONIC MEDIA; and TELECOMMUNICATIONS POLICY: A SURVEY BIBLIOGRAPHY.

See 0230. University of Illinois. CATALOG OF THE COMMUNICATIONS LIBRARY.

0011 **ULRICH'S INTERNATIONAL PERIODICALS DIRECTORY.** New York: Bowker, 1932–date, annual. Available online from DIALOG and other services. CD-ROM version—ULRICH'S PLUS—available from Bowker. Premier international descriptive source for magazines, newspapers, annuals, and irregularly issued publications. All publications are classified by subject, fully described (publisher, address, frequency, date first published, editors, circulation, price, indexes, publishing code, abstracting services, Copyright Clearance Center registrations, document delivery suppliers). Since the 1993/94 edition, it has included over 7,000 daily and weekly U.S. newspapers, providing "comprehensive worldwide newspaper coverage." In addition to the subject classification, all entries are indexed by title.

1-A-2. Print Media and Journalism

0012 Cates, Jo A. **JOURNALISM: A GUIDE TO THE REFERENCE LITERATURE.** Englewood, CO: Libraries Unlimited, 1997 (2nd ed.), 225 pp. More than 700 annotated sources divided by type of publication, with good author/title and subject indexing.

0013 Paine, Fred K., and Nancy E. Paine. **MAGAZINES: A BIBLIOGRAPHY FOR THEIR ANALYSIS, WITH ANNOTATIONS AND STUDY GUIDE.** Metuchen, NJ: Scarecrow Press, 1987, 690 pp. Most comprehensive guide on the industry; includes some 2,200 items in more than 30 topical sections, with indexes. Part 1 includes an annotated list of popular, trade, and scholarly journals and articles that cover magazines and the industry, all annotated, and also lists reference books (bibliographies, directories, handbooks, statistical sources, and indexes to material published in and about magazines). Part 2 is a bibliography of over 2,000 magazine, journal, and newspaper articles, as well as books and dissertations about magazines.

0014 Schwarzlose, Richard A. **NEWSPAPERS: A REFERENCE GUIDE.** Westport, CT: Greenwood, 1987, 417 pp. Nine topical chapters detail what is known of and published about the industry, with references for each chapter. Schwarzlose describes, evaluates, and provides a context for the abundant literature about newspapers and news people. Extensive bibliographies. Topics include histories; newspaper people before the 20th century; newspaper people during the 20th century; newspaper work; producing newspapers; newspapers and society; newspapers and the law; newspapers and technology; and references and periodicals about newspapers. Appendices provide a chronology of newspapers and descriptions of major research collections of newspapers and about newspapers. Index.

0015 Wolseley, Roland E., and Isabel Wolseley. **THE JOURNALIST'S BOOKSHELF: AN ANNOTATED AND SELECTED BIBLIOGRAPHY OF UNITED STATES PRINT JOURNALISM.** Indianapolis, IN: R.J. Berg Co., 1986 (8th ed.), 400 pp. Some 2,400 items are included in this indexed volume, which first appeared in 1939.

1-A-3. Electronic Media

0016 **BCTV: BIBLIOGRAPHY ON CABLE TELEVISION.** San Francisco: Communications Library, 1984–date, annual. Compilation of selected materials on cable television published during a given year. Entries arranged by format: book, dissertation, thesis, ephemera, magazine, newspaper, and trade press. Appendix provides a master cross-reference index to books and dissertations from 1975 to the year of publication. The cross-reference index features the following subject headings: access, advertising/marketing, audience/subscribers, business/finance, international, legislation/regulations, operations, programming-local, programming-network, satellites, social effects/education, technical, teletex and videotex. This series was inaugurated by a volume that annotated cable television from 1975 to 1983.

0017 Carothers, Diane Foxhill. **RADIO BROADCASTING FROM 1920 TO 1990: AN ANNOTATED BIBLIOGRAPHY.** New York: Garland, 1991, 564 pp. Very wide coverage—probably the most inclusive listing with some 1,800 resources on radio—with chapters on background, economic aspects, production, programming, international, public, regulation, amateur and ham radio, women and minorities, careers, and reference sources. Author/title indexes. (See Greenfield, 0298a.)

0018 Cassata, Mary, and Thomas Skill. **TELEVISION: A GUIDE TO THE LITERATURE.** Phoenix, AZ: Oryx Press, 1985, 148 pp. Ten topical chapters (including history, reference, process and effects, children, television news, television and politics, the industry, criticism, and anthologies of television writing) offer discussions and listings of several thousand titles with good author and title indexes.

0019 Chin, Felix. **CABLE TELEVISION: A COMPREHENSIVE BIBLIOGRAPHY.** New York: Plenum Publishing, 1978, 285 pp. The first book-length survey of the medium's literature, this includes some 650 annotated entries (about 10% of what the author estimates to have appeared prior to publication), plus appendices on the 50 largest cable systems, large cable system owners, a chronology, major federal agencies concerned with cable, FCC rules, glossary, and indexes. (See Garay, 0021, for an update.)

0020 Fisher, Kim N. **ON THE SCREEN: A FILM, TELEVISION, AND VIDEO RESEARCH GUIDE.** Littleton, CO: Libraries Unlimited, 1986, 209 pp. Annotated and indexed guide to more than 700 publications and associations, arranged by subject. Author/title and subject indexes.

0021 Garay, Ronald. **CABLE TELEVISION: A REFERENCE GUIDE TO INFORMATION.** Westport, CT: Greenwood, 1988, 177 pp. Comprehensive narrative discussion about, and citations on general sources, business and industry/economic resources, program services and content as well as cable uses and effects, cable law and regulations, and videotex. Appendices on association and agency addresses. Index. (See Chin, 0019, for earlier material.)

0022 Hill, Susan M. **BROADCASTING BIBLIOGRAPHY: A GUIDE TO THE LITERATURE OF RADIO & TELEVISION.** Washington: National Association of Broadcasters, 1989 (3rd ed.), 74 pp. More than 500 items are listed (not annotated) under topical headings. Indexed.

0023 McCavitt, William E. **RADIO AND TELEVISION: A SELECTED, ANNOTATED BIBLIOGRAPHY,** and **SUPPLEMENT ONE: 1977–1981.** Metuchen, NJ: Scarecrow, 1978, 229 pp.; 1982, 167 pp. First attempt since Rose (0156) at a comprehensive bibliography of broadcasting, this includes some 1,500 items in both volumes, topically divided and indexed. Many items are not annotated and there is some confusion in topical arrangement. Indexes. See Pringle and Clinton (0024) for update.

0024 Pringle, Peter K, and Helen H. Clinton. **RADIO AND TELEVISION: A SELECTED, ANNOTATED BIBLIOGRAPHY, SUPPLEMENT TWO: 1982–1986.** Metuchen, NJ: Scarecrow Press, 1989, 249 pp. Another 1,000 items are added to the work begun by McCavitt (0023). Indexed.

1-B. Abstracts, Indexes, Databases

0025 **ACCESS: THE SUPPLEMENTARY INDEX TO PERIODICALS.** Evanston, IL: John Gordon Burke, 1975–date, 3/year. Subscription includes disk from Electronic Information Services. Online version available from NLIGHTN. Intends to complement READERS' GUIDE (0049) in journal and subject coverage. Author and subject indexes for local and regional magazines such as CLEVELAND MAGAZINE, NEW JERSEY MONTHLY, and SAN DIEGO MAGAZINE, as well as such journals as WIRED and MONITORING TIMES. Useful for articles on local media companies and public relations pieces about technology and social issues as well as for regional perspectives on topics of current interest, such as the information superhighway. Also covers radio and television program reviews.

0026 **ALTERNATIVE PRESS INDEX.** Baltimore: Alternative Press Center, 1969–date, quarterly. Contact: P.O. Box 33109, Baltimore, MD 21218. Voice: 410-243-2471. Fax: 410-235-5325. Internet: www.igc.apc.org./altpress/api.html. CD-ROM version available from National Information Services Corporation. Indexes 222 alternative and radical publications and provides subject access to periodical literature on subcultures (African-Americans, gays/lesbians, feminists, ethnic groups, religious alternatives, environmental groups, and political activists) and to reviews (films, books, recorded music, television programs, theater), and to persons (autobiographies, biographies, obituaries). Does not index comic strips and cartoons, although the articles are coded for illustrations in the index.

0027 **ARTICLE 1ST.** [Online service.] Columbus, OH: OCLC, 1992–date, updated daily. Covers 1990–date. Offers subject, author, title, keyword, and selected field searching of "nearly 12,500 journals in science, technology, medicine, social science, business, the humanities, and popular culture," with OCLC holdings. Journal title searching provided by CONTENTS 1ST (see 0036). Both services mainly valuable for accessing periodical contents in advance of more sophisticated systematic indexing.

0028 **BIBLIOGRAPHIC INDEX.** New York: H. W. Wilson, 1938–date, 3/year. Online version available from Wilsonline, Ovid, OCLC, and other services: covers November 1984–date, updated twice weekly. For more information, see Wilson's homepage: www.hwwilson.com/humani.html. Offers subject access (based on Library of Congress Subject Headings) to bibliographies published separately as books and articles and as parts of books. Selectively indexes about 2,600 journals and also book-length bibliographies and other works with bibliographies listed in CUMULATIVE BOOK INDEX (0037). Detailed subject headings and frequent cross-references make it a good starting point for comprehensive literature searches.

0029 **BIOGRAPHY AND GENEALOGY MASTER INDEX.** Detroit: Gale, 1980 (2nd ed.), 8 vols. SUPPLEMENT. 1981/82–date, annual, with 5-year cumulations. Online version BIOGRAPHY MASTER INDEX available from Dialog and GaleNext: cumulates all editions and supplements, updated annually. CD-ROM version available from Gale: cumulates all editions, updated annually. Cross references more than 4 million biographies published in over 400 current and retrospective biographical dictionaries and other sources. Cumulative editions index an extensive number of older and standard biographical reference works useful for historical research such as DICTIONARY OF AMERICAN BIOGRAPHY, early volumes of WHO'S WHO IN AMERICA and AMERICAN MEN AND WOMEN OF SCIENCE, and subject-specific works. More recent volumes cover reference series such as CONTEMPORARY THEATRE, FILM, AND TELEVISION (0030), and magazine and newspaper journalists in the DICTIONARY OF LITERARY BIOGRAPHY (0169, 0163). Also indexes persons covered in BIOGRAPHY INDEX (0030).

0030 **BIOGRAPHY INDEX: A QUARTERLY INDEX TO BIOGRAPHICAL MATERIAL IN BOOKS AND MAGAZINES.** New York: H. W. Wilson, 1946–date, quarterly, annual, and 3-year cumulations. Online version available from Wilsonline, Ovid, OCLC; covers August 1984–date, updated twice weekly. CD-ROM version available from H. W. Wilson. For more information, see Wilson's homepage: www.hwwilson.com/humani.html. Indexes works of individual biography and autobiography, works of collective biography, and biographical features in journals. Arranged by biographee. More selective than BIOGRAPHY AND GENEALOGY MASTER INDEX (0029), but includes a useful Index to Professions and Occupations that cross references entries under headings such as actors and actresses, advertising, press agents, radio and television executives, radio and television talk show hosts.

0031 **BOOK REVIEW DIGEST.** New York: H. W. Wilson, 1905–date, monthly, annual cumulations. Online version available from Wilsonline, Ovid, OCLC; covers January 1983–date, updated twice weekly. For more information, see Wilson's homepage: www.hwwilson.com/humani.html. CD-

ROM version available from SilverPlatter; covers 1983–date, updated quarterly. Indexes book reviews featured in major book trade and library journals such as PUBLISHERS WEEKLY and LIBRARY JOURNAL and major reviewing journals such as NEW YORK TIMES BOOK REVIEW and NEW YORK REVIEW OF BOOKS. Also indexes COLUMBIA JOURNALISM REVIEW. Arranged by author; provides excerpts of reviews. Subject index offers useful access under headings such as motion pictures, radio, and television. Coverage from 1905 to the present makes it important for historical research. The first place to check for reviews of books on popular mass media topics published by mainstream publishers.

0032 **BOOK REVIEW INDEX.** Detroit: Gale, 1965–date, bimonthly. Online version available from Dialog: covers 1969–date, updated quarterly. CD-ROM version available from Gale: 1965–date, updated quarterly. Complements coverage of reviews in BOOK REVIEW DIGEST (0031), indexing many more scholarly reviewing journals (nearly 500) including AMERICAN JOURNALISM REVIEW, JOURNAL OF COMMUNICATION, JOURNAL OF FILM AND VIDEO, JOURNAL OF POPULAR FILM AND TELEVISION, JOURNALISM AND MASS COMMUNICATIONS QUARTERLY, and TELEVISION QUARTERLY. Limited to author listing with separate title index; provides neither subject access nor excerpts of reviews. Electronic version allows useful key word in title access.

See 0051. BUSINESSORGS.

See 0446. BUSINESS PERIODICALS INDEX.

See 0909. CIS INDEX TO PUBLICATIONS OF THE UNITED STATES CONGRESS.

0033 **COMINDEX** [Electronic file]. Rotterdam Junction, NY: CIOS (Communication Institute for Online Scholarship), 1993–date, irregular. For more information, see WWW homepage: cios.llc.rpi.edu/INDEX.HTM. "Electronic author and title index to the core literature of communication discipline and communication related topics... Complete bibliographic information from more than 19,000 articles from 60 key international journals and annuals from the communication field." Lack of key words or abstracts makes COMINDEX less useful for subject searching than COMMUNICATION ABSTRACTS (0035) or other electronic indexes. Can support Boolean search techniques. Also offers unique co-occurence analysis of authors and title keywords.

0034 **COMMSEARCH95.** Annandale, VA: Speech Communication Association with Science Press, 1995 [release 1]. CD-ROM replication of Ronald Matlon and Sylvia P. Ortiz's 4th ed. of INDEX TO JOURNALS IN COMMUNICATION STUDIES THROUGH 1990 (1158), with several notable enhancements, including the full texts of articles in SCA journals COMMUNICATION EDUCATION, COMMUNICATION MONOGRAPHS, CRITICAL STUDIES IN MASS COMMUNICATION, QUARTERLY JOURNAL OF SPEECH, JOURNAL OF APPLIED COMMUNICATION RESEARCH, and TEXT AND PERFORMANCE QUARTERLY; abstracts of these SCA journals, 1972–1994; title and author indexes for 22 journals through 1994; and keyword index for 19 journals through 1990. Offers access by any combination of year, journal, subject keyword, author, title, abstract, and full text. Networked version forthcoming.

0035 **COMMUNICATION ABSTRACTS.** Thousand Oaks, CA: Sage, 1978–date, 6/year. Indexes and abstracts about 50 books and book chapters and articles from about 250 journals, with annual cumulative author and subject indexes. Mainly useful for its abstracts written by a panel of scholars. Usefulness for advanced research on mass media topics is limited by its relatively brief publication history. Covers the most significant English-language communication research journals, including smaller ones like JOURNAL OF MEDIA LAW AND PRACTICE, JOURNAL OF MEDIA ECONOMICS, and JOURNAL OF MASS MEDIA ETHICS. The subject access is a controlled keyword approach, requiring experimentation. The user is prompted by a listing of index terms assigned to each abstract (e.g., MTV and audiences). Despite wonderfully specific subject headings such as television advertising, television characters, television commercials, television effects, and television programming, there is no way to cross reference one heading with a different one—economic issues, for instance—without consulting the entries/abstracts. Several more quickly updated and more readily searchable electronic versions of standard indexes such as HUMANITIES INDEX (0044), SOCIAL SCIENCES INDEX (0741), and PSYCHOLOGICAL ABSTRACTS (0739), as well as new indexes in the field, like COMINDEX (0033), make this less central for indexing communication's scholarly literature.

See 1031. COMMUNICATION CONTENTS SISALLOT.

0036 **CONTENTS 1ST** [Online service]. Columbus, OH: OCLC, 1992–date, updated daily. Covers 1990–date. Offers "complete table of contents page and holdings information for nearly 12,500 journals." Covers major mass communications trade and scholarly journals. CONTENTS 1ST and its companion service, ARTICLE 1ST (0027), which offers subject and keyword searching of the same journals, combine features of traditional indexes and current contents services with OCLC's bibliographic holdings information. Like CURRENT CONTENTS (0038), mainly useful as current awareness service.

0037 **CUMULATIVE BOOK INDEX.** New York: H.W. Wilson, 1898–date, monthly. Online version available from Wilsonline, Ovid, and OCLC: covers 1982–date, updated twice weekly. CD-ROM version available from H.W. Wilson: covers 1982–date, updated quarterly. Amounts to an "international author, subject, and title bibliography of books published in the English language." For more information, see Wilson's homepage: www.hwwilson.com/humani.html. Subject headings based on LIBRARY OF CONGRESS SUBJECT HEADINGS (see Appendix B to this volume). Includes directory of publishers and distributors. Useful for identifying new books on mass communications.

0038 **CURRENT CONTENTS.** Philadelphia: Institute for Scientific Information, 1961–date, weekly. Online version available from Ovid, Dialog, and others: covers current 6 months, updated weekly. CD-ROM and magnetic tape versions also available; for more information see ISI's homepage: www.isinet.com/prodserv/cc/cchp.html. Each service reprints tables of contents of recent issues of 6,600 journals and selected "new, multi-authored books" analyzed in ISI's citation indexes. Covers many mass communications core journals. Title word indexes include media issues, modeled on the citation indexes ("Permuterm Index"), alphabetically listing "significant words in every article and book title." Field- and discipline-specific services relevant to electronic mass media include:

1 ARTS & HUMANITIES. 1978–date.
2 ENGINEERING, TECHNOLOGY, & APPLIED SCIENCES. 1970–date.
3 SOCIAL AND BEHAVIORAL SCIENCES. 1961–date.

See 0738. CURRENT INDEX TO JOURNALS IN EDUCATION.

See 0450. DISCLOSURE.

0039 **ESSAY AND GENERAL LITERATURE INDEX.** New York: H. W. Wilson, 1934–date, semiannual with annual and 5-year cumulations. Online version available from Wilsonline, Ovid, and OCLC: covers January 1985–date, updated twice yearly. CD-ROM version available from H. W. Wilson and SilverPlatter: covers 1985–date, updated annually. For more information, see Wilson's homepage: www.hwwilson.com/humani.html. Offers important access to critical works that fall between books and articles. Indexes book chapters, sections of collective works (like entries on journalists, screenwriters, and magazine publishers in volumes of the DICTIONARY OF LITERARY BIOGRAPHY), and other parts of collections, such as published proceedings or symposia papers. Emphasis on humanities and social science disciplines. Useful subject headings include, newspapers, radio broadcasting, and television broadcasting. See also the cumulative index to nearly 10,000 analyzed collections: ESSAY AND GENERAL LITERATURE INDEX: WORKS INDEXED 1900–1969 (1972).

0040 **EXPANDED ACADEMIC INDEX** [Online service]. Foster City, CA: Information Access Company, 1976–date, updated weekly. One of the several electronic reference databases available on the InfoTrac system; for more information, see IAC homepage: library.iacnet.com/over/aca_over.html. Useful place to begin a literature search. Academic Index provides bibliographic references and abstracts to 1,000 scholarly and general interest journals. Coverage for the research-oriented journals begins in January 1987. The database is updated and cumulated monthly and offers an excellent searching system. Among the journals included are COMMUNICATION QUARTERLY, COMMUNICATION

RESEARCH, HUMAN COMMUNICATION RESEARCH, CRITICAL STUDIES IN MASS COMMUNICATION, JOURNAL OF COMMUNICATION, JOURNALISM & MASS COMMUNICATION QUARTERLY, POLITICAL COMMUNICATION, TELECOMMUNICATIONS POLICY, QUARTERLY JOURNAL OF SPEECH, and JOURNAL OF BROADCASTING & ELECTRONIC MEDIA.

0041 **FILM LITERATURE INDEX.** Albany, NY: State University of New York at Albany, Film and Television Documentation Center, 1973–date, quarterly. Offers comprehensive author and subject access to the international trade and scholarly periodical literature of film and television/video around the world. Covers journals ranging from VARIETY to SMPTE JOURNAL as well as more specialized titles. Reviews of films listed under film titles.

0042 **GALE DIRECTORY OF DATABASES.** Detroit, MI: Gale Research, 1993–date, twice yearly, 2 vols. Available online through Orbit/Questel, GaleNet, and others. CD-ROM version available through SilverPlatter. Also available in diskette and magnetic tape. Includes Vol.1: ONLINE DATABASES; Vol. 2: CD-ROM, DISKETTE, MAGNETIC TAPE, HANDHELD, AND BATCH ACCESS DATABASE PRODUCTS. Formed by merger of COMPUTER-READABLE DATABASES (1975–1992) and DIRECTORY OF ONLINE DATABASES (1979–1992) and DIRECTORY OF PORTABLE DATABASES (1990–1992). Comprehensive coverage of electronic database industry, containing contact and descriptive information on 10,000 databases, 3,550 producers, 860 online services, and 1,000 vendors and distributors. Geographic, subject, and master indices.

0043 **GENERAL SCIENCE INDEX.** New York: H. W. Wilson, 1978–date, monthly. Online version available from Wilsonline, Ovid, and OCLC: covers May 1984–date, updated twice weekly. CD-ROM version available from H.W. Wilson, Ovid, and SilverPlatter: covers 1984–date, updated quarterly. For more information, see Wilson's homepage: www.hwwilson.com/humani.html. Indexes a selection of the most readily available science and technology journals. Useful for coverage of topics of current and perennial interest, such as tobacco advertising and television's impact on children, featured in frequently cited journals like NATURE, SCIENCE, and SCIENTIFIC AMERICAN.

0044 **HUMANITIES INDEX.** New York: H. W. Wilson, 1974–date, quarterly with annual cumulations. Online version available from Wilsonline, Ovid, OCLC, and others: covers February 1984–date, updated twice weekly. CD-ROM version available from H. W. Wilson, Ovid, and SilverPlatter: covers 1984–date, updated quarterly. For more information, see Wilson's homepage: www.hwwilson.com/humani.html. Formerly INTERNATIONAL INDEX (1907–1965) and SOCIAL SCIENCES AND HUMANITIES INDEX (1965–1974): these volumes offer important historical coverage. One of the most useful and important indexes for identifying scholarly studies of electronic media's social and cultural impacts. Covers a significant core of mass media journals including AMERICAN JOURNALISM REVIEW, COLUMBIA JOURNALISM REVIEW, COMMUNICATION QUARTERLY, COMMUNICATION RESEARCH, JOURNAL OF BROADCASTING & ELECTRONIC MEDIA, JOURNAL OF COMMUNICATION, JOURNAL OF POPULAR CULTURE, JOURNAL OF POPULAR FILM AND TELEVISION, JOURNALISM HISTORY, JOURNALISM & MASS COMMUNICATION QUARTERLY, MASS COMM REVIEW, QUILL, and SIGHT AND SOUND. Also covers full range of scholarly journals in literature, music, art, history, religion, and philosophy that address such topics as freedom of expression and the press and obscenity and rock lyrics. Major subject headings include journalism, mass media, radio, and television and provide extensive crossreferences to alternatives. Also covers reviews of radio and television programs and videotapes. An all-purpose index for scholarship on electronic media, especially artistic content.

See 0449. INDEX OF ECONOMIC ARTICLES.

See 1157. INDEX TO JOURNALS IN MASS COMMUNICATION.

See 0910. INDEX TO LEGAL PERIODICALS.

See 0048. F & S INDEX UNITED STATES.

See 0911. LEGAL TRAC.

See 0912. LEXIS/NEXIS.

See 1034. MASS COM PERIODICAL LITERATURE INDEX.

See 1158. Matlon, INDEX TO JOURNALS IN COMMUNICATIONS.

See 0931. MONTHLY CATALOG OF UNITED STATES GOVERNMENT PUBLICATIONS.

0045 **NEWSPAPER ABSTRACTS DAILY** [Online service]. Louisville, KY: UMI, 1989–date, updated daily. Covers 1989–date; preceded by NEWSPAPER ABSTRACTS for coverage of 1984–1988. Available from Dialog, OCLC, and others. CD-ROM version available from UMI. Indexes and abstracts 27 selected major national and regional newspapers, including NEW YORK TIMES, WALL STREET JOURNAL, WASHINGTON POST. Useful service for current awareness, but LEXIS/NEXIS (0912) offers wider (and full-text) coverage of local and regional newspapers.

0046 **NEWSPAPERS ONLINE.** Needham Heights, MA: BiblioData, 1992–date, annual. A directory of nearly 200 daily newspapers worldwide that are available as full-text electronic files. Covers major database vendors. See also: Worldwide List of Online Newspapers homepage: www.intercom.com.au/intercom/newsprs/index.htm.

0047 **PAIS BULLETIN.** New York: Public Affairs Information Service, 1914–date, monthly. Online version available from Dialog, Knowledge Index, OCLC, and others: coverage varies (Dialog 1972–date), updated monthly. CD-ROM version available from PAIS, SilverPlatter, and others: covers 1972–date, updated quarterly. Subject indexing of international scholarly and professional publications (monographs, 1,400 journals, U.S. and foreign governmental, quasi-governmental, and organizational documents) in English-language public policy literature—law, political science, economic and social conditions, public administration, and international relations. Covers MEDIA STUDIES JOURNAL, JOURNAL OF BROADCASTING & ELECTRONIC MEDIA, and JOURNALISM & MASS COMMUNICATION QUARTERLY. Also gives bibliographic data for publications from major mass media publishers such as Artech, Erlbaum, and Sage; and for publications from the FCC, ITU, and UNESCO. Annual cumulative author index. Useful subject headings include communication in politics, mass media, and propaganda. Very helpful crossreferences.

0048 **PERIODICAL ABSTRACTS** [Online service]. Louisville, KY: UMI, 1988–date, updated weekly. Available from Dialog, OCLC, and others. CD-ROM version available from UMI. Includes abstracts of articles published since 1986 in more than 1,500 periodicals. Covers general and academic journals in all areas as well as electronic media; particularly useful for brief accounts of network news programs and specials, with information on transcript availability. Covers ADVERTISING AGE, BILLBOARD, BROADCASTING AND THE LAW, COLUMBIA JOURNALISM REVIEW, COMMUNICATIONS AND THE LAW, EDITOR AND PUBLISHER, ELECTRONIC NEWS, JOURNALISM & MASS COMMUNICATION QUARTERLY, MEDIA REPORT ON WOMEN, MEDIA STUDIES JOURNAL, SIGHT AND SOUND, TV GUIDE, VARIETY, and WIRED, as well as popular journals like NEWSWEEK, TIME, and BUSINESS WEEK. An alternative to the READERS' GUIDE and other Wilson indexes.

See 0739. PSYCHOLOGICAL ABSTRACTS.

0049 **READERS' GUIDE TO PERIODICAL LITERATURE.** New York: H. W. Wilson, 1900–date, monthly. Online version available from Wilsonline, Ovid, OCLC: covers January 1983–date, updated twice weekly. Online READGUIDEABS (READERS GUIDE ABSTRACTS) also available from Wilsonline, Ovid, OCLC, and others. CD-ROM versions of READERS' GUIDE and READERS' GUIDE ABSTRACTS available from H. W. Wilson, SilverPlatter, Ovid: covers 1983–date, updated quarterly. For more information, see Wilson's homepage: www.hwwilson.com/humani.html. Useful for identifying mass media content as well as articles on communication and new communication technologies in society. Coverage back to 1900 makes it important for historical research. Indexes popular periodicals such as TIME, NEWSWEEK, U.S. NEWS AND WORLD REPORT, ROLLING STONE, and MS; also indexes many basic mass communication journals, including AJR: AMERICAN JOURNALISM REVIEW, COLUMBIA JOURNALISM REVIEW, TELEVISION QUARTERLY, TV GUIDE, and VIDEO REVIEW. Includes reviews of radio and television programs and videotapes. There are abundant relevant mass media subject headings and cross references. Good starting point for research on all aspects of mass media.

See 0372. SCIENCE CITATION INDEX.

See 0740. SOCIAL SCIENCE CITATION INDEX.

See 0741. SOCIAL SCIENCES INDEX.

See 0742. SOCIOLOGICAL ABSTRACTS.

See 0109. STATISTICAL MASTERFILE.

0050 **TOPICATOR: CLASSIFIED ARTICLE GUIDE TO THE ADVERTISING /COMMUNICATIONS/MARKETING PERIODICAL PRESS.** Clackamas, OR: Lakemoor, 1965–date, bimonthly. Indexes core professional and trade literature of advertising, marketing, and mass media, including ADVERTISING AGE, EDITOR & PUBLISHER, and TV GUIDE. Useful for convention reports from professional organizations as well as information and descriptions of current events and hot products. Loaded with relevant citations, but complex subject headings make for difficult use. No electronic versions.

See 0384. U.S. Department of Commerce. Patent and Trademark Office. CASSIS.

See 0914. WESTLAW.

1-C. Directories and Yearbooks

1-C-1. General Business

0051 **BUSINESS ORGANIZATIONS, AGENCIES, AND PUBLICATIONS DIRECTORY.** Detroit: Gale, 1986–date, annual. Online version BUSINESSORGS available from OCLC: covers 1993–date, updated annually. Subtitle: "Directory of more than 26,000 new and established organizations, agencies, and publications worldwide." Subject, organization name, geographic (city), and other searching.

0052 **CORPORATE TECHNOLOGY DIRECTORY.** Wellesley Hills, MA: Corporate Technology Information Services, 1986–date, annual. Online version available from Orbit, DataStar, and others: covers current edition, updated quarterly. CD-ROM version available from Bowker Electronic Publishing in SCI-TECH REFERENCE PLUS: covers current edition, updated annually. Brief profiles of more than 35,000 high technology domestic and foreign companies arranged by "Corporate Technology Codes." Company name, geographical, technology, product kind "who makes what" indexes. Glossary.

See 0373. DIRECTORY OF AMERICAN RESEARCH AND TECHNOLOGY.

0053 **DIRECTORY OF CORPORATE AFFILIATIONS.** New Providence, NJ: National Register Publishing (Reed Reference), 1973–date, annual. Online version CORPORATE AFFILIATIONS ONLINE available from Dialog and others: covers current edition, updated quarterly. CD-ROM versions available from Knight-Ridder Information (CORPORATE AFFILIATIONS ONDISC) and Bowker Electronic Publishing (CORPORATE AFFILIATIONS PLUS). Acquisition and merger information for more than 16,000 major domestic corporations and 140,000 divisions, subsidiaries, and affiliates. Geographic, SIC Code, brand name and personal name indexes. Electronic versions cumulate DIRECTORY OF CORPORATE AFFILIATIONS, INTERNATIONAL DIRECTORY OF CORPORATE AFFILIATIONS, and DIRECTORY OF LEADING PRIVATE COMPANIES.

0054 **MILLION DOLLAR DIRECTORY.** Parsippany, NJ: Dun's Marketing Services, 1979–date, annual. Continues DUN AND BRADSTREET MILLION DOLLAR DIRECTORY and DUN AND BRADSTREET MIDDLE MARKET DIRECTORY (1959–1978). Information from MILLION DOLLAR DIRECTORY consolidated in online DUN'S MARKET IDENTIFIERS available from Dialog, DataStar, Compuserve, and others. CD-ROM version DUN'S MILLION DOLLAR DISC available from Dun's Marketing Services: covers current edition, udpated quarterly (also includes information from Dun's REFERENCE BOOK OF CORPORATE MANAGEMENT). Identifies 160,000 U.S. businesses and domestic subsidiaries of foreign companies with net worth of $500,000. Geographic and SIC Code indexes. Access to the same information and more is available in CD-ROM version DUN'S BUSINESS LOCATOR from Dun and Bradstreet Information Services: covers current edition; updated semiannually. Cumulating MILLION DOLLAR DIRECTORY, DUN'S BUSINESS RANKINGS, DUN'S INDUSTRIAL GUIDE, DUN'S CONSULTANTS DIRECTORY, DUN'S REGIONAL BUSINESS DIRECTORIES, DUN'S DIRECT ACCESS, and DUN'S EMPLOYMENT OPPORTUNITIES DIRECTORY, this gives data for 8.6 million U.S. companies in 15,000 categories.

0055 **ELECTRONICS MANUFACTURERS DIRECTORY: A MARKETER'S GUIDE TO MANUFACTURERS IN THE UNITED STATES AND CANADA.** Twinsburg, OH: Harris, 1969–date, annual. Formerly U.S ELECTRONICS INDUSTRY DIRECTORY and WHO'S WHO IN ELECTRONICS. Basic information for companies: telephone and fax numbers, sales, top personnel, SIC Codes for products. Geographical and product (SIC Codes) indexes.

See 0478 ENCYCLOPEDIA OF ASSOCIATIONS.

0056 **ENCYCLOPEDIA OF BUSINESS INFORMATION SOURCES.** Detroit: Gale, 1970–date, irregular. 10th ed. for 1995–1996. Subject listings for research resources (printed and electronic indexes, bibliographies, handbooks, directories, trade and professional organizations, research centers); very specific headings with elaborate cross references. Relevant materials under many headings, including cable television industry, college and school newspapers, freedom of information, media research, radio and television, television apparatus industry, videotex/teletext. Formerly EXECUTIVE'S GUIDE TO INFORMATION SOURCES (1965).

0057 **HOOVER'S GUIDE TO MEDIA COMPANIES.** Austin, TX: Hoover's Business Press, 1996–date, annual. Company profiles available online by subscription at Internet address: www.hoovers.com. Directory of 675 information and entertainment companies with indepth profiles of 205 leading media companies. Profiles include financial data, company history, personnel, product information, and key competitors. Includes public and private companies. Covers traditional media—books, magazines, newspapers, radio, television, and other content providers.

See 0151a. INTERNATIONAL DIRECTORY OF COMPANY HISTORIES.

0058 **NATIONAL TRADE AND PROFESSIONAL ASSOCIATIONS OF THE UNITED STATES.** Washington: Columbia Books, 1966–date, annual. 32nd ed. for 1997. Formerly NATIONAL TRADE AND PROFESSIONAL ASSOCIATIONS OF THE UNITED STATES AND CANADA AND LABOR UNIONS and variant titles. Gives directory data, describes activities, and lists publications for 7,600 active national trade associations, labor unions, professional scientific or technical societies, and other national organizations. Indexes for subjects, geographic, budget, executives, and acronyms. Relevant listings under such headings as actors, audio visual, authors, press, communications, journalism, newspapers, and radio–TV, and writers.

See 0748. RESEARCH SERVICES DIRECTORY.

0059 **STANDARD AND POOR'S REGISTER OF CORPORATIONS, DIRECTORS AND EXECUTIVES.** New York: Standard and Poor's, 1928–date, annual. Supplements issued in April, July, and October. Online version (in several similarly named files) available from Dialog, LEXIS/NEXIS (0912): covers current edition; updated quarterly. CD-ROM version available in STANDARD AND POOR'S CORPORATIONS from Knight-Ridder Information: covers current edition; updated quarterly. 70th ed. for 1997. Standard directory of U.S. companies. Data for 56,000 companies in vol. 1;

brief biographical information for over 71,000 executives in vol. 2; SIC, geographical, and corporate family indices in vol. 3. Relevant SIC numbers include 2700 for printing, publishing, and allied industries; 3663 for radio–TV broadcasting equipment; and 4800 for communications.

1-C-2. Media Industries

i) General and Print

0060 **AMERICAN LIBRARY DIRECTORY: A CLASSIFIED LIST OF LIBRARIES IN THE UNITED STATES AND CANADA.** New York: R. R. Bowker, 1923–date, annual. Online version available from Dialog. CD-ROM version available in PUBLISHING MARKETPLACE REFERENCE PLUS from Bowker Electronic Publishing. A standard reference source for addresses, phone numbers, personnel, and brief information on U.S. libraries, including those in media organizations and companies. Information arranged by state for all varieties of libraries (corporate, state, academic, research), with brief information on special collections. This is the place to check for contacts before traveling to visit a library collection.

0061 American Marketing Association. New York Chapter. **GREEN- BOOK: INTERNATIONAL DIRECTORY OF MARKETING RESEARCH COMPANIES AND SERVICES.** New York: AMA New York Chapter, 1962–date, annual (title has varied). Standard directory of marketing research organizations.

0062 **BACON'S MAGAZINE DIRECTORY.** Chicago: Bacon's Information Inc., 1993–date, annual. Formerly (through 41st ed.) part of BACON'S PUBLICITY CHECKER. Designed to serve advertisers and public relations practitioners, this provides detailed information for more than 10,400 business, trade, professional, and consumer publications, including circulation, advertising rates, news executives and editors names, types of unsolicited materials materials accepted, descriptions and profiles of content and targeted audience.

0063 **BACON'S NEWSPAPER DIRECTORY.** Chicago: Bacon's Information Inc., 1993–date, annual. Formerly (through 41st ed.) part of BACON'S PUBLICITY CHECKER. Covers more than 10,700 daily newspapers, weekly newspapers, weekly multiple publisher chains, news services, syndicates, and Sunday supplements in the United States and Canada. Information includes population of city, newspaper's name, address and telephone number, circulation, ad rate, titles and names of management and news executives, editors, reporters, local and syndicated colunmists. Separate sections: Black Press Newspaper Index, Hispanic Bilingual Newspaper Index (both list daily and weekly newspapers); Markets (daily newspapers in 209 major markets); Daily Newspapers Over 50,000 Circulation; Daily Newspaper Locator (place of publication given for newspapers whose banners do not include town name).

See 1037 BENN'S MEDIA.

0064 **EDITOR & PUBLISHER INTERNATIONAL YEARBOOK.** New York: Editor & Publisher, 1924–date, annual. CD-ROM version available from Editor and Publisher: covers current volume. Standard directory for the newspaper industry. First appeared in 1920/21 as a regular part of the trade magazine, EDITOR & PUBLISHER. The main section is a list of daily newspapers published in the United States, giving address, circulation, personnel directory, advertising rates, special editions, broadcast affiliates, political leanings for some newspapers, groups, and mergers. A new section, beginning in 1993, indexes the names of editors and journalists listed in the year book. Other directory sections include U.S. weekly and special newspapers, selected foreign newspapers, Canadian newspapers (daily, weekly, and foreign languages), national and international associations related to newspapers, employees and education, pay scales for guild reporters, industry organizations and supply companies, roster of the Newspaper Association of America, foreign correspondents, journalism schools, newsprint statistics, and clipping bureaus (print and electronic), descriptions of films about newspapers and journalism. Annual statistics for newsprint, including estimated consumption of U.S. users, stock in metric tons, shipments, and production. Data are from the Newspaper Association of America, American Forest and Paper Association, and Canadian Pulp and Paper Association.

0065 **FORBES MEDIA GUIDE 500: A CRITICAL REVIEW OF THE PRINT MEDIA.** Bedminster, NJ: Forbes, 1986–date, annual. Intended to be a news consumer's guide. Reviews journals, rates individual journalists, reprints representative articles, and gives biographical information. Also useful as a summary of top news stories of the year. Beginning with the 1993 review, some political cartoons are represented. Name and topic index. Supplements quarterly FORBES MEDIACRITIC (1170).

0066 **GALE DIRECTORY OF PUBLICATIONS AND BROADCAST MEDIA: AN ANNUAL GUIDE TO PUBLICATIONS AND BROADCASTING STATIONS INCLUDING NEWSPAPERS, MAGAZINES, JOURNALS, RADIO STATIONS, TELEVISION STATIONS, AND CABLE SYSTEMS.** Detroit: Gale, 1869–date, annual. Online version available from Dialog and GaleNet: updated twice yearly. A comprehensive and authoritative directory of media in the United States, Canada, and Puerto Rico, this continues a publishing history begun in 1869 as ROWELL'S AMERICAN NEWSPAPER DIRECTORY, continued in 1880 as AYER'S AMERICAN NEWSPAPER DIRECTORY, and more recently known as AYER DIRECTORY OF PUBLICATIONS and IMS DIRECTORY OF PUBLICATIONS. Broadcast stations and cable systems were added beginning with vol. 122 (1990). A strength of the directory is its combination of publications with broadcast stations and cable systems in a single geographic list. This arrangement offers an overall description of local media in the towns and cities. The Gale directory also includes tables of industry statistics, the number of newspapers and periodicals published in each state and province, and a count of publications by category (e.g., Black publications). Custom-made maps show cities and towns in which listed publications and stations are located. Vol. 3 includes useful indexes for publishers, formats, fields, languages, racial, gender, and religious groups.

0067 **INTERNATIONAL DIRECTORY OF NEWS LIBRARIES INCLUDING NEWSPAPER BANNERS.** Bayside, NY: LDA Publishers, 1996 (5th ed.). Gives access information to 800 newspaper libraries around the world. Published in cooperation with the News Division of the Special Libaries Association.

0068 **LITERARY MARKET PLACE.** Providence, NJ: R.R. Bowker, 1940–date, annual. LMP is the standard directory for the North American book publishing business. A new section in (56th volume, 1996) contains new section on electronic publishing and portends the blurring of book publishing and periodical publishing. Includes a directory of book reviewers who write for newspapers and magazines. Using this directory is more efficient than searching through standard newspaper and magazine directories. A similar section about magazines and newspapers featuring news about the book business also included.

0069 Katz, Bill, and Linda Sternberg Katz. **MAGAZINES FOR LIBRARIES.** New Providence, NJ: R.R. Bowker, 1969–date, annual. Carefully written descriptive and evaluative summaries of 6,600 periodicals give reasons why they were selected to represent best and most useful titles for public and academic libraries. Information is given about the publishing history, where the magazine is indexed, the intended audience, and the bibliographic information of frequency, publisher, and editor(s).

See 0748 RESEARCH SERVICES DIRECTORY.

0070 **WORKING PRESS OF THE NATION.** New Providence, NJ: National Register Publishing, 1950–date, annually. Began publication in 1947 under Farrell Publishing. 46th ed. published in 3 vols.: Newspaper Directory, Magazine and Internal Publications, and TV and Radio Directory. These comprehensive guides are organized to assist users to select the optimum media outlets. These directories list 180,000 individuals and 28,000 media locations. Subject indexes for newspaper editorial personnel and syndicate services. The directories give standard information with additional information of freelance pay scale, deadlines, materials accepted and included.

0071 **WRITER'S MARKET.** Cincinnati, OH: Writer's Digest Books, 1930–date, annual. Subtitled: "Where and how to sell what you write: 4,000 places to sell your articles, books, short stories, novels, plays, scripts, greeting cards, and fillers." A comprehensive guide for writers looking for a publisher and general help with getting published. Offers excellent advice and information about selling one's writings. Includes directories of consumer magazines, book publishers, small presses, book producers; information about contracts, copyright, finances and taxes, and illustrated instructions about correspondence and packaging the proposal. Indexed.

ii) Electronic

0072 **BIA'S RADIO YEARBOOK.** Chantilly, VA: BIA Publications, 1993–date, annual. Formerly DUNCAN'S RADIO YEARBOOK (1993). Station listings by market showing format, city of license, frequency, power, owner, date of acquisition, address, with listings of non-metro stations, group owners, service providers.

0073 **BIA'S TELEVISION YEARBOOK.** Chantilly, VA: BIA Publications, 1992–date, annual. Station listings by market showing city of license, power, affiliation, owner, date of acquisition, address, with listings of group owners and service providers.

0074 **BROADCASTING & CABLE YEARBOOK.** New Providence, NJ: R.R. Bowker, 1935–date, annual, two volumes in recent years (title has varied). Standard reference work for the industry featuring directories of radio and television stations in the U.S. and Canada. Entries include frequency, channel, power, date station began broadcasting, licensee, ownership, and date of acquisition. Includes format and programming information and market data. Lists radio stations by frequency and tv stations by channel. Cable section features directory of multiple systems operators, independent owners, and cable systems in U.S. and Canada. Yearbook also includes directories of programming, satellite, advertising and marketing, technical, and professional services; equipment manufacturers, and government agencies. Lists associations, schools, awards, books. Includes charts, statistics, brief history of broadcasting and cable, and selected regulations. Vol.2 contains the Radio, Television & Cable Yellow Pages, an alphabetical listing with telephone numbers of stations, companies, and personnel included in Vol. 1.

0075 **BURRELLE'S MEDIA DIRECTORY: BROADCAST MEDIA: RADIO.** Livingston, NJ: Burrelle's Information Services, 1981–date, annual. Lists more than 11,000 radio stations in the U.S., Canada, and Mexico. Entries include format, target audience, coverage area, and station policy regarding use of news releases and PSAs. Local programming information included as new feature with 1995 edition. Listings include program names, airtimes, and contact personnel. Radio networks and syndicated programs listed separately. Indices include network affiliated stations and programs by title (about 850 programs). BROADCAST MEDIA: RADIO is one of five volumes that compose BURRELLE'S MEDIA DIRECTORY. Other volumes include TELEVISION AND CABLE (0076) and three volumes concerned with print media. CD-ROM available from SilverPlatter: cumulates information in all five printed services; updated twice yearly.

0076 **BURRELLE'S MEDIA DIRECTORY: BROADCAST MEDIA: TELEVISION AND CABLE.** Livingston, NJ: Burrelle's Information Services, 1981–date, annual. Lists more than 1,500 television stations in the U.S., Canada, and Mexico and more than 500 cable systems in the U.S. Station entries include network affiliation, coverage area, station's policy on PSAs, type of information station would like to receive, and interview format used by station. Local programming information included as new feature with 1995 edition. Listings include program names, airtimes, and contact personnel. Cable section includes coverage area, ownership, policy on PSAs and local advertising. Separate listings of TV networks and syndicators. Lists and indices include radio and TV stations by DMA, and MSA, state capitals and key cities, and indices by program titles (about 600 programs). One of five volumes that compose BURRELLE'S MEDIA DIRECTORY. Others include BROADCAST MEDIA: RADIO (0075) and three volumes concerned with print media.

0077 **CABLE YELLOW PAGES.** Torrance, CA: CYP, 1989–date, annual. Internet: www.cableyellowpages.com. Provides alphabetical and subject-classified information. The 1994 edition includes over 8,000 listings for cable television systems, independent telephone companies, broadcast television stations, equipment suppliers, and cable programmers. Includes area codes, time zone map, international calling guide, coupons, scrambling assistance hotlines and U.S. federal mini-directory. Some of these features were dropped in 1995 edition. Indexes for product and service vendors are provided.

0078 **CABLE & STATION COVERAGE ATLAS.** Washington: Warren Publishing, Inc., 1966–date, annual. Title has varied. Provides zone and contour maps for television station and cable system coverage in 50 states, plus directory and statistical information. Includes some copyright and cable regulations text.

0079 **COMPLETE CABLE BOOK: THE MULTI-CHANNEL TELEVISION DIRECTORY.** Los Angeles: Homily Press, 1994–date, annual. Provides directory information for four categories: networks, pay-per-view, MSOs and noncable services. Each entry lists executives, address, phone and fax numbers. Some entries also delineate launch dates, ownership, and description of service. Index.

0080 **CPB PUBLIC BROADCASTING DIRECTORY.** Washington: Corporation for Public Broadcasting, 1982–date, annual. Directory of public radio and TV stations as well as national, regional, and state public broadcasting organizations, networks, and related agencies.

0081 **INTERNATIONAL TELEVISION & VIDEO ALMANAC.** New York: Quigley, 1929–date. Title has varied—long known as INTERNATIONAL TELEVISION ALMANAC. Detailed guide to broadcast, cable and home video markets with directories and statistics.

0082 **THE M STREET RADIO DIRECTORY.** Nashville, TN: M Street Corp., 1989–date, annual. Directory of U.S. and Canadian AM and FM stations, listing formats and station personnel as well as addresses, owners, current power and facilities, LMA data, and market area served. Includes listings by frequencies, call letters, markets (with Arbitron and Willhight ratings), and essays about FCC activities and procedures.

0083 **R&R RATINGS REPORT & DIRECTORY.** Los Angeles: Radio&Records, 1978–date, annual. Top 100 radio market profiles, listed by market rank, featuring Arbitron 1-year trends and rankings in five key demographics. Directory section includes schools, software, consultants, employment services, equipment suppliers, financial services, organizations, marketing firms, brokers, program suppliers, research firms, and show prep services.

0084 **RADIO SOURCE GUIDE AND DIRECTORY.** Springfield, VA: Radio Business Report, 1993–date, annual. Guide to radio business with directory sections and considerable market audience information, clearly arranged and indexed.

0085 Standard Rate and Data Service (SRDS). Des Plaines, IL. Issues the following:

1 **RADIO ADVERTISING SOURCE.** 1929–date, monthly. Title varies. Directory of commercial radio stations showing personnel, format, audience profile, and special programming. Separate listings of sales reps, networks, syndicators, and group owners. For many years, this monthly publication (as SPOT RADIO RATES AND DATA) was the source of station advertising rates for media buyers. Ad rate cards have not been included for many years.

2 **TV & CABLE SOURCE.** 1947–date, quarterly. Title varies as does frequency of publication. Directory of television stations (commercial and public), showing personnel, affiliation, facilities, production specifications, and programming schedules (for some entries). Also includes DMA maps and profiles, syndicators, networks, reps, interconnects, and cable systems. For many years, this was a monthly publication (as SPOT TELEVISION RATES AND DATA) and the source of station advertising rates for media. Ad rate cards have not been included for many years.

0086 **TELEVISION & CABLE FACTBOOK.** Washington: Warren Publishing, Inc., 1947–date, annual, three volumes since 1990. Title and frequency have varied. A volume each on cable, television stations, and services, with prodigious information on each subject. The stations volume provides contour maps, plus directory and historical information. The cable volume describes cable television systems arranged by city within state. The services volume provides alphabetical and classified listings of services such as associations, brokers, attorneys, program sources, and publications. Some Canadian information provided. Tables, figures, industry charts, glossary, indexes.

1-D. Dictionaries and Glossaries

(See also: 3-A-4 for technical dictionaries/glossaries)

0087 Bognár, Desi K. **AN INTERNATIONAL DICTIONARY OF BROADCASTING AND FILM.** Newton, MA: Focal Press, 1995, 256 pp. Includes several thousand terms and reference appendices. Illustrated.

0088 Delson, Donn and Edwin Michalov. **DELSON'S DICTIONARY OF CABLE, VIDEO & SATELLITE TERMS.** Thousand Oaks, CA: Bradson Press, 1983, 63 pp. Definitions provided for words and phrases commonly used in four industries: cable, satellite, programming, and home video.

0089 Devito, Joseph A. **THE COMMUNICATION HANDBOOK: A DICTIONARY.** New York: Harper & Row, 1986, 337 pp. Some 2,000 brief definitions plus about 100 longer essays on academic and research terminology.

0090 Diamant, Lincoln. **DICTIONARY OF BROADCAST COMMUNICATIONS.** Westport, CT: Greenwood, 1989 (3rd ed.), 255 pp. Some 6,000 terms are briefly defined.

0091 Ellmore, R. Terry. **NTC'S MASS MEDIA DICTIONARY.** Lincolnwood, IL: National Textbook, 1991, 668 pp. Some 20,000 terms across all media.

0092 Hansen, Douglas E. **EDUCATIONAL TECHNOLOGY TELECOMMUNICATIONS DICTIONARY WITH ACRONYMS.** Englewood Cliffs, NJ: Educational Technology Publications, 1991, 55 pp. Nontechnical definitions of about 750 common terms and acronyms; intended for educational administrators and teachers as well as business and community leaders.

0093 Jones, Glenn R. **JONES CABLE TELEVISION AND INFORMATION INFRASTRUCTURE DICTIONARY.** Englewood, CO: Jones Interactive, Inc., 1994 (4th ed.), 216 pp. This dictionary defines 350 acronyms, 2,900 terms and provides 750 cross references. Available on 3.5 diskettes for Macintosh or IBM Windows and on CD-ROM.

0094 **THE RADIO DICTIONARY: A NEW TESTAMENT OF RADIO.** Dublin, OH: Riverview Press, 1993, 352 pp. Pocket-sized dictionary of the radio industry with emphasis on advertising and marketing.

0095 Reed, Robert M. **DICTIONARY OF TELEVISION, CABLE & VIDEO.** New York: Facts on File, Inc., 1994, 256 pp. Terms are defined as they relate to electronic media: advertising, agencies/ associations/companies/unions, broadcasting/cablecasting, educational/corporate communications, engineering, general terms and processes, government/legal, home video, production, programming. Extensive cross references, abbreviations.

0096 Watson, James, and Anne Hill. **A DICTIONARY OF COMMUNICATION AND MEDIA STUDIES.** London: Edward Arnold, 1989 (2nd ed.), 190 pp. British-oriented, but only existing guide to several hundred research-related terms and the academic study of communications.

0097 Weiner, Richard. **WEBSTER'S NEW WORLD DICTIONARY OF MEDIA AND COMMUNICATIONS.** New York: Simon & Schuster, 1990. 533 pp. More than 30,000 definitions covering all fields of media communication.

1-E. Encyclopedias

0098 Brown, Les. **LES BROWN'S ENCYCLOPEDIA OF TELEVISION.** Detroit: Gale, 1992 (3rd ed.), 723 pp. A standard reference source first issued in 1977. Useful and concise insight into programs, people, and major firms. (see also Slide 0313)

0099 Inge, M. Thomas, ed. **HANDBOOK OF AMERICAN POPULAR CULTURE.** Westport, CT: Greenwood, 1989 (2nd ed., 3 vols.), 1,580 pp. Arranged in separately authored chapters by headings such as animation, film, magazines, and advertising. Each section provides an historic and bibliographic overview in both standard bibliographic format and an essay. Includes only monographic citations and a list of relevant U.S. periodicals.

0100 **INTERNATIONAL ENCYCLOPEDIA OF COMMUNICATIONS.** New York: Oxford, 1989 (4 vols.), 1,700 pp. Valuable for its broad-ranging social science and humanities scholarship-based entries—some quite extensive—on communication and its wide variety of expert contributors. Strong historical tone throughout. Tables, charts, bibliographic references.

See 1049. Kurian, WORLD PRESS ENCYCLOPEDIA.

0101 Pool, Ithiel de Sola, with Wilbur Schramm, et al. **HANDBOOK OF COMMUNICATION.** Chicago: Random House, 1973, 1,011 pp. Thirty-one chapters by a variety of experts cover the entire academic field and its various media. Notes, bibliographies, charts, tables, index.

0102 Reed, Robert M. and Maxine K. Reed. **THE ENCYCLOPEDIA OF TELEVISION, CABLE, AND VIDEO.** New York: Van Nostrand Reinhold, 1992, 622 pp. Provides 3,100 entries in 14 areas: advertising, agencies/associations/companies/unions, awards, educational/corporate communications, engineering, events, general terms/processes, government/legal, home video, people, personnel, production, programing, programs. Initials and acronyms index, bibliography, cross references.

0103 Thomas, Erwin K., and Brown H. Carpenter, eds. **HANDBOOK ON MASS MEDIA IN THE UNITED STATES.** Westport, CT: Greenwood, 1994, 325 pp. Brief descriptions of the history, organization, role, current issues, and outlook for the mass media industry. Analyzes different media audiences including minorities, women, children, and the disabled, plus those for religion and sports. Directs the user to significant sources of data and interpretation. Tables, figures, notes, bibliography, index.

1-F. Biographical Directories

(See also: 2-A-4.)

0104 **NEWS MEDIA YELLOW BOOK: WHO'S WHO AMONG REPORTERS, WRITERS, EDITORS, AND PRODUCERS IN THE LEADING NATIONAL NEWS MEDIA.** New York: Leadership Directories, 1993–date, quarterly. Detailed directory of U.S. news media personnel, including news services, newspapers, broadcasting networks, television stations, radio stations, independent and syndicated programs, periodicals of all types (associations, consumer, government, newsletters, trade, weekly newspapers), and non-U.S. media with U.S. bureaus. The Personnel Index is a unique source for locating working journalists and media professionals, 31,000 listed in a 1997 issue. Note: Given the dearth of monographic resources, *see also* the "Who's Where: The Directory of Newspaper Professionals," in EDITOR & PUBLISHER INTERNATIONAL YEAR BOOK (0064), beginning in 1993; and BROADCASTING & CABLE (1199) "Profile" features as indexed in Business Periodicals Index (0046) and online via LEXIS/NEXIS (0912), Dialog, and DowJones (0047). Vol. 2 of the BROADCASTING & CABLE YEARBOOK (0074) lists personnel at stations included in vol. 1.

0105 **WHO'S WHO IN ENTERTAINMENT.** Wilmette, IL: Marquis Who's Who, 1992 (2nd ed.), 700 pp. Over 18,000 biographical sketches of prominent individuals in the entertainment industry, including broadcast executives, television producers, and radio and television personalities.

1-G. Statistics

1-G-1. Guides to & Indexes of Statistics

0106 **GUIDE TO U.S. GOVERNMENT STATISTICS.** McLean, VA: Documents Index, 1990–date, biennial. First published in 1956; with 1990–91 (5th) edition revised in alternate years. Arranges statistical sources by departments and agencies. Agency, world area, and U.S. area indexes.

0107 Kurian, George Thomas. **SOURCEBOOK OF GLOBAL STATISTICS.** London: Longman/New York: Facts on File, 1985, 413 pp. Describes 209 sources of statistical information; international in scope. Subject index.

0108 **PREDICASTS.** Foster City, CA: Information Access. IAC Customer Service: Voice: 415-378-5398; 800-227-8431. Fax: 415-378-5329. Various PREDICASTS services available online on Dialog, DataStar, and other services. Information Access Company issues major statistical resources on markets, including:

1 **PREDICASTS BASEBOOK.** 1973–date, annual. Measures market size and cyclical sensitivity of products and industries. Arranged by SIC code with alphabetical list of products.

2 **PREDICASTS FORECASTS.** 1960–date, quarterly. Available online from DataStar. Formerly published by Predicasts. Short- and long-term statistics for economic indicators, products, markets, and industries, arranged by SIC code, extracted from trade and business press. Data cross references sources (journal title, date, page). Alphabetical list of products: "Electrical and electronic equipment" and "Communications" under SIC code 480. Coverage complements that provided in STATISTICAL MASTERFILE (0109).

0109 **STATISTICAL MASTERFILE** [CD-ROM]. Washington: Congressional Information Service, 1980–date, quarterly. CD-ROM indexing and abstracting service which cumulates CIS's printed AMERICAN STATISTICS INDEX (1973–date), INDEX OF INTERNATIONAL STATISTICS (1983–date), and STATISTICAL REFERENCE INDEX (1980–date). Online version only of AMERICAN STATISTICS INDEX available from Dialog: covers 1973–date, updated monthly. The CD-ROM version of ASI, IIS, and SRI is the most comprehensive and convenient index for statistics sources, covering the mid-1960s to the present. Detailed analyses of statistical data featured in wide range of publications issued by U.S. and international government and quasi-qovernment agencies, trade, and professional organizations, and in financial, business, and industry journals. Covers publications relevant to electronic mass media issued by departments of Commerce, FCC, NTIA, OTA; EC, OECD, foreign governments; and EIA and other trade associations as well as research centers. Also identifies statistics in selected popular journals like BUSINESS WEEK and FORBES, complementing coverage of PREDICASTS FORECASTS (0108). Full texts of selected statistical documents available in ASI, IIS, and SRI microfiche collections.

0110 **STATISTICS SOURCES.** Detroit: Gale Research, 1995. 20th ed. 2 vols. Subtitle: "A Subject Guide to Data on Industrial, Business, Social, Educational, Financial, and Other Topics for the United States and Internationally." For U.S., see topical headings (e.g., newspapers, radio) directly; for other countries and states, topical headings listed under main headings for countries and states. Source publications and sources of nonpublished data appendixed. For state statistical sources, see STATE AND LOCAL STATISTICS SOURCES, 2nd ed. (Detroit, MI: Gale Research, 1993).

1-G-2. U.S. Government Statistics Sources

0111 Department of Commerce. Bureau of the Census. Washington. All publications are published by GPO:

1 **ANNUAL SURVEY OF COMMUNICATION SERVICES.** 1992–date, annual. Series begins with data for 1990 (published 1992) and covers telephone, broadcast, and cable industries (all part of the 48 series in the SIC code). A dozen charts and as many tables plus appendices on the research process behind the report are provided. Includes revenue and expense estimates for telephone, broadcast and cable industries, and pay services.

2 **CURRENT INDUSTRIAL REPORTS.** 1959–date, monthly. This series consists of more than 100 monthly, quarterly, and annual reports giving current data on different industries arranged by SIC codes. Series MA 26M "Radio and Television Receivers, Phonographs, and Related Equipment." Based on CENSUS OF MANUFACTURING. Indexed in STATISTICAL MASTERFILE (0109).

3 Bureau of Economic Analysis. **SURVEY OF CURRENT BUSINESS.** 1921–date, monthly. Formerly issued by Bureau of Census and other offices. Comprehensive report on economic conditions and business activities. Indexed in STATISTICAL MASTERFILE (0109).

4 **STATISTICAL ABSTRACT OF THE UNITED STATES,** 1878–date, annual. Key media data, much of it from commercial sources, are included in the chapter, "Communication and Information Technology," which covers basic cable, books, home video, daily newspapers, recorded music, magazines, and movies in theaters. International statistics for the mass media industries are provided in "Comparative International Statistics."

0112 Department of Commerce. National Telecommunications and Information Administration. (see 0947). Minority Telecommunications Development Program. **MINORITY COMMERCIAL BROADCAST OWNERSHIP IN THE UNITED STATES.** 1990–date, annual. Title has varied. Minority broadcast ownership list by state showing station owner, address, and format. Minority ownership is deemed to exist when Blacks, Hispanics, Asian Americans, Native Americans, or any combination thereof own more than 50% of a broadcast corporations's stock or have voting control in a broadcast partnership.

See 0950. Federal Communications Commission ANNUAL REPORT.

0113 International Trade Commission. **U.S. INDUSTRIAL OUTLOOK.** Washington: GPO, 1961–1994, annual. Trends and projections for over 350 manufacturing and nonmanufacturing industries, arranged by SIC code for "Information and Communications." Data on employment, worker earnings, capital expenditures, imports and exports, etc. Cumulates data from other Department of Commerce publications. Indexed in STATISTICAL MASTERFILE (0000). NOTE: 1994 issue was last issued in hard-copy format.

1-G-3. Commercial Statistics Sources

i) General Media

0114 **INVESTEXT** [Online service]. Boston: Thomson Financial Services, 1982–date, daily. Available from Dialog, LEXIS/NEXIS (0912), and other services. CD-ROM version available from Thomson and SilverPlatter. Full texts of investment analyses and reports on companies and industries by more than 300 leading investment banks, consulting and research firms, and other financial authorities. Global coverage.

0115 **KAGAN'S MEDIA TRENDS: THE ESSENTIAL GUIDE TO THE ECONOMICS OF ENTERTAINMENT & COMMUNICATIONS MEDIA.** Carmel, CA: Paul Kagan Associates, 1993–date, annual. Compilation of charts showing historical and projected revenues for television, cable, direct broadcast satellite, home video, interactive multimedia, newspapers, video games, and wireless telecom. Includes consumer entertainment expenditures and usage data, developments in consumer media technology, and trends in mergers and acquisitions.

0116 **MARKETER'S GUIDE TO MEDIA.** New York: BPI Communications, 1978–date, twice yearly but issued annually effective 1996. Pocket-sized resource containing media industry rates and audience demographics for major media, including broadcast and syndicated television, cable, radio, out-of-home, promotion, custom publishing, magazine, and newspapers. Prepared by the publishers of Adweek magazines. Charts drawn from many sources including editors' projections. Strategically placed glossaries and definitions help user to interpret rate and circulation tables and audience estimates.

0117 **MEDIAMARK RESEARCH.** New York: Mediamark Research Inc., 1979–date, annual. Online MEDIAMARK RESEARCH DATA BASE available from Mediamark MEMRI and other services: updated twice yearly. Survey data for audiences of individual mass media (radio, television, newspapers, magazines, and outdoor advertising) in the U.S. Characteristics statistically described by various categories (e.g., age, sex, homemakers, working women, income, education, race, presence of children in the home, value of owned home, geographical area). Also describes audiences of specific titles or programs (e.g., ROLLING STONE or *60 Minutes*).

0118 **SIMMONS STUDY OF MEDIA AND MARKETS.** New York: Simmons Market Research Bureau, 1963–date, annual. Online and CD-ROM versions available from Simmons and other services. Statistical report on continental U.S. consumer market measuring adult use of particular products and mass media. The 1992 data are presented in "Product Volumes" (25 vols.) and as audience analyses (8 vols.) covering print, broadcast, and cable media. Used by advertising and public relations specialists. Simmons also publishes a technical guide and a code book for each annual survey.

0119 **STANDARD AND POOR'S INDUSTRY SURVEYS.** New York: Standard and Poor's, 1959–date, quarterly. Basic data on 69 domestic industries, including electronics and communications. Information on prospects, trends, problems, with composite industry statistical data, and financial comparisons of leading companies. Kept up to date by weekly loose-leaf service.

0120 **THE VERONIS, SUHLER & ASSOCIATES COMMUNICATIONS INDUSTRY FORECAST: HISTORICAL AND PROJECTED EXPENDITURES FOR 10 INDUSTRY SEGMENTS.** New York: Veronis, Suhler, 1987–date, annual. Compendium of historical and projected domestic media expenditure data by industry. Includes market growth and trend data for television, radio, cable TV, recorded music, filmed entertainment, newspaper publishing, book publishing, magazine publishing, business information, and advertising and promotion. Extensive charts, tables, and graphs cover most areas of communications industry spending and growth.

0121 **THE VERONIS, SUHLER & ASSOCIATES COMMUNICATIONS INDUSTRY REPORT: FIVE-YEAR HISTORICAL REPORT OF 400 PUBLIC COMPANIES.** New York: Veronis, Suhler, 1983–date, annual. Yearly and 5-year financial data of 11 communication industry segments, including television and radio, cable, filmed entertainment, recorded music, newspaper publishing, book publishing, magazine publishing, business information, advertising agencies, interactive digital media, and miscellaneous communications. Examines individual performances of over 400 publicly reporting companies. Tables and graphs summarize revenues, profits, margins, assets deployed, and returns of assets and growth.

ii) Print Media

0122 **MAGAZINE MARKET COVERAGE REPORT.** Schaumburg, IL: Audit Bureau of Circulations, 1984–date, annual, with supplements. Circulation data issued in several reports: by metropolitan statistical areas (MSAs), designated market areas (DMAs), and by publication and market. The analyses provide circulation for all magazines that voluntarily participate in the ABC Circulation Data Bank.

0123 Chin, Harry. **NEWSPAPER ADVERTISING SALES: THE COMPLETE GUIDE TO JOB FINDING, FACTS, AND FORECASTS.** Redmond, WA: Newspaper Research Press, 1994, 239 pp. Useful sources for information about professional opportunities as well as statistical information.

0124 **CIRCULATION.** Wilmette, IL: SRDS, 1991–date, annual. Subtitle: "The Annual Comprehensive Analysis of Penetration and Circulation of Major Print Media." A unique presentation of data representing circulation of U.S. print media based on standardized geographic areas down to the county level. Statistical information is presented in four sections: (a) Metropolitan Area Print Analysis, using geographic areas as defined by the U.S. Census, which includes population, households, retail sales, average household effective buying income, circulation of all U.S. daily and Sunday newspapers, total weekly newspaper circulation, newspaper groups and magazine circulation; (b) State Section that includes a summary of newspapers circulating within the state and an analysis for each county with a circulation breakdown; (c) County Section that includes magazines with top national circulations as well as penetration of newspapers and magazines across county lines; and (d) Television Viewing Areas as defined by Nielsen Media Research.

0125 **FACTS ABOUT NEWSPAPERS.** Reston, VA: The Newspaper Center of the Newspaper Association of America, 1966–date, annual. A pamphlet, displaying in tabular and graphic formats, statistical information about newspapers in the U.S. and Canada. Culled from private sources, the data are organized in 24 categories, including number of dailies, daily newspaper circulation, largest newspapers by circulation, largest newspaper companies, reading audience, readership demographics, advertising expenditures, employment, and newsprint consumption and prices.

0126 **NEWSPAPER INDUSTRY COMPENSATION SURVEY.** Park Ridge, IL: Inland Press Association, 1988–date, annual. The 1994 report is titled: NAA NEWSPAPER INDUSTRY COMPENSATION SURVEY. Reports salaries of 63 newspaper jobs. Custom reports are also available from Inland. Co-sponsored by the National Newspaper Association, New England Newspaper Association, Newspaper Association of America, Newspaper Personnel Relations Association, Pacific Northwest Newspaper Association, and International Newspaper Financial Executives.

0127 **NEWSPAPER INDUSTRY COST AND REVENUE STUDY.** Park Ridge, IL: Inland Daily Press Association, 1915–date, annual. 80th year in 1995. Industry standard study of newspaper cost and revenue, used to analyze performance. Custom reports are available from Inland. Co-sponsored by the International Newspaper Financial Executives.

0128 **NEWSPRINT DIVISION MONTHLY STATISTICAL REPORT.** Washington: American Forest and Paper Association, 1995–date, monthly with an ANNUAL STATISTICAL SUMMARY. Monthly report on newsprint production, shipments, inventory, and plant capacity for U.S. and Canada. Also reports U.S. consumption, foreign trade, publishers' stock, and shipments and capacity for various foreign countries. Data provided by the Newspaper Association of America, American Forest and Paper Association, Canadian Pulp and Paper Association, and other sources. See also PRESSTIME (1191) and FACTS ABOUT NEWSPAPERS (0125).

0129 **SRDS NEWSPAPER CIRCULATION ANALYSIS.** DesPlaines, IL: Standard Rate and Data Service, 1959–1990, annual. Detailed circulation analysis for all daily U.S. newspapers and news groups in standard market areas, showing market penetration and comparisons with competing media. Ceased with the 1990 edition.

iii) Electronic Media

0130 BIA Publications. Chantilly, VA. Issues:

1 **INVESTING IN RADIO: MARKET REPORT.** 1986–date, quarterly. Also available on MasterAccess database disks. Profiles Arbitron-rated radio markets and stations within those markets by presenting market overviews and competitive overviews for each. The market overview includes historical and projected gross revenue estimates, demographics, number of stations, and average shares. Competitive overview lists stations with ownership data, format, estimated revenue, and average quarter-hour shares, recent and historical.

2 **INVESTING IN RADIO: OWNERSHIP FILE.** 1986–date, annual. Also available on MasterAccess database disks. Lists over 3,100 commercial radio station owners in the U.S., including group and individual owners. Profiles their radio holdings, including rating data, performance, and estimated revenues.

3 **INVESTING IN TELEVISION: MARKET REPORT.** 1984–date, quarterly. Also available on MasterAccess database disks. Profiles Nielsen-rated television markets and stations within those markets. (Prior to 1994, Artibron ratings data were used.) Market trend analysis shows DMA rank, cable penetration, number of stations and average households using television (HUT) levels. Daypart share analysis profiles key daypart shares. Market overview includes demographics and estimated revenues, historical and projected. Competitive overview lists stations with ownership data, estimated revenues, and recent viewing shares.

4 **INVESTING IN TELEVISION: OWNERSHIP FILE.** 1987–date, annual. Also available on MasterAccess database disks. Profiles more than 750 individual and group owners. Lists

their station holdings and includes ratings data and estimated revenues. Includes over 1,300 commercial television stations in U.S. arranged alphabetically by owner.

0131 Corporation for Public Broadcasting. Washington. Issues following publications. See also 0519.

1 **AVERAGE REVENUE PROFILES FOR PUBLIC BROADCASTING STATIONS.** ca 1985–date, annual (issued as a RESEARCH NOTE). Shows average revenue sources for public radio and television stations by licensee type and budget size.

2 **INVENTORY OF FEDERAL FUNDS DISTRIBUTED TO PUBLIC TELECOMMUNICATIONS ENTITIES BY FEDERAL DEPARTMENTS AND AGENCIES.** ca 1982–date, annual. Submitted by CPB to president for transmittal to Congress, the report provides information about federal grants and contracts awarded directly to public telecommunications entities for services such as noncommercial radio and television programming, production facilities, interconnection, and captioning.

3 **PUBLIC BROADCASTING INCOME.** ca 1978–date, annual. Income analysis for public television and radio stations, including charts showing funding sources by percentages for current and previous years.

4 **VIEWER AND LISTENER MEMBERSHIP INCOME FOR PUBLIC TELEVISION AND RADIO GRANTEES.** ca 1985–date, annual (issued as a RESEARCH NOTE). Charts number of individual contributors to public broadcasting as well as average contribution.

0132 Duncan's American Radio. Cincinnati, OH. Voice: 513-731-1800.

1 **AMERICAN RADIO,** 1976–date, quarterly (spring and fall editions; summer and winter supplements). Individual market reports showing Arbitron ratings and programming information for reporting stations. Data provided for each station include number of listeners, recent and historical shares, cume ratings, demographics, and daypart rankings. Capsule station descriptions for many entries include format and revenue level. Market information includes Arbitron rank, population, time spent listening by average radio listener, household income, retail sales, and market revenues. Spring and fall are primary editions with spring edition including a national rankings supplement. Summer and winter supplements provide updated summaries of the 97 markets that Arbitron surveys on quarterly basis.

2 **AMERICAN RADIO: SMALL MARKET EDITION** complements the primary edition by providing coverage of about 100 small radio markets in the U.S. not included in the other issues.

3 **DUNCAN'S RADIO GROUP DIRECTORY.** 1989–date, annual. The 1996–1997 edition is the 6th ed. Includes groups with two or more rated stations in two or more Arbitron markets and revenues over $3 million. 1996–97 edition covers nearly 200 radio groups and includes ratings performance, station purchase prices, revenue estimates, group financial data, major shareholders, board of directors, and senior management.

4 **DUNCAN'S RADIO MARKET GUIDE.** 1984–date, annual. Source book showing economic conditions for over 170 radio markets. Provides market radio revenue histories and projections, revenue estimates for over 1,600 radio stations; salary estimates for many of the top 100 markets; revenue estimates for competitive media; radio station sales over past 5 years; population and retail sales histories and projections.

5 **THE RELATIONSHIP BETWEEN RADIO AUDIENCE SHARES AND RADIO REVENUE SHARES AND RADIO STATION AUDIENCE BREAKDOWNS.** 1989–date, annual. Study of the mathematical relationship (known as power ratio or conversion ratio) between the ratings of an individual station and the revenue that station is able to generate. Lists over 1,200 leading stations and outlines revenues and revenue shares for each. Provides national means for formats and by market size.

0133 Electronic Industries Association. Arlington, VA. Issues:

1 **CONSUMER ELECTRONICS: U.S. SALES.** 1984–date, semiannual. Current and historical unit and dollar sales for product categories (e.g., audio, video, home information, accessories) and total factory sales for industry; trends and household penetration rates. Indexed in STATISTICAL MASTERFILE (0109).

2 **U.S. CONSUMER ELECTRONICS INDUSTRY IN REVIEW.** 1968–date, annual. Title has varied. Issue for 1995 has 120 pp. of text, tables, and charts covering data from the late 1980s into the early 1990s. Details units sold and factory value for a wide variety of consumer electronics. Indexed in STATISTICAL MASTERFILE (0109).

0134 National Association of Broadcasters. Washington. See also: 0513.

1 **ADVERTISING REVENUES PER TELEVISION HOUSEHOLD: A MARKET-BY-MARKET ANALYSIS.** 1990–date, annual. Analyzes revenues of local television markets on a market-by-market basis for 116 markets. Because revenue per TV household is purest form of the product of the local television market, this analysis shows how markets are faring, controlling for influence of fluctuations in market size (i.e., population). Data are from NAB/BCFM's TELEVISION MARKET ANALYSIS (see below).

2 **A FINANCIAL PROFILE OF TELEVISION STATIONS BY NETWORK AFFILIATION.** 1992–date, annual. An evaluation of the relative performance of local affiliates of the four major television networks. Analyzes and compares pre-tax profits, expenses, ad revenues, and cash flow figures over a 5-year period. Includes summary tables for each affiliate group, nationwide and by market size for most recent years. Data are taken from NAB's TELEVISION FINANCIAL REPORT. (see below)

3 **RADIO FINANCIAL REPORT.** 1953–1992, annual. Title varies. Survey report showing average revenues, expenses, cash flow, profit margins, and number of employees of radio stations by revenue size and station type. The final edition (1992) features 80 charts in five categories: all stations, daytime AM, fulltime AM, AM/FM, and FM. Revenue categories include national/regional advertising, local advertising, political advertising, tradeouts, and barter. Expense items include compensation, music license fees, outside news services, and ratings services. All charts provide average figures as well as 25, 50, and 75 percentile figures.

4 **TELEVISION FINANCIAL REPORT.** 1950–date, annual. Title varies. (Issued in recent years in cooperation with Broadcast Cable Financial Management Association.) Survey report showing average revenues, expenses, and pre-tax profit, profit margins, cash flow, capital expenditures, and number of employees of television stations by market size, affiliate type, and revenue category. The 1996 edition features 85 tables in nine categories: all stations; affiliate stations: ABC, CBS, NBC; ABC; CBS; Fox; NBC; independent stations; VHF independent stations; and UHF independent stations. Revenue categories include network compensation, national/regional advertising; local advertising, political advertising. Expense items include compensation, broadcast rights, amortization, music license fees, and departmental expenses for seven areas. Charts provide average figures as well as 25, 50, 75 percentile figures. Detailed anaylsis allows comparison of revenue and expense items with national averages.

5 **THE TELEVISION INDUSTRY: MARKET-BY-MARKET REVIEW.** 1992–date, annual. (Issued with Bond & Pecaro.) Financial and market data on 211 DMAs. Demographic summary includes population, number of households, retail sales, effective buying income, and cable and VCR penetration. Financial data, including historical and projected revenues, are provided where available. Includes local cable ad sales. Station summary shows ratings history for recent years plus technical data.

6 **TELEVISION MARKET ANALYSIS.** 1981–date, annual. (Issued with Broadcast Cable Financial Management Association.) Aggregate television market revenue and expense data. Title varies as does coverage. 1996 edition contains data on 117 TV markets and includes figures for network compensation, total advertising revenues, tradeouts, political advertising revenues, expenses, cash flow, and profit margin. Not all information is available in all markets because station response is voluntary.

0135 Paul Kagan Publications. Carmel, CA. Issues a variety of electronic media industry statistical and other (see 0115, 1048) publications, including:

1 **BROADCAST FINANCIAL RECORD.** 1984–date, annual. Summary of key financial data for publicly held U.S. radio and television companies. Includes income statement,

operating margins, return on investment, balance sheets, debt coverage, and cash flow. Appendices include directories of bankers, venture capital contacts, brokers, and appraisers.

2 **KAGAN'S RADIO DEAL RECORD.** 1988–date, annual. Summarizes data regarding radio station transactions proposed since 1981, including cash flow multiples, prior sales prices, terms of deals, years held, and seller financing. Data are drawn from financial reports filed by owners of radio stations, documents filed with FCC by station buyers and sellers, and estimates of Paul Kagan Associates. Includes sections for most recent deals as well as historical transactions.

3 **KAGAN'S TV DEAL RECORD.** 1988–date, annual. Summarizes data regarding television station transactions proposed since 1981, including cash flow multiples, prior sales prices, terms of deals, years held, seller financing. Data are drawn from financial reports filed by owners of TV stations, documents filed with the FCC by station buyers and sellers, and estimates of Paul Kagan Associates. Includes sections for most current deals as well as historical transactions.

0136 Radio Advertising Bureau. **RADIO MARKETING GUIDE AND FACTBOOK FOR ADVERTISERS.** New York: RAB, 1959–date, annual. Title varies. Compilation of statistics designed to sell radio as an effective advertising medium. Includes charts showing radio's reach, listener trends and profiles, top radio advertisers, revenue growth, and format data.

0137 Schutz, David E. **TRENDS IN RADIO STATION SALES.** Washington: National Association of Broadcasters, 1990–date, annual. Provides open market selling prices and reviews patterns in station values during the preceding 2-year period. Material compiled from FCC documents and trade press. Transaction information includes technical data, date sale was announced, and sale price of station. Separate sections rank largest sales in terms of price for each type of station and chart appreciation in station values.

0138 Television Bureau of Advertising. **TRENDS IN TELEVISION.** New York: TVB, ca. 1983–date, annual. Collection of charts showing current and historical statistics about television. Numbers include TV households, time spent viewing, set sales, number of stations, ad volume, and commercial activity.

0139 **TV DIMENSIONS.** New York: Media Dynamics, 1983–date, annual. Report on revenue trends, audience dynamics, intermedia comparisons, reach and frequency factors, with emphasis on television as an advertising vehicle. Heavily illustrated with charts showing both quantitative and qualitative factors that impact on television.

1-G-4. Historical Media Statistics

0140 Chapin, Richard E. **MASS COMMUNICATIONS: A STATISTICAL ANALYSIS.** East Lansing: Michigan State University Press, 1957, 148 pp. Pioneering survey of historical statistics with chapters on newspaper, book, magazine, radio and television, and motion-picture industries. Important early work on what are today referred to as cultural indicators. Tables, notes, appendix, bibliography.

0141 Rubin, Michael Rogers and Mary Taylor Huber. **THE KNOWLEDGE INDUSTRY IN THE UNITED STATES, 1960–1980.** Princeton, NJ: Princeton University Press, 1986, 213 pp. Economic and other measures of knowledge production and distribution in dozens of tables and supporting text. Notes, index.

0142 Sterling, Christopher H. and Timothy R. Haight. **THE MASS MEDIA: ASPEN INSTITUTE GUIDE TO COMMUNICATION INDUSTRY TRENDS.** New York: Praeger, 1978, 457 pp. Some 200 tables of historical statistics and supporting text on growth of media industries, ownership and control, economics, employment and training, content trends, media audiences, and U.S. media abroad. Within each chapter are tables on the major media: books, newspapers, magazines, motion pictures, recordings, radio, and television. Tables, references, subject index.

0143 Sterling, Christopher H. **ELECTRONIC MEDIA: A GUIDE TO TRENDS IN BROADCASTING AND NEWER TECHNOLOGIES: 1920–1983.** New York: Praeger, 1984, 337 pp. Reprints, updates, and expands the electronic media material presented in the book immediately above. Adds new tables and text on pay cable, home VCRs, and media regulation. Tables, notes, and references.

2

History

Chapter 2 begins with several standard bibliographies that describe mass communications' historical literature published as books and journals. Particularly useful starting points among these resources are Caswell's GUIDE TO SOURCES IN AMERICAN JOURNALISM HISTORY (0146) and Pollay's INFORMATION SOURCES IN ADVERTISING HISTORY (0152). Although Startt and Sloan's HISTORICAL METHODS IN MASS COMMUNICATION (0261) offers solid information on historical research methods, similar guides are needed for the other fields of mass communications.

This chapter includes references to significant collections of unpublished materials located in museums, archives, libraries, and other repositories. These references clearly reflect mass communications' technological and business/labor interests. Section 2-B includes a limited selection of federal, state, and local museums, archives, historical collections, public and academic libraries, and other repositories containing important manuscripts and unpublished materials on mass communications.

Standard guides and databases described in this chapter identify many more collections; no single guide, however, can locate and describe the full richness of archived resources. U.S. newspapers are the primary example. Newspapers are extensively archived by each of the state libraries and state historical societies as well as by myriad local institutions. In the 1980s a national program to identify, catalog, and preserve U.S. state newspapers was funded by the National Endowment for the Humanities. The cataloging records from this comprehensive inventory are available in the Online Computer Library Center's database (OCLC). On the other hand, no existing guides even attempt to describe the full range of corporate archives—and some archivists and librarians are hesitant to even admit their existance. We apologize for likely omissions and welcome additional information about other significant collections available for mass communications research.

Entries for collections frequently cite standard NATIONAL UNION CATALOG OF MANUSCRIPT COLLECTIONS (NUCMC; 0182) numbers (MS) to facilitate obtaining more information about their contents. The recent publication of its subject and corporate names index makes NUCMC all the more useful. Users are advised to consult DeWitt's outstanding GUIDE TO ARCHIVES AND MANUSCRIPT COLLECTIONS IN THE UNITED STATES (0148) to identify published guides, finding aids, and calendars for repositories. DeWitt's selection of guides to the collections of the Library of Congress, National Archives, Smithsonian, and presidential libraries will save researchers valuable time. It is noteworthy that these institutions and many others now publish guides to their collections on their www homepages and similar electronic gateway services. This chapter concludes with selected listings of general secondary historical studies of mass communications.

2-A. Bibliographic Resources

2-A-1. Bibliographies

0144 Brigham, Clarence S., comp. **HISTORY AND BIBLIOGRAPHY OF AMERICAN NEWSPAPERS, 1690–1820.** Worcester, MA: American Antiquarian Society, 1947, 2 vols. Classic and important source listing newspapers in the United States. Organized geographically; locates and describes newspaper collections. Contains a list of libraries, private owners, and an index to titles and printers. Complements Gregory's AMERICAN NEWSPAPERS (0150).

0145 Cannon, Carol L. **JOURNALISM: A BIBLIOGRAPHY.** New York: New York Public Library, 1924 (reprinted by Gale Research, 1967), 360 pp. Comprehensive annotated discussion of sources on both U.S. and British journalism to time of publication. Extensively subject divided.

0146 Caswell, Lucy Shelton, ed. **GUIDE TO SOURCES IN AMERICAN JOURNALISM HISTORY.** New York: Greenwood, 1989, 319 pp. Carefully annotated guide to research methods and resources, especially on newspaper history. Section on archival and manuscript sources describes newspaper holdings in 172 repositories in 34 states. Indexed.

0147 Cooper, Isabella M., comp. **BIBLIOGRAPHY ON EDUCATIONAL BROADCASTING.** Chicago: University of Chicago Press, 1942 (reprinted by Arno Press, 1971), 576 pp. Far more comprehensive than title suggests, this covers all of pre-war radio, annotating some 1,800 studies, reports, books, and articles in a subject-divided volume with good indexes.

0148 DeWitt, Donald L. **GUIDE TO ARCHIVES AND MANUSCRIPT COLLECTIONS IN THE UNITED STATES: AN ANNOTATED BIBLIOGRAPHY.** Westport, CT: Greenwood, 1994, 478 pp. Describes 2,062 published finding aids for governmental, academic, institutional, corporate, and other collections. Classified arrangement: relevant entries in sections for "Radio/Television"; other useful listings in geographical and professional sections. An important starting point for historical research.

0149 Flannery, Gerald V. **MASS MEDIA: MARCONI TO MTV 1900–1988: A SELECTED BIBLIOGRAPHY OF *NEW YORK TIMES* SUNDAY MAGAZINE ARTICLES ON COMMUNICATION.** Lanham, MD: University Press of America, 1989, 342 pp. Chronological listing divided by subject within each year, with good indexes, although not annotated.

0150 Gregory, Winnifred, ed. **AMERICAN NEWSPAPERS, 1821–1936: A UNION LIST OF FILES AVAILABLE IN THE UNITED STATES AND CANADA.** New York: Wilson, 1937, 791 pp. An exhaustive listing of the holdings of U.S. newspapers in 5,700 depositories, including libraries, county courthouses, newspaper offices, and private collections. Continues Brigham's HISTORY AND BIBLIOGRAPHY OF AMERICAN NEWSPAPERS (0144).

0151 Humphreys, Nancy K. **AMERICAN WOMEN'S MAGAZINES: AN ANNOTATED HISTORICAL GUIDE.** New York: Garland, 1989, 303 pp. The hundreds of American women's magazines included cover three centuries, all regions in the U.S., all ages, racial and class background, sexual preference, and ideology. Two sections cover alternative and mainstream publications. Detailed subject index.

0151a **INTERNATIONAL DIRECTORY OF COMPANY HISTORIES.** Detroit: St. James Press, 1988–date, in progress. Exceptionally useful for informative histories of mass communications and related companies, global in scope. Entries in first six vols arranged by industry (e.g., vol. 2 includes entertainment—broadcasting and motion pictures; vol. 4 includes publishing) while from vol. 7 on arranged alphabetically, and include classified index to the complete set.

0152 Pollay, Richard W., ed. **INFORMATION SOURCES IN ADVERTISING HISTORY.** Westport, CT: Greenwood, 1979, 330 pp. Bibliographic essays with annotated bibliographies on all aspects of the topic including most media of communication. Indexed.

0153 Price, Warren C. **THE LITERATURE OF JOURNALISM: AN ANNOTATED BIBLIOGRAPHY.** Minneapolis: University of Minnesota Press, 1959, 489 pp. A classic reference work with some 3,100 titles annotated in subject-divided categories. Index.

0154 _____ and Calder M. Pickett. **AN ANNOTATED JOURNALISM BIBLIOGRAPHY.** Minneapolis: University of Minnesota Press, 1970, 283 pp. Continues book immediately above with 2,100 more entries, but is arranged alphabetically with subject indexing.

0155 Rivers, William L. and Wallace Thompson, eds. **ASPEN HANDBOOK ON THE MEDIA: 1977–79 EDITION: A SELECTIVE GUIDE TO RESEARCH, ORGANIZATIONS AND**

PUBLICATIONS IN COMMUNICATIONS. New York: Praeger, 1977 (3rd ed.), 438 pp. First issued in 1973, this volume surveys the field broadly in sections on universities with research programs, nonacademic research groups, those supporting research, organizations, media action groups, government policymaking, communication law courses, international and overseas organizations, special libraries, periodicals, books, bibliographies, and films. It is useful today as a record of older materials. Index.

0156 Rose, Oscar. **RADIO BROADCASTING AND TELEVISION: AN ANNOTATED BIBLIOGRAPHY.** New York: H.W. Wilson, 1947, 120 pp. Useful for its details on and annotations of early literature, especially more ephemeral booklets and pamphlets. Television material covers five pages. Indexes.

0157 Shiers, George, assisted by May Shiers. **BIBLIOGRAPHY OF THE HISTORY OF ELECTRONICS.** Metuchen, NJ: Scarecrow Press, 1972, 323 pp. Well-annotated guide including topical chapters on radio and television, broadcasting, and both individual and company biographies—some 1,800 items in all. Index.

0158 _____. **EARLY TELEVISION: A BIBLIOGRAPHIC GUIDE TO 1940.** New York: Garland, 1996, 616 pp. Exhaustive and definitive with nearly 9,000 entries, this chronologically arranged and extensively annotated guide covers developments in all countries through 1939 and provides a highly selective listing of major monographs published since then. Indexed by subject and name.

2-A-2. Abstracts, Indexes, Databases

0159 **AMERICA: HISTORY AND LIFE**. Santa Barbara, CA: ABC-Clio, 1964–date, 5/year. Online version available from Dialog and other services: covers 1964–date; updated quarterly. CD-ROM version available from ABC-Clio: covers 1982–date; updated 3/year. The best index to the scholarly literature (books, journals, dissertations) on U.S. mass communications history. Selectively indexes about 2,000 journals in history, economics, law, political science, and other disciplines as well as major interdisciplinary journals, in 40 languages, including CRITICAL STUDIES IN MASS COMMUNICATION, JOURNAL OF COMMUNICATION, JOURNAL OF POPULAR CULTURE, JOURNALISM & MASS COMMUNICATION QUARTERLY, and TECHNOLOGY AND CULTURE. Classified arrangement: relevant listings in transportation and communication, culture, arts, and ideas; entries relevant to political communication, propaganda, public opinion, are ubiquitous. Indexes for authors, book reviews, and subjects: relevant headings include names of companies and organizations and full range of media. Scholarly historical literature on international media history indexed in complementary HISTORICAL ABSTRACTS (Santa Barbara, CA: ABC-Clio, 1955–date). Several separately published selected topical bibliographies in the Clio Bibliography Series, based on ABC-Clio databases, also include listings relevant to communications history: LABOR IN AMERICA: A HISTORICAL BIBLIOGRAPHY (1985); and CORPORATE AMERICA: A HISTORICAL BIBLIOGRAPHY (1984).

0160 **WRITINGS ON AMERICAN HISTORY**. Washington: American Historical Association, 1902–date, annual. Formerly ANNUAL REPORT of the American Historical Association (1902–1960) and other variant titles. Standard authoritative bibliography of studies of U.S. history. More comprehensive, but also more difficult to use, than AMERICA: HISTORY AND LIFE (0159). Classified listings: relevant entries under communication history; cultural and intellectual history (journalism, visual arts, popular culture, communication, public opinion, and publishing); and cultural relations with other countries (political communication and propaganda); and under social history and public world. No subject indexing, no cumulations; but covers everything, international in scope. Must be used in a comprehensive literature search.

2-A-3. Chronologies

0161 Hudson, Robert V. **MASS MEDIA: A CHRONOLOGICAL ENCYCLOPEDIA OF TELEVISION, RADIO, MOTION PICTURES, MAGAZINES, NEWSPAPERS, AND BOOKS**

IN THE UNITED STATES. New York: Garland, 1987, 435 pp. This media chronology from 1638 to 1985 can be approached by year, as arranged, or by its detailed subject index. The work was inspired by and complements Edwin and Michael Emery's THE PRESS AND AMERICA (0255).

0162 Nelson, Richard Alan. **A CHRONOLOGY AND GLOSSARY OF PROPAGANDA IN THE UNITED STATES**. Westport, CT: Greenwood, 1996, 341 pp. Includes 115 pages of chronology, 150 pages of glossary, and 30 pages of selected references on the subject broadly defined (many media-relevant dates are included).

2-A-4. Biographical Sources

(See also: 1-F)

0163 Ashley, Perry J., ed. **AMERICAN NEWSPAPER JOURNALISTS**. Detroit: Gale Research, 4 vols. to date for U.S. journalists:

1 **1690–1872**. 1985, 527 pp. (Dictionary of Literary Biography, v. 43)
2 **1873–1900.** 1983, 392 pp. (Dictionary of Literary Biography, v. 23)
3 **1901–1925**. 1984, 385 pp. (Dictionary of Literary Biography, v. 25)
4 **1926–1950**. 1984, 410 pp. (Dictionary of Literary Biography, v. 29)

Lengthy illustrated essays on hundreds of journalists. Preface to each volume provides historical context for the period. Other volumes of DLB cover screenwriters and book publishers.

See 0029. BIOGRAPHY AND GENEALOGY MASTER INDEX.

See 0030. BIOGRAPHY INDEX.

0164 Bloxham, James L., ed. **WHO'S WHO IN CABLE COMMUNICATIONS**. El Cajon, CA: Communications Marketing, Inc., 1980, 190 pp. Although billed as the inaugural edition of an annual, no sequel appeared. Biographies for 1,500 people at all levels of industry employment were compiled from a biographical data form and followup telephone calls. Provides 19 items of information for each entry. Gaps exist where a person did not want to be listed or could not be located. Abbreviations.

0165 Downs, Robert B., and Jane B. Downs. **JOURNALISTS OF THE UNITED STATES: BIOGRAPHICAL SKETCHES OF PRINT AND BROADCAST NEWS SHAPERS FROM THE LATE 17TH CENTURY TO THE PRESENT**. Jefferson, NC: McFarland, 1991, 391 pp. Alphabetically arranged biographies of major persons in U.S. newspaper and broadcast journalism. Introduction surveys issues and topics in U.S. journalism history, including censorship, muckraking, women journalists, wartime journalism. Bibliography and index.

0166 Dziki, Sylwester, Janina Maczuga, and Walery Pisarek, compilers. **WORLD DIRECTORY OF MASS COMMUNICATION RESEARCHERS**. Cracow, Poland: Bibliographic Section of IAMCR and CECOM and Press Research Centre in Cracow, 1984, unpaged. Project of the Bibliographic Section of the International Association for Mass Communication Research, the Press Research Centre and Comnet: International Network for Documentation of Communication Research and Policies, the directory provides personal information about active scholars in the 1980s. The entries give biographical and directory information and list each scholar's publications and describe areas of research interests.

0167 Ingham, John N. **BIOGRAPHICAL DICTIONARY OF AMERICAN BUSINESS LEADERS.** Westport, CT: Greenwood, 1983, 4 vols. Entries for 1,159 "historically most significant business leaders" with bibliographies. Useful indexes for industries (entertainment and allied fields), companies, and subjects.

0168 McKerns, Joseph P., ed. **BIOGRAPHICAL DICTIONARY OF AMERICAN JOURNALISM**. Westport, CT: Greenwood, 1989, 820 pp. Biographical essays about both living and deceased journalists, describing the lives and professional contributions of nearly 1,000 women and men in U.S. journalism. Well-written entries by scholars of journalism history include standard biographical information and nonstandard evaluative information about careers and contributions.

Appendices include an index of personal names, publication titles, and list of entries by category (e.g. columnist, humorist), minority and ethnic journalism, and women in journalism.

0169 Riley, Sam G., ed. **AMERICAN MAGAZINE JOURNALISTS.** Detroit: Gale Research, 4 vols. to date:

1 **1741–1850**. 1988, 430 pp. (Dictionary of Literary Biography, v. 73).
2 **1850–1900**. 1988, 387 pp. (Dictionary of Literary Biography, v. 79).
3 **1900–1960: FIRST SERIES.** 1990, 401 pp. (Dictionary of Literary Biography, v. 91).
4 **1900–1960: SECOND SERIES.** 1994, 411 pp. (Dictionary of Literary Biography, v. 137). These DLB volumes provide solid, heavily illustrated, scholarly biographies of both living and dead U.S. editors, publishers, and writers, with primary and secondary bibliographies.

0170 _____ . **BIOGRAPHICAL DICTIONARY OF AMERICAN NEWSPAPER COLUMNISTS**. Westport, CT: Greenwood, 1995, 411 pp. Some 600 figures are included, ranging from a few sentences to two pages. Bibliography.

0171 Taft, William H. **ENCYCLOPEDIA OF TWENTIETH-CENTURY JOURNALISTS**. New York: Garland, 1986. 408 pp. Biographical sketches of over 1,000 media personalities with emphasis on post-World War II period. Inclusion based on achievement and reputation.

2-B. Museums, Archives, and Libraries

2-B-1. Directories and Guides to Libraries and Archives

0172 Ash, Lee, and William G. Miller, comps. **SUBJECT COLLECTIONS: A GUIDE TO SPECIAL BOOK COLLECTIONS AND SUBJECT EMPHASES AS REPORTED BY UNIVERSITY, COLLEGE, PUBLIC, AND SPECIAL LIBRARIES AND MUSEUMS IN THE UNITED STATES AND CANADA.** New York: R. R. Bowker, 1993 (7th ed.), 2 vols. Standard guide to collections, including institutional and corporate archives. Subject arrangement includes detailed listings under communications, newspapers, radio, and television.

0173 Bedi, Joyce E., Ronald R. Kline, and Craig Semsel. **SOURCES IN ELECTRICAL HISTORY: ARCHIVES AND MANUSCRIPT COLLECTIONS IN U.S. REPOSITORIES**. New York: Center for the History of Electrical Engineering, 1989, 234 pp. Sponsored by the Friends of the IEEE Center. Describes 1,008 collections in 158 repositories, mainly university archives and state historical societies. Entries arranged by collection titles, with notes on size, contents, finding aids, and data for repositories and access. Repository and subject indexes. An important resource for historical research.

0174 **BIBLIOGRAPHIC CHECKLIST OF AFRICAN AMERICAN NEWSPAPERS**. Baltimore, MD: Genealogical Publishing Co., 1995, 206 pp. Identifies more than 5,000 titles and describes collections in libraries and other repositories.

0175 Danilov, Victor J. **AMERICA'S SCIENCE MUSEUMS.** New York: Greenwood, 1990, 483 pp. Classified descriptions of national, regional, local, and private museums, including the National Museum of Communications, Hagley Museum and Library, and others. Museum name index.

0176 **DIRECTORY OF ARCHIVES AND MANUSCRIPT REPOSITORIES IN THE UNITED STATES**. Phoenix, AZ: Oryx Press, 1988 (2nd ed.), 853 pp. Compiled by National Historical Publications and Records Commission. Especially useful for collections in university and state and local historical and institutional collections. Arranged geographically with repository and subject indexes.

0177 **DIRECTORY OF BUSINESS ARCHIVES IN THE UNITED STATES AND CANADA**. Chicago: Society of American Archivists, Business Archives Section, 1990 (4th ed.), 96 pp. Brief descriptions and contact information for about 100 selected mass communication company archives, including ABC, N.W. Ayer, Inc., CBS News, Walt Disney Company, and Tribune Company. Geographical and business-type indexes.

0178 **DIRECTORY OF SPECIAL LIBRARIES AND INFORMATION CENTERS.** Detroit: Gale, 1963–date, irregular. 18th ed. for 1995. International in scope. Vol. 1 (in two parts) includes brief descriptive entries arranged by repository with subject index: relevant listings cross referenced under advertising, broadcast journalism, journalism, newspapers, radio, and television. Vol. 2 is geographic and name index. Updated by NEW SPECIAL LIBRARIES (1988–date).

0179 Godfrey, Donald G. **RERUNS ON FILE: A GUIDE TO ELECTRONIC MEDIA ARCHIVES**. Hillsdale, NJ: Erlbaum, 1992, 322 pp. Arranged by state and then by archive, this is a useful annotated search guide to recorded material including radio and television programs.

0180 Heintze, James R. **SCHOLARS' GUIDE TO WASHINGTON, D.C. FOR AUDIO RESOURCES: SOUND RECORDINGS IN THE ARTS, HUMANITIES, AND SOCIAL, PHYSICAL, AND LIFE SCIENCES.** Washington: Smithsonian Institution Press, 1985, 395 pp. Classified descriptions of resources in libraries, archives, museums, embassies, organizations, research centers, academic programs, government offices, and other entities, with name, subject, and organization indexes. Sections for broadcasting organizations and publications and print media most useful.

0181 Library of Congress Manuscript Division. **NATIONAL INVENTORY OF DOCUMENTARY SOURCES IN THE UNITED STATES.** Teaneck, NJ: Chadwyck-Healey, 1983–date, irregular. Microfiche collection. The most powerful access tool for U.S. archive collections, comprising a topical index to published and unpublished finding aids for individual collections, with the full text of those finding aids. CD-ROM version, INDEX TO NIDS (Alexandria, VA: Chadwyck-Healey, 1992–date), essentially makes this key word access to collection descriptions.

0182 _____. **NATIONAL UNION CATALOG OF MANUSCRIPT COLLECTIONS.** Washington: Library of Congress, 1962–date, annual, with 5-year cumulative indexes. Usually referred to as NUCMC. Essential for historical research. As of 1992 includes more than 70,000 manuscript collections reported by nearly 1,400 libraries and other repositories since 1959. Subject index. Access greatly facilitated with INDEX TO PERSONAL NAMES IN THE NATIONAL UNION CATALOG OF MANUSCRIPT COLLECTIONS, 1959–1984, 2 vols. (Alexandria, VA: Chadwyck-Healey, 1988); and INDEX TO SUBJECTS AND CORPORATE NAMES IN THE NATIONAL UNION CATALOG OF MANUSCRIPT COLLECTIONS, 1959–1984, 2 vols. (Alexandria, VA: Chadwyck-Healey, 1994). Latter provides useful headings for organizations; heading for television subdivided into directing and production, news and commentary, and programs and scripts.

0183 Meckler, Alan M., and Ruth McMullin, eds. **ORAL HISTORY COLLECIONS.** New York: R.R. Bowker, 1975, 344 pp. Name and subject index to oral history collections in U.S. and selected foreign centers and archives. Relevant listings under radio and popular culture.

0184 Mehr, Linda Harris, comp. and ed. **MOTION PICTURES, TELEVISION, AND RADIO: A UNION CATALOGUE OF MANUSCRIPT AND SPECIAL COLLECTIONS IN THE WESTERN UNITED STATES**. Boston: G.K. Hall, 1977, 201 pp. Dated but solid information on special collections of film, television, and radio in academic and public libraries, historical societies, and other research centers in Arizona, California, Colorado, Idaho, New Mexico, Oregon, Utah, and Washington. "Index of Occupations" and general index.

0185 **OFFICIAL MUSEUM DIRECTORY**. Washington: American Association of Museums, 1961–date, biennial. Briefly annotated listings by state with indexes for institutions by collections (see listings under "Tools and Equipment for Communication" and "Audiovisual and Film") and by category (see "Communications Museums" and "Audiovisual and Film Museums").

0186 Prelinger, Richard, and Celeste R. Hoffnar, eds. **FOOTAGE...: NORTH AMERICAN FILM AND VIDEO SOURCES**. New York: Prelinger Associates, 2 vols.

1 **1989**. 795 pp.
2 **1991**. 246 pp.

Directory of nearly 2,000 moving image collections in institutions, organizations and corporations. Geographical arrangement with source/collection index and detailed subject index. Entries are descriptive and intended to characterize nature, strength, and research value of the collection. Includes information on access, rights, licensing, restrictions, viewing and duplicating facilities. Also available in CD-ROM edition.

0187 Rowan, Bonnie G., and Cynthia J. Wood. **SCHOLAR'S GUIDE TO WASHINGTON, D.C., MEDIA COLLECTIONS**. Baltimore: Johns Hopkins University Press, 1994, 189 pp. Details on collections of (and sometimes dealing with) newsreels and television news, print media, news photos, photographs, film and television, sound recordings, and radio. Entries by type, bibliography, index.

0188 Vanden Heuvel, Jon. **UNTAPPED SOURCES: AMERICA'S NEWSPAPER ARCHIVES AND HISTORIES**. New York: Gannett Foundation Media Center, 1991, 101 pp. Discusses research on newspapers, books on journalists, and offers an inventory of major newspaper archives.

0189 Wheeler, Mary Bray, ed. **DIRECTORY OF HISTORICAL ORGANIZATIONS IN THE UNITED STATES AND CANADA**. Nashville, TN: AASLH Press, American Association for State and Local History, 1990 (14th ed.), 1,108 pp. Arranged by state and province. Descriptions of historical organizations, with brief notes on collections. Access is difficult; "Major Program Areas" index lacks specificity. Organizational name index.

2-B-2. National Libraries and Archives

0190 **Library of Congress**. 10 First St. SE, Washington 20540. Voice 202-707-5000. Fax 202-707-5844. Internet: www.loc.gov. (See also: THOMAS, 0913.) The nation's library with close to 100 million items located in three buildings next to each other: Jefferson (the original building), Adams (the 1939 annex), and James Madison Memorial Bldg. Open with restrictions on use. Researchers must show photo identification to request materials in all public reading rooms.

1 **Manuscript Division.** Rm. 101, Madison Bldg., 101 Independence Ave. S.E. Washington 20540. Voice: 202-707-5387. Fax: 202-707-6336. E-mail: mss@loc.gov. Broadcast-related collections open to researchers include papers of Eric Sevareid, Lawrence Spivak, Lee De Forest, Stanford C. Hooper, Raymond Swing, 5,000 CBS Radio scripts, major collections of scripts representing the careers of Goodman and Jane Ace and Fred Allen and the series *Amos 'n' Andy* and *Vic and Sade*. Copyright deposits of radio scripts (1920s-1977). Limited photocopying.

2 **Newspaper and Current Periodical Room, Serial and Government Publications Division.** Madison Bldg, 101 Independence Ave. S.E., Washington 20540. 202-707-5647, Fax: 202-707-6128. Holds the largest newspaper collection in the U.S. Consult the library's biennal (since 1980) NEWSPAPERS RECEIVED CURRENTLY IN THE LIBRARY OF CONGRESS. Information about using the collections is available on the division's homepage: lcweb.loc.gov./global/NCP/ncp.html. The library has approximately 14,350 U.S. newspaper titles—900,000 issues. The combined collection includes current serial publications of U.S. federal, state, and local governments; foreign governments; and international organizations.

3 **Motion Picture, Broadcasting, and Recorded Sound Division.** Rm. 336, Madison Bldg., 101 Independence Ave. SE., Washington 20540. Voice: 202-707-1000. Fax: 202-707-2371. E-mail: mbrs@loc.gov. Maintains several important collections, with published guides like Iris Newsom's WONDERFUL INVENTIONS: MOTION PICTURES, BROADCASTING, AND RECORDED SOUND AT THE LIBRARY OF CONGRESS (1985, 384 pp.), a lavish pictorial with text describing key parts of the Library's extensive media collections; A. Balkansky's "Through the Electronic Looking Glass: Television Programs in the Library of Congress," QUARTERLY JOURNAL OF THE LIBRARY OF CONGRESS, 37: 458–475 (Summer/Fall 1980); James R. Smart's RADIO BROADCASTS IN THE LIBRARY OF CONGRESS, 1924–1941 (1982, 149 pp.); and Sarah Rouse and Katharine Loughney's 3 DECADES OF TELEVISION: A CATALOG OF TELEVISION PROGRAMS ACQUIRED BY THE LIBRARY OF CONGRESS, 1949–1979 (1989). Provides access to collections and important services in different locations:

*__Motion Picture and Television Reading Room.__ Rm. 336, Madison Bldg., 101 Independence Ave. SE., Washington 20540. Voice: 202-707-8572. Fax: 202-707-2371. E-mail: mbrs@loc.gov. Access limited to qualified researchers. Extensive collection of television programs acquired by copyright deposit, gift, exchange, and purchase. Includes 18,000 NBC television programs (1948–1977), 10,000 NET (National Educational Television) programs, and *Meet the Press* Collection (1949–date). Duplication of copyright deposits not permitted; limited duplication of other materials. Printed and electronic finding aids.

*__Recorded Sound Reference Center.__ Rm. 113, Madison Bldg., 101 Independence Ave SE, Washington 20540. Voice: 202-707-7833. Fax: 202-707-8464. Reference room open to the public. Listening facilities available only to researchers. Radio broadcasts include the NBC Collection of 175,000 items (1935–70); WOR Radio Collection of 18,000 items, documenting the station's programming from 1930s–1970s; NPR (1973–date), with a 5-year delay; Mary Margaret McBride Collection (1937–1954); Raymond Swing Collection (1944–1964). Limited duplication if copyright and other restrictions are met. Printed and electronic finding aids.

0191 **National Archives**. Constitution Ave. and 8th St. NW, Washington 20408. Voice: 202-501-5402. Fax: 202-523–4357. Internet: www.nara.gov. Contains the largest and most important American collection of documents related to mass communications. Among the most prominent record groups are documents of the Federal Communication Commission (RG 173) partially detailed in the dated but still useful Albert W. Winthrop, PRELIMINARY INVENTORY OF THE RECORDS OF THE FEDERAL COMMUNICATIONS COMMISSION (1956). Other National Archives collections are described in GUIDE TO THE NATIONAL ARCHIVES OF THE UNITED STATES (1974), which is updated in turn by GUIDE TO RECORDS IN THE NATIONAL ARCHIVES series of 11 regional guides (1989–90). Index to record groups (by name, office, and RG number) is LIST OF RECORD GROUPS IN THE NATIONAL ARCHIVES AND THE FEDERAL RECORDS CENTERS (1984). Specialized guides identifying Congressional documents related to mass communication topics include Robert W. Coren's GUIDE TO THE RECORDS OF THE UNITED STATES SENATE IN THE NATIONAL ARCHIVES, 1789–1989 (Washington: U.S. Senate, 1989); and Charles E. Schamel's GUIDE TO THE RECORDS OF THE UNITED STATES HOUSE OF REPRESENTATIVES IN THE NATIONAL ARCHIVES, 1789–1989 (Washington: U.S. House of Representatives, 1989); as well as Brightbill's COMMUNICATIONS AND THE UNITED STATES CONGRESS (0904). See also: S.L. Shamley, TELEVISION INTERVIEWS, 1951–1955: A CATALOG OF LONGINE'S CHRONOSCOPE INTERVIEWS IN THE NATIONAL ARCHIVES. (1991).

1. **Motion Picture, Sound, and Video Branch.** Archives II, 8601 Adelphi Rd., College Park, MD 20740-6001. Voice: 301-713-7060. Fax: 301-713-6904. Fax-on-Demand: 301-713-6905—from handset of fax machine. Internet: www.nara.gov. Houses historical materials created for and acquired by the U.S. government as well as donated materials from private sources. Arranged by record groups. Extensive media collections including television newscasts from ABC, CBS, NBC (mid-1970s-date), ABC Radio News Collection (1943–1967), National Public Radio Collection (1971–1980). Open to the public. Users must obtain a researcher's card. Duplication facilities available.

0192 Presidential Libraries. **Office of Presidential Libraries.** National Archives and Records Administration, Washington 20408. Voice: 202-501-5700. The nine Presidential Libraries and two Presidential Projects (the Nixon Presidential Materials Staff and the Bush Presidential Materials Project) include collections totalling "more than 260 million pages of textual materials, 5 million still photographs, 13.5 million feet of motion picture film, 68,000 hours of disc, audiotape, and videotape recordings, and more than 280,000 museum objects." The most important are White House files followed by personal papers and historical materials donated by individuals closely associated with the President. Materials for mass communications research common to all Presidential Libraries include papers of White House offices for media and the press and speechwriting, press releases, private papers and oral histories of personnel, and audiovisual records. Most presidential libraries and museums have been described in published finding aids, which are usually identified on Internet sites.

1 **Herbert Hoover Library**. Parkside Drive, P.O. Box 488, Branch, IA 52358. Voice: 319-643-5301. Fax: 319-643-5825. Internet: gopher.nara.gov:70/1/inform/library/hoover.

2 **Franklin D. Roosevelt Library**. 511 Albany Post Road, Hyde Park, NY 12538. Voice: 914-229-8114. Fax: 914-229-0872. Internet: www.academic.marist.edu/fdr/fdrintro.htm.

3 **Harry S. Truman Library**. U.S. Highway 24 & Delaware Street, Independence, MO 64050-1798. Voice: 816-833-1400. Voice: 816-833-4368. Internet: gopher.nara. gov: 70/1/inform/ library/truman.

4 **Dwight D. Eisenhower Library**. Southeast Fourth Street, Abilene, KS 67410. Voice: 913-263-4751. Fax: 913-263-4218. Internet: gopher.nara.gov:70/1/inform/library/eisen.

5 **John Fitzgerald Kennedy Library**. Columbia Point, Boston, MA 02125. Voice: 617-929-4500. Fax: 617-929-4538. Internet: gopher.nara.gov:70/1/inform/library/jfk

6 **Lyndon Baines Johnson Library**. 2313 Red River Street, Austin, TX 78705. Voice: 512-482-5137. Fax: 512-478-9104. Internet: www.lbjlib.utexas.edu/

7 **Nixon Presidential Materials Staff**. National Archives at College Park, 8601 Adelphi Road, College Park, MD 20740-6001. Voice: 301-713-6950. Fax: 301-713-6916. Internet: gopher.nara.gov:70/1/inform/library/nixon

8 **Gerald R. Ford Library.** 1000 Beal Avenue, Ann Arbor, MI 48109. Voice: 313-741-2218. Fax: 313-741-2341. Internet: gopher.nara.gov:70/1/inform/library/ford (A seperatly operated and located organization is the Gerald R. Ford Museum. 303 Pearl Street, NW, Grand Rapids, MI 49504-5353. Voice: 616-451-9263. Fax: 616-451- 9570)

9 **Jimmy Carter Library**. One Copenhill Avenue, Atlanta, GA 30307. Voice: 404-331-3942. Fax: 404-730-2215. Internet: gopher.nara.gov:70/1/inform/library/carter

10 **Ronald Reagan Library**. 40 Presidential Drive, Simi Valley, CA 93065. Voice: 805-522-8444. Fax: 805-522-9621. Internet: gopher.nara.gov:70/0/inform/library/reagan/ nlspart3.txt.

11 **George Bush Presidential Library.** 701 University Drive, East, Suite 300, College Station, TX 77840. Voice: 409-260-9554. Fax: 409-260-9557. Internet: csdl.tamu.edu/ bushlib/ bushpage.html

0193 **Smithsonian Institution**. **National Museum of American History.** Archives Center, 12th and Constitution Ave. NW, Washington 20560. Voice: 202-357-3270. Fax: 202-787-2866. A small selection of important collections in history of electronics and mass communications including George H. Clark (MS 80-197) [National Electric Signaling Company, RCA, radio and television broadcasting, Fessenden]; and Allen Balcom Dumont (MS 80-198) [radio and television standards and policy]. Several of these collections are described in GUIDE TO MANUSCRIPT COLLECTIONS IN THE NATIONAL MUSEUM OF HISTORY AND TECHNOLOGY (1978). Guides to specific collections include Robert S. Harding's REGISTER OF THE GEORGE H. CLARK RADIOANA COLLECTION, c. 1880–1950 (1985)

2-B-3. Other Archives, Libraries, Societies

Note: U.S. newspapers are extensively archived by state libraries and historical societies. In the 1980s a national program (the U.S. Newspaper Project) to identify, catalog, and preserve state newspapers was sponsored by the National Endowment for the Humanities. The cataloging records from this comprehensive inventory are available on the OCLC's database. In general, U.S. newspapers maintain archives of the content of their own papers, including text, graphics, and photographs. These archives are not open to the public; however, the library staff may respond to requests for information on a fee basis. EDITOR & PUBLISHER INTERNATIONAL YEARBOOK (0064) lists daily newspaper personnel, including librarians, with voice and fax numbers. See also, Caswell's GUIDE TO SOURCES IN AMERICAN JOURNALISM HISTORY (0146) and Jon Vanden Heuvel's UNTAPPED SOURCES (0188) for descriptions of many U.S. newspaper archives in the United States. Only a few of the larger collections have individual entries here.

0194 **American Antiquarian Society**. 185 Salisbury St., Worcester, MA 01609-1634. Voice: 508-755-5221. Fax: 508-753-3311. Primary repository for early American newspapers—15,000 titles in 20,000 volumes, with nearly 1,500 pre-1821 titles. Emphasis on Eastern states and the nation's first century. Research library specializes in American history through 1876. Collections are described in the cataloging records created under the U.S. Newspaper Project discussed in the note above. Founded in 1812.

0195 **American Film Institute.** 2021 N. Western Ave., Box 27999, Los Angeles 90027. Voice: 213-856-7600. Fax: 213-467-4578. Internet: www.afionline.org/. Maintains National Center for Film and Video Preservation which coordinates American film and television preservation activities by acquiring and preserving films and programs in the AFI collection at the Library of Congress and other archives. The Louis B. Mayer Library holds reference collection of over 14,000 volumes and 100 journals, extensive clipping files, and over 40 special collections of film and television scripts, oral history transcripts, and materials related to the likes of Fritz Lang, Martin Scorsese, Sergei Eisenstein. Founded in 1967.

0196 **American Library of Radio and Television.** Thousand Oaks Library, 1401 E. Janss Rd., Thousand Oaks, CA 91362. Voice: 805- 497-6282. Open to the public. Access to special collections by appointment. Broadcast-related materials include radio and television scripts, books, photographs, manuscripts, and special collections including the papers of Norman Corwin, Rudy Vallee, Clete Roberts, Fletcher Markle, and Carlton E. Morse. Publishes guide to radio series scripts, RADIO SERIES SCRIPTS 1930–1990: MANUSCRIPT HOLDINGS OF THOUSAND OAKS LIBRARY SPECIAL COLLECTIONS DEPARTMENT (Thousand Oaks, CA: Thousand Oaks Library, 1994). Founded in 1984.

0197 **Friends of Old-Time Radio.** PO Box 4321, Hamden, CT 06514. Voice: 203-248-2887. Fax: 203-281-1322. Internet: www.old-time.com/. Loosely-organized local groups of individuals who trade and collect historical radio materials. Publishes bimonthly newsletter, HELLO AGAIN. Holds annual meetings. Founded in 1976.

0198 **New York Historical Society**. 170 Central Park West, New York 10024-5194. Voice: 212-873-3400. Collections include some 8,800 newspaper titles and 1.5 million issues, most 19th century and early 20th century. Collection is open to the public.

0199 **New York Public Library**. 521 West 43rd St., The Annex, New York, NY 10036. Voice: 212-714-8520. Important collection of New York City and state newspapers.

0200 **Pacific Pioneer Broadcasters.** 5841 McDonie Ave., Woodland Hills, CA 91367. Voice: 818-346-6363. Fax: 818-346-1225. Membership organization. Open to researchers by appointment. No duplication. Collection includes transcriptions, radio programs, kinescopes, scripts, photographs, music scores, publications, equipment, and other memorabilia. Collection is stored in vaults provided by Home Savings of America on the site of NBC studios at Sunset and Vine, Hollywood. Founded in 1966.

0201 **Society to Preserve and Encourage Radio Drama, Variety and Comedy (SPERDVAC).** P.O. Box 7177, Van Nuys, CA 91409-9712. Membership organization. Works to preserve history of radio broadcasting by collecting recordings of radio programs, including soap operas, children's shows, comedy, music shows, variety, dramas, and news broadcasts. Offers members over 7,000 hours of old-time radio shows in open reel or cassette formats through lending libraries that operate by mail. Program catalogs available to members. Printed materials library, including radio scripts, also available to members by mail. Publishes newsletter. Sponsors annual convention. Founded in 1974.

0202 **State Historical Society of Wisconsin Library**. Archives Division, 816 State St., Madison, WI 53706. Voice: 608-264-6534. Fax: 608-264-6520. A major archive for mass communications research including the second largest (after Library of Congress) collection of historical newspapers. Important collections include papers of Walter R. Baker (MS 68-2105) [National Television System Committee, Radio-Television Manufacturer's Association, color television]; Kenneth Allen Cox (MS 78-982) [Federal Communications Commission]; Malcolm Parker Hanson (MS 62-2357) [radio communication for Admiral Byrd's expeditions]; Herbert Clark Hoover (MS 68-2218) [President Hoover's role in radio regulation, Federal Radio Commission]; Lee Loevinger (MS 78-1009) [Federal Communications Commission]; National Broadcasting Company]; Sig Mickelson (MS 78-1016) [communications satellites]; and National Broadcasting Company, 1930–1960 (MS 64-1619) [Engineering department records]. Collections described in Janice O'Connell's THE COLLECTIONS OF THE MASS COMMUNICATIONS HISTORY CENTER OF THE STATE HISTORICAL SOCIETY OF WISCONSIN AND THE COLLECTIONS OF THE WISCONSIN CENTER FOR FILM AND THEATER RESEARCH OF THE UNIVERSITY OF WISCONSIN (1979); SOURCES FOR MASS COMMUNICATIONS, FILM, AND THEATER RESEARCH: A GUIDE (1982); and F. Gerald Ham and Margaret Hedstrom's A GUIDE TO LABOR PAPERS IN THE STATE HISTORICAL LIBRARY OF WISCONSIN (1978). NEWSPAPERS ACQUIRED BY THE STATE HISTORICAL SOCIETY OF WISCONSIN LIBRARY (1974–date, irregular) details extensive newspaper collections with a concentration on African-American and labor newspapers; and NEWSPAPERS IN THE STATE HISTORICAL SOCIETY OF WISCONSIN: A BIBLIOGRAPHY WITH HOLDINGS (New York: Norman Ross Publishing, 1995) covers Wisconsin papers in Vol I, and U.S. and foreign papers in Vol II. Founded in 1846.

2-B-4. Corporate and Industry Archives

NOTE: Newspaper archives are often part of that paper's library collection. See note at 2-B-3.

0203 **ABC News.** 47 W. 66th St., New York 10023. Voice: 212-456-7777. Fax: 212-887-4968. News programs (1963–date). Materials are for internal use only.

See 0231. University of Maryland, Broadcast Pioneers American Library of Broadcasting

0204 **CBS News Archives.** 524 W. 57th St., New York 10019. Voice: 212-975-2875. Fax: 212-975-5442. Television network archives, including newsfilm and videotape (1954–date), newscasts (1975–date), and documentaries (1951–date). Designed to aid internal staff and to license stock footage to outside producers. Offers only limited access for scholarly research. Apply for admission. Research and screening fees.

0205 **CLIO Awards**. 276 Fifth Ave., Ste., 401, New York 10001. Voice: 212-683-4300. Fax: 212-683-4796. E-Mail: clioawards.com or clioawards@aol.com. Open to researchers by appointment. Begun as a television commercial competition, Clio has developed in recent years into an international advertising festival and exposition honoring advertising excellence in many media. The Clio collection includes award winning television commercials (1960–date). Recent winning presentations available on CD-ROM (1994–date). Founded in 1959; added radio in 1967, print in 1971, and international radio in 1974. Known as the New Clios in 1991 and 1992. Recent winning presentations available on CD-ROM (1994–date). Limited access to earlier commercials.

0206 **Los Angeles Times History Center.** Times Mirror Square, Los Angeles 90053. Voice: 213-237-5000. Although now inactive, the archive includes materials on the Chandler family, corporate papers, manuscripts, official records, 75 oral histories, 37,000 photographs, and audio recordings.

See 0513. National Association of Broadcasters.

0207 **NBC News Video Archives.** 30 Rockefeller Plaza, Rm. 922, New York 10112. Voice: 212-664-3797. Fax: 212-957-8917. E-mail: ychin@NBC.com. Television network archives, including complete newscasts (mid-1970s-date) stock footage, major news events and documentary and magazine show footage. Designed for use by internal staff and for stock footage sales. Open to researchers by appointment. Apply for admission. Research fees.

0208 **The National Cable Television Center Library**. The Pennsylvania State University, 301 James Bldg., University Park, PA 16802. Voice: 814-865-1875. Fax: 814-863-7808. Information center on the subject of cable television. The noncirculating collection contains cable specific items in all formats: paper, audiovisual, photographic and equipment. The collection encompasses all aspects of the industry: technical, financial, legal, regulatory, administrative, managerial, public relations, marketing and advertising. Represents development of the industry from the 1940s to the present. Bibliographic information for documents and serials in the collection can be viewed on The Penn State

University Libraries' online catalog—Library Information Access System (LIAS). Other items are found inhouse through finding aids. Open to the public. Founded in 1989.

0209 **New York Times Archives**, 229 West 43rd St., New York, 10036. Voice: 212-556-1234. Internet: www.nytimes.com/. The library is closed to the public; researchers should inquire by letter. Research can be done on a fee basis. The same location and telephone can be used to reach the Photo Syndicate holding some three million items.

0210 **Pacifica Radio Archive.** 3729 Cahuenga Blvd. West, North Hollywood, CA 91604. Voice: 818-506-1077. Part of Pacifica Foundation. Oldest and largest collection of community radio programs. Holds over 40,000 recordings—documentaries, interviews, speeches, news reports—on contemporary history, including civil rights movement, Vietnam War era, women's movement, gay and lesbian rights movement. Includes programming from Pacifica stations, Pacifica Radio National Programming and News units, and independent radio producers. Finding aids include catalog available on microfiche. Commercial services include program distribution to stations and cassette sales to the public. Founded in 1968.

0211 **David Sarnoff Research Center.** 201 Washington Rd., Princeton, NJ 08543-5300. Voice: 609-734-2608. Created by RCA, it is now owned by SRI. David Sarnoff Library collections (founded in 1966) include materials on the development of wireless technology and electronics and on David Sarnoff, longtime head of RCA. Founded in 1941.

0212 **Time Inc. Archives**. Time-Life Bldg, Room 33-23f, Rockefeller Center, New York 10020. Voie: 212-556-4122. Collection of business and editorial records, memos and correspondence, promotion, and publicity related to company activities.

2-B-5. College and University Archives

0213 **Brooklyn College of the City University of New York. Celia Nachatovitz Diamant Memorial Library of Classic Television Commercials**. Dept. of Radio and Television, 2900 Bedford Ave., Brooklyn, NY 11210-2889. Voice: 718-951-5555. Fax: 718-951-4418. Available to qualified researchers and nonprofit organizations and schools. Duplication fee. Collection of 69 classic television commercials produced during the decade prior to 1958. Donated to the college by advertising and broadcast executive producer Lincoln Diamant in memory of his wife. Diamant's TELEVISION'S CLASSIC COMMERCIALS: THE GOLDEN YEARS 1948–1958 (New York: Hastings House, 1971) is companion book with scripts and background information on the commercials.

0214 **Columbia University**. New York 10027.

1 **Alfred I. duPont-Columbia Awards Archive.** Alfred I. duPont Center for Broadcast Journalism at the Graduate School of Journalism, 701 Journalism Bldg., Mail Code 3805, 2950 Broadway, New York, 10027. Voice: 212-854-5047. Fax: 212-854-7837. Internet: www.dupont.org. Open by appointment for in-house use. No duplication. Collection of broadcasts that received the Alfred I. duPont-Columbia University Awards in broadcast journalism. Awards program established in 1942 in memory of Alfred I. duPont and expanded to include radio, television, and cable coverage of news and public affairs programming. Collection includes work of winners since archive was established at Columbia in 1968.

2 **Rare Books and Manuscripts, Butler Library.** 535 W. 114th St., New York, 10027. Voice: 212-854-2231.The most important collections include papers of Edwin Howard Armstrong (MS 80-1888) [some 200,000 items related to research and inventions, frequency modulation, U.S. Air Force communications, Radio Club of America, RCA, Zenith Radio Corp., lawsuits,]; author Eric Barnouw (MS 77-73) [communications history]; and James Lawrence Fly [Federal Communications Commission, Board of War Communications]. Collection also includes oral histories.

0215 **Duke University. John W. Hartman Center for Sales, Advertising, and Marketing History.** Special Collections Library, Duke University, Box 90185, Durham, NC 27708-0185. Voice: 919-660-5820. Fax:919-684-2855. Internet: scriptorium.lib.duke.edu/hartman/. Open to the public.

Reference, research, and photoduplication services; fees charged. Country's largest advertising archive includes the J. Walter Thompson Company Archives; the D'Arcy, Masius Benton & Bowles collection; the Wayne P. Ellis Collection of Eastman Kodak Advertising, Sales, and Marketing; and records of the Charles W. Hoyt agency. Detailed guides to collections available at the Center. Founded in 1992 and named for the former CEO of Bill Communications, a major benefactor.

0216 **Ernie Pyle State Memorial.** P.O. Box 338, Dana IN 47847. Voice: 317-665-3633. Maintains important collection of the correspondent's papers and columns. See also: 0221.

0217 **George Washington University. Special Collections, Gelman Library**, Washington 20052. Voice: 202-994-7549. Fax: 202-994-1340. Includes papers of Joseph Charyk, founding CEO of Comsat and Albert Rose, color television pioneer. Library published TELEVISION NEWS RESOURCES: A GUIDE TO COLLECTIONS (Television News Study Center, 1981).

0218 **Georgia State University, Special Collections Dept.**, Library, 100 Decatur St., SE, Atlanta, GA 30303-3202. Voice: 404-651-2477. Fax: 404-651-2476. Internet: www.lib.gsu.edu/library/dept/spcoll/htm. Open to public. Closed stacks. Finding aids available. Broadcast collection features WSB radio archives including correspondence, news clippings, program log books, photographs, and artifacts (1922–1984) and sound recordings (1944-1956). WGST radio scripts, fan mail, and recordings (1930s-1950s). Founded in 1970.

0219 **Harvard University.** Cambridge, MA 02138.

1 **Graduate School of Education. Action for Children's Television Library Collection.** Monroe C. Gutman Library, Appian Way, Cambridge, MA 02138. Voice: 617-495-4228. Fax: 617-495-0540. Open to the public. Materials created and collected since the late 1960s by Action for Children's Television (founded 1968), a national organization working to encourage diversity in children's television. Includes books, periodicals, videotapes, clippings, and manuscripts pertaining to the impact of television on children. Donated by Peggy Charren, ACT founder and president. Founded in 1986.

2 **Harvard College Library**. Cambridge, MA 02138. Voice: 617-495-2411. Harvard's extensive collections of U.S. newspapers are dispersed in several campus libraries, the largest single collection being housed in the Widener Library. Their strength is in Massachusetts and New England papers. The Houghton Library includes original issues of colonial era papers. There are also extensive holdings of ethnic and underground papers.

0220 **Howard University. Black Press Archives and Gallery of Distinguished Newspaper Publishers. Moorland-Spingam Research Center.** Washington 20059. Tel: 202-806-7239. Fax: 202-806-6405. Extensive collection of African-American newspapers. Holdings include private and professional papers as well as oral histories of journalists, editors, and publishers.

0221 **Indiana University.** Bloomington, IN 47405.

1 **The Roy W. Howard Archive**. School of Journalism, Ernie Pyle Hall. Voice: 812-855-9247. Fax: 812-855-0901. Includes 13,000 letters, drafts of Howard's news columns, and video interviews. Complements related collection at Library of Congress.

2 **The Scripps-Howard Foundation Ernie Pyle Collection**. The Lilly Library. Voice: 812-855-2452. Fax: 812-855-3143. Includes copies of the World War II war correspondent's columns, photographs, and personal letters. See also 0216.

0222 **Marquette University. Special Collections & University Archives.** Memorial Library, P.O. Box 3141, Milwaukee, WI 53201-3141. Voice: 414-288-7256. Fax: 414-288-3123. Internet: 970Frunkel@VMS.CSD.MU.EDU. Open to public. Finding aids available. Broadcast-related materials include the Don McNeill collection (1928–1969) which features papers, scripts, photographs, films, audiotapes. Also holds records of Catholic Broadcasters Association (1956–1972) and UNDA USA (International Catholic Association for Radio and Television) (1973–date).

0223 **Michigan State University. The G. Robert Vincent Voice Library.** East Lansing, MI 48824-1048. Voice: 517-355-5122. Fax: 517-432-1445. Internet: web.msu.edu/vincent/index.html.

Open to the public. No fees. Over 50,000 utterances cataloged by speaker and subject. Includes broadcasts as well as interviews, home recordings, and memoirs. Features political figures, labor leaders, show business, sports and literary figures. Includes radio and television broadcasts. Published catalog: A DICTIONARY CATALOG OF THE G. ROBERT VINCENT VOICE LIBRARY AT MICHIGAN STATE UNIVERSITY (New York: G.K. Hall, 1975). Founded in 1962.

0224 **Purdue University. Public Affairs Video Archives.** 1000 Liberal Arts and Education Bldg., West Lafayette, IN 47907-1000. Voice: 800-423-9630; 317-494-9630. Fax: 317-494-3421. E-Mail: info@pava.purdue.edu. Internet: archives.pava.purdue.edu/pava. Open to the public. Duplication available for educators only. Duplication fee. Archive of programming on both channels of the Cable-Satellite Public Affairs Network (C-SPAN), preserved specifically for teaching and research. Publishes PUBLIC AFFAIRS VIDEO ARCHIVES CATALOG (1988–date). Founded in 1987.

0225 **San Francisco State University. San Francisco Bay Area Television News Film Archives.** Archives/Special Collections, J. Paul Leonard Library, San Francisco State University, 1630 Holloway Ave., San Francisco 94132. Voice: 415-338-1856. Fax: 415-338-1504. Open to qualified researchers. Access and duplication fees. Core collections include KQED (PBS affiliate) local newsfilm (1967-1980) and KPIX (CBS affiliate) Film Library of local newsfilm created between early 1950s to 1980. Collections portray San Francisco Bay Area history from the 1950s to the 1980s. Additional collections include the local Emmy Award-winning programs from the Northern California Chapter of the National Academy of Television Arts and Sciences, 1974–date. Founded in 1981.

0226 **Temple University.** Samuel Paley Library. Special Collections Department. Philadelphia 19122. Voice: 215-204-8230. Fax: 215-204-5201. Internet: www.library.temple.edu/speccoll/rare_boo.htm. Collections include scripts and other papers of long-time radio serial writer Carleton E. Morse and scripts of the *Lux Radio Theater.*

0227 **Texas Tech University. Southwest History Center** Lubbock, TX 79409. Voice: 806-742-3749. Fax: 806-742-0496. Includes professional and personal records of Gordon L. McClendon, important radio broadcasting pioneer, plus recordings from his stations and the Liberty Broadcasting Network.

0228 **University of California Los Angeles. UCLA Film and Television Archive.** Archive Research and Study Center, 46 Powell Library, 405 Hilgard Ave., Los Angeles 90095-1517. Voice: 301-206-5388. Fax: 310-206-5392. Commercial Services, 1015 N. Cahuenga Blvd., Los Angeles 90038. Voice: 213-466-8559. Fax: 213-461-6317. Open to researchers by appointment. Major international center for preservation and study of film and television. On-site viewing access to over 25,000 titles covering every form of U.S. telecasting from 1946 to the present, including classic anthology dramas from the Golden Age; national and local Emmy winners (early 1960s–date); Hallmark Hall of Fame programs (1951–date); and the Paramount Television Collection (early 1960s–date). News and Public Affairs Collection includes national and local newscasts, cable programming, press discussion and interview formats, debates, documentaries, and entertainment news (1970–date). Guides include ATAS/UCLA TELEVISION ARCHIVES CATALOG: HOLDINGS IN THE STUDY COLLECTION OF THE ACADEMY OF TELEVISION ARTS & SCIENCES/ UNIVERSITY OF CALIFORNIA, LOS ANGELES TELEVISION ARCHIVES (Los Angeles, CA: Department of Theater Arts, University of California; Pleasantville, NY: Redgrave Publishing, 1981). Contact Commercial Services regarding duplication, licensing, or reuse of material. Founded in 1965.

0229 **University of Georgia. George Foster Peabody Collection**. College of Journalism and Mass Communication, Athens, GA 30602-3018. Voice: 706-542-3787. Fax: 706-542-9273. E-Mail: peabody@uga.cc.uga.edu. Open to the public. On-site use by appointment. Extensive archive of Peabody Award-winning television and radio programs from 1940–date. Founded in 1940.

0230 **University of Illinois at Urbana-Champaign.** Urbana, IL 61801.

1 **D'Arcy Collection.** Communications Library, Gregory Hall, Urbana, IL 61801. Voice: 217-333-2216. Maintains some 2 million original newspaper and magazine advertisements from 1890 to 1970.

2 **University Archives.** University Library, 1408 West Gregory Dr., Urbana, IL 61801. Voice: 217-333-0798. Fax: 217-244-0398. Open to the public. Collection includes archives of the Advertising Council (founded in 1942) including campaign promotional materials and copies of ads in major advertising formats—magazines, newspapers, radio, television, billboards, and posters; publications, photos, and files documenting the origin and growth of the National Association of Farm Broadcasters (1943–date); and materials pertaining to the campus radio and television stations. Limited duplication facilities. Founded in 1963.

3 **CATALOG OF THE COMMUNICATIONS LIBRARY**. Boston: G.K. Hall, 198x. Reproduces the card catalog of one of the stronger communications collections in the United States.

0231 **University of Maryland.** College Park, MD 20742-7011.

1 **[Broadcast Pioneers] Library of American Broadcasting**. Hornbake Library. Voice: 301-405-9160. Fax: 301-314-9419. E-mail: bp50@umail.umd.edu. Internet: www.itd.umd.edu/UMS/UMCP/BPL/bplintro.html. Open to the public. Wide-ranging collection of recordings, books, pamphlets, journals, photographs, scripts, clipping files, and personal papers devoted to the history of broadcasting. Includes 1,000 oral histories, interviews, and speeches; 3,300 transcription discs; 10,000 books; 250 periodical titles; 1,300 scripts from radio and television programs; 25,000 photographs, slides, and negatives; and papers of many industry notables including William S. Hedges and Elmo N. Pickerill (MS 78-1182) with materials on wireless telegraphy and radio communication related to Lee de Forest, Marconi, and others. Also relevant are papers of Federal Communications Bar Association (MS 79-1172). Founded in 1971 and housed in the National Association of Broadcasters Building in Washington, DC, until 1994 when the Library was moved to the University of Maryland-College Park.

2 **National Public Broadcasting Archives**. Hornbake Library, Voice: 301-405-9988. Fax: 301-314-9419. E-mail: pb99@umail.umd.edu. Internet: www.itd.umd.edu /UMS/UMCP/NPBA/npba.html. Open to the public by appointment. Textual archival records of major entities of noncommercial broadcasting in the United States, including Corporation for Public Broadcasting, Public Broadcasting Service, National Public Radio, Midwest Program for Airborne Television Instruction, Public Service Statellite Consortium, America's Public Television Stations, Children's Television Workshop, and Joint Council for Education Telecommunications. Selected audio and video program records of public broadcasting's national production and support centers and stations WETA, WAMU-FM, and Maryland Public Television. Founded in 1990.

0232 **University of Memphis. Radio Program Archive.** Dept. of Communication, Broadcasting & Electronic Media Concentration, University of Memphis, Memphis, TN 38152. Voice: 901-678-3174. Fax: 901-678-4331. Internet: www.people.memphis.edu/~bensmanm/. Open to the public. Duplication fees. Collection of representative radio programs from radio's golden years. Developed from personal collection of Professor Marvin R. Bensman, founder and director of the archive. Catalog available only on www. Founded in early 1970s.

0233 **University of Missouri**. **Archive of Investigative Reporters and Editors.** The Paul Williams Memorial Resource Center, 26A Walter Williams Hall, Columbia, MO 65211. Voice: 314-882-2042. Fax: 314-882-5431. Contains more than 8,000 clips, tapes, and transcripts of investigative stories from U.S. publications. See also 0611.

0234 **University of Oklahoma. Political Commercial Archive.** Political Communication Center, Dept. of Communication, 610 Elm Ave., Norman, OK 73019-0335. Voice: 405-325-3114. Fax: 405-325-1566. Open to researchers. World's largest collection of political commercials. Holds 55,000 radio (1936–date) and television (1950–date) commercials representing candidates running for offices ranging from the U.S. presidency to school boards throughout the country. Includes commercials by political action committees, ads sponsored by corporations and special interest groups on public issues, and commercials done for elections in other countries. Duplication subject to copyright restrictions. Fee schedule applies for research and duplication. Publishes POLITICAL COMMERCIAL

ARCHIVE: A CATALOG AND GUIDE TO THE COLLECTION, and POLITICAL ADVERTISING RESEARCH REPORTS. Founded by private collector in 1959; acquired by the university in 1985.

0235 **University of South Carolina. Newsfilm Library.** Film Center, 1139 Wheat St., Columbia, SC 29208. Voice: 803-777-6841. Fax: 803-777-4756. Internet: www.sc.edu/newsfilm. Open to the public. Duplication charges. Operates as commercial stock footage house as well as research center. Collection features Fox Movietone News (1942–1944 and outtakes from 1919–1934). Also includes film footage from local television stations WIS, WLTX, and WBTW from 1950s to mid-1970s. Founded in 1980.

0236 **University of Southern California.** University Park, Los Angeles 90089-0182. Collections include:

1 **Cinema-Television Library and Archives of Performing Arts. USC - Doheny Library.** Voice: 213-740-8906. Open to the public. Over 200 collections of personal papers and studio resources including scripts, production records, memos and correspondence, stills, scrapbooks, sketches, music scores, and editing notes. Emphasis is on television and film, although several of the collections include radio holdings. Television script collection features dramatic and comedic shows of the 1950s and 1960s. Founded in the 1930s.

2 **Warner Bros. Archives.** School of Cinema-Television. Voice 213-748-7747. Fax: 213-747-3301. Open to researchers by appointment. Photocopying available. Fee Schedule. Records of Warner Bros. Pictures Inc. from 1914 and the company's first feature film until 1967. Brings together production, distribution, and exhibition records to document activities of vertically ingegrated studio. Includes papers, scripts, photos, film music, animation, and art collections. Also includes television shows from 1968–date. Given to USC by Warner Communications in 1977. Note: Turner Broadcasting owns rights on films released up to December 31, 1949.

0237 **University of Texas. Eugene C. Barker Texas History Center**. General Libraries, Austin, TX 78713-7330. Voice: 512-471-5961. Includes extensive collection of newspapers from 19th and 20th centuries.

0238 **University of Washington. Educational Media Collection/ Milo Ryan Phonoarchive.** Classroom Support Services, 23 Kane Hall, Box 353090, University of Washington, Seattle, WA 98195. Voice: 206-543-9907. Collection of World War II radio broadcasts by the Columbia Broadcasting System, given to the University by affiliate station KIRO. Chronicles rise of radio as a force in 20th-century journalism, 1939–1962. Cataloged in Milo Ryan's HISTORY IN SOUND: A DESCRIPTIVE LISTING OF THE KIRO-CBS COLLECTION OF BROADCASTS OF THE WORLD WAR II YEARS AND AFTER, IN THE PHONOARCHIVE OF THE UNIVERSITY OF WASHINGTON (Seattle: University of Washington Press, 1963).

0239 **Vanderbilt University. Vanderbilt Television News Archive**. 110 21st. Ave. South, Ste. 704, Nashville, TN 37203. Voice: 615-322-2927. Fax: 615-343-8250. E-Mail: tvnews@tvnews.vanderbilt.edu. Internet: tvnews.vanderbilt.edu; gopher: tvn. vanderbilt.edu. Open to public. Loan copies available by mail for fee. Collection of over 18,000 network evening news broadcasts and 5,000 hours of news-related programming. Current newscasts taped off air daily. Publishes guides and indexes to collection, including monthly TELEVISION NEWS INDEX AND ABSTRACTS: A GUIDE TO THE VIDEOTAPE COLLECTION OF THE NETWORK EVENING NEWS PROGRAMS IN THE VANDERBILT TELEVISION NEWS ARCHIVES (1968–date). Founded in 1968.

2-B-6. Museums

0240 **American Museum of the Moving Image**. 35 Ave. at 36 St., Astoria, NY 11106. Voice: 718-784-4520. Fax: 718-784-4681. Open to public. Fee schedule. Repository for material culture of motion pictures and television. Houses nation's largest collection of moving image artifacts, including cameras; televisions; sound, lighting, and editing equipment; costumes; production design models and drawings; fan magazines; and photographs. Dedicated to educating the public about the art, history, technique, and technology of film, television, video, and digital media. Core exhibition features artifacts, computer-based interactive experiences, film and video presentations, and demonstrations of professional equipment used to produce "Behind the Screen," a look at the process of producing, marketing, and exhibiting moving images. Presents more than 300 programs annually. Mounts traveling exhibitions. Founded in 1981; building opened to public in 1988.

0241 **The Electronics Museum of the Perham Foundation.** 101 First St., Ste 394, Los Altos, CA 94022 Voice: 408-734-4453. Fax: 408-736-2685. E-mail: anyone@perham.org. Foundation formed in 1959 to display collection of some 20,000 devices gathered by Douglas Perham on all aspects of electronics in Silicon Valley area. Displayed for many years at Foothill College in Los Altos, the collection is now in storage pending construction of a dedicated museum at the San Jose Historical Museum campus. Highlights include the early technology of broadcast pioneer Charles Herrold, Federal Telegraph arc transmitters of C.F. Elwell, the personal papers and audio tubes of Lee de Forest and a sample or prototype of practically every electronic device made in California from commercial Klystron tubes to consumer radio receivers. Produced BROADCASTING'S FORGOTTEN FATHER: THE CHARLES HERROLD STORY (VHS, 60 min., 1994).

0242 **John Rivers Communications Museum. College of Charleston.** 58 George St., Charleston, SC 29424. Voice: 803-953-5810. Open to the public. Collection includes early radio and television receivers, phonographs, motion-picture projectors, magic lanterns, and early sound recordings. Begun as an educational extension of WCSC. Founded in the 1970s; moved to the college in 1986. Named for broadcast executive John M. Rivers, Sr.

0243 **McKissick Museum. South Carolina Broadcasting Archives. University of South Carolina.** Columbia, SC 29208. Voice: 803-771-7251. Fax: 803-777-2829. E-mail: Robertsonl@garnet.cla.sc.edu. Open to the public. Collection devoted to South Carolina broadcasting. Includes papers, tapes, scripts, photographs, and sound recordings from South Carolina broadcasters and stations. Includes minutes and newsletters of the South Carolina Broadcasters Association. Maintains Hall of Fame. Founded in 1976.

0244 **Museum of Broadcast Communications**. Chicago Cultural Center, Michigan Ave. at Washington St., Chicago 60602-3407. Voice: 312-629-6000. Fax: 312-629-6009. Open to public for in-house viewing. Duplication of programs not permitted. No charge for admission. Collection includes 10,000 television shows, 50,000 hours of radio, 9,000 television commercials, and 2,500 newscasts. Collection is national in scope, with emphasis on Chicago and midwest. Midwest home of the George F. Peabody Collection (see also: 0229). Has since 1991 administered the Radio Hall of Fame, established by Emerson Radio Corporation in 1988. Founded in 1987.

0245 **Museum of Television & Radio.** 25 West 52 St., New York 10019-6101. Voice: 212-621-6600. Fax: 212-621-6715. Open to the public for in-house viewing. Collection maintained for research and viewing only; duplication of programs not permitted. Admission fee. Research fee. Collection of over 60,000 television and radio programs and commercials, covering 70 years of broadcasting history, including news, public affairs programs, documentaries, performing arts, children's programming, sports, comedy, and advertising. Published guides include SUBJECT GUIDE TO THE RADIO AND TELEVISION COLLECTION OF THE MUSEUM OF BROADCASTING (1979, 2nd ed.). Features exhibitions, special screening and listening series, and seminars. Duplicate collection housed in museum's West Coast facility which opened in 1996 at 465 North Beverly Dr., Beverly Hills, CA 90210. Voice: 310-786-1000. Fax: 310-786-1086. Founded in 1975 as Museum of Broadcasting; name changed in 1991.

0246 **National Jewish Archive of Broadcasting.** Jewish Museum, 1109 Fifth Ave., New York 10128. Voice: 212-423-3200. Fax: 212-423-3232. Open to researchers by appointment. No duplication. Collection of 3,000 television programs and 600 radio programs (1948–date) pertaining to the Jewish experience. Founded in 1979.

0247 **National Museum of Communications.** 2001 Plymouth Rock Dr., Richardson, TX. 75081-3946. Voice: 214-690-3636. Fax: 214-644-2473. Internet: www.audionet.com. Located outside of Dallas, museum combines displays and hands-on exhibits tracing history of mass communications from cave paintings and smoke signals to the modern era. Operates a satellite-delivered station broadcasting old radio shows.

See 0595. National Public Radio Program Library

0248 **Newseum**. The Freedom Forum, 1101 Wilson Blvd., Arlington, VA 22209. Voice: 703-284-3700. Fax: 703-284-3777. Toll free: 1-888-newseum. Internet: www.newseum.org. Described as the world's only museum dedicated to telling the story of the past, present, and future of news, this large facility opened in April 1997 with 72,000 sq. feet on four levels of the Freedom Forum World Center. Major features include a 126-foot-long display of current global news feeds, interactive exhibits, broadcast studios, a theater, and artifacts from news reporting history.

0249 **Pavek Museum of Broadcasting.** 3515 Raleigh Ave. St. Louis Park, MN 55416. Voice: 612-926-8198. Fax: 612-926-9761. Open to the public. Admission free. Collection of antique radio, television, and broadcast equipment, including crystal radios, vacuum tubes, transmitters and receivers, microphones, speakers, antennas, television cameras. Library includes service literature for radio receivers built before 1950. Includes a Minnesota Room, devoted to equipment manufactured in Minnesota and to local programming. Publishes newsletter. Founded in 1985.

0250 **Washington Press Club Foundation**. National Press Building, Suite 1067, Washington 20045. Voice: 202-393-0613. Fax: 202-783-0841. Oral history project on "Women in Journalism," begun in 1986, includes 50 oral histories of women journalists that have been distributed to participating research libraries in the U. S. Includes female publishers, editors, foreign correspondents, sportswriters, columnists—women of various backgrounds who worked in news and information media.

0251 **WGBH Educational Foundation Media Archives and Preservation Center**, 125 Western Ave., Boston 02134. Voice: 617-492-2777, ext. 4206. Fax: 617-787-0714. One of the largest collections of public television programming in the U.S. Preserves program materials produced by WGBH, award-winning PBS affiliate in Boston and supplier of one third of all prime-time programming offered nationwide by PBS. Open to researchers by appointment. Stock footage and production footage available for sale through the Film and Video Resource Center (ext. 3195). Collection includes WGBH television and radio programs (1956–date). Includes 19,000 reels of film, 11,000 programs on videotape, 32,000 audiotapes, and outtakes. Includes programs from the series *Advocates, NOVA, Frontline, The French Chef, Crockett's Victory Garden, Evening at Pops, In Search of the Real America, Making Things Work (Grow).* Founded in 1979.

2-C. Selected Secondary Resources

2-C-1. Survey Histories

0252 Baughman, James L. **THE REPUBLIC OF MASS CULTURE: JOURNALISM, FILMMAKING AND BROADCASTING IN AMERICA SINCE 1941.** Baltimore: Johns Hopkins University Press, 1992, 257 pp. Useful integrated assessment of print, film, and broadcasting development. Emphasizes television's dominance. Bibliographic essay, index.

0253 Covert, Catherine L., and John D. Stevens, eds. **MASS MEDIA BETWEEN THE WARS: PERCEPTIONS OF CULTURAL TENSION 1918–1941**. Syracuse, NY: Syracuse University Press, 1984, 252 pp. Twelve scholarly papers focus on different aspects of print media with one chapter each on motion pictures and radio. Bibliographic essay, index.

0254 Czitrom, Daniel J. **MEDIA AND THE AMERICAN MIND FROM MORSE TO McLUHAN**. Chapel Hill: University of North Carolina Press, 1982, 254 pp. Insightful scholarly analysis with chapters on the telegraph and telephone, motion pictures, radio, and three chapters assessing the overall impact of media and the development of research about media. Notes, bibliography, index.

0255 Emery, Michael, and Edwin Emery. **THE PRESS IN AMERICA: AN INTERPRETIVE HISTORY OF THE MASS MEDIA**. Englewood Cliffs, NJ: Prentice Hall, 1996 (8th. ed.), 715 pp. Encyclopedic text describes changes in dominant media, complexity of the media industry, and key media figures. Photos, notes, bibliography, index.

0256 Flichy, Patrice. **DYNAMICS OF MODERN COMMUNICATION: THE SHAPING AND IMPACT OF NEW COMMUNICATION TECHNOLOGIES**. Newbury Park, CA: Sage, 1995, 181 pp. A French scholar places media in historical context with telecommunications and discusses the social impact of constantly changing technologies. References, index.

0257 Folkerts, Jean, and Dwight L. Teeter, Jr. **VOICES OF A NATION: A HISTORY OF MASS MEDIA IN THE UNITED STATES**. New York: Macmillan, 1994 (2nd ed.), 570 pp. Survey text of mass media in the U.S. provides historical, social and legal context, and detail about media professionals/journalists and media organizations, including newspapers, magazines, and news services. Excellent bibliograpy.

0258 Halberstam, David. **THE POWERS THAT BE**. New York: Knopf, 1979, 770 pp. Powerfully written history of four media: *Time*, the *Los Angeles Times,* CBS, and *The Washington Post,* focusing on key personnel, major events and trends, and the impact of these news services on U.S. history. Notes, bibliography, index.

See 0099. Inge, M. Thomas, ed. HANDBOOK OF AMERICAN POPULAR CULTURE.

0259 Lacy, Dan. **FROM GRUNTS TO GIGABYTES: COMMUNICATIONS AND SOCIETY**. Urbana: University of Illinois Press, 1996, 193 pp. Wide-ranging historical essay tracing rise of communications systems and their impact. Bibliography, index.

0260 Nye, Russel B. **THE UNEMBARRASSED MUSE: THE POPULAR ARTS IN AMERICA**. New York: Dial Press, 1970, 497 pp. Readable scholarly survey of print (books, magazines, newspaper), motion picture and broadcast media through U.S. history. Bibliography, index.

0261 Startt, James D., and William David Sloan. **HISTORICAL METHODS IN MASS COMMUNICATION**. Hillsdale, NJ: Erlbaum, 1989, 210 pp. Basic procedures and techniques, searching for historical materials, sources and their evaluation, with good bibliography.

2-C-2. News Agencies

0262 Blondheim, Menahem. **NEWS OVER THE WIRES: THE TELEGRAPH AND THE FLOW OF PUBLIC INFORMATION IN AMERICA, 1844–1897**. Cambridge, MA: Harvard University Press, 1994, 301 pp. Explores role of the telegraph in creation of news agencies and their reportorial product, and the trend to monopolization in news. Notes, sources, index.

0263 Desmond, Robert W. **WORLD NEWS REPORTING**. Iowa City: University of Iowa Press, 1978–1984, 4 vols. Unique narrative of the development of news as a worldwide commodity. Bibliography, index.

1 **THE INFORMATION PROCESS: TO THE TWENTIETH CENTURY.** 1978, 495 pp. Beginnings of newspapers in Europe and America, news reporting processes, news agency development, reporting of wars.

2 **WINDOWS ON THE WORLD: 1900–1920.** 1980, 608 pp. Flow of news, establishment of wireless and its role, British and U.S. developments, reporting World War I, photojournalism, news magazines.

3 **CRISIS AND CONFLICT: BETWEEN TWO WORLD WARS, 1920–1940.** 1982, 518 pp. Flow of news in and around various parts of the world, news agenices, newspaper services, media coverage of the rising world crisis of the 1930s.

4 **TIDES OF WAR: 1931–1945.** 1984, 544 pp. Media reporting of the pre-war and wartime period.

0264 Read, Donald. **THE POWER OF NEWS: THE HISTORY OF REUTERS 1849–1989**. New York: Oxford University Press, 1992, 431 pp. History of the London-based news service. Photos, appendices, glossary, index.

0265 Schwarzlose, Richard A. **THE NATION'S NEWSBROKERS**. Evanston, IL: Northwestern University Press, 2 vols. Notes, bibliography, index.

1 **THE FORMATIVE YEARS: FROM PRETELEGRAPH TO 1865.** 1989, 370 pp. Details the creation and early operation of Associated Press and other lesser news agencies, building on the telegraph.

2 **THE RUSH TO INSTITUTION: FROM 1865 TO 1920.** 1990, 366 pp. Includes the development of the United Press and the International News Service, among others, showing how the telephone assisted news reporting.

0266 UNESCO. **NEWS AGENCIES: THEIR STRUCTURE AND OPERATION**. Paris: UNESCO, 1953, 208 pp. Historical review, legal organization, telegraphic news agencies (the major organizations), telecommunication and transmission of news, international regulation, news agencies and radio broadcasting, and how the public receives news. Valuable early record of news agencies around the world. Maps, charts, appendix, index.

2-C-3. Newspapers

0267 Altschull, J. Herbert. **FROM MILTON TO MCLUHAN: THE IDEAS BEHIND AMERICAN JOURNALISM**. White Plains, NY: Longman, 1990, 447 pp. An historical approach based on the seminal ideas and thinkers about journalism's social and cultural roles. Notes, recommended readings, index.

0268 Bagdikian, Ben H. **THE INFORMATION MACHINES: THEIR IMPACT ON MEN AND THE MEDIA**. New York: Harper & Row, 1971, 359 pp. Rand study of changing technology in print and broadcast news and its likely impact. Charts, tables, bibliography, index.

0269 Compaine, Benjamin M. **THE NEWSPAPER INDUSTRY IN THE 1980s: AN ASSESSMENT OF ECONOMICS AND TECHNOLOGY**. White Plains, NY: Knowledge Industry Publications, Inc., 1980, 290 pp. Synthesis of newspapers with numerous tables. Valuable historical record of newspaper production history to 1980.

0270 Fischer, Heinz-Dietrich, and Erika J. Fischer, eds. **THE PULITZER PRIZE ARCHIVE: A HISTORY AND ANTHOLOGY OF AWARD-WINNING MATERIALS IN JOURNALISM, LETTERS, AND ARTS.** Munich and New York: K. G. Saur, 1987–1995, 8 vols. Each volume focuses on one of Pulitzer categories, analysed chronologically and documented. One of the intentions of the series is to document and describe the annual process of selecting the winning entries for the Pulitzer Prizes. Volumes include:

1 **INTERNATIONAL REPORTING 1928–1985. FROM THE ACTIVITIES OF THE LEAGUE OF NATIONS TO PRESENT-DAY GLOBAL PROBLEMS.** 1987, 352 pp. The 84-page introduction is an excellent description of Joseph Pulitzer's publishing career and his ideas on education for journalism.

2 **NATIONAL REPORTING, 1941–1986: FROM LABOR CONFLICTS TO THE CHALLENGER DISASTER**. 1988, 388 pp. Texts of Pulitzer-winning journalistic reporting stories are introduced by a history of the national reporting prize.

3 **LOCAL REPORTING, 1947–1987: REPORTAGE JOURNALISM.** 1989, 388 pp. After a brief history of the prize for local reporting, the 41 entries provide a record of the awards for local reporting.

4 **POLITICAL EDITORIALS, 1916–1988: FROM WAR-RELATED CONFLICTS TO METROPOLITAN DISPUTES.** 1990, 376 pp. Anthology of opinion journalism receiving the

Pulitzer award since 1917.

5 **SOCIAL COMMENTARY, 1969–1989: FROM UNIVERSITY TROUBLES TO A CALIFORNIA EARTHQUAKE.** 1991, 400 pp.

6 **CULTURAL CRITICISM, 1969–1990: FROM ARCHITECTURAL DAMAGES TO PRESS IMPERFECTIONS.** 1992, 420 pp.

7 **AMERICAN HISTORY AWARDS, 1917–1991: FROM COLONIAL SETTLEMENTS TO THE CIVIL RIGHTS MOVEMENT**. 1994, 366 pp.

8 **BIOGRAPHY/AUTOBIOGRAPHY AWARDS 1917–1992: FROM THE LUCKY DISCOVERER OF AMERICA TO AN UNFORTUNATE VIETNAM VETERAN**. 1995, 406 pp.

0271 Gordon, Gregory, and Ronald E. Cohen. **DOWN TO THE WIRE: UPI'S FIGHT FOR SURVIVAL**. New York: McGraw-Hill, 1990, 429 pp. The decline of UPI in the face of AP competition—and the reasons for that decline. Photos, index.

0272 Hardt, Hanno, and Bonnie Brennen, eds. **NEWSWORKERS: TOWARD A HISTORY OF THE RANK AND FILE**. Minneapolis: University of Minnesota Press, 1995, 237 pp. Essays describe the history of newsworkers as laborers amid the growth of media capitalism between 1890 and 1940.

0273 Harris, Michael, ed. **STUDIES IN NEWSPAPER AND PERIODICAL HISTORY.** Westport, CT.: Greenwood, 1993–date, annual. Anthology of newspaper and periodical history covering both the U.S. and Great Britain.

0274 Knightley, Phillip. **THE FIRST CASUALTY: FROM THE CRIMEA TO VIETNAM—THE WAR CORRESPONDENT AS HERO, PROPAGANDIST, AND MYTH MAKER**. New York: Harcourt, Brace Jovanovich, 1975, 465 pp. Details century and a half of war reporting. Photos, notes, bibliography, index.

0275 Lee, Alfred McClung. **THE DAILY NEWSPAPER IN AMERICA: THE EVOLUTION OF A SOCIAL INSTRUMENT**. New York: Macmillan, 1937, 797 pp. Classic social and economic history focusing on larger trends rather than specific papers or editors—one of the first such studies. Tables, bibliography, index.

0276 Marbut, F.B. **NEWS FROM THE CAPITAL: THE STORY OF WASHINGTON REPORTING**. Carbondale: Southern Illinois University Press, 1971, 304 pp. Narrative history covering nearly 200 years. Notes, index.

0277 Monmonier, Mark. **MAPS WITH THE NEWS: THE DEVELOPMENT OF AMERICAN JOURNALISTIC CARTOGRAPHY**. Chicago: University of Chicago Press, 1989, 330 pp. Discusses changing printing technology, the impact of wire services, different ways of using maps within news stories and the like. Notes, illustrations, bibliography, index.

0278 Mott, Frank Luther. **AMERICAN JOURNALISM: A HISTORY 1690–1960.** New York: Macmillan, 1962 (3rd ed.), 901 pp. Long-standard history of newspapers emphasizing editors and publishers and their roles. Notes, bibliographic notes, index.

0279 Pratte, Paul Alfred. **GODS WITHIN THE MACHINE: A HISTORY OF THE AMERICAN SOCIETY OF NEWSPAPER EDITORS, 1923–1993.** Westport, CT: Greenwood, 1995, 231 pp. A critical and thorough history of this national and politically active association of newspaper editors.

0280 Stephens, Mitchell. **A HISTORY OF NEWS FROM THE DRUM TO THE SATELLITE**. New York: Viking Press, 1988, 400 pp. A wide-ranging history emphasizing the long history of printed news. Notes, bibliography, index.

2-C-4. Magazines

0281 **HISTORICAL GUIDES TO THE WORLD'S PERIODICALS AND NEWSPAPERS.** Westport, CT: Greenwood Press, various dates as shown. Extensive series of exhaustive bibliographies and guides, providing history and profiles of periodicals and newspapers. Each provides detailed historical information and essays summarizing development of magazines and newspapers to the present. Titles include:

1 Chielens, Edward E., ed. **AMERICAN LITERARY MAGAZINES: THE EIGHTEENTH AND NINETEENTH CENTURIES.** 1986, 503 pp. See next entry.

2 _____. **AMERICAN LITERARY MAGAZINES: THE TWENTIETH CENTURY.** 1992, 474 pp. Solid "biobibliographical" introductions to major U.S. literary magazines, with briefer information on additional titles. Entries identify title and publisher changes, editors, availability in reprints and in major microform sets, like UMI'S AMERICAN PERIODICALS, and indexing. Entries also include useful secondary bibliographies. Index.

3 Cook, Michael L., ed. **MYSTERY, DETECTIVE, AND ESPIONAGE MAGAZINES.** 1983, 795 pp. Profiles some 400 magazines, describing contents and publication histories, with secondary bibliographies. Survey of foreign book clubs. Appendixes, chronology, bibliography.

4 Danky, James P., and Maureen E. Hady, eds. **NATIVE AMERICAN PERIODICALS AND NEWSPAPERS 1828–1982.** 1984, 352 pp. A bibliography with precise publishing records and holdings of 1,164 titles of American Indian periodicals, newspapers, and magazines.

5 Daniel, Walter C., ed. **BLACK JOURNALS OF THE UNITED STATES**. 1982, 432 pp. More than 100 African-American periodicals, published between 1857 and the 1980s, are examined. Each entry includes an historical essay describing the personnel and the social, political and business climate in which each magazine emerged and published.

6 Endres, Kathleen, L., ed. **TRADE, INDUSTRIAL, AND PROFESSIONAL PERIODICALS OF THE UNITED STATES**. 1994, 467 pp. Some 70 selected magazines are detailed as to history and current operations. Bibliography, index.

7 Ireland, Sandra L. Jones, compiler. **ETHNIC PERIODICALS IN CONTEMPORARY AMERICA: AN ANNOTATED GUIDE.** 1990. 222 pp. A guide limited to current ethnic periodicals published in the U. S. Designed to guide freelance writers who want to submit articles for publication.

8 Kelly, R. Gordon, ed. **CHILDREN'S PERIODICALS OF THE UNITED STATES.** 1984, 591 pp. Surveys histories of some 100 children's periodicals from 1789 to 1980. Bibliography of periodicals, chronological and geographical indexes.

9 Lippy, Charles W., ed. **RELIGIOUS PERIODICALS OF THE UNITED STATES: ACADEMIC AND SCHOLARLY JOURNALS.** 1986, 607 pp. Introduction includes a bibliography of scholarly articles about religious periodicals. Carefully edited and organized. Includes list of contributors, identified by their home universities.

10 Littlefield, Daniel Jr., and James W. Parins, eds. **AMERICAN INDIAN AND ALASKA NATIVE NEWSPAPERS AND PERIODICALS.** 1984–1986, 3 vols. Historical profiles of native U.S. publications, giving bibliographies, indexing sources, location sources, title changes, publishers with addresses, and editors. Volumes cover: **1826–1924** (1984, 482 pp.); **1925–1970** (1984, 553 pp.) and **1971–1985** (1986, 629 pp.)

11 Nourie, Alan, and Barbara Nourie, eds. **AMERICAN MASS MARKET MAGAZINES.** 1990, 611 pp. Describes and assesses about 100 of the most important including *Cosmopolitan, Reader's Digest,* and *Modern Maturity.* Some profiles give Simmons market data. Index.

12 Riley, Sam G., ed. **MAGAZINES OF THE AMERICAN SOUTH.** 1986, 346 pp. Useful discussions of major library collections as well as the magazines themselves.

13 _____. **INDEX TO SOUTHERN PERIODICALS**. 1986, 459 pp. Identifies 7,000 non-newspaper periodicals published from 1764 to 1984 in Alabama, Arkansas, Florida, Georgia, Kentucky, Louisiana, Mississippi, North Carolina, South Carolina, Tennessee, and Texas. Maryland is included until the Civil War. Covers consumer, business, legal, medical, and other titles, but excludes leaflets, proceedings, collections, occasional papers, yearbooks, bibliography series, abstracts, almanacs, handbooks, and tracts. Two appendices: an alphabetical list of titles and a list arranged by state.

14 _____, and Gary W. Selnow, eds. **REGIONAL INTEREST MAGAZINES OF THE UNITED STATES**. 1991, 418 pp. Regional interest publications are arranged alphabetically by title,

providing a full description of each magazine with publishing history, development, editorial policies, content, and bibliographies.

15 _____. **INDEX TO CITY AND REGIONAL MAGAZINES OF THE UNITED STATES.** 1989, 130 pp. Covers regional interest magazines published between 1950 and 1988. Identifies 920 magazines and sorts them into alphabetical, chronological, and geographical lists.

16 Sloane, David E., ed. **AMERICAN HUMOR MAGAZINES AND COMIC PERIODICALS**. 1987, 648 pp. Describes historical and cultural development, and 100 "important" magazines. Includes briefer descriptions of 400 minor journals, a citing of unverified titles identified from copyright lists; and essays on magazine types.

17 Tymm, Marshall B., and Mike Ashley, eds. **SCIENCE FICTION, FANTASY, AND WEIRD FICTION MAGAZINES.** 1985, 970 pp. Includes English language magazines (279 titles), English-language anthologies (15 titles), academic periodicals and major fanzines (72 titles) and non-English language magazines (184 titles).

18 Unsworth, Michael E., ed. **MILITARY PERIODICALS: UNITED STATES AND SELECTED INTERNATIONAL JOURNALS AND NEWSPAPERS**. 1990, 404 pp. Includes those that had an "impact on the armed forces of the United States and on American military thought."

0282 Mott, Frank Luther. **A HISTORY OF MAGAZINES IN AMERICA**. Cambridge, MA: Harvard University Press, 1930–1968, 5 vols. Magisterial study from 1741 to 1905 in the first four volumes, with the last volume profiling 21 magazines of 1905–1930 era and containing a cumulative index. Standard and definitive for 18th- and 19th-century coverage. Notes, photos, bibliography, index.

0283 Peterson, Theodore. **MAGAZINES IN THE TWENTIETH CENTURY**. Urbana: University of Illinois Press, 1964 (2nd ed.), 484 pp. Detailed treatment of all aspects of the industry, including its history. Tables, index.

0284 Swanberg, W.A. **LUCE AND HIS EMPIRE**. New York: Scribner's, 1972, 529 pp. Exhaustive critical biography of Henry R. Luce and his Time-Life publishing house and its impact. Photos, index.

0285 Tebbel, John, and Mary Ellen Zuckerman. **THE MAGAZINE IN AMERICA 1741–1990**. New York: Oxford University Press, 1991, 433 pp. The latest overall survey history. Bibliography, notes, photos, index.

2-C-5. Broadcasting

0286 Barnouw, Erik. **A HISTORY OF BROADCASTING IN THE UNITED STATES.** New York: Oxford, 3 vols:

1 **A TOWER IN BABEL: TO 1933.** 1966, 344 pp.
2 **THE GOLDEN WEB: 1933–1953.** 1968, 391 pp.
3 **THE IMAGE EMPIRE: FROM 1953.** 1970, 396 pp.

Perhaps the best narrative on U.S. broadcasting development based on both primary and secondary sources—a wonderfully readable account full of people and events and social impact. Bibliography, chronology, photos, notes, index.

0287 _____. **THE SPONSOR: NOTES ON A MODERN POTENTATE**. New York: Oxford University Press, 1978, 220 pp. History and critique of radio and television sponsors and advertising, focusing on television. Notes, index.

0288 Bergreen, Laurence. **LOOK NOW, PAY LATER: THE RISE OF NETWORK BROADCASTING**. New York: Doubleday, 1980, 300 pp. Overall survey of both radio and television network development before the inception of cable competition. Index.

0289 Hilliard, Robert L., and Michael C. Keith. **THE BROADCAST CENTURY: A BIOGRAPHY OF AMERICAN BROADCASTING**. Stoneham, MA: Focal Press, 1997 (2nd ed.),

310 pp. Chronological telling with many sidebars on key figures in the radio–television businesses. Photos, index.

0290 Hilmes, Michele. **HOLLYWOOD AND BROADCASTING FROM RADIO TO CABLE**. Champaign: University of Illinois Press, 1990, 221 pp. Reviews the changing relationship of Hollywood studios to the radio and television industry (and the more recent rise of cable systems and networks), showing growing symbiosis between the two. Notes, bibliography, index.

0291 Inglis, Andrew F. **BEHIND THE TUBE: A HISTORY OF BROADCASTING TECHNOLOGY AND BUSINESS**. Stoneham, MA: Focal Press, 1990, 527 pp. Topic-by-topic approach to technical history is useful, though with something of an RCA bias. The business history is less insightful. Tables, charts, notes, photos, index.

0292 Shawcross, William. **MURDOCH**. New York: Simon & Schuster, 1992, 492 pp. Best biography thus far of a key figure in print and broadcast news around the world—how his empire developed and operates. Photos, notes, bibliography, index.

0293 Smith, Sally Bedell. **IN ALL HIS GLORY: THE LIFE OF WILLIAM S. PALEY, THE LEGENDARY TYCOON AND HIS BRILLIANT CIRCLE**. New York: Simon & Schuster, 1990, 782 pp. Exhaustive and insightful biography telling the story of CBS through life of its long-time leader. Photos, notes, index.

0294 Sterling, Christopher H., and John M. Kittross. **STAY TUNED: A CONCISE HISTORY OF AMERICAN BROADCASTING**. Belmont, CA: Wadsworth, 1990 (2nd ed.), 705 pp. Integrated treatment of major periods in development of radio–TV (and related services) from its prehistory to the late 1980s. Tables, bibliography, chronology, technical appendix, index. (Third edition due in 1998 from Lawrence Erlbaum Publishers.)

i) Radio and Recording

(NOTE: for historical directories of radio programming, see 5-C-6)

0295 Dearling, Robert and Celia Dearling. **THE GUINNESS BOOK OF RECORDED SOUND**. Enfield, England: Guinness Books, 1984, 225 pp. The story of recordings from wax cylinders to laser discs and the people who made it happen. Photos, bibliography, index.

0296 Douglas, Susan J. **INVENTING AMERICAN BROADCASTING 1899–1922**. Baltimore: Johns Hopkins University Press, 1987, 363 pp. Best assessment of the "prehistory" of radio focusing on its technical development and early thinking about a potential "business." Notes, bibliography, index.

0297 Eberly, Philip K. **MUSIC IN THE AIR: AMERICA'S CHANGING TASTES IN POPULAR MUSIC, 1920–1980**. New York: Hastings House, 1982, 406 pp. Interrelates the story of recorded music and radio. Appendices, bibliography, discography, index.

0298 Garay, Ronald. **GORDON McLENDON: THE MAVERICK OF RADIO**. Westport, CT: Greenwood, 1992, 248 pp. First biography of a key figure in development of modern AM "formula" radio. Notes, bibliography, index.

0298a Greenfield, Thomas Allen. **RADIO: A REFERENCE GUIDE.** Westport, CT: Greenwood, 1989, 173 pp. Review of the historical literature on radio, each chapter being followed by specific references. Chapters discuss the medium in general, networks and station histories, drama, news, music, comedy and variety, sports, and miscellaneous subjects. The guide concludes with information on organizations, collections, journals, and indexes.

0299 Lewis, Tom. **EMPIRE OF THE AIR: THE MEN WHO MADE RADIO**. New York: HarperCollins, 1991, 421 pp. Excellent biographical study of Lee de Forest, Edwin Armstrong, and David Sarnoff and their varied and interrelated roles in the development of radio broadcasting. Photos, bibliography, index.

0300 Read, Oliver, and Walter L. Welch. **FROM TIN FOIL TO STEREO: EVOLUTION OF THE PHONOGRAPH**. Indianapolis, IN: Howard W. Sams, 1976 (2nd ed.), 550 pp. Most detailed technical history of recording technology. Photos, appendix, bibliography, index. (Welch and L.B.S. Burt authored a later version, subtitled THE ACOUSTIC YEARS OF THE RECORDING INDUSTRY, 1877–1929, University Press of Florida, 1994, 212 pp.)

0301 Schiffer, Michael Brian. **THE PORTABLE RADIO IN AMERICAN LIFE.** Tucson: University of Arizona Press, 1991, 259 pp. A social/technical history of the portable radio from the 1920s into the 1960s with many photos and reproductions of ads—an archeologist writing a technical and social history of the changing shape and function of radios. Photos, notes, bibliography, index.

ii) Television

(NOTE: for historical directories of television programming, see 5-C-7)

0302 Abramson, Albert. **THE HISTORY OF TELEVISION, 1880–1941**. Jefferson, NC: McFarland & Co., 1987, 354 pp. Definitive history of technical developments to the dawn of U.S. commercial operation with clear discussion of key people, firms, and technical devices. Photos, notes, diagrams, index.

0303 Auletta, Ken. **THREE BLIND MICE: HOW THE TV NETWORKS LOST THEIR WAY**. New York: Random House, 1991, 642 pp. Journalistic account of the three major television networks under siege before and after they changed hands in the mid-1980s. Focus on people and anecdotes. Index.

0304 Barnouw, Erik. **TUBE OF PLENTY: THE EVOLUTION OF AMERICAN TELEVISION.** New York: Oxford, 1990, 3rd ed., 607 pp. Well-written although somewhat anecdotal discussion in an updated one-volume history of television based on his three-volume history (0000). Bibliography, index.

0305 Boddy, William. **FIFTIES TELEVISION: THE INDUSTRY AND ITS CRITICS**. Urbana: University of Illinois Press, 1990, 294 pp. Chapters on television regulation and policy, the industry and its major issues, programs and sponsors, and critical reactions to television's first decade. Notes, bibliography, index.

0306 Goldenson, Leonard. **BEATING THE ODDS: THE UNTOLD STORY BEHIND THE RISE OF ABC.** New York: Scribner's, 1991, 495 pp. The long-time head of the network relates its story. Photos, index.

0307 Hawes, William. **AMERICAN TELEVISION DRAMA: THE EXPERIMENTAL YEARS**. University: University of Alabama Press, 1986, 271 pp. Covers the 1937–1946 era on network experimental and commercial stations. Appendices, notes, bibliography, index.

0308 Kisseloff, Jeff. **THE BOX: AN ORAL HISTORY OF TELEVISION, 1920–1961**. New York: Viking Press, 1995, 592 pp. Hundreds of interviews woven into a continuing narrative. Bibliography, index.

0309 Luke, Carmen. **CONSTRUCTING THE CHILD VIEWER: A HISTORY OF THE AMERICAN DISCOURSE ON TELEVISION AND CHILDREN, 1950–1980**. New York: Praeger, 1990, 231 pp. Assesses the popular, scholarly, and policy writings and their impact. References, index.

0310 MacDonald, J. Fred. **ONE NATION UNDER TELEVISION: THE RISE AND DECLINE OF NETWORK TV.** New York: Pantheon, 1990, 335 pp. Well-written history focusing on programs and programming, exploring the trend from network success to today's competitive tension, especially with cable television. Index.

0311 Marling, Karal Ann. **AS SEEN ON TV: THE VISUAL CULTURE OF EVERYDAY LIFE IN THE 1950s**. Cambridge, MA: Harvard University Press, 1994, 328 pp. Assessment of popular culture in chapters on Mamie Eisenhower's clothes, painting by numbers, Disneyland, cars in the television age, popular music and mobility, aesthetics of food, and Nixon's visit to Moscow. Photos, notes, index.

0312 Murray, Michael D., and Donald G. Godfrey, eds. **TELEVISION IN AMERICA: LOCAL STATION HISTORY FROM ACROSS THE NATION.** Ames: Iowa State University Press, 1997, 428 pp. First video history to approach the medium from point of view of 22 local stations from markets, large to small, all over the U.S. Notes, bibliography, index.

0312a Newcomb, Horace, ed. **ENCYCLOPEDIA OF TELEVISION.** Chicago: Fitzroy Dearborn, 1997, 3 vols., 1,948 pp. Lavish illustrated guide to the people, programs, and other topics concerning the U.S., British, Australian, and Canadian television businesses. Most entries include further references, videographies, and other details.

0313 Slide, Anthony. **THE TELEVISION INDUSTRY: A HISTORICAL DICTIONARY.** Westport, CT: Greenwood, 1991, 374 pp. As the title suggests, this is broad-ranging with hundreds of entries—the longer ones include references to further reading. Programs, whole genres, companies, individuals. Index. (See also Brown 0098)

0314 Watson, Mary Ann. **THE EXPANDING VISTA: AMERICAN TELEVISION IN THE KENNEDY YEARS**. New York: Oxford, 1990, 273 pp. Good social history on all aspects of the medium in the early 1960s. Photos, notes, index.

iii) Noncommercial/Public Broadcasting

0315 Blakely, Robert J. **TO SERVE THE PUBLIC INTEREST: EDUCATIONAL BROADCASTING IN THE UNITED STATES**. Syracuse, NY: Syracuse University Press, 1979, 274 pp. Focuses primarily on radio and the early development of noncommercial television. The first scholarly history. Tables, notes, index.

0316 Carnegie Commission on Educational Television. **PUBLIC TELEVISION: A PROGRAM FOR ACTION**. New York: Harper & Row, 1967, 254 pp. The landmark study that led within a year to creation of Corporation for Public Broadcasting and the public broadcasting system. Tables.

0317 Carnegie Commission on the Future of Public Broadcasting. **A PUBLIC TRUST**. New York: Bantam, 1979, 401 pp. Assessment of the national system's first decade and the need for greatly increased funding. Appendices, bibliography, index.

0318 Day, James. **THE VANISHING VISION: THE INSIDE STORY OF PUBLIC TELEVISION**. Berkeley: University of California Press, 1995, 443 pp. Best overall history to date, written by a participant. Photos, notes, bibliography, index.

0319 Engleman, Ralph. **PUBLIC RADIO AND TELEVISION IN AMERICA: A POLITICAL HISTORY**. Newbury Park, CA: Sage, 1996, 342 pp. Places the modern story in context of battles over public service radio in 1930s. Several chapters each on public radio, public television, and community television. References, index. (Compare to Gibson, 0320)

0320 Gibson, George H. **PUBLIC BROADCASTING: THE ROLE OF THE FEDERAL GOVERNMENT, 1912–1976**. New York: Praeger, 1977, 237 pp. The changing roles of the FRC and FCC as well as Congress and the battle for long-range funding. Notes, index. (Compare to Engleman, 0319.)

0321 Koenig, Allen E., and Ruane B. Hill, eds. **THE FARTHER VISION: EDUCATIONAL TELEVISION TODAY**. Madison: University of Wisconsin Press, 1967, 369 pp. Useful snapshot of the situation on the eve of the Public Broadcasting Act. Appendix, index.

0322 Nyhan, Michael J., ed. **THE FUTURE OF PUBLIC BROADCASTING**. New York: Praeger, 1976, 372 pp. About 20 papers assess the status of the national system a decade after creation of the modern system. Annotated bibliography, index.

0323 Stone, David M. **NIXON AND THE POLITICS OF PUBLIC TELEVISION**. New York: Garland, 1985, 370 pp. Analysis of the upheaval in the public broadcasting system in the early 1970s under pressure from the Nixon administration's unwillingness to approve long-range funding. Notes, index.

iv) Broadcast Journalism
(NOTE: See also 5-C-7)

0324 Bliss, Edward Jr. **NOW THE NEWS: THE STORY OF BROADCAST JOURNALISM**. New York: Columbia University Press, 1991, 575 pp. The only book-length study of both radio and television news, written by a long-time CBS producer. Chronology, notes, bibliography, index.

0325 Bluem, A. William. **DOCUMENTARY IN AMERICAN TELEVISION: FORM, FUNCTION, METHOD**. New York: Hastings House, 1965, 311 pp. The first and classic assessment of the televised documentary with many examples from the medium's first 15 years. Photos, bibliography, index. (Continued with Hammond, 0329)

0326 Chester, Edward W. **RADIO, TELEVISION, AND AMERICAN POLITICS**. New York: Sheed & Ward, 1969, 342 pp. Traces the role of radio and then television in national elections. Bibliography, index.

0327 Culbert, David Holbrook. **NEWS FOR EVERYMAN: RADIO AND FOREIGN AFFAIRS IN THIRTIES AMERICA**. Westport, CT: Greenwood, 1976, 238 pp. Six chapters on as many correspondents, plus two overview discussions of the era. Bibliography, index.

0328 Donovan, Robert J., and Ray Scherer. **UNSILENT REVOLUTION: TELEVISION NEWS AND AMERICAN LIFE 1948–1991**. New York: Cambridge University Press, 1992, 357 pp. Valuable assessment of four decades of political newsmaking divided into two parts: a review of coverage of 12 specific news events followed by a broader contextual review of TV news impacts. Notes, index.

0329 Hammond, Charles Montgomery Jr. **THE IMAGE DECADE: TELEVISION DOCUMENTARY 1965–1975**. New York: Hastings House, 1981, 285 pp. Continues Bluem (0325) in sections on major themes, producers, reporters, and events. Sources, bibliography, index.

0330 Henson, Robert. **TELEVISION WEATHERCASTING: A HISTORY**. Jefferson, NC: McFarland, 1990, 192 pp. Only study of its kind. Photos, appendices, bibliography, index.

0331 Hosley, David H. **AS GOOD AS ANY: FOREIGN CORRESPONDENCE ON AMERICAN RADIO, 1930–1940**. Westport, CT: Greenwood, 1984, 165 pp. Narrative of the men and their reporting roles. Notes, bibliography, index.

0332 MacDonald, J. Fred. **TELEVISION AND THE RED MENACE: THE VIDEO ROAD TO VIETNAM**. New York: Praeger, 1985, 277 pp. Study of the changing news and propagandistic content of network television news in the 1950s and 1960s. Tables, notes, bibliography, index.

2-C-6. Cable and Newer Media

0333 Denisoff, R. Serge. **INSIDE MTV**. New Brunswick, NJ: Transaction Books, 1988, 373 pp. Creation and first 5 years of the cable music service. Bibliography, index.

0334 Goldberg, Robert and Gerald Jay Goldberg. **CITIZEN TURNER: THE WILD RISE OF AN AMERICAN TYCOON**. New York: Harcourt Brace, 1995, 525 pp. Based on documentary and interview research, this saga begins with Ted Turner's father. Notes on sources, photos, index.

0335 Graham, Margaret B.W. **RCA AND THE VIDEODISC: THE BUSINESS OF RESEARCH.** New York: Cambridge University Press, 258 pp. Valuable study of the corporate decision-making process within RCA leading to marketing of a non-laser videodisc that failed. Notes, index.

0336 Lardner, James. **FAST FORWARD: HOLLYWOOD, THE JAPANESE, AND THE VCR WARS**. New York: Norton, 1987, 344 pp. Development and impact of the home video recorder stressing film industry concern—pinpointed in a landmark Supreme Court case—over the machine's abilities to violate their copyrights.

0337 Marlow, Eugene, and Eugene Secunda. **SHIFTING TIME AND SPACE: THE STORY OF VIDEOTAPE**. New York: Praeger, 1991, 174 pp. Just that—plus some material on video's impact over the years.

0338 Nmungwun, Aaron Foisi. **VIDEO RECORDING TECHNOLOGY: ITS IMPACT ON MEDIA AND HOME ENTERTAINMENT**. Hillsdale, NJ: Erlbaum, 1989, 289 pp. Broadcast video, home video, video disc, and related services are historically detailed.

0339 Phillips, Mary Alice Mayer. **CATV: A HISTORY OF COMMUNITY ANTENNA TELEVISION**. Evanston: Northwestern University Press, 1972, 209 pp. The first such history, it focuses primarily on slowly developing policy issues. Notes, bibliography, index.

2-C-7. Policy and Regulation

0340 Bensman, Marvin R. **BROADCAST REGULATION: SELECTED CASES AND DECISIONS**. Lanham, MD: University Press of America, 1985 (2nd ed.), 227 pp. Abstracts nearly 650 cases covering over 60 years. Subject index.

0341 Chafee, Zechariah Jr. **GOVERNMENT AND MASS COMMUNICATIONS**. Chicago: University of Chicago Press, 1947 (two vols.; reprinted in one by Shoestring Press in 1968), 823 pp. Combining philosophy with details of trends in specific media, this classic study is one of a series of reports from the Commission on Freedom of the Press. Notes, appendix, index.

0342 Conant, Michael. **ANTITRUST IN THE MOTION PICTURE INDUSTRY: ECONOMIC AND LEGAL ANALYSIS**. Berkeley: University of California Press, 1960, 240 pp. The best study of the changing relationship of government antitrust efforts and the studio system, focusing on the postwar Paramount decrees. Bibliography, notes, index of cases, index.

0343 Flannery, Gerald V. **COMMISSIONERS OF THE FCC 1927–1994**. Lanham, MD: University Press of America, 1994, 228 pp. Useful brief (average three pages) biographies of chairs and members of the Federal Radio Commission and Federal Communications Commission.

0344 Kahn, Frank J., ed. **DOCUMENTS OF AMERICAN BROADCASTING**. Englewood Cliffs, NJ: Prentice-Hall, 1984 (4th ed.), 501 pp. More than 40 of them are reproduced with brief contextual introductions. Index.

0345 Le Duc, Don R. **CABLE TELEVISION AND THE FCC: A CRISIS IN MEDIA CONTROL**. Phialdelphia: Temple University Press, 1973, 289 pp. Policy history of cable television's early years. Appendices, glossary, notes, bibliography, index.

0346 McChesney, Robert W. **TELECOMMUNICATIONS, MASS MEDIA, AND DEMOCRACY: THE BATTLE FOR THE CONTROL OF U.S. BROADCASTING, 1928–1935**. New York: Oxford University Press, 1993, 393 pp. Insightful analysis of the arguments leading to the 1934 Act. Notes, bibliography, index.

0347 Paglin, Max D., ed. **A LEGISLATIVE HISTORY OF THE COMMUNICATIONS ACT OF 1934**. New York: Oxford University Press, 1989, 981 pp. Collects the relevant documents and adds useful historical essays. Index.

0348 **REGULATION OF BROADCASTING: HALF A CENTURY OF GOVERNMENT REGULATION OF BROADCASTING.** House of Representatives, Committee on Interstate and Foreign Commerce, 85th Cong, 2nd Sess., 1958, 171 pp. In part based on a dissertation, this is a useful survey of regulation to that point. Notes.

2-C-8. International

0349 Hudson, Heather E. **COMMUNICATION SATELLITES: THEIR DEVELOPMENT AND IMPACT**. New York: Free Press, 1990, 338 pp. Solid analytical history of both domestic and international satellite development. Notes, glossary, bibliography, index.

0350 Schwoch, James. **THE AMERICAN RADIO INDUSTRY AND ITS LATIN AMERICAN ACTIVITIES, 1900–1939**. Urbana: University of Illinois Press, 1990, 184 pp. Interesting telling of early outreach activities by U.S. wireless, manufacturing, and broadcasting companies. Notes, index.

0351 Smith, Anthony, ed. **TELEVISION: AN INTERNATIONAL HISTORY**. New York: Oxford University Press, 1995, 419 pp. Fifteen chapters by as many authorities place television in its varied historical contexts. Some deal with programs across countries, others focus on specific regions. Photos, further reading, list of museums and archives, index.

0352 UNESCO. **PRESS FILM RADIO.** Paris: UNESCO, 1947–52, five vols. and two supplements (reprinted in three vols. by Arno Press, 1972), ca 2,000 pp. Perhaps the most detailed record in English of the immediate postwar status (and earlier history) of newspapers, news agencies, motion picture business, and radio in most parts of the world. Tables, maps.

0353 _____. **TELEVISION: A WORLD SURVEY**. Paris: UNESCO, 1953, 184 pp. **SUPPLEMENT**, 1955, 47 pp. (both reprinted in one vol. by Arno Press, 1972). A country-by-country survey that is now an invaluable record of the inception of television service. Maps, tables.

2-C-9. Propaganda Media

0354 Browne, Donald R. **INTERNATIONAL RADIO BROADCASTING: THE LIMITS OF THE LIMITLESS MEDIUM**. New York: Praeger, 1982, 369 pp. Very detailed analysis of the many official and private international services over the years. Appendices, bibliography, index.

0355 Dougherty, William E., ed. **A PSYCHOLOGICAL WARFARE CASEBOOK**. Baltimore: Johns Hopkins Press, 1958, 880 pp. Impressive and important collection based primarily on World War II incidents: history, doctrine, organization and personnel, policy goals and planning, operational objectives, role of intelligence and research, media and methods, evaluation, and Soviet psychological warfare. References, indexes.

0356 Lasswell, Harold D. et al., eds. **PROPAGANDA AND COMMUNICATION IN WORLD HISTORY**. Honolulu: University of Hawaii Press, 1979–1980, three vols., 1,800 pp. Massive collection of primary and secondary material on the changing role and definition of propaganda in history from the earliest times to the present. Index.

0357 Lerner, Daniel. **SYKEWAR: PSYCHOLOGICAL WARFARE AGAINST GERMANY—D-DAY TO VE-DAY.** New York: Stewart, 1949 (reprinted by MIT Press in 1971), 463 pp. The standard history of Allied methods and practice in the European Theater, 1944–1945. Charts, bibliography and sources, appendices, index.

0358 Mickelson, Sig. **AMERICA'S OTHER VOICE: THE STORY OF RADIO FREE EUROPE AND RADIO LIBERTY**. New York: Praeger, 1983, 269 pp. A 23-chapter historical review of both radio services from the days of "private" operation to those of acknowledged government support. Sources, chronology, appendices, index.

0359 Mock, James R., and Cedric Larson. **WORDS THAT WON THE WAR: THE STORY OF THE COMMITTEE ON PUBLIC INFORMATION 1917–1919**. Princeton, NJ: Princeton University Press, 1939, 372 pp. Standard history of the "Creel Committee," U.S. propaganda in World War I. Illustrations, notes, index.

0360 Shulman, Holly Cowan. **THE VOICE OF AMERICA: PROPAGANDA AND DEMOCRACY, 1941–1945**. Madison: University of Wisconsin Press, 1991, 282 pp. Careful study of the origins of VOA and its initial years. Notes, bibliography, index.

0361 Simpson, Christopher. **SCIENCE OF COERCION: COMMUNICATION RESEARCH AND PSYCHOLOGICAL WARFARE, 1945–1960**. New York: Oxford University Press, 1994, 204 pp. Study of the relations between scholars and the government at the height of the cold war. Appendix, notes, bibliographic essay, index.

0362 Wood, James. **HISTORY OF INTERNATIONAL BROADCASTING**. Piscataway, NJ: IEEE Service Center, 1992, 258 pp . Good overall history stressing the technical development of international services. Bibliography, appendices, index.

3

Technology

Chapter 3 includes bibliographies and other basic research resources on mass communications technology. APPLIED SCIENCE AND TECHNOLOGY INDEX (0371), available electronically from several services, analyzes the field's highly technical research journals as well as others (the journals themselves appear in chapter 9). Equally significant is the complex documentation of patents and technical standards, somewhat simplified and rendered more accessible via the Patent and Trademark Office's Internet site.

Our emphasis is to identify the few basic tools for research in very complex and highly technical areas. Often the most convenient way to obtain up-to-date information of a technical nature is to take advantage of the electronic document ordering and delivery services offered by the likes of the IEEE (0394) or by contacting an organization like SCTE (0396) or SMPTE (0397). We include selected secondary works on various modes of distributing mass communications, including spectrum management that offer explanations of many of these technologies.

3-A. Bibliographic Resources

3-A-1. Bibliographies

0363 **BIBLIOGRAPHIC GUIDE TO TECHNOLOGY**. New York: G.K. Hall, 1987–date, annual. "Comprehensive annual subject bibliography" cumulating holdings of New York Public Library and Library of Congress. Useful for international coverage.

0364 **LIBRARY HI TECH BIBLIOGRAPHY**. Ann Arbor, MI: Pierian Press, 1986–date, annual. Volumes include 10 to 12 extensively annotated bibliographies identifying recent literature on a variety of high technology topics, including cable television (vols. 1 and 7), interactive video (vol. 2), privacy in the electronic age (vol. 7), multimedia and virtual reality, desktop publishing, and open systems interconnection (vol. 8), and e-mail and faxes (vol. 9). A time-saver for current cites on new media technologies.

0365 Saffady, William. **HIGH DEFINITION TELEVISION: A BIBLIOGRAPHY**. Westport, CT: Meckler, 1990, 121 pp. Unannotated listing divided into sections on books, reports, journals, and magazines; papers and conference proceedings; and newspapers and news magazine stories. No index.

0366 Sanchez, James Joseph. **TELETEXT SYSTEMS: A SELECTIVE, ANNOTATED BIBLIOGRAPHY.** Monticello, IL: Vance Bibliographies, 1987, 9 pp. (Public Administration Series, P-2265). About 25 items from trade journals, ERIC documents, with international focus.

0367 _____. **VIDEOTEX SYSTEMS: A SELECTIVE, ANNOTATED BIBLIOGRAPHY.** Monticello, IL: Vance Bibliographies, 1987, 17 pp. (Public Administration Series, P-2262). About 60 annotated items with an international focus (Prestel, Minitel).

0368 Sudalnik, James E. and Victoria A. Kuhl, comps. **HIGH-DEFINITION TELEVISION: AN ANNOTATED MULTIDISCIPLINARY BIBLIOGRAPHY 1981–1992**. Westport, CT: Greenwood Press, 1994, 368 pp. Some 1,400 citations are arranged in seven areas: historical treatises and overviews, Japanese and European development, U.S. development, socioeconomic implications, development of standards, program production, and alternative delivery systems. Author, title, and subject indices.

0369 Taggart, Dorothy T. **A GUIDE TO SOURCES IN EDUCATIONAL MEDIA AND TECHNOLOGY**. Metuchen, NJ: Scarecrow, 1975, 156 pp. Some 400 items in 18 topical sections. Indexed.

0370 **THE VIDEOTEX/TELETEXT BIBLIOGRAPHY**. Rosslyn, VA: Videotex Industry Association, 1985 (2nd. ed.), 87 pp. Unannotated listing of over 100 books, 150 reports, and 750 articles on videotex and teletext. Books and reports are listed alphabetically. Articles are listed by 10 broad categories. Videotex Industry Association is now Interactive Services Association.

3-A-2. Abstracts, Indexes, Databases

0371 **APPLIED SCIENCE AND TECHNOLOGY INDEX**. New York: H. W. Wilson, 1958–date, monthly. Online version available from Wilsonline, Ovid, and OCLC: covers October 1983–date, updated twice weekly. CD-ROM version available from H.W. Wilson, SilverPlatter, and Ovid: covers 1983–date, updating varies. For more information, see Wilson's homepage: www.hwwilson.com/ Author and subject indexing of major English-language technical and scientific journals in new communication technologies journals, including SMPTE JOURNAL, TECHNOLOGY REVIEW, NEW SCIENTIST, and IEEE journals. Far less comprehensive than SCIENCE CITATION INDEX (next entry) but also less intimidating for users.

0372 **SCIENCE CITATION INDEX**. Philadelphia: Institute for Scientific Information, 1961–date, bimonthly with annual cumulations. Online version SCISEARCH available from Dialog, Data-Star, and others: coverage varies, updated weekly. CD-ROM version available from ISI: current coverage only, updated quarterly. Author, cited reference, and keyword indexes for some 4,500 journals.

3-A-3. Directories

See 0052. CORPORATE TECHNOLOGY DIRECTORY.

0373 **DIRECTORY OF AMERICAN RESEARCH AND TECHNOLOGY**. New Providence, NJ: R.R. Bowker, 1965–date, annual. Formerly INDUSTRIAL RESEARCH LABORATORIES OF THE UNITED STATES (1920–1964). CD-ROM version available from Bowker Electronic Publishing in SCI-TECH REFERENCE PLUS: covers current edition, updated annually. Subtitle: "Organizations active in product development for business." 31st ed. for 1997 (1996). Profiles private and public companies listed alphabetically under parent company. Entries give brief information, identify numbers and academic disciplines of PhDs, technicians. Geographic, personnel, and R&D classification (subject) indexes.

3-A-4. Dictionaries

0374 **BKSTS DICTIONARY OF IMAGE TECHNOLOGY**. Newton, MA: Focal Press, 1994 (3rd ed.), 168 pp. Pocket-size collection of definitions. Illustrations.

See 0087. Bognár, Desi K. INTERNATIONAL DICTIONARY OF BROADCASTING AND FILM.

0375 Browne, Steven E. **FILM-VIDEO TERMS AND CONCEPTS**. Newton, MA: Focal Press, 1992, 181 pp. Icons lead reader to terms for the specific medium sought.

0376 **CONSUMER ELECTRONICS PRODUCT TERMINOLOGY DICTIONARY**. Washington: Electronic Industries Association, 1991 (2nd ed.), 101 pp. Brief definitions of 1,000 terms used in conjunction with electronic consumer products, including camcorders, computers, home audio products, fax machines, mobile electronics, telecommunications products, TVs, and VCRs. Intended for consumers and retailers. Subject arrangement with index.

0377 Ferncase, Richard K. **FILM AND VIDEO LIGHTING TERMS AND CONCEPTS**. Newton, MA: Focal Press, 1994, 176 pp. More than 1,000 of them are defined and many are illustrated in a general approach suitable for nontechnical readers.

0378 **A GUIDE TO UNDERSTANDING TECHNOLOGY TERMS**. Washington: U.S. Department of Commerce, Office of the Chief Financial Officer, October 1994, 329 pp. Wide-ranging (beyond communications) but highly useful plain-language definitions. Readings, topical indexes include information and communication.

0379 Jeffers, Mike. **NCTA/SCTE: GLOSSARY OF CABLE TELEVISION TECHNICAL TERMS**. Washington: National Cable Television Association, 1988, 66 pp. Created by members of NCTA Engineering Committee. Labeled "draft," it represents compromises agreed on by the committee. Acronyms, bibliography.

3-B. Patents and Technical Standards

3-B-1. Patents

0380 Bertin, Gilles Y., and Sally Wyatt. **MULTINATIONALS AND INDUSTRIAL PROPERTY: THE CONTROL OF THE WORLD'S TECHNOLOGY**. Brighton: Harvester, 1988, 177 pp. Discusses tensions between inventors and imitators and developed and developing countries in high technology, including telecommunications and electronics.

0381 Bowie, Norman E. **UNIVERSITY-BUSINESS PARTNERSHIPS: AN ASSESSMENT.** Lanham, MD: Rowman & Littlefield, 1994, 287 pp. Discusses business versus values issues of corporate-sponsored academic research and development in advanced technologies. Emphasis on technology transfer at MIT in telecommunications and information technologies, with historical documents on patents and licensing agreements.

0382 Kraeuter, David W. **RADIO AND TELEVISION PIONEERS: A PATENT BIBLIOGRAPHY.** Metuchen, NJ: Scarecrow, 1992, 319 pp. Identifies by patent number, date, and descriptive title more than 3,000 patents for Armstrong, de Forest, Dolbear, Farnsworth, Du Mont, Loomis, Marconi, Sarnoff, and many others. Companion volume to Kraeuter's BRITISH RADIO AND TELEVISION PIONEERS: A PATENT BIBLIOGRAPHY (Metuchen, NJ: Scarecrow, 1993).

0383 McKnelly, Michele, and Johanna Johnson. **PATENTS AND TRADEMARKS: A BIBLIOGRAPHY OF MATERIALS AVAILABLE FOR SELECTION**. Washington: Patent Depository Library Association, 1989, 63 pp. Guide to major information resources about U.S. patents.

0384 **U.S. Department of Commerce, Patent and Trademark Office**. 2021 Jefferson Davis Highway, Arlington, VA 22202. Patent or Trademark information, voice: 703-557-4636. The repository of the nation's patent history (although some older records are in the National Archives, 0191). Holds as public records all patents (primarily in paper files, although computerization project is making headway). Patent searching sites, many offering for-a-fee searching and document delivery services, are proliferating on the Internet. The Patent and Trademark Office's Internet site (www.uspto.gov/) provides access to full texts of patents since 1976, with a very user-friendly search engine, as well as other information on patents and the Patent and Trademark Office's services and fees.

1 **U.S. Department of Commerce, Patent and Trademark Office. CASSIS** [CD-ROM]. 1969–date, bimonthly. Searching U.S. patent information typically requires using the U.S. Patent and Trademark Office's INDEX TO THE U.S. PATENT CLASSIFICATION, MANUAL OF CLASSIFICATION, and PATENT CLASSIFICATION DEFINITIONS; in combination, these cross reference classification and subclassification numbers and descriptive titles provide an index to the OFFICIAL GAZETTE OF THE UNITED STATES PATENT AND TRADEMARK OFFICE, a weekly abstracting and announcing service that gives details for patents granted. CASSIS, or the "Classification and Search Support Information System," designed for use in numerically organized patent collections (especially patent depository libraries), simplifies research by providing current classification information and electronic versions of Patent Office publications. CASSIS includes two complementary parts: CASSIS/CLSF indexes all U.S. patents from 1790 to the present by classification and subclassification and patent number (including some 10,000 X-numbered patents issued in 1790–1836 without numbers); and CASSIS/BIB, covering 1969 to the present, accesses patents by classifications,

descriptive titles, names of patentees and assignees, dates, geographic locations, and most usefully, keywords in titles and abstracts.

2 **PATENT AND TRADEMARK OFFICE COLLECTION OF HISTORICAL AND INTERESTING U.S. PATENTS IN CELEBRATION OF OUR NATION'S BICENTENNIAL.** GPO, 1976, one microfilm reel. A very convenient packaging of full texts of patents for radio, television, and the like of historical significance, including those of Edison, Berliner, Poulsen, de Forest, Armstrong, Farnsworth, Zworykin, and others.

3 **TELEPHONE DIRECTORY.** 1989–date, annual. Identifies telephone numbers of sections responsible for electronic media classifications. This useful directory information, as well as U.S. Patent Classifications, is reprinted in Richard C. Levy's INVENTING AND PATENTING SOURCEBOOK: HOW TO SELL AND PROTECT YOUR IDEAS (Detroit: Gale, 1990).

3-B-2. Technical Standards

0385 **Advanced Television Systems Committee (ATSC).** 1750 K St.NW, Suite 800, Washington 20006. Voice: 202-828-3130. Fax: 202-828-3131. Internet: www.atsc.org. Coordinates and develops voluntary technical standards for advanced television systems, including enhanced conventional television as well as high definition television (HDTV). Develops national positions for presentation to governmental executive departments and regulatory agencies. Proposes standards to the Federal Communications Commission. Charter members are Electronic Industries Association, Institute of Electrical and Electronics Engineers, National Association of Broadcasters, National Cable Television Association, and Society of Motion Picture and Television Engineers. Published ATSC DIGITAL TELEVISION STANDARD (1995), which was proposed by the FCC as the ATV broadcasting standard. Founded in 1982 by the Joint Committee on Inter-Society Coordination.

0386 **Advanced Television Technology Center, Inc. (ATTC).** 1330 Braddock Pl., Suite 200, Alexandria, VA 22314-1650. Voice: 703-739-3850. Fax: 703-739-3230. Private nonprofit corporation formed by the television broadcast and manufacturing companies to develop technical solutions to problems facing broadcasters in implementing digital advanced television broadcasting, including high definition service. Founded as Advanced Television Test Center (to test competing HDTV systems) in 1988; changed name in 1996.

0387 **American National Standards Institute (ANSI).** 11 West 42nd St., New York 10036. Voice: 212-642-4900. Fax: 212-302-1286. ANSI membership includes more than 1,200 professional and technical societies, trade associations, and companies. ANSI approves standards developed and voluntarily submitted by trade, technical, and other organizations; coordinates and assigns ANSI numbers; represents U.S. interests in nongovernmental standards forums with ISO and IEC. Supplies ANSI and other national and international standards; accepts orders by phone, fax, and mail. Publishes CATALOG OF AMERICAN NATIONAL STANDARDS; ANSI REPORTER (1967–date), biweekly newsletter, reports on standards news and activities of its membership. ANSI's Information Infrastructure Standards Panel is charged with identifying requirements for new or modified standards for the National Information Infrastructure (NII).

0388 **EIA, JEDEC, AND TIA STANDARDS AND ENGINEERING PUBLICATIONS: 1995 CATALOG.** Englewood, CO: Global Engineering Documents, 1995, 169 pp. Comprehensive listing of Electronic Industries Association and Telecommunications Industry Association standards, specifications, bulletins, and publications as well as documents developed by the Joint Electronic Device Engineering Council. Entries are arranged by subject and include corresponding ANSI reference number, brief document summary, respective committee number of the formulating committee responsible for the document, and purchase information. Entries are indexed under document number and product category code. Global is the primary distributor of EIA/JEDEC/TIA standards and related publications.

See 0392. Electronic Industries Association (EIA).

See 0950. Federal Communications Commission.

0389 **National Data Broadcasting Committee (NDBC)**. Contact either EIA (0392) or NAB (0513) which share roles as secretariat in odd and even-numbered years, respectively. Has as its purpose to develop voluntary national technical standards for high-speed data broadcasting using the National Television Systems Committee television service as a delivery medium. Membership on the committee may be extended to representatives of companies and organizations having substantive U.S. commercial interest in the committee's work. Includes Evaluation Working Group and Testing Working Group. Founded in 1993.

0390 **National Radio Systems Committee (NRSC)**. Contact either EIA (0392) or NAB (0513), which share roles as secretariat in odd and even numbered years, respectively. Has as its purpose to make recommendations for technical standards which relate to radio broadcasting and reception of radio broadcast signals. Open to those with a business interest in the technology. Most members are engineers, scientists, or technicians. Has three active subcommittees: Digital Audio Broadcasting (DAB; formed in 1993); High-Speed FM Subcarrier (formed ca 1993); and Radio Broadcast Data System (RBDS; formed in 1991). DAB Subcommittee oversees testing and evaluation of proposed systems for transmitting and receiving digital radio signals and includes Report-Writing Working Group, Field Test Task Group, and Compatibility Working Group. High-Speed FM Subcarrier Subcommittee oversees testing and evaluation of proposed high-speed, digital subcarrier transmissions systems for use by FM radio stations. RBDS Subcommittee produced U.S. RBDS Standard (1993) and includes AM RBDS Working Group and Emergency Alert System Working Group (formed in 1995). Founded in 1979; reactivated in 1986.

See 0947. National Institute of Standards and Technology (NIST).

See 0947. National Technical Information Service (NTIS).

0391 Office of Technology Assessment. **GLOBAL STANDARDS: BUILDING BLOCKS FOR THE FUTURE**. Washington: GPO, 1992, 114 pp. Discusses the role and process of standard setting in general, comparing U.S. and European experience. Diagrams, tables, notes, index.

See 0396. Society of Cable Telecommunications Engineers.

3-C. Engineering Organizations

3-C-1. Manufacturing Associations

0392 **Electronic Industries Association (EIA)**. 2500 Wilson Blvd., Arlington, VA 22201. Voice: 703-907-7500. Fax: 703-907-7501. Internet: www.eia.org. 1250 members. Annual budget $42 million. Major trade association of U.S. electronics manufacturers, organized into groups and divisions, including Consumer Electronics Manufacturers Association (formerly Consumer Electronics Group) and Telecommunications Industry Association. Seeks to enhance the competitiveness of the U.S. producer. Promulgates technical standards, collects and tabulates marketing data on production and sales of electronic products. Monitors legislation and regulation and represents industry interests in competitiveness, common distribution, trade, and government procurement. Publications include ELECTRONIC DATA MARKET BOOK (annual), CONSUMER ELECTRONICS U.S. SALES (annual), ELECTRONIC MARKET TRENDS (monthly). Publishes directories, proceedings, reports, and member newsletter. Sponsors award programs, semiannual meetings, and trade shows. Library; fee-based research service (EIA Research Center). Founded in 1924 as the Radio Manufacturers Association; became Radio–Television Manufacturers Association in 1950; Radio–Electronics–Television Manufacturers Association in 1953; Electronic Industries Association in 1957.

0393 **International Communications Industries Association**. 3150 Spring St., Fairfax VA 22031-2399. Voice: 703-273-7200. Fax: 703-278-8082. 1,200 members, including video, audiovisual, and computer hardware and software dealers, manufacturers, and users. Interests in competition and regulation, legislation, small business issues, postal rates, copyright, education, and taxation. Participates in standards development. Sponsors Audio-Visual Communications Fund Political Action Committee. Operates Educational Communications Foundation. Headquarters for INFOCOMM International, annual trade show. Publishes COMMUNICATIONS INDUSTRY REPORT (1983–date, monthly); DIRECTORY OF VIDEO, COMPUTER, AND AUDIO-VISUAL PRODUCTS (1953–date), formerly AUDIO VISUAL EQUIPMENT DIRECTORY and variant titles; industry studies, including AUDIO-VISUAL EQUIPMENT SURVEY (1989–date); and other resources, including FOUNDATION GRANTS GUIDE: GRANTS WITH A SLICE FOR COMMUNICATIONS TECHNOLOGY PRODUCTS (1984). Holds annual meetings. Absorbed Association of Media Producers and International Media Producers Association. Formerly National Audio-Visual Association (1939–1983).

3-C-2. Engineering Societies

0394 **Institute of Electrical and Electronics Engineers (IEEE)**. 345 East 47th St., New York 10017-2394. Voice: 212-705-7900. Fax: 212-752-4929. Customer Service Center: 445 Hoes Ln., P.O. Box 1331, Piscataway, NJ 08855-1331. Voice: 908-981-0060. Fax: 908-981-9667; Washington office: 1828 L St., NW, Suite 1202, Washington 20036, voice: 202-785-0017, fax: 202-785-0835. Internet: www.ieee.org/ti.html. 310,000 members in 150 countries. Annual budget $110 million. International technical professional society devoted to advancing theory and application of electrical engineering, electronics, and computing. Includes 37 technical societies and councils devoted to specific technical areas, including Broadcast Technology. Promotes development of electrotechnology and allied sciences. Promulgates over 700 technical standards. Conducts over 300 conferences and 5,000 local meetings around the world annually. Publishes magazines, journals, books, conference records, and CD-ROMS, including IEEE SPECTRUM (monthly), IEEE TRANSACTIONS ON BROADCASTING, (quarterly), IEEE TRANSACTIONS ON CONSUMER ELECTRONICS (quarterly), PROCEEDINGS OF THE IEEE (monthly), STANDARD DICTIONARY OF ELECTRICAL AND ELECTRONICS TERMS (5th ed. 1993), and IEEE STANDARDS CATALOG. Sponsors awards program. Maintains library, Center for History of Electrical Engineering, at Rutgers University, New Brunswick, NJ. Formed in 1963 by merger of American Institute of Electrical Engineers (founded in 1884) and the Institute of Radio Engineers (founded in 1912).

0395 **Society of Broadcast Engineers (SBE)**. 8445 Keystone Crossing, Suite 140, Indianapolis, IN 46240-2454. Voice: 317-253-1640. Fax: 317-253-0418. Internet: www.sbe.org. 5000 members. Annual budget $445,000. Nonprofit organization devoted to advancement of all levels and types of broadcast engineering. Represents interests of broadcast engineers with federal agencies, legislatures, and industry organizations. Members include studio and transmitter operators and technicians, announcer-technicians, chief engineers of stations, consultants, and broadcast engineers in other facilities. Administers certification program for broadcast engineers. Sponsors jobline, career placement referral service, regional conferences, and annual engineering conference. Founded in 1963 as Institute of Broadcast Engineers. Name changed in 1964.

0396 **Society of Cable Telecommunications Engineers (SCTE)**. 140 Philips Road, Exton, PA 19341. Voice: 610-363-6888, 800-542-5040. Fax: 610-363-5898. Internet: www.scte.org. Designed to develop, increase, and spread both theoretical and practical technical knowledge of cable television and broadband communications sytems. Membership over 15,000 with over 70 chapters and meeting groups. Engineering Committee is responsible for all standards and recommended practices activity of the Society. Publishes monthly membership newsletter, INTERVAL and COMMUNICATIONS TECHNOLOGY, books, pamphlets and videotapes on technical aspects of cable television. Implements BCT/E (Broadband Communication Technician/Engineer) and Installer certification programs. Develops standards. Sponsors and publishes proceedings of two annual conferences—Emerging Technologies and Cable-Tec Expo. Founded in 1969 as Society of Cable Television Engineers; name changed in 1995.

0397 **Society of Motion Picture and Television Engineers (SMPTE)**. 595 West Hartsdale Ave., White Plains, NY 10607-1224. Voice: 914-761-1100. Fax: 914-761-3115. Internet: www.smpte.org. 10,000 members. Annual budget $2.5 million. Devoted to advancing the theory and application of film, television, video, computer imaging, telecommunications, and related arts and sciences. Members include engineers, technical directors, cameramen, editors, technicians, and specialists in film processing, production and postproduction. Develops technical standards in motion-imaging. Provides subcription service to SMPTE Standards, Recommended Practices, and Engineering Guidelines and offers test materials based on these standards. Administers Secretariat of the International Organization for Standardization Technical Committee on Cinematography and the U.S. Technical Advisory Group for the International Electrotechnical Commission. Publishes proceedings of annual conferences, SMPTE JOURNAL (monthly) and member newsletter (monthly). Sponsors awards program. Sponsors two annual conferences: Technical Conference and the Advanced Motion Imaging Conference. Founded in 1916 as the Society of Motion Picture Engineers; name changed in 1950.

3-D. Selected Secondary Resources

3-D-1. Print Media

0398 Fidler, Roger. **MEDIAMORPHOSIS: UNDERSTANDING NEW MEDIA**. Thousand Oaks, CA: Pine Forge Press, 1997, 250 pp. History of the newspaper with discussion of its future as an electronic product. Includes discussion of digital newspapers.

0399 Marshall, Alan. **CHANGING THE WORD: THE PRINTING INDUSTRY IN TRANSITION**. London: Comedia, 1983, 144 pp. British study of how technology changed newspaper and other printing businesses. Index.

0400 Smith, Anthony. **GOODBYE GUTENBERG: THE NEWSPAPER REVOLUTION OF THE 1980s**. New York: Oxford University Press, 1980, 367 pp. The coming impact of the computer and changes in printing technology and their likely impact are discussed. Notes, glossary, index.

3-D-2. Radio and Recording

0401 Anderton, J.T., ed. **THE FACILITIES OF AMERICAN RADIO: FM STATIONS, MARKETS 1–100**. 1997 ed. Cincinnati, OH: Duncan's American Radio, 1996, unpaged. Unique collection of coverage maps for 1,300 FM stations with charts showing technical data, including transmitting power, height above average terrain, tower height, coordinates, and location. Compiled from FCC technical and application files. Additional volume on markets 101–200 in preparation.

0402 Benson, K. Blair and Jerry C. Whitaker. **TELEVISION AND AUDIO HANDBOOK: FOR TECHNICIANS AND ENGINEERS**. New York: McGraw-Hill, 1990, unpaged. Comprehensive reference data for maintenance and operation of television and audio equipment, including analog and digital signal processing, video and audio signal processing, television receiver design and operation, loudspeakers and sound systems, compact disk and magnetic tape recording, measurement and test methods.

0403 Braun, Mark J. **AM STEREO AND THE FCC: CASE STUDY OF A MARKETPLACE SHIBBOLETH**. Norwood, NJ: Ablex, 1994, 206 pp. Discussion of technical standards and who should set them, exemplified by the 1978–1992 policy wrangle over AM stereo. References, index.

0404 National Association of Broadcasters. **ENGINEERING HANDBOOK**. Washington: NAB, 1992 (8th ed.), 1,345 pp. Over 70 broadcast engineering experts contributed to this comprehensive technical resource on the radio and television industries. First published in 1935, the NAB Engineering Handbook is an essential engineering reference, covering antennas, towers, transmitters, program transmission facilities, production facilities, remote program origination, color TV, closed captioning systems, emergency systems, and low power TV systems.

0405 Talbot-Smith, Michael. **BROADCAST SOUND TECHNOLOGY**. Newton, MA: Focal Press, 1990, 234 pp. Approachable introduction to the main items in the broadcast process: studio acoustics, microphones, speakers, consoles, recording and replay, and principles of stereo. Photos, diagrams, index.

0406 Watkinson, John. **AN INTRODUCTION TO DIGITAL AUDIO**. Newton, MA: Focal Press, 1994, 256 pp. Describes key technologies and their applications in tape and disc (DAT, DCC, CD, and MiniDisc) recorders, and editing with digital formats. Diagrams, index.

3-D-3. Television

0407 Beltz, Cynthia A. **HIGH-TECH MANEUVERS: INDUSTRIAL POLICY LESSONS OF HDTV**. Washington: AEI Press, 1991, 142 pp. Argues the rationale for government support for HDTV research and development. Notes.

0408 Benson, K. Blair and Donald G. Fink. **HDTV: ADVANCED TELEVISION FOR THE 1990s**. New York: McGraw-Hill, 1991, ca 300 pp. Technical basics of a fast-changing area. Diagrams, tables, notes, index.

0409 Benson, K. Blair and Jerry C. Whitaker. **TELEVISION ENGINEERING HANDBOOK; FEATURING HDTV SYSTEMS.** Rev. ed. New York: McGraw-Hill, 1992, 1500+pp. Covers basic theory of television, signal transmission and distribution, image generation, hardware, reference standards and data, and HDTV.

See 0402. Benson and Whittaker. TELEVISION AND AUDIO HANDBOOK: FOR TECHNICIANS AND ENGINEERS.

0410 Beson, Stanley M., and Leland Johnson. **COMPATIBILITY STANDARDS, COMPETITION AND INNOVATION IN THE BROADCASTING INDUSTRY**. Santa Monica: Rand, 1986, 60 pp. The best discussion of why such technical standard setting is important—and how it works.

0411 Brinkley, Joel. **DEFINING VISION: THE BATTLE FOR THE FUTURE OF TELEVISION.** New York: Harcourt, Brace, 1996, 402 pp. Useful narrative on how the all-digital "Grand Alliance" standard was developed, with interesting details on people, technical development, industry competition and changing views, and the role of the FCC. Photos, notes, index.

0412 Hartwig, Robert L. **BASIC TV TECHNOLOGY**. Newton, MA: Focal Press, 1995 (2nd ed.), 176 pp. Brief illustrated survey of the technology behind the pictures. Diagrams.

0413 Jackson, K.G. and G.B. Townsend, eds. **TV & VIDEO ENGINEER'S REFERENCE BOOK**. Oxford, UK: Butterworth-Heinemann, 1991, 700 pp. Comprehensive survey of television technology including transmission, distribution, DBS, studies, equipment, sound, receivers, recorders, HDTV, and TV performance measurements.

See 0404. National Association of Broadcasters ENGINEERING HANDBOOK.

0414 Noll, A. Michael. **TELEVISION TECHNOLOGY: FUNDAMENTALS AND FUTURE PROSPECTS**. Norwood, MA: Artech House, 1988, 184 pp. Clear explanation of how television works, including principles, monochrome transmission, color receivers, picture and camera tubes, video tape recording, video discs, cable and alternative technologies, HDTV, and international standards. Diagrams, index.

0415 Rice, John F., ed. **HDTV: THE POLITICS, POLICIES, AND ECONOMICS OF TOMORROW'S TELEVISION**. New York: Union Square Press, 1990, 332 pp. Some 30 brief articles on the search for standards. Tables.

0416 Sargent, Ralph N. **PRESERVING THE MOVING IMAGE**. Washington: National Endowment for the Arts, 1974, 152 pp. Detailed analysis of archiving for film and video images with illustrations and some how-to examples. Photos, diagrams, index.

0417 Weiss, S. Merrill. **ISSUES IN ADVANCED TELEVISION TECHNOLOGY**. Newton, MA: Focal Press, 1996, 334 pp. Useful discussion of the many problems and issues in bringing an advanced system online in the late 1990s. Charts, diagrams, index.

3-D-4. Cable and Newer Media

0418 Bartlett, Eugene R. **CABLE TELEVISION TECHNOLOGY AND OPERATIONS: HDTV AND NTSC SYSTEMS**. New York: McGraw-Hill, Inc., 1990, 421 pp. Describes the building and maintenance of cable television systems in the context of two specifications: National Television Systems Committee (NTSC) and HDTV. Material drawn from series of training lectures. Index.

0419 Ciciora, Walter S. **CABLE TELEVISION IN THE UNITED STATES: AN OVERVIEW**. Boulder, CO: Cable Television Laboratories, Inc., 1995 (revised 2nd ed.), 91 pp. Primer on cable television technology, including historical perspective and technical detail. Fifteen appendices provide data and specifications on 330-MHz channel lineup and 14 aspects of a generic cable distribution network. Bibliography. (See also Deschler 0420 and Grant 0425.)

0420 De Sonne, Marcia L., ed. **CONVERGENCE: TRANSITION TO THE ELECTRONIC SUPERHIGHWAY**. Washington: National Association of Broadcasters, 1994, 260 pp. Enabling technologies and business outcomes as media and telecommunications converge. Tables, charts, endnotes.

0421 Deschler, Kenneth T. **CABLE TELEVISION TECHNOLOGY**. New York: McGraw-Hill, 1987, 262 pp. Textbook for cable technician training courses. Discusses cable technology from coaxial cable to satellite antennas and fiber-optic links. Describes studio and broadcast technology found in program production facilities. Glossary, appendices, reading list, index.

0422 Dholakia, Ruby, et al. eds. **THE INFOTAINMENT TECHNOLOGIES IN THE HOME: DEMAND-SIDE PERSPECTIVES**. Mahwah, NJ: Lawrence Erlbaum, 1996, 291 pp. Fourteen papers divided into managerial, user, and policy perspectives. Notes, references, index.

0423 Dodds, Philip V.W., ed. **THE DIGITAL MULTIMEDIA CROSS-INDUSTRY GUIDE**. Newton, MA: Focal Press, 1995, 350 pp. Chapters by experts review broadcasting and cable, consumer electronics, handheld electronics devices, computer hardware and software. Diagrams, index.

0424 Grant, August, ed. **COMMUNICATION TECHNOLOGY UPDATE**. Newton, MA: Focal Press, 1996 (5th ed.), 440 pp. Useful and concise survey, regularly revised, with 40 chapters including 12 on various electronic media. Offers updates on related web page. Tables, charts, bibliography, glossary.

0425 Grant, William O. **CABLE TELEVISION**. Schoharie, NY: GWG Associates, 1994 (3rd ed.), 599 pp. Thirty-one chapters cover aspects of radio frequency (RF) broadband transmission systems utilizing both coaxial cable and optical fiber with particular emphasis on cable television applications. Equivalency tables, units of measure, glossary, formulas, review questions, review answers, explanations, and index.

0426 Greenberg Baron Simon and Miller, Inc. **A VISION OF THE FUTURE: 1993 CONVERGENCE CONFERENCE, BERMUDA**. Denver: Daniels and Associates, 1994, 88 pp. During this conference, sponsored by Daniels and Associates and General Instruments, nearly 200 senior executives from the cable, computer and telephone industries discussed the future. Summaries of eight panel discussions and four keynote speeches.

0427 Lyle, Jack, and Douglas McLeod. **COMMUNICATION, MEDIA AND CHANGE**. Mountain View, CA: Mayfield, 1993, 264 pp. Broad introductory text emphasizing fast-changing technological base of media. Glossary, bibliography, index.

0428 Mirabito, Michael M.A. **THE NEW COMMUNICATIONS TECHNOLOGIES**. Newton, MA: Focal Press, 1994, 223 pp. Eleven chapters include computer technology, information storage, fiber-optic distribution, satellites, desktop publishing, personal media, and interactive systems. Photos, diagrams, index.

0429 Pavlik, John, and Everette E. Dennis, eds. **DEMYSTIFYING MEDIA TECHNOLOGY: READINGS FROM THE FREEDOM FORUM CENTER**. Mountain View, CA: Mayfield, 1993, 194 pp. Collects 28 papers on current and projected trends in the field. Glossary, annotated bibliography, index.

0430 Rutkowski, Katherine, ed. **THE NCTA TECHNICAL PAPERS**. Washington: National Cable Television Association, 1972–date, annual. Papers delivered by industry experts at the annual NCTA convention.

0431 Silverstone, Roger and Eric Hirsch, eds. **CONSUMING TECHNOLOGIES: MEDIA AND INFORMATION IN DOMESTIC SPACES**. New York: Routledge, 1992, 241 pp. Thirteen papers focus on the applications and impact of such technologies in the consumer market. References, index.

0432 **TECHNOLOGY IN THE AMERICAN HOUSEHOLD**. Washington: Times Mirror Center for the People and the Press, 1994, 143 pp. Telephone survey poll of 3,667 adults and 400 adolescents (13 to 17) in early 1994. Queries use of technology in U.S. households. Appendices summarize survey methodology and statistically detail responses.

0433 Van Tassel, Joan M. **ADVANCED TELEVISION SYSTEMS: BRAVE NEW TV**. Newton, MA: Focal Press, 1996, 417 pp. Broad-scale survey of changing television (including but not restricted to HDTV). Photos, diagrams, glossary, references, index.

0434 Wells, Robert. **THE INTERACTIVE HOME: TECHNOLOGIES, STRATEGIES AND BUSINESS OPPORTUNITIES**. Washington: Warren Publishing Inc., 1994, 184 pp. Lennox Research summarizes research of the emerging technological market in the 1990s. Intended for corporate strategists, entrepreneurs, and investors, the analysis assesses enabling technology, regulatory and political environment, and home interactivity. Strategic profiles encompass carriers, vendors, and providers. Glossary, a directory of key players (mentioned in the book), and index.

0435 Williams, Frederick. **THE NEW TELECOMMUNICATIONS: INFRASTRUCTURE FOR THE INFORMATION AGE**. New York: Free Press, 1991, 246 pp. Description and assessment of telecommunication technologies from user point of view. Glossary, notes, bibliography, index.

0436 Wilson, Kevin G. **TECHNOLOGIES OF CONTROL: THE NEW INTERACTIVE MEDIA FOR THE HOME**. Madison: University of Wisconsin Press, 1988, 180 pp. Argues business and government may be able to centralize their control of people through the new networks. References, index.

0437 Wood, James. **SATELLITE COMMUNICATIONS AND DBS SYSTEMS**. Newton, MA: Focal Press, 1992, 288 pp. Comprehensive account of development and technologies of various communications satellite services and how they relate to terrestrial systems. Photos, diagrams, index.

4

Industry and Economics

This chapter describes resources on economic and business aspects of mass communications, including bibliographies, indexes, and other resources that identify business/trade, economics, and management/scholarly literature. Readers should also consult the statistical resources discussed at the end of chapter 1. Of considerable importance is DISCLOSURE SEC (0450), containing full texts of annual reports and other federally required company documents. Section 4-D identifies a selection of major trade and industry associations, professional organizations, and public interest groups because we believe their offices can provide supplemental industry statistics. Selected secondary resources include industry surveys, economic analyses, and management studies.

4-A. Bibliographic Resources

4-A-1 Bibliographies

0438 Du Charme, Rita and John M. Lavine. **BIBLIOGRAPHY OF MEDIA MANAGEMENT AND ECONOMICS**. Minneapolis: University of Minnesota Media Management and Economics Resource Center, 1988 (2nd ed.), 131 pp. Some 400 titles are gathered into 36 subject areas and indexed. Not annotated.

0439 Fuld, Leonard M. **THE NEW COMPETITOR INTELLIGENCE: THE COMPLETE RESOURCE FOR FINDING, ANALYZING, AND USING INFORMATION ABOUT YOUR COMPETITORS.** New York: John Wiley, 1995, 482 pp. Guide to printed, electronic, and organizational resources and strategies for their uses in researching companies and industries. International in scope, especially strong for Japanese high technologies. Directory, subject index.

0440 **HOW TO FIND INFORMATION ABOUT COMPANIES**. Washington: Washington Researchers, 1995 (12th ed.), three vols. Detailed descriptions of company information sources: vol. 1 covers published printed and electronic resources; federal, state, and local documents, organizations, trade and professional associations; vol. 2 offers advice and case studies on how to research companies and corporate culture, plants and facilities, research and development, mangement and labor, products and services, finances, strategic plans; vol. 3 is an index.

0441 Miller, E. Willard, and Ruby M. Miller. **UNITED STATES TRADE—INDUSTRIES: A BIBLIOGRAPHY.** Monticello, IL: Vance Bibliographies, 1991, 25 pp. (Public Administration Series, P-3059). Pages 11–17 list about 70 unannotated references on U.S. international trade in semiconductors, home electronics, fiber optics, communications equipment, magnetic recorders, electronics equipment, and computers.

0442 Picard, Robert G., and Stephen Lacy. **NEWSPAPER ECONOMICS BIBLIOGRAPHY.** Columbia, SC: Media Management and Economics Division, Association for Education in Journalism and Mass Communication, 1991, 17 pp. Selective unannotated bibliography covering the U.S. newspaper industry is presented in four parts: books and serials, articles and monographs, unpublished material, and government reports and documents.

0443 Popovich, Charles J., and M. Rita Costello. **DIRECTORY OF BUSINESS AND FINANCIAL INFORMATION SERVICES.** Washington: Special Libraries Association, 1994 (9th ed.), 471 pp. Detailed descriptions of printed and electronic business, economic, and industry information sources. Title, publisher, and subject indexes. Very convenient for identifying numerous communications newsletters available from Dialog, Dow Jones, LEXIS/NEXIS (0912), NewsNet, and other electronic services. Relevant publications listed under communication among other headings.

4-A-2. Abstracts, Indexes, Databases

0444 **ABI/INFORM** [Machine-readable data]. Louisville, KY: UMI/Data Courier, 1971–date, weekly and monthly. Online service available from Dialog, Ovid, Orbit/Questel, OCLC, and other services: Online coverage and updating varies. ABI/INFORM GLOBAL CD-ROM available from UMI/Data Courier; updated monthly. No printed version. Important for access to trade and scholarly literature on telecommunication business, economics, and management. Coverge more inclusive than WILSON BUSINESS ABSTRACTS (0446). Indexes about 1,400 business and management-related periodicals. Includes full-text of selected articles from 550 publications since 1991.

0445 **BUSINESS NEWS** [Online service]. Columbus, OH: OCLC, 1992–date, updated daily. Database updated by Individual, Inc.'s HEADSUP service. "Brief summaries of news stories drawn from over 350 sources. ...Business News contains 1 to 2 weeks' worth of summaries and includes such subjects as information technology, telecommunications, health care, and defense. News summaries are added to the database daily. Once a week, summaries from the oldest week are deleted." Subject, source, and other indexing. Covers industry-monitoring newsletters; wire services (Reuters, PR Newswire); and selected major newspapers. Also covers press releases from the FCC. An alternative to similar services offered by LEXIS/NEXIS (0912), NewsNet, Dialog, and other vendors.

0446 **BUSINESS PERIODICALS INDEX**. New York: H. W. Wilson, 1958–date, monthly. Online version WILSON BUSINESS ABSTRACTS available from Wilsonline, Ovid, and OCLC: covers 1982–date, updated twice weekly. CD-ROM version WILSON BUSINESS ABSTRACTS available from H. W. Wilson and SilverPlatter: covers 1983–date, updated monthly. For more information, see Wilson's homepage: www.hwwilson.com. Indexes communications trade and scholarly business, management, and economics literature. Covers over 300 English-language periodicals in advertising, broadcasting, communications, computer technologies and applications, industrial relations, international business, marketing, printing, publishing, public utilities, regulation of industry, and public relations. Particularly useful for identifying business literature on mass communications technologies and organizations. Electronic versions offer abstracts.

0447 **DOW JONES NEWS/RETRIEVAL** [Online service]. Princeton, NJ: Dow Jones, updated monthly. Full texts of selected articles in about 1,200 international business journals. Comparable to coverage of business journals in LEXIS/NEXIS (0912).

0448 **F & S INDEX UNITED STATES**. Foster City, CA: Information Access, 1968–date, monthly. Online version included in F & S INDEXES available from Dialog and Data-Star; coverage varies, updated weekly. CD-ROM version included in PREDICASTS F & S INDEX PLUS TEXT available from SilverPlatter: covers current year only, updated monthly. Covers over 2,400 financial, business, trade and industry journals and special reports. Part 1 indexes articles about industries by SIC codes; part 2 indexes articles about specific companies. Black dots identify major articles. Complemented by F & S INDEX INTERNATIONAL (1968–date) as well as PREDICASTS FORECASTS (1960–date) for statistics. Electronic versions combine printed indexes and feature full texts of 80% of articles.

0449 **INDEX OF ECONOMIC ARTICLES**. Pittsburgh: American Economics Association, 1886–date, annual. Variant titles. Online version ECONOMIC LITERATURE INDEX available on Dialog, OCLC, and other services: covers 1984–date, updated quarterly. CD-ROM version ECONLIT available from SilverPlatter: covers 1969–date, updated quarterly. Comprehensive bibliography covers 400 major economic journals, books, and collections.

4-B. Annual Reports and 10-K Forms

0450 **DISCLOSURE SEC** [Electronic service]. Bethesda, MD: Disclosure Incorporated, 1985–date, monthly. Online DISCLOSURE SEC available from Dialog, LEXIS/NEXIS (0912), Data-Star, OCLC, and other services: covers 1977–date, updated weekly. CD-ROM version COMPACT D/SEC available from Disclosure: covers 1985–date; updated monthly. Information on more than 12,000 public companies extracted from 10Ks, 20Fs, 10Qs, 8Ks, annual reports, tender offer and acquisitions reports, and proxy statements. No printed version. Information includes 2-year comparisons of balance sheets, 3-year comparisons of income statements, 5-year summary of operating income, sales and earnings per share.

0451 **FAIRCHILD'S ELECTRONIC INDUSTRY FINANCIAL DIRECTORY.** New York: Fairchild Publications, 1962–date, annual. Formerly ELECTRONIC NEWS FINANCIAL FACT BOOK AND DIRECTORY (1962–1991). Covers about 1,000 companies. Concise profiles detail products and services, subsidiaries, acquisitions, transfer agents, employees, sales and earnings, common stock, income accounts, assets, liabilities.

0452 **MOODY'S MANUALS**. New York: Moody's Investors Services, 1909–date, annual. Contents of the several different manuals are cumulated in online MOODY'S CORPORATE NEWS-U.S. available from Dialog (1983–date): updated weekly. CD-ROM version of each manual also available (see below): updated quarterly. Manuals contain information on publicly owned companies in particular sectors, including income statements, balance sheets, financial and operating ratios based on company reports and SEC filings; historical and current descriptions with lists of subsidiaries; details on capital structure, capital stock and long-term debt. Each manual includes geographical and business classification indexes (blue pages) and is updated by looseleaf NEWS REPORTS. Complete historical series of manuals available on microfiche, MOODY'S MANUALS ON MICROFICHE. Most useful volumes for mass communications include:

1 **MOODY'S INTERNATIONAL MANUAL** (1981–date). Covers about 7,000 companies in 90 countries, excluding the U.S.

2 **MOODY'S OTC INDUSTRIAL MANUAL** (1909–date). Many variant titles. Covers about 2,000 companies traded on NASDAQ and regional stock exchanges. CD-ROM version is MOODY'S INDUSTRIAL DISC.

3 **MOODY'S PUBLIC UTILITIES MANUAL** (1914–date). Title has varied. Covers U.S. publicly held, privately held, and subsidiary utilities. CD-ROM version is MOODY'S PUBLIC UTILITY DISC.

0453 **STANDARD & POOR'S CORPORATION RECORDS**. New York: Standard and Poor's, 1940–date, bimonthly. Updated by STANDARD AND POOR'S DAILY CORPORATION NEWS. Online version corresponding in part to STANDARD AND POOR'S CORPORATE DESCRIPTIONS available on LEXIS/NEXIS (0912) and other services: covers current edition; updated biweekly; also in STANDARD AND POOR'S CORPORATE DESCRIPTIONS PLUS NEWS available from Dialog: covers current edition; updated biweekly. CD-ROM version corresponding in part to STANDARD AND POOR'S CORPORATIONS available from Knight-Ridder: covers current edition; updated monthly. Information on publicly owned companies: capitalization, corporate background, stock data, bond descriptions, earnings, and finance. Useful features include CEO annual messages to stockholders and management discussions.

4-C. Employment

4-C-1. General Media

0454 Bureau of Labor Statistics, U.S. Department of Labor. **OCCUPATIONAL OUTLOOK HANDBOOK**. Washington: GPO, 1949–date, annual. (BULLETIN OF THE UNITED STATES BUREAU OF LABOR STATISTICS, number varies). CD-ROM version available from GPO. Also available and searchable on Internet: stats.bls.gov/ocohome.htm. A standard reference source giving data for employment trends by occupation. Describes occupations and gives basic employment data for job outlook and trends, working conditions, training and qualifications, earnings, as well as identifying related occupations and sources of additional information. Entries arranged by DOT (Dictionary of Occupational Titles) class numbers, with cross-referenced SOC (Standard Occupational Classification) numbers. Subject index offers common access.

4-C-2. Print Media

0455 **APME JOURNALIST SATISFACTION STUDY: A NATIONAL STUDY COMMISSIONED BY THE ASSOCIATED PRESS MANAGING EDITORS ASSOCIATION.** Minneapolis, MN: MORI Research, Inc., September, 1993, 55 pp. Presents data and analysis about retention of journalists.

0456 Johnstone, John W. C., Edward J. Slawski, and William W. Bowman. **THE NEWS PEOPLE: A SOCIOLOGICAL PORTRAIT OF AMERICAN JOURNALISTS AND THEIR WORK.** Urbana: University of Illinois Press, 1976, 257 pp. Based on a national study of news media journalists in the U.S. in 1971, a time of struggle between the press and the Nixon administration. The results of the survey are represented in 73 tables. See Weaver and Wilhoit (0459).

0457 Newspaper Association of America. Reston, VA. See also: 0495.

1 **NAA NEWSPAPER INDUSTRY COMPENSATION SURVEY.** 1987–date, annual. Provides salary information to allow for comparison of compensation among job categories. Data organized by the U.S. as a whole as well as regions and circulation. Includes list of participating newspapers.

2 **LABOR & EMPLOYMENT LAW LETTER.** 1992–date, monthly. Publishes texts of arbitration decisions, NLRB and court decisions, regulatory actions, labor and personnel issues, and contract settlements.

0458 Tan, Alexis S. **WHY ASIAN AMERICAN JOURNALISTS LEAVE JOURNALISM AND WHY THEY STAY.** San Francisco: Asian American Journalists Association, 1990, 22 pp. Results of a national survey concluding lack of advancement opportunities and need for other challenges are key factors.

0459 Weaver, David H., and G. Cleveland Wilhoit. **THE AMERICAN JOURNALIST IN THE 1990s: U.S. NEWS PEOPLE AT THE END OF AN ERA.** Mahwah, NJ: Erlbaum, 1996, 299 pp. Update of authors' 1982 and 1991 studies of print and broadcast journalists—their characteristics and background, job conditions and satisfactions, professionalism and ethics, women journalists, minority journalists and other issues, based on national survey. Tables, charts, notes, index. See also: Johnstone et al. (0456).

4-C-3. Electronic Media

0460 Corporation for Public Broadcasting. Washington. See also: 0519. **FULL-TIME EMPLOYEES OF PUBLIC BROADCASTING.** 1993–date, annual. Research Note consisting of charts showing 15-year history of employment by major job category and by gender and ethnicity.

0461 Corporation for Public Broadcasting. Washington. **SALARY REPORT...** There are four series:

1 **SALARY REPORT FOR JOINTLY OPERATED PUBLIC BROADCASTING LICENSEES.** 1985–date, annual.

2 **SALARY REPORT FOR NPPAG, SOLE SERVICE AND STEP GRANTEES.** 1992–date, annual.

3 **SALARY REPORT FOR PUBLIC RADIO LICENSEES.** ca 1975–date, annual.

4 **SALARY REPORT FOR PUBLIC TELEVISION LICENSEES.** ca 1975–date, annual. Series of reports providing average annual salaries for full-time employees by job category and operating budget size.

0462 Federal Communications Commission. Washington. See also: 0950. Two employment reports are issued:

1 **EQUAL EMPLOYMENT OPPORTUNITY TREND REPORT.** 1972–date, annual. See next item.

2 **MINORITY EMPLOYMENT REPORT FOR U.S. BROADCASTING SERVICES.** 1972–date, annual. Two separate but related reports compiled by the EEO Division of the FCC from data supplied by stations in FCC Form 395. Both are computer printouts by state showing numbers of persons employed in broadcasting by sex and ethnicity. The Trend Report charts full-time employees in nine categories: officials and managers, professionals, technicians, sales workers, office/clerical, craftsmen, operatives, laborers, services. The second report tracks full-time and part-time employees. Multivolume.

0463 National Association of Broadcasters. Washington. See also: 0512.

1 **RADIO EMPLOYEE COMPENSATION & FRINGE BENEFITS REPORT**. 1955–1992, biannual. Provides average salary data for most positions in a radio station although title and coverage have varied throughout its history. The 1992 edition (the last in the series) reports average and median base salary plus bonus data for 12 department heads and average, median, and starting salaries for 12 support staff positions, along with definitions of those positions. Sales compensation reported in separate section. Benefits information includes insurance, vacation, pension, and sick leave. Data provided in 35 tables ranked by revenue categories, population, and type of station.

2 (with Miller, Kaplan, Arase & Co.), **RADIO STATION SALARIES.** 1994–date, annual. Over 40 charts showing average, median, low, and high salaries and compensation for 38 station positions. Charts are grouped by market size, station revenues, format, and regions of country.

3 **TELEVISION EMPLOYEE COMPENSATION AND FRINGE BENEFITS REPORT**. 1954–date, biannual. Compares salary schedules and fringe benefits in television stations ranked by revenues, market, region, and affiliate status. Provides average and median base salary and bonus data for 15 department heads and average, median, and starting salaries for 17 support staff positions, along with definitions of these positions. Sales compensation reported separately. Benefits information includes insurance, vacation, pension, and sick leave. Data provided in over 20 tables.

0464 Stone, Vernon A. **LET'S TALK PAY IN TELEVISION AND RADIO NEWS**. Chicago: Bonus Books, 1993, 194 pp. Compilation of 20 years of survey research showing trends in broadcast journalism salaries and benefits. Stone is a journalism professor emeritus at the University of Missouri and research director for Radio Television News Directors Association which has sponsored his annual surveys on salaries since 1972.

4-C-4. Career Guides

0465 Alexander, James P. **INTERNSHIPS IN COMMUNICATIONS**. Ames: Iowa State University Press, 1995, 207 pp. How to get and keep internships. Appendices, index.

0466 Bone, Jan. **OPPORTUNITIES IN CABLE TELEVISION CAREERS**. Lincolnwood, IL: NTC Publishing Group, 1993, 150 pp. Chapters discuss cable development, how a cable system works, advertising, the business of cable, and job hunting tips. Includes discussion on international markets and the hiring of women and minorities. Directory of associations, photos, figures, bibliography, glossary.

0467 Guiley, Rosemary. **CAREER OPPORTUNITY FOR WRITERS**. New York: Facts on File, 1995 (3rd ed.), 230 pp. Includes options in television, newspapers, book publishing, arts and entertainment, business communications, and related fields.

0468 Gross, Lynne S. **THE INTERNSHIP EXPERIENCE**. Prospect Heights, IL: Waveland Press, 1993 (2nd ed.), 125 pp. Useful guide for students, teachers, and media professionals.

0469 Horwin, Michael. **CAREERS IN FILM AND VIDEO PRODUCTION**. Newton, MA: Focal Press, 1990, 206 pp. Details the positions and background required.

0470 Mogel, Leonard. **MAKING IT IN THE MEDIA PROFESSIONS**. Chester, CT.: Globe Pequot Press, 1988, 291 pp. Chapters offer detailed advice by medium: newspapers, magazines, books, television, radio, movies, and advertising. Bibliographies, index.

0471 Morgan, Bradley J., ed. **RADIO AND TELEVISION CAREER DIRECTORY**. Detroit: Visible Ink, 1993, 334 pp. Twenty-five chapters combine advice from pros, practical first-job tips, ideas on resumes and tapes. Extensive annotated guide to career resource organizations and publications. Index.

0472 Noble, John H. **THE HARVARD GUIDE TO CAREERS IN MASS MEDIA**. Cambridge, MA: Harvard University Office of Career Services, 1987, 200 pp. Individual media are covered in major sections on the entertainment media, the news media, book and magazine publishing, and promotional media (advertising and PR). Index.

0473 **PETERSON'S INTERNSHIPS**. Princeton, NJ: Peterson's Guides, 1996, 517 pp. First edition of comprehensive directory covering all fields including many in communication. Internet site: www.petersons.com.

0474 Reed, Maxine K., and Robert M. Reed. **CAREER OPPORTUNITIES IN TELEVISION, CABLE, AND VIDEO**. New York: Facts on File, 1990 (3rd ed.), 260 pp. Describes 70 jobs in broadcasting and 30 in cable, video, and media. Descriptions gleaned from printed job descriptions, research studies, salary surveys, organizational charts, and discussions with professional colleagues. Descriptions provide career profile, career ladder, and narrative text. Appendices include degree and non-degree programs, directory information for unions and associations, and bibliography. Index.

4-C-5. Unions

0475 **American Federation of Television Radio Artists (AFTRA)**. 260 Madison Ave., New York 10016. Voice: 212-532-0800. Fax: 212-545-1238. 75,000 members. Annual budget under $5 million. Union of radio and television performers. Affiliated with AFL-CIO. Publishes member magazine (three times year). Sponsors biennial meeting. Founded in 1937 as American Federation of Radio Artists. Merged with Television Authority and changed name in 1952.

0476 **National Association of Broadcast Employees and Technicians-Communications Workers of America (NABET)**. 501 3rd St. NW, Washington 20001-27901. Voice: 202-434-1254. Fax: 202-434-1426. 10,000 members. Annual budget $5 million. Union concerned with improving the status of workers employed in broadcasting, distributing, telecasting, recording, cable, video, sound recording, and related industries in North America. Represents over 9,000 employees at CapitalCities/ABC, NBC and over 100 private radio and television, film and videotape companies. Members include engineers, technicians, news writers, announcers, directors, clerical employees, photographers, traffic, communications, and stage service. Publishes member newsletter (bimonthly). Sponsors scholarship program and quadrennial conference. Founded in 1933 as the Association of Technical Employees, a company union within the National Broadcasting Co. Broke away in 1940 and changed name to National Association of Broadcast Engineers and Technicians. Affiliated with Congress of Industrial Organizations in 1951 and changed name to National Association of Broadcast Employees and Technicians. Merged with Communications Workers of America in 1994.

0477 **The Newspaper Guild (TNG)**. 8611 Second Ave., Silver Spring, MD 20910. Voice: 301-585-2990. Fax: 301-585-0668. 34,000 members. Annual budget under $5 million. Union of editorial and commercial department employees of newspapers, wire and news services, magazines. Affiliated with AFL-CIO. Publishes member newspaper (monthly). Sponsors award and annual meeting. Founded in 1933 as American Newspaper Guild; changed name in 1971.

4-D. Selected Associations and Organizations

(Note: See also: 4-C-5, Unions.)

0478 **ENCYCLOPEDIA OF ASSOCIATIONS**. Detroit: Gale, 1956–date, annual. Online version available from Dialog, GaleNet, and other services: covers current edition, updated semiannually. CD-ROM and online versions available from Gale and SilverPlatter: covers current edition, updated semiannually. 32nd ed. for 1997. See Gale Internet homepage for more information: galenet.gale.com/db.html.

Standard directory describing more than 22,000 national and international organizations in all fields. Classified listings relevant to mass communications appear in all chapters, especially those for trade and business; labor unions; engineering and technology professions; and public affairs. Careful use of name and keyword index is essential. Electronic versions cumulate entries for some 87,000 organizations listed in Gale's ENCYCLOPEDIA OF ASSOCIATIONS, INTERNATIONAL ORGANIZATIONS (1984–date), and REGIONAL, STATE, AND LOCAL ORGANIZATIONS (1987–date).

0479 **EVENTLINE** [Electronic service]. Amsterdam: Elsevier Science Publishers, 1989–date, updated monthly. Available online from Dialog, OCLC, and other services. Diskette version available from Elsevier Publishing Group: updated monthly. For more information about access, see Elsevier Internet homepage: www.elsevier.com. Offers subject, event, location, and other indexing for international "conventions, conferences, symposia, trade fairs, and exhibits scheduled between the present time and the 21st century." Entries give data for contacts, sponsoring organizations, exhibits (telephone, fax numbers). Useful supplement to calendars in professional and trade journals.

4-D-1. Newspapers

0480 **Alicia Patterson Foundation**. 1001 Pennsylvania Ave., N.W., Suite 1250, Washington 20004. Voice: 202-393-5995 or 301-951-8512. Offers $30,000 for 1 year to support candidates with at least 5 years experience at a newspaper or magazine (writer/editor/photojournalists) to research/report/prepare a visual report on a subject of the candidate's choosing.

0481 **American Society of Newspaper Editors (ASNE).** P.O. Box 4090, Reston, VA 22090-1144. Voice: 703-648-1144. e-mail: ASNE@AOL.COM. Internet: www.infi.net/asne/index.htm. Its nearly 900 members are editors of U.S. daily newspapers who are responsible for directing editorial and news policy. Annual budget under $1 million. Sponsors annual convention and THE AMERICAN EDITOR. Publishes regular reports about issues affecting the news staff, manuals, and research reports. An excellent history of the society is recorded in PROBLEMS OF JOURNALISM: THE PROCEEDINGS OF THE AMERICAN SOCIETY OF NEWSPAPER EDITORS, a series of annual reports 1923–1988. Founded in 1922.

0482 **Asian American Journalists Association.** 1765 Sutter St. Suite 1000, San Francisco 994115. Voice: 415-346-2051. Fax: 415-346-2261. Internet: www.aaja.org. Encourages Asian Pacific American journalists (some 1,500 members) by providing career advice, offering fellowships, maintaining a resume file, and recognizing achievement in journalism. Budget of $250,000. Meets in conjunction with the national associations for Black and Hispanic journalists, sponsors occasional training workshops, and co-sponsors an annual Journalism Opportunities Conference.

0483 **Associated Press Managing Editors (APME).** 50 Rockefeller Plaza, New York 10020. Voice: 212-621-1552. Internet: www.apme.com. Some 2,000 members are managing editors or executives on the staff of newspapers that are members of Associated Press (AP). Budget under $250,000. The editors and news executives monitor the services of the AP to attune the services to meet newspaper needs. Issues (since 1964) APME NEWS. Published details of its annual meeting 1949 to late 1980s as APME RED BOOK. Publishes a newsletter, AP LOG, for member newspapers and an annual report. Sponsors annual meeting. Founded in 1933.

0484 **The Freedom Forum**. 1101 Wilson Blvd., Arlington, VA 22209. Voice: 703-284-2804. Fax: 703-522-4831. Internet: www4.nando.net/prof/freedom/1994/info/brochure.html. A foundation supporting international, national, and community programs to foster freedom of the press. Provides 1-year scholarships annually to students in news-editorial, broadcasting, or advertising. Sponsors professional-in-residence programs. Also operates the New York-based Freedom Forum Media Studies Center (0787), educational programs for Washington, DC-based reporters, and the First Amendment Center at Vanderbilt University (0964).

See 0787. Freedom Forum Media Studies Center.

0485 **Gay and Lesbian Press Association**. P.O. Box 8185, Universal City, CA 91608. Voice: 818-902-1476. An association for gay and lesbian employees of periodical publishing firms and organizations, news and features agencies and syndicates, radio and television enterprises, and other mass media institutions. Publications include a quarterly newsletter, THE MEDIA REPORTER, and a mailing list of gay/lesbian newspapers and magazines. Promotes the growth of gay media through workshops and legal defense support. Some 325 members with budget of $50,000. Biennial meetings/exhibits in May. See also: National Lesbian and Gay Journalists Association (0491). Founded in 1980.

0486 **Inland Daily Press Association**. Inland Newspaper Center, 777 Busse Highway, Park Ridge, IL 60068. Voice: 708-696-1140. Fax: 708-696-2463. e-mail: Inlander1@AOL.COM. Serves 570 newspaper members in 45 states, Canada, and Bermuda, concerned with practical issues of newspaper publishing. Two of its annual reports are used as national standards, NEWSPAPER INDUSTRY COST AND REVENUE STUDY and the NEWSPAPER INDUSTRY COMPENSATION. Also publishes a bimonthly magazine, INLANDER, providing seminar listings, revenue ideas and other practical information. Offers training seminars, confidential custom employee surveys, a lending library of newspaper training videos, contests, and an online bulletin board for members. Founded in 1885.

0487 **Jaws: Journalism & Women Symposium**. P.O. Box 838, School of Journalism, University of Missouri, Columbia, MO 65205. Voice: 314-882-1110. Fax: 314-884-4735. Supports professional and personal growth of women in newsrooms. Membership is open to journalists, present and past, and researchers and publishers in the fields of journalism and feminism. Founded in 1985.

0488 **Knight Foundation**. One Biscayne Tower, Suite 300, 2 South Biscayne Blvd., Miami, FL 33131-1803. Voice: 305-539-0009. Awards national grants to organizations and institutions for the education of working and future journalists. Founded in 1950.

0489 **National Association of Black Journalists (NABJ).** 3100 Taliaferro Hall, University of Maryland, College Park, MD 20742. Voice: 301-405-8500. Fax: 301-405-8555. Internet: www.nabj.org. Some 3,000 members work in newspapers, magazines and broadcast stations. Under $2 million budget. The association recognizes outstanding achievement among Black journalists, provides a national clearinghouse for jobs, identifies and rewards promising high school journalists. Publishes NABJ JOURNAL. Founded in 1975.

0490 **National Federation of Hispanic Owned Newspapers**. 1309 South Highway 427, Longwood, FL 32750-6403. Voice: 407-767-0070. Fax: 407-767-5478. The federation promotes U.S. Hispanic print media and encourages recruitment and training of Hispanics as print journalists. Members (60) are publishers and editors of 103 U. S. Hispanic newspapers. Budget of $40,000. The association maintains a library of 170 Hispanic newspapers, newsletters, magazines, and journals. Founded in 1992.

See 0611. For National Institute of Computer-Assisted Reporting, see Investigative Reporters and Editors.

0491 **National Lesbian and Gay Journalists Association**. P.O. Box 423048, San Franciso 94142-3048. Voice: 415-905-4690. Fax: 707-829-3365. Internet: www.tcp.com:800 /qrd/orgs/NLGJA. Has over 800 members. Serves as a support group for gays and lesbians in the media industry. Encourages fair media coverage of gay issues through workshops, seminars, and an annual award for journalistic excellence. Publishes a quarterly newsletter, ALTERNATIVES, and has an annual conference. See also Gay and Lesbian Press Association (0485). Founded in 1990.

0492 **National Newspaper Association (NNA)**. 1525 Wilson Blvd., Ste. 550, Arlington, VA 22209. Voice: 703-907-7900. Fax: 703-907-7901. Serving weekly, semiweekly, and daily newspapers, the association serves over 4,000 members with $1.6 million budget. Compiles statistics and publishes the NATIONAL DIRECTORY OF WEEKLY NEWSPAPERS, annual; PUBLISHERS' AUXILIARY, a biweekly tabloid covering the newspaper business. Sponsors annual spring meetings in Washington, DC. Founded 1885 as National Editorial Association; took present name in 1960.

0493 **National Press Club**. National Press Building, 529 14th St. NW, Washington 20045. Voice: 202-662-7500. Fax: 202-662-7521. Internet: town.hall.org/places/npc. More than 4,300 members, including reporters, writers, and news people employed by newspapers, wire services, magazines, broadcast stations, and other news media. Sponsors many annual awards including the Washington Correspondent award. Maintains a reference library of more than 7,000 books and periodicals. Publishes the NATIONAL PRESS CLUB DIRECTORY, an annual, available to members only, and a weekly newsletter, NATIONAL PRESS CLUB RECORD; conducts an annual workshop on Washington reporting. See also National Press Foundation (0494). Founded in 1908.

0494 **National Press Foundation**. 1282 National Press Building, 529 14th St. NW, Washington 20045. Voice: 202-662-7350. Fax: 202-662-1232. Funds the National Press Club Library and Reference Center and NPC journalism awards; administers the Washington Journalism Center and many annual awards for distinguished journalism. Budget of $700,000. Founded in 1975.

0495 **Newspaper Association of America (NAA).** 1921 Gallows Rd., Ste. 600, Vienna, VA 22182. Voice: 703-902-1600. Internet: www.infi.net/naa. The industry association for newspapers in the United States and Canada and newspapers from Europe and the Pacific Rim. Some 3,000 members; budget over $5 million. Compiles and publishes information on advertising and marketing, circulation and readership, labor relations, workforce diversity, legislation, research, telecommunications, newsprint, and literacy. The Information Resource Center is open to outside researchers. Formed in 1992 through merger of American Newspaper Publishers Association, International Circulation Managers Association, International Newspaper Advertising and Marketing Executives, Newspaper Advertising Bureau of ANPA, Association of Classified Advertising Managers, Newspaper Advertising Co-Op Network, and Newspaper Research Council. Sponsors annual meeting. Publishes the monthly PRESSTIME (1191), an annual FACTS ABOUT NEWSPAPERS (0125), and a monthly newsletter UPDATE.

See 0500. Publishers Information Bureau

0496 **Society of Professional Journalists (SPJ).** 16 South Jackson St., Greencastle, IN 46135-0077. Voice: 317-653-3333. Fax: 317-653-4631. e-mail: SPJ@internetmci.com. Internet: town.hall.org/places/spj/. Membership (13,500) includes broadcast, print, and wire service journalists at all levels. Budget under $2 million. Dedicated to preservation of press freedom and to stimulating high professional standards and ethical behavior. Maintains First Amendment Center to provide resources on First Amendment and Freedom of Information issues. Regional and national awards, including the annual Mark of Excellence Awards in 27 journalistic categories for students. Publishes monthly THE QUILL. Founded in 1909 as Sigma Delta Chi; added present name in 1972 (dropped old name entirely in 1989).

4-D-2. Magazines

0497 **American Business Press**. 675 3rd Ave., Ste. 400, New York, 10017. Voice: 212-661-6360. Fax: 212-370-0736. Assists business, technical, scientific, trade, and marketing magazines that are independently owned and have audited circulations. Over 700 members; budget of $2 million. Develops and promotes industry standards, provides analyses of costs, compiles statistics, monitors postal laws and regulations, maintains a library, offers educational programs. Founded in 1965.

0498 **American Society of Magazine Editors (ASME).** 919 Third Ave., New York 10022. Voice: 212-872-3700. Fax: 212-888-4217. Internet: www.magazine.org/asme/asmeinfo.html. Members are senior editors of magazines affiliated with the larger association, Magazine Publishers of America. Sponsors an annual internship program for college juniors and the National Magazine Award. Annual convention.

0499 **Magazine Publishers of America (MPA).** 919 Third Ave., New York 10022. Voice: 212-872-3700. Fax: 212-888-4217. Internet: www.magaine.org/menv/mgnet.home.html. An association of publishers of more than 800 consumer and other magazines. Budget over $5 million. MPA surveys the members (200) on topics of magazine finance, paper usage, and salaries and publishes a newsletter, MAGAZINE NEWSLETTER OF RESEARCH, also cited as MPA NEWSLETTER OF RESEARCH. Monitors federal legislation and postal rates and regulations. At the New York headquarters, the association maintains extensive library. An advertising auditors service, Publishers Information Bureau, measures advertising in magazines and newspaper supplements and issues monthly reports, print and online. The Publishers Information Bureau is housed and administered by the MPA (see 0050). Founded in 1919 as the National Association of Periodical Publishers, its name has changed five times, most recently from Magazine Publishers Association to Magazine Publishers of America.

0500 **Publishers Information Bureau.** 919 Third Avenue, New York 10022. Voice: 212-872-3700. Fax: 212-888-4217. Measures the amount and type of advertising in magazines and newspaper supplements and publishes the data in PUBLISHERS INFORMATION BUREAU-REPORTS, also cited as PIB REPORTS. Some 200 members; budget of $200,000. Maintains an electronic database of consumer magazine information. The Bureau is administered by the Magazine Publishers of America (0499). Founded in 1945.

4-D-3. Broadcasting

i) Commercial

0501 **Academy of Television Arts and Sciences (ATAS).** 5220 Lankershim Blvd., North Hollywood, CA 91601-3109. Voice: 818-754-2800. Fax: 818-761-2827. Internet: www.emmys.org. 6500 members. Works to advance telecommunication arts and sciences and to foster creative leadership in the telecommunications industry. Membership open to individuals who have contributed their professional and creative talents to the enhancement of the telecommunications industry. Honors outstanding national nighttime television programming and Los Angeles area television programming. Recognizes individual achievements and engineering achievements in television. Sponsors annual Prime-time Emmy Awards telecast. Publishes EMMY Magazine (bimonthly). Companion organization Television Academy Foundation supports Television Academy Hall of Fame; the College Television Awards; the ATAS/UCLA Television Archives, housed at UCLA (0228); and the ATAS Foundation Library in the USC Cinema-Television Library. Founded in 1946 as the Hollywood Chapter of National Academy of Television Arts and Sciences; name changed in 1977.

0502 **American-Hispanic Owned Radio Association (AHORA).** 1400 Central SE, Ste. 2300, Albuquerque, NM 87106. Voice: 505-243-1744. Fax: 505-842-1990. 110 members. Promotes interests of American-Hispanic owned radio stations. Sponsors research, educational programs, and lobbying efforts. Publishes periodic member newsletter. Quarterly meetings. Founded in 1990.

0503 **American Women in Radio & Television (AWRT).** 1650 Tysons Blvd., Ste. 200, McLean, VA 22102. Voice: 703-506-3290. Fax: 703-506-3266. 1,800 members. Annual budget under $500,000. Professional organization of women and men who work in electronic media and related fields. Seeks to advance the impact of women in the electronic media. Publishes member newsletter (biweekly) and CAREERLINE, which lists job openings for members. Sponsors local chapters and awards programs for achievement in the industry and positive portrayal of women in programming. Sponsors annual convention. Founded in 1951.

0504 **Association for Maximum Service Television (AMST).** 1776 Massachusetts Ave. NW, Ste. 310, Washington 20036. Voice: 202-861-0344. Fax: 202-861-0342. 250 members. Annual budget under $2 million. Association of television stations working to protect and improve the technical quality of television pictures and sound. Works to preserve interference-free spectrum and to assure broadcaster access to technologies that expand business opportunities. Promotes governmental policies that foster improved NTSC services, flexible digital advanced television options, and competitive access to the national information superhighway. Publishes member newsletter. Annual meeting. Founded in 1956 as Association of Maximum Service Telecasters; name changed in 1990.

0505 **Association of Local Television Stations (ALTA).** 1320 19th St. NW, Ste. 300, Washington 20036. Voice: 202-887-1970. Fax: 202-887-0950. 302 members. Annual budget under $5 million. Nonprofit organization representing the interests of local commercial independent television stations before Congress and the Federal Communications Commission. Speaks for independent stations in industry councils. Publishes member newsletter (monthly). Sponsors annual convention and summer Washington rally. Founded in 1972 as Association of Independent Television Stations; took present name in 1996.

0506 **Broadcast Cable Financial Management Association (BCFM).** 701 Lee St., Ste. 640, Des Plaines, IL 60016-4555. Voice: 708-296-0200. Fax: 708-296-7510. 1,100 members. Annual budget $1 million. Professional society for financial executives of the broadcast and cable industry. Seeks to develop progressive concepts of financial management for television, radio, and cable and to formulate source material relating to the applications of the controllership, treasureship, and related functions. Involved in broadcast industry credit matters through its whollyowned subsidiary, Broadcast Cable Credit Association, which provides credit reports on credit worthiness of advertising agencies and advertisers and offers credit and collection seminars. BCFM/BCCA publishes member newsletter (monthly), member magazine FINANCIAL MANAGER (six times a year), OPERATIONAL GUIDELINES, and THE FINANCIAL HANDBOOK FOR NON-FINANCIAL MANAGERS. Sponsors annual BCCA seminar and BCFM conference. Founded in 1961 as the Institute of Broadcasting Financial Management; name changed to Broadcast Financial Management Association in 1977 and to current name in 1990.

0507 **Broadcast Designers' Association International (BDA).** 145 West 45th St., 11th Floor, New York 10036. Voice: 212-376-6222. Fax: 212-376-6202. 1100 members. Annual budget under $500,000. Professional association advocating value of design in television, video, and multimedia production. Members include designers, art directors, animators, and illustrators. Seeks to promote the efficiency of the design process and the quality of the design product in electronic media. Publishes DESIGN ANNUAL, compilation of BDA Design Award winners (annual); DIEM: DESIGN IN THE ELECTRONIC MEDIA, member journal (quarterly); and member newsletter fax (biweekly). Sponsors annual international design competition, resume referral service, annual conference, and scholarship program. Library of over 4,000 design pieces. Founded in 1978.

0508 **Broadcasters' Foundation.** 296 Old Church Road, Greenwich, CT 06830. Voice: 203-862-8577. Fax: 203-629-5739. 1400 members. Seeks to encourage broadcasting industry's future leaders by distinguishing individuals and companies making contributions to the radio and television industry. Members are those who have worked for minimum of 15 years as a broadcast professional. Promotes fellowship, friendship, education, and the sharing of wisdom. Recognizes and honors industry professionals. Sponsors Golden Mike Award. Founded and helps support Broadcast Pioneers Library of American Broadcasting (0231). Publishes member newsletter (quarterly). Chapters in Indiana, Florida, Philadelphia, PA, and Washington, DC. Founded in 1942 as The Twenty-Year Club; name changed to Radio Pioneers Club in 1947, Broadcast Pioneers in 1957, and current name in 1995.

0509 **Community Broadcasters Association (CBA).** P.O. Box 9556, Panama City Beach, FL 32417. Voice: 904-234-2773. Fax: 904-234-1179. Organization of low power television station owners and others involved in the community broadcasters field. Has as its mission to promote community broadcasters by protecting their legal rights and interests and by promoting their importance in the community. Publishes member newsletter (bimonthly). Sponsors annual convention and trade show. Founded in 1985 through merger of National Association of Community Broadcasters, the Community Broadcasters of America, and the American Low Power Television Association.

0510 **International Radio & Television Society Foundation (IRTS).** 420 Lexington Ave., Ste. 1714, New York 10170-0101. Voice: 212-867-6650. Fax: 212-867-6653. 1,900 members. Offers communication professionals and industry enthusiasts the opportunity to gather and exchange ideas. Educational programs include the monthly Newsmaker Luncheon series, Minority Career Workshop, Summer Fellowship Program, annual Faculty/Industry Seminar, and annual Foundation Dinner. Sponsors Gold Medal Award Dinner and Foundation Awards Luncheon. Founded in 1952 as the Radio and Television Executives Society by merger of Radio Executives Club of New York and American Television Society. Changed name in 1962 to International Radio and Television Society and in 1994 to current name.

0511 **National Academy of Television Arts and Sciences (NATAS).** 111 West 57th St., New York 10019. Voice: 212-586-8424. Fax: 212-246-8129. 14,000 members. Annual budget under $5 million. Seeks to advance the arts and sciences of television and to foster creative leadership in the television industry. Members must be engaged in profession of television or related fields. Active chapters in 17 major television markets. Sponsors Emmy Awards for documentary, popular arts, children's, drama, and performing arts categories. Sponsors educational programs, scholarships, workshops. Publishes TELEVISION QUARTERLY and member newsletter (quarterly). Library. Sponsors semiannual meeting. Founded in 1946.

0512 **National Association of Black-Owned Broadcasters (NABOB).** 1333 New Hampshire Ave. NW, Suite 1000, Washington 20036. Voice: 202-463-8970. Fax: 202-429-0657. 150 members. Annual budget under $250,000. NABOB represents the interests of Black radio and television stations. Members include blacks who own broadcast stations or cable systems and related businesses. Publishes member newsletter (monthly). Founded in 1976.

0513 **National Association of Broadcasters (NAB).** 1771 N St. NW, Washington 20036-2891. Voice: 202-429-5300. Fax: 202-429-5406. Internet: www.nab.org. 7500 members. Annual budget $40 million. Broadcasting industry's largest, most inclusive organization, representing radio and television stations, networks, and a variety of companies that serve the broadcasting industry. Provides legislative, regulatory and judicial representation in Washington, DC to ensure the viability and success of America's free, over-the-air broadcasters. Serves as an informational resource for the industry through its vigorous publication program that includes financial studies, technical manuals, management guides, and new technology reports. Major publications include NAB ENGINEERING HANDBOOK (0404); NAB LEGAL GUIDE TO BROADCAST LAW AND REGULATION (1003); RADIO ADVERTISING'S MISSING INGREDIENT: THE OPTIMUM EFFECTIVE SCHEDULING SYSTEM, 2nd ed. (1993); BUYING OR BUILDING A BROADCAST STATION IN THE '90s, 3rd ed. (1991); RADIO STATION SALARIES (0463); NAB/BCFM TELEVISION FINANCIAL REPORT (0134); THE TELEVISION INDUSTRY: MARKET-BY-MARKET REVIEW (0134); NAB/BCFM TELEVISION EMPLOYEE COMPENSATION AND FRINGE BENEFITS REPORT (0463); and NAB PROCEEDINGS: ANNUAL BROADCAST ENGINEERING CONFERENCE (annual). New technology publications include RDS APPLICATIONS: OPPORTUNITIES FOR RADIO BROADCASTERS (1995); DIGITAL TELEVISION BROADCASTING: A STANDARD FOR THE FUTURE WITH LESSONS FROM THE PAST (1995) A COMPILATION OF ADVANCED TELEVISION SYSTEMS COMMITTEE STANDARDS (1996); THE DBS REVOLUTION: EMERGING SYSTEMS AND MARKETS BRING NEW COMPETITION (1996); INTERNATIONAL DTH/DBS: GLOBAL BUSINESS DEVELOPMENTS, STRATEGIC DIRECTIONS AND MARKET PROSPECTS IN LATIN AMERICA, CANADA, EUROPE, JAPAN, CHINA, AND ASIA-PACIFIC REGIONS (1996); THE DATACASTING BUSINESS: FUTURE APPLICATIONS, BUSINESS DEVELOPMENT STRATEGIES AND INTERNATIONAL MARKET DEVELOPMENTS (1996); and WIRELESS COMMUNICATIONS: CRITICAL NEW LINKS ON THE INFO-HIGHWAY (1996). NAB also publishes newsletters for its membership, sponsors over one dozen awards and honors to outstanding industry leaders, both stations and individuals, and offers a minority placement service, employment clearinghouse, and research grants program. NAB manages two industry trade shows annually: an all-industry convention in the spring, covering radio, television, advanced television, engineering, multimedia, post production, law and regulation, and the Radio Show in the fall. Fee-based library. Founded in 1922/1923. Absorbed Television Broadcasters Association in 1951 and known as National Association of Radio and Television Broadcasters from 1951 to 1958. Absorbed Daytime Broadcasters Association in 1985 and National Radio Broadcasters in 1986.

0514 **National Captioning Institute**. 1900 Gallows Rd., Ste. 3000, Vienna, VA 22182. Voice: 703-917-7600. Fax: 703-917-9878. Internet: mail@ncicap.org. Private company that provides closed captioning service for the television and home video industries. Founded in 1979.

0515 **PROMAX International**. 2029 Century Park East, Ste. 555, Los Angeles 90067-2906. Voice: 310-788-7600. Fax: 310-788-7616. Internet: www.promax.com. 1900 members. Annual budget $3.2 million. Association of promotion and marketing executives in the electronic media, including radio, television, cable, networks, syndicators. Seeks to advance role and increase effectiveness of promotion and marketing within the industry, related industries, and the academic community. Publishes PROMAX IMAGE magazine (quarterly), DIRECTORY AND PROMOTION PLANNER (annual), and member newsletter (weekly). Sponsors jobline, annual conference, and awards program. Founded in 1956 as Broadcasters Promotion Association; name changed to Broadcast Promotion & Marketing Executives in 1985 and to current name in 1993.

0516 **Radio Advertising Bureau (RAB).** 304 Park Ave. South, New York, NY 10010. Voice: 212-254-4800. Fax: 212-254-8713. Services & Administrative Center, 1320 Greenway Drive, Irving, TX 75038. Voice: 214-753-6750. Fax: 214-753-6727. Internet: www.rab.com. 3400 members. Annual budget $5.5 million. Promotes sale of radio time as an advertising medium. Members include radio stations and allied industry services. Has as its mission to increase awareness, credibility, and salability of radio by designing, developing and implementing appropriate programs, research, tools, and activities for member stations and their clients. Provides faxed newsletter and marketing kits to members. Publishes RADIO MARKETING GUIDE AND FACT BOOK FOR ADVERTISERS (0136), RADIO CO-OP DIRECTORY (annual), and INSTANT BACKGROUND: PROFILES OF 100 BUSINESSES (annual). Sponsors Radio Sales University training seminars, Radio-Mercury Awards for outstanding radio commercials, and annual meeting. Awards the CRMC (Certified Radio Marketing Consultant) designation. Founded in 1951 as the Broadcast Advertising Bureau; assumed current name in 1955.

0517 **Television Bureau of Advertising (TvB).** 850 Third Ave., New York 10022. Voice: 212-486-1111. Fax: 212-935-5631. 300 members. Annual budget $5 million. Represents broadcast television industry to the advertising community. Seeks to develop and increase spot television dollars. Members include television stations and others interested in improving and expanding the use of television as an advertising medium. Provides faxed newsletter (bimonthly) and marketing data resources for members. Publishes TRENDS IN TELEVISION (0138), a series of statistical summaries pertaining to television usage and advertising. Sponsors annual marketing conference and Innovative Television Retailer of the Year Award. Founded in 1954.

ii) Noncommercial/Public

0518 **Association of America's Public Television Stations (APTS)**. 1350 Connecticut Ave. NW, Ste. 200, Washington 20036. Voice: 202-887-1700. Fax: 202-293-2422. Internet: info@apts.org. 165 members. Annual budget $2.9 million. Nonprofit organization whose members are public television stations. Supports development of a financially sound noncommercial television service. Advocates for public television stations on funding, taxation, budget, education, cable, and advanced television issues. Works to protect distribution technologies for public service programming that originates from member stations and to minimize federal regulations that impede public television stations. Publishes research reports including A PLAIN ENGLISH GUIDE TO TECHNOLOGY: TELECOMMUNICATIONS TRENDS AND THEIR IMPACT ON PUBLIC TELEVISION STATIONS (1993) and PUBLIC TELEVISION IN THE INFORMATION AGE (1994). Publishes member newsletter (monthly). Sponsors annual meeting. Founded in 1980 as the Association for Public Broadcasting; became National Association of Public Television Stations, then America's Public Television Stations/Association for Public Broadcasting in 1990; changed to present name in 1991.

0519 **Corporation for Public Broadcasting (CPB).** 901 E St. NW, Washington 20004-2037. Voice: 202-879-9600. Fax: 202-783-1019. Internet: www.cpb.org. Annual budget $285.6 million. Nonprofit corporation created by Congress to develop public television, radio, and online services. Oversees distribution of annual federal contribution to the national public broadcasting system. Fosters educational, informational and cultural programming and outreach services. Funds diverse and innovative television and radio programs, distributes grants to public stations, supports development of nonbroadcast services such as community computer networking, and provides leadership to public broadcasting system through training, technical assistance, and research. Supports outreach programs such as literacy, childcare, education, and the environment. Publishes weekly member newsletter as well as statistical and financial reports, including AVERAGE REVENUE PROFILES FOR PUBLIC BROADCASTING STATIONS; INVENTORY OF FEDERAL FUNDS DISTRIBUTED TO PUBLIC TELECOMMUNICATIONS ENTITIES BY FEDERAL DEPARTMENTS AND AGENCIES; PUBLIC BROADCASTING INCOME REPORT (0131); SALARY REPORT FOR CPB QUALIFIED RADIO, TV, JOINT LICENSEES (0461); and PUBLIC BROADCASTING DIRECTORY (0080). Sponsors awards program. Founded in 1968.

0520 **National Association of College Broadcasters (NACB).** 71 George St., Box 1824, Providence, RI 02912-1824. Voice: 401-863- 2225. Fax: 401-863-2221. Internet: nacb@aol.com. 1,000 members. Annual budget $250,000. Trade association for student-operated radio and television stations. Fosters growth, prestige, and recognition of student media community. Members are student stations, media departments, professionals, students, and faculty. Provides programming for student TV outlets via student-produced network. Helps fund student radio underwriting cooperative. Publishes magazine (quarterly). Maintains placement service. Sponsors awards program and national and regional conferences. Founded in 1988.

0521 **National Federation of Community Broadcasters (NFCB).** Fort Mason Center, Bldg. D, San Francisco 94123. Voice: 415-771-1160. Internet: nfcb@soundprint.brandywine.american.edu. 230 members. Annual budget under $450,000. Membership organization of community-oriented non-commercial radio stations. Represents community radio on national policy and funding criteria. Provides technical assistance to member stations. Publications include NFCB'S GUIDE TO POLITICAL BROADCASTING FOR PUBLIC RADIO STATIONS, Rev. ed., (1992) and member newsletter (monthly). Hosts annual conference. Founded in 1975.

0522 **National Public Radio (NPR).** 635 Massachusetts Ave. NW, Washington 20001-3753. Voice: 202-414-2000. Fax: 202-414-3329. Internet: www.npr.org. 530 members. Annual budget $62 million. Private nonprofit organization that produces and distributes news and cultural programming to member public radio stations. Also provides members with professional develoment, promotional support, and representation in Washington on issues affecting public broadcasting. Operates national satellite program distribution system. Sponsors annual conference. Founded in 1970; absorbed Association of Public Radio Stations in 1977.

0523 **Public Broadcasting Service (PBS).** 1320 Braddock Place, Alexandria, VA 22314-1698. Voice: 703-739-5000. Fax: 703-739-0775. Internet: www.pbs.org. 346 members. Annual budget $161.9 million. Private nonprofit program distribution company owned by its member public television stations. Funds creation and acquisition of children's, cultural, educational, news and public affairs, science and nature, fundraising, and skills programs for its member stations. Provides technical services including program distribution and educational services including instructional programs for classroom use in Grades K-12 and college-credit television courses. Publishes SETTING THE RECORD STRAIGHT: THE FACTS ABOUT PUBLIC TELEVISION (1995). Sponsors annual conference. Founded in 1969.

4-D-4. Cable and Newer Media

0524 **Cable Positive, Inc**. c/o HBO-3rd floor, 1100 Avenue of the Americas, New York 10036-6740. Voice: 212-512-7650. Fax: 212-512-1520. Internet: www.cablepositive.org. Through this public service organization, the cable industry sponsors AIDS fundraisers and raises AIDS awareness. POSITIVE OUTLOOK, a quarterly newsletter, provides a voice for these efforts.

0525 **Cable Telecommunications Association, Inc. (CATA)**. 3950 Chain Bridge Rd., P.O. Box 1005, Fairfax, VA 22030-1005. Voice: 703-691-8875. Fax: 703-691-8911. Founded to protect the interests of small independent system operators, this organization has grown to represent many interests through lobbying and providing cable specific information through publications, seminars, and training sessions. Publishes CATABRIEF, summarizes federal law or regulation in a manner stripped of legalese and CATACABLE, a bimonthly newsletter. CATA implements two fax services: CATAFAX and StatusFax. With the cooperation of CTPAA (0615), CATA implements the NCTA (0529) Cable Industry Public Affairs Training Program providing operators with communication skills. The PAR EXCELLENCE newsletter complements this training program. Founded in 1974 as Community Antenna Television Association; name changed in 1994.

0526 **Cabletelevision Advertising Bureau (CAB)**. 757 3rd Ave., New York, NY 10017. Voice: 212-751-7770. Fax 212-832-3268. Advocates advertising via cable television. Sponsors an annual conference. Publishes CABLE TV FACTS (1985–date, annual) which provides statistics on the demographics of cable television viewing. CAB also publishes marketing case studies, television research updates and a cable network profile handbook. Founded in 1980.

0527 **Interactive Multimedia Association (IMA)**. 48 Maryland Ave., Ste. 202, Annapolis, MD 21401-8011. Voice: 410-626-1380. Fax: 410-263-0590. Internet: www.ima.org. 745 members. Annual budget $1 million. Oldest and largest multimedia trade association. Fosters development of multimedia markets and works to simplify technology for end user. Members include platform/system manufacturers, application software and tools vendors, publishers, custom developers, consultants, and government agencies. Tracks and reports on government policy issues; testifies before select committees and government agencies. Through its Interactive Media Forum, seeks to develop technical initiatives including recommendations for cross-platform compatibility of multimedia data and applications and the interoperability of multimedia systems. Publishes proceedings, including INTELLECTUAL PROPERTY PROJECT PROCEEDINGS, the journal of the Intellectual Property Project, white papers, and membership journal (bi-monthly). Sponsors job bank. Co-sponsors annual conference. Founded in 1988 as Interactive Video Industry Association; name changed in 1990.

0528 **The Marketing Society of the Cable and Telecommunications Industry (CTAM).** 201 North Union St., Ste. 440, Alexandria, VA 22314. Voice: 703-549-4200. Fax: 703-684-1167. This national professional organization with 4,300 members and an annual budget under $5 million has striven to improve cable marketing. CTAM annually publishes PAY PER VIEW CASE STUDY DIGEST, RESEARCH DIGEST & RESOURCE DIRECTORY, NATIONAL MARKETING CASE STUDY DIGEST and MEMBERSHIP DIRECTORY. CTAM also publishes monthly CTAM MEMBER UPDATE. CTAM QUARTERLY MARKETING JOURNAL examines marketing issues and industry trends. The quarterly CTAM PULSE summarizes consumer research on timely topics. CTAM sponsors five annual conferences: National Marketing, Research, New Revenue, Customer Satisfaction and National Pay Per View. Sponsors Mark and Customer is Key awards programs. Commissions research. Operates CTAM ONLINE which features bulletin boards, chat opportunities and news about CTAM. Founded in 1976 as Cable Television Administration and Marketing Society; name changed in 1995.

0529 **National Cable Television Association, Inc. (NCTA)**. 1724 Massachusetts Ave., NW, Washington 20036-1969. Voice: 202-775-3550. Fax: 202-775-3604. Members include 2,700 cable television systems and 400 associated manufacturers, distributors, hardware suppliers and programmers. Budget of $30 million. Sponsors ACE awards and Cable Television Political Action Committee (Cable-PAC). Publishes informational pieces for its membership, for example, CABLE PRIMER (1984) and COMPLETE CABLE BOOK (1994). Publishes industry reports and studies, for example, AMERICA'S STUDENTS: TRAVELERS ON CABLE'S INFORMATION HIGHWAYS (0712), CABLE DEVELOPMENTS (bimonthly), INTERNATIONAL FACTS AT-A-GLANCE (twice yearly). Publishes conference proceedings, membership newsletters, and NCTA TECHNICAL PAPERS. Sponsors ACE awards (for programing), signal theft competition (for papers on signal theft) and Vanguard Awards (for outstanding cable personnel). Provides operating base for National Cable Programming Academy and Cable Office of System Theft (C.O.S.T.). Founded in 1952 as National Community Television Association; name changed in 1967.

0530 **Walter Kaitz Foundation**. Preservation Park, 660 13th St., Ste. 200, Oakland, CA 94612. Voice: 510-451-9000. Fax: 510-451-3315. Internet: www.wkl.com. The Foundation promotes diversity hiring in the industry. To this end, the Foundation sponsors two programs: Cable Management and Engineering Technology Careers. Through these annual programs, the Foundation matches minorities with industry employers and provides an orientation to the industry.

0531 **Women in Cable and Telecommunications (WICT)**. 230 West Monroe St., Ste. 730, Chicago 60606. Voice: 312-634-2330. Hotline: 800-628-WICT. Fax: 312-634-2345. Internet: www.cable-online.com/wict.htm. Organization with 2,600 members designed to help advance the careers of women working in telecommunications. Publishes newsletter, THE SOURCE. Hosts management seminars, an annual conference, and mentoring breakfasts. Sponsors two programs that target future senior management: The Betsy Magness Leadership Institute and The Executive Development Seminar. Sponsors three scholarships and a job bank. Launched a speakers bureau in 1995. Founded in 1969 as Women in Cable; name changed in 1994.

0532 **Women in Communications, Inc. (WICI)** 10605 Judicial Dr., Ste. A-4, Fairfax, VA 22030. Voice: 703-359-9000. Fax: 703-359-0603. 10,000 members. Annual budget under $2 million. Seeks to improve women's opportunities in the communications professions. Publishes THE PROFESSIONAL COMMUNICATOR (5/year). Sponsors awards and annual conference. Founded in 1909 as Theta Sigma Phi; name changed in 1972.

4-D-5. Resources on Consultants

0533 **CONSULTANTS AND CONSULTING ORGANIZATIONS DIRECTORY**. Detroit: Gale, 1966–date, annual. Online version available from HRIN (Human Resources Information Network): covers current edition; updated semiannually. Classified descriptions include personnel, addresses, telephone and fax numbers, with brief notes on consulting activities and publications. Supplemented by NEW CONSULTANTS (1973–date).

0534 **DUN'S CONSULTANTS DIRECTORY.** Parsippany, NJ: Dun's Marketing Service, 1985–date, annual. CD-ROM version available in DUN'S BUSINESS LOCATOR from Dun and Bradstreet Information Services: covers current edition; updated semiannually. Directory of U.S. consulting firms. Geographic, consulting area/speciality, branch offices indexes.

4-E. Selected Secondary Resources

4-E-1. General Surveys

0535 Albarran, Alan B. **MEDIA ECONOMICS: UNDERSTANDING MARKETS, INDUSTRIES AND CONCEPTS**. Ames: Iowa State University Press, 1996, 227 pp. Principles of media economics, electronic media, film and recording industries, print industries, future of media economics research. Appendices, tables, charts, glossary, index.

0536 Alexander, Alison et al. eds. **MEDIA ECONOMICS: THEORY AND PRACTICE**. Hillsdale, NJ: Erlbaum, 1993, 391 pp. Fifteen chapters by as many contributors on all aspects of print and electronic media. Tables, notes, glossary, index.

0537 Compaine, Benjamin M. et al. **WHO OWNS THE MEDIA?** White Plains, NY: Knowledge Industry Publications, Inc., 1982 (2nd ed.), 529 pp. Old, but still the only available such compedium of information and data about the media, compiled and analyzed by four authors: Compaine on newspapers and magazines, Christopher Sterling on broadcasting and cable, Thomas Guback on film, and J. Kendrick Noble on books. (A new edition is in preparation.)

0538 Lacy, Stephen et al. **MEDIA MANAGEMENT: A CASEBOOK APPROACH**. Hillsdale, NJ: Erlbaum, 1993, 391 pp. Ten categories of management issues with several cases provided for each. References, index.

0539 Maney, Kevin. **MEGAMEDIA SHAKEOUT: THE INSIDE STORY OF THE LEADERS AND THE LOSERS IN THE EXPLODING COMMUNICATIONS INDUSTRY.** New York: Wiley, 1995, 358 pp. Useful snapshot of the dramatic impact of convergence between media and telecommunications industries—and the reasons behind the mergers. Photos, index.

0540 Owen, Bruce M. **ECONOMICS AND FREEDOM OF EXPRESSION: MEDIA STRUCTURE AND THE FIRST AMENDMENT.** Cambridge, MA: Ballinger, 1975, 202 pp. One of the earliest economic assessments of the industry and how the First Amendment's image and impact changed amidst technical and competitive pressures. Tables, notes, index.

0541 Picard, Robert G. **MEDIA ECONOMICS: CONCEPTS AND ISSUES.** Newbury Park, CA: Sage, 1989, 136 pp. Brief conceptual overview of the topic—a good introduction to basic trends and issues. Glossary, bibliography, index.

0542 Steinbock, Dan. **TRIUMPH & EROSION IN THE AMERICAN MEDIA & ENTERTAINMENT INDUSTRIES.** Westport, CT: Quorum, 1995, 328 pp. Integrated study of the financial and economic performance of these businesses, emphasizing the impact of increased competition. Tables, notes, index.

0543 Turow, Joseph. **MEDIA INDUSTRIES: THE PRODUCTION OF NEWS AND ENTERTAINMENT.** White Plains, NY: Longman, 1984, 213 pp. Analysis of the production process and the key players across all media. Bibliography, index.

0544 Vogel, Harold L. **ENTERTAINMENT INDUSTRY ECONOMICS: A GUIDE FOR FINANCIAL ANALYSIS.** New York: Cambridge University Press, 1994 (3rd ed.), 446 pp. About half devoted to film, broadcasting and cable, but also including sports, performing arts, and theme parks. Only book of its kind. Tables, glossary, references, index.

4-E-2. Newspapers

0545 Busterna, John C. and Robert G. Picard. **JOINT OPERATING AGREEMENTS: THE NEWSPAPER PRESERVATION ACT AND ITS APPLICATION.** Norwood, NJ: Ablex, 1993, 170 pp. Focuses on the 1970 legislation and its economic impact on the industry. Tables, charts, references, index.

0546 Cose, Ellis. **THE PRESS.** New York: William Morrow and Company, 1989, 380 pp. A review of the work of editors at the "national" U.S. newspapers—*The Washington Post, Times Mirror,* and *The New York Times*—and major group newspapers—Gannett and Knight-Ridder. A general theme is the need to print news to serve a defined market.

0547 Lacy, Stephen, and Todd F. Simon. **THE ECONOMICS AND REGULATION OF UNITED STATES NEWSPAPERS.** Norwood, NJ: Ablex, 1993, 296 pp. Chapters on newspaper demand, supply, competition, ownership, the impact of technology, antitrust and market regulation, newspaper economics and antitrust, and the business regulation of newspapers. One of the few recent sources of such information. Tables, charts, endnotes, author and subject indexes.

0548 Picard, Robert G. et al. **PRESS CONCENTRATION AND MONOPOLY: NEW PERSPECTIVES ON NEWSPAPER OWNERSHIP AND OPERATION.** Norwood, NJ: Ablex Publishing, 1988, 231 pp. A report of multiple studies of the practices and economics of U.S. newspapers. The information is presented in the context of concern over preserving the multiplicity of opinion and information available to the public as chain ownership increases.

4-E-3. Magazines

0549 Compaine, Benjamin M. **THE BUSINESS OF CONSUMER MAGAZINES.** White Plains, NY: Knowledge Industry Publications, 1982. 197 pp. Using data from 1960s through early 1980s, the author identifies trends and creates a snapshot of the consumer magazines publishing business in the U.S. The data and information are organized and illustrated by tables and appendixes.

Builds on author's earlier CONSUMER MAGAZINES AT THE CROSSROADS (White Plains, NY: KIP, 1974).

4-E-4. Broadcasting

0550 Blumenthal, Howard J. and Oliver R. Goodenough. **THIS BUSINESS OF TELEVISION**. New York: Billboard Books, 1991, 660 pp. Guide to the business and legal aspects of television production and distribution. Includes over 30 sample industry contracts and forms.

0551 **THE ECONOMICS OF TV PROGRAMMING AND SYNDICATION 1996.** Carmel, CA: Paul Kagan Associates, 1996, 202 pp. Analysis of financial and viewing trends in network television, first-run and off-network syndication, and cable network programming.

0552 Head, Sydney W. et al. **BROADCASTING IN AMERICA: A SURVEY OF ELECTRONIC MEDIA**. Boston: Houghton-Mifflin, 1994 (7th ed.), 650 pp. A standard descriptive and analytic text on all aspects of the field including history, technology, economics, programming, audiences, regulation, and international comparisons. Tables, photos, charts, bibliography, index.

0553 Krasnow, Erwin G., et al. **BUYING OR BUILDING A BROADCAST STATION IN THE 1990s**. Washington, DC: NAB, 1991 (3rd ed.), 98 pp. Step-by-step guide details what is involved in the process.

0554 Pringle, Peter K. et al. **ELECTRONIC MEDIA MANAGEMENT**. Stoneham, MA: Focal, 1995 (3rd ed.), 425 pp. Covers radio, television, and related media services—all aspects of management. Glossary, bibliography, index.

i) Radio

0555 Ditingo, Vincent M. **THE REMAKING OF RADIO**. Newston, MA: Focal Press, 1994, 160 pp. Surveys the dramatic changes in the industry in the late 1980s and early 1990s. Index.

0556 Keith, Michael. **THE RADIO STATION**. Newton, MA: Focal Press, 1997 (4th ed.), 322 pp. Probably the standard radio management text, updated to include radio's likely digital future. Photos, diagrams, glossary, index.

0557 Pease, Edward C. and Everette E. Dennis, eds. **RADIO: THE FORGOTTEN MEDIUM**. New Brunswick, NJ: Transaction, 1995, 213 pp. Based on an issue of MEDIA STUDIES JOURNAL, this looks at the economics, operation, programming and impact of commercial and public radio. References, index.

ii) Television

0558 American Association of Advertising Agencies. **A.A.A.A.TELEVISION PRODUCTION COST SURVEY: REPORT OF FINDINGS**. New York: AAAA, 1987–date, annual. Analysis of TV production costs based on survey of 22 agencies with database of nearly 2,000 national commercials, providing average costs by commercial length, shoot location, product category.

0559 American Association of Advertising Agencies and Association of National Advertisers. **TELEVISION COMMERCIAL MONITORING REPORT**. New York: AAAA and ANA, 1989–date, annual. Tracks nonprogram material (clutter) including commercials, public service announcements, program credits and promotional announcements. Surveys four TV broadcast networks, 16 cable networks, and a cross-section of the syndication market.

0560 Eastman, Susan Tyler, and Robert Klein, eds. **PROMOTION AND MARKETING FOR BROADCASTING AND CABLE**. Prospect Heights, IL: Waveland, 1991 (2nd ed.), 444 pp. Original articles by industry experts discuss all aspects.

0561 Jankowski, Gene F. and David C. Fuchs. **TELEVISION TODAY AND TOMORROW: IT WON'T BE WHAT YOU THINK**. New York: Oxford University Press, 1995, 237 pp. Two former senior officials of CBS predict the medium's likely economic, programming, content, and policy future. Photos, tables, notes, index.

0562 Owen, Bruce M., and Steven Wildman. **VIDEO ECONOMICS**. Cambridge: Harvard University Press, 1992, 364 pp. Details the economics of network television, cable and VCRs in terms of supply and demand and both traditional and new models of program choice. The final 100 pages focus on public policy alternatives, including public and children's TV. Bibliography, notes, index.

0563 Wasko, Janet. **HOLLYWOOD IN THE INFORMATION AGE**. Austin: University of Texas Press, 1994, 308 pp. How Hollywood film and television studios are adapting to changing technology and distribution patterns. Notes, index.

iii) Noncommercial/Public

0564 Hoynes, William. **PUBLIC TELEVISION FOR SALE: MEDIA, THE MARKET, AND THE PUBLIC SPHERE**. Boulder, CO: Westview, 1994, 207 pp. A strongly critical study that focuses on funding problems and options. Includes case studies. Tables, figures, notes, references, index.

0565 Lashley, Marilyn. **PUBLIC TELEVISION: PANACEA, PORK BARREL, OR PUBLIC TRUST?** Westport, CT: Greenwood, 1992, 147 pp. Study of the organization and budgeting of the national system. Diagrams, references, index.

0566 Looker, Thomas. **THE SOUND AND THE STORY: NPR AND THE ART OF RADIO**. Boston: Houghton Mifflin, 1995, 421 pp. Combines informal history and current survey of National Public Radio programs and key figures.

0567 **QUALITY TIME? THE REPORT OF THE TWENTIETH CENTURY FUND TASK FORCE ON PUBLIC TELEVISION**. New York: Twentieth Century Fund, 1993, 188 pp. First such assessment since the 1967 (0316) and 1979 (0317) Carnegie commissions, this calls for substantial changes in the structure and operations of public broadcasting as it celebrated 25 years. Index.

4-E-5. Cable and Newer Media

0568 Baldwin, Thomas F. and D. Stevens McVoy. **CABLE COMMUNICATION**. Englewood Cliffs, NJ: Prentice-Hall Inc., 1988 (2nd ed.), 434 pp. Concise chapters recapitulate four aspects of the industry: technology, services, organizations, and future. Appendices provide information on public access channel rules, pay services, the Cable Communications Policy Act of 1984, audience survey methods, and sample advertising production rates. Index.

0569 Batra, Rajeev and Rashi Glazer, eds. **CABLE TV ADVERTISING: IN SEARCH OF THE RIGHT FORMULA**. New York: Quorum Books, 1989, 187 pp. Papers delivered by academic researchers and industry professionals attending a 1987 conference co-sponsored by the Center for Telecommunications and Information Studies at Columbia Graduate School of Business and the firm of Coopers and Lybrand. Comments of respondents are also included. The themes summarized are industry analysis, implications for advertisers, and new developments. Figures, tables, bibliography, index.

0570 Nicholson, Margie. **CABLE ACCESS: COMMUNITY CHANNELS AND PRODUCTIONS FOR NONPROFITS**. Washington: Benton Foundation, 1990, 59 pp. The book is divided into three sections: background, use, and 12 case studies. Appendix, notes.

0571 Picard, Robert G., ed. **THE CABLE NETWORKS HANDBOOK**. Riverside, CA: Carpelan Publishing, 1993, 216 pp. Twenty-eight chapters on as many cable networks, each telling the story of the network's development, organization, programming, and audiences. References.

0572 Sherman, Barry L. **TELECOMMUNICATIONS MANAGEMENT: BROADCASTING/CABLE AND THE NEW TECHNOLOGIES.** New York: McGraw-Hill, 1995 (2nd ed.), 431 pp. The basics plus case studies, with more material on the "core" business, international developments, and newer technologies. Photos, diagrams, index.

0573 Warner, Charles, and Jack Buchman. **BROADCAST AND CABLE SELLING**. Belmont, CA: Wadsworth, 1993 (updated 2nd ed.), 447 pp. All types and approaches to selling ad time. Photos, notes, index.

0574 Yates, Robert K., Nolwen Mahe and Jerome Masson. **FIBER OPTICS AND CATV BUSINESS STRATEGY**. Norwood, MA: Artech House, 1990, 159 pp. Discusses the deployment and use of fiber by cable television, including business implications. Index.

5

Content

This chapter includes resources that describe and assess the application and impact of mass communications on all aspects of daily life, including recreation and entertainment, information and news, education, consumerism, and employment. Many of the useful topical bibliographies listed first, notably Signorelli's ROLE PORTRAYAL AND STEREOTYPING ON TELEVISION (0588), address timely and controversial issues. Because they were published in the mid-1980s, most need updating. Researchers should consult the various relevant indexing and abstracting services for more recent work.

In addition to bibliographies and directories, we have included selected corporate, academic, and private organizations that conduct research on economic, social, political, and cultural implications. Selected secondary resources include studies on the impact of mass communications on business, the individual, and U.S. society, and culture.

5-A. Bibliographic Resources

5-A-1. Bibliographies

0575 Alali, A. Odasuo, ed. **MASS MEDIA SEX AND ADOLESCENT VALUES: AN ANNOTATED BIBLIOGRAPHY AND DIRECTORY OF ORGANIZATIONS**. Jefferson, NC: McFarland, 1991, 138 pp. Over 200 listings of studies and articles concerning media sex role stereotypes, sexual curricula and media use, adolescents' attitudes and values, and contraception, pregnancy, and health issues. Most of the entries were published in the 1980s. Describes over 50 organizations that conduct relevant research or provide services to adolescents.

0576 Alali, A. Odasuo and Gary W. Byrd. **TERRORISM AND THE NEWS MEDIA: A SELECTED, ANNOTATED BIBLIOGRAPHY.** Jefferson, NC: McFarland, 1994, 213 pp. Some 600 entries.

0577 Cooper, Thomas W. **TELEVISION & ETHICS: A BIBLIOGRAPHY**. Boston: G.K. Hall, 1988, 203 pp. Includes 1,170 references, many of them annotated, with both author and subject index.

0578 Dillman, Don A., and Jurg Gerber. **SOCIOLOGICAL IMPLICATIONS OF INFORMATION TECHNOLOGY: A BIBLIOGRAPHY OF RECENT PUBLICATIONS**. Chicago: Council of Planning Librarians, 1985, 32 pp. (CPL Bibliography 170). 530 references on cable television, computer crime, and electronic mail. Detailed subject index.

0579 Friedman, Leslie J. **SEX ROLE STEREOTYPING IN THE MASS MEDIA: AN ANNOTATED BIBLIOGRAPHY**. New York: Garland, 1977, 324 pp. Includes about 1,000 items, divided by topic. Indexed.

0580 Gray, John. **BLACKS IN FILM AND TELEVISION; A PAN-AFRICAN BIBLIOGRAPHY OF FILMS, FILMMAKERS, AND PERFORMERS**. Westport, CT: Greenwood, 1990, 496 pp. Over 6,000 unannotated entries on Africa, South America, and the Caribbean and, more selectively, the United States. Includes books, dissertations, unpublished papers, newspapers, and magazines, videotapes, and audiotapes in major Western European languages. Reference works and film resources listed in appendices. Artist, title, subject, and author indices.

0581 Greenberg, Gerald S. **TABLOID JOURNALISM: AN ANNOTATED BIBLIOGRAPHY OF ENGLISH-LANGUAGE SOURCES**. Westport. CT: Greenwood Press, 1996, 187 pp. Listing and brief summary of books, scholarly journal research, popular magazine articles and trade periodical pieces plus theses and dissertations concerning sensationalized journalism. Emphasis on the U.S. genre.

0582 Hill, George H. **BLACK MEDIA IN AMERICA: A RESOURCE GUIDE.** Boston: G.K. Hall, 1984, 333 pp. Includes books, dissertations, theses, journal articles, and newspaper and magazine articles. Author and subject indexes.

0583 _____, and Lenwood Davis, eds. **RELIGIOUS BROADCASTING 1920–1983: A SELECTED ANNOTATED BIBLIOGRAPHY**. New York: Garland, 1984, 243 pp. Some 1,600 items are included and indexed.

0584 Kaid, Lynda Lee and Anne Johnston Wadsworth. **POLITICAL CAMPAIGN COMMUNICATION: A BIBLIOGRAPHY AND GUIDE TO THE LITERATURE.** Metuchen, NJ: Scarecrow Press, 2 vols. Unannotated listing of works on U.S. political campaign communication (political advertising, debates, television news coverage, election coverage).

1 [to 1973]. 1974, 220 pp.
2 **1973–1982**. 1985, 217 pp.

0585 **MARXISM AND THE MASS MEDIA: TOWARDS A BASIC BIBLIOGRAPHY**. New York: International Mass Media Research Center, 1972–1980, 7 vols. published in 3. "Global, multilingual, annotated bibliography of Marxist studies on all aspects of communications." 825 entries: vols. 1, 2, 3, entries 1–453, "revised edition" (1978); vols. 4, 5, entries 454–658 (1976); vols. 6, 7, entries 659–825 (1980). Subject, author, and country indexes.

0586 Nuessel, Frank. **THE IMAGE OF OLDER ADULTS IN THE MEDIA: AN ANNOTATED BIBLIOGRAPHY**. Westport, CT: Greenwood, 1992, 181 pp. Divided into 21 media-defined chapters, this includes some 550 entries. Indexed.

0587 Poteet, G. Howard. **PUBLISHED RADIO, TELEVISION, AND FILM SCRIPTS: A BIBLIOGRAPHY**. Troy, NY: Whitson Publishing, 1975, 245 pp. Lists some 2,300 scripts that have appeared in print.

0588 Signorelli, Nancy, ed. **ROLE PORTRAYAL AND STEREOTYPING ON TELEVISION: AN ANNOTATED BIBLIOGRAPHY OF STUDIES RELATING TO WOMEN, MINORITIES, AGING, SEXUAL BEHAVIOR, HEALTH AND HANDICAPS**. Westport, CT: Greenwood, 1985, 214 pp. Only 423 entries, but clearly arranged and well indexed and annotated.

0589 Smith, Myron J., Jr. **U.S. TELEVISION NETWORK NEWS: A GUIDE TO SOURCES IN ENGLISH**. Jefferson, NC: McFarland, 1984, 233 pp. Includes some 3,200 entries divided by topic (but not annotated), and indexed.

5-A-2. Abstracts, Indexes, Databases

(NOTE: for historical statistics resources, see 1-G-4.)

0590 **ABC NEWS TRANSCRIPTS AND INDEX** [CD-ROM]. Primary Source Media, 12 Lunar Dr., Woodbridge, CT 06525. Voice: 203-397-2600. Fax: 203-397-3893. Internet: www.thomson. com. Transcripts of 11 network news programs on microfiche (1969–date). ABC NEWS INDEX references information in transcripts by subject, name of person interviewed, and program titles. Cumulative index available for 1970–1985. Index for individual years 1986–date. ABC Transcripts also available on Burrelle's Broadcast Database, DataTimes, and Lexis-Nexis.

0591 **BROADCAST NEWS** [CD-ROM]. Primary Source Media, 12 Lunar Dr., Woodbridge, CT 06525, 1993–date, monthly. Voice: 203-397-2600. Fax: 203-397-3893. e-mail: sales@rpub.com. Broadcast news database on CD-ROM provides access to full-text transcripts from ABC News, CNN, PBS, and National Public Radio from 1992–date.

0592 **BURRELLE'S BROADCAST DATABASE** [Online service]. Livingston, NJ: Burrelle's Broadcast Database, 1990–date (available day following broadcast). Available from Burrelle's Information Services, 75 E. Northfield Rd., Livingston, NJ 07039-9873. Voice: 201-992-6600. Fax: 201-992-7675. Online service offering full-text transcripts of news and public affairs programs, including ABC, CBS, and NBC television networks; selected syndicated television programs, National Public Radio, and Financial News Network.

0593 **Cable News Network.** 100 Industrial Blvd., Box 105366, Atlanta, GA 30348. Transcripts and new footage can be ordered from Journal Graphics. Voice: 800-366-6397 or 303-831-9000. Internet: www.footage.net. CNN Headline News programs can be ordered from Video Monitoring Services. Voice: 212-564-2887. Information can also be found on LEXIS/NEXIS.

0594 **CBS NEWS TRANSCRIPTS** [CD-ROM]. Livingston, NJ: Burrelle's Information Services, 1991–date, updated monthly. Available from UMI, 620 S. Third St., Louisville KY 40202-2475. Voice: 502-583-4111. Fax: 502-589-5572. Full text and indexing database of news transcripts, including news and current events programs. CBS transcripts also available on BURRELLE'S BROADCAST DATABASE (0000), DataTimes, DowJones News/Retrieval, and LEXIS/NEXIS (0912).

0595 **National Public Radio Program Library and Audio Archive**, 635 Mass. Ave., NW, Washington 20001-3753. Voice: 202-414-2060. Fax: 202-414-3056. Internet: rrobinson@npr.org. Open to the public by appointment. Listening facilities available. Collection of 80,000 tapes of programs produced or distributed by NPR. Cataloged by keyword/subject, person talking, and person talked about. News shows available from 1982 to date; performance shows from 1989 to date. Pre-1982 news tapes available at Public Broadcasting Archives in College Park, MD (0231) and pre-1989 performance tapes at Library of Congress. Collection includes transcripts of *Morning Edition, All Things Considered,* and *Weekend Edition* from Sept. 1, 1990 to date. NPR Audience Services (202-414-3232) sells cassette tapes and transcripts of these programs and cassette tapes of *Talk of the Nation.*

0596 **NBC NEWS TRANSCRIPTS ONDISC**. Louisville, KY: UMI, 1990–date. Full text and indexing database of news transcripts, including news and current events programs. NBC transcripts also available on Burrelle's Broadcast Database, DataTimes, Dow Jones News/Retrieval, and LEXIS/NEXIS.

0597 **PUBLIC TELEVISION TRANSCRIPTS AND INDEX** [CD-ROM]. Primary Source Media, 12 Lunar Dr., Woodbridge, CT 06525. Voice: 203-397-2600. Fax: 203-397-3893. Transcripts from original air dates forward of WNET/New York interview programs. Cumulative index for 1973-1986. Annual indexes for years 1987–date.

See 0251. WGBH EDUCATIONAL FOUNDATION

5-A-3. Directories

i) Print Media

(Note: See also: 2-C-4 for extensive Greenwood series on periodicals.)

0598 Ellenbogen, Glenn C., ed. **THE DIRECTORY OF HUMOR MAGAZINES AND HUMOR ORGANIZATIONS IN AMERICA (AND CANADA).** New York: Wry-Bred Press, 1989. 186 pp. A detailed listing of magazines and organizations, primarily devoted to humor. Excludes magazines mixing humor with serious material.

0599 Wynar, Lubomyr R., and Anna T. Wynar. **ENCYCLOPEDIC DIRECTORY OF ETHNIC NEWSPAPERS AND PERIODICALS IN THE UNITED STATES.** Littleton, CO: Libraries Unlimited, 1976 (2nd ed.), 248pp. A carefully researched "encyclopedic directory" of ethnic periodicals published in the U.S., first published in 1972. The information for this edition, which lists nearly 1,000 titles, was gathered through a comprehensive survey. The introduction provides references to directories of the press of the Native American and Black American periodicals.

ii) Electronic Media

(Note: includes current directories only; for historical directories see 5-C.)

0600 **BACON'S RADIO DIRECTORY: DIRECTORY OF RADIO STATIONS PROGRAMMING CONTACTS.** Chicago: Bacon's Information, 1987–date, annual. Guide to programming information at more than 10,000 radio stations in the U.S. Emphasis is on news and talk show programs. Station profiles include format, target audience, descriptions of talk shows (where applicable), use of guests data, major league sports play-by-play programming, and policy concerning use of releases or scripts for news segments. Host and guest contact names are included for news/talk programs. Radio networks and syndicators listed in separate sections. Indices include radio programs by title (over 2,400 programs), by topic, and syndicated radio programs. Also available on CD-ROM.

0601 **BACON'S TV/CABLE DIRECTORY: DIRECTORY OF TV/CABLE STATIONS PROGRAMMING CONTACTS.** Chicago: Bacon's Information, 1987–date, annual. Guide to local programming information at more than 2,200 TV stations and cable systems in the U.S. Station profiles include local programs with air time, description, guest usage, host, and guest contact. Cable section includes cable satellite systems that have locally produced news/interview/panel discussion programs or provide time segments for public access programming. System profile for each entry includes number of channels devoted to local programming. Networks and syndicators listed in separate sections. Indices include TV programs (over 4,600 programs) by title and by topic. Includes maps for 50 top U.S. radio and TV markets showing cities and towns having radio and TV stations within 50-mile radius. Also available on CD-ROM.

0602 Bension, Shmuel, ed. **THE PRODUCER'S MASTERGUIDE: THE INTERNATIONAL PRODUCTION MANUAL FOR MOTION PICTURES, BROADCAST TELEVISION, COMMERCIALS, CABLE, AND VIDEOTAPE INDUSTRIES**. New York: Producer's Masterguide, 1979–date, annual. 16th ed. (1996); publisher has varied. Guide to logistics, contacts, union requirements, and other information needed for onsite TV and motion picture production.

0603 **BIB TELEVISION PROGRAMMING SOURCE BOOKS.** Philadelphia: North American Publishing, 1950s–date, annual. Available on CD-ROM with 1993 ed. Four-volume guide to available television programming. Vols. 1 and 2 list 32,000 theatrical films, made-for-TV and cable movies, with descriptions, credits, and current distributors. Vol. 3 lists films in packages (including foreign language packages and holiday and theme films), which have corresponding and complete listings in Vol. 1 and 2. Vol. 4 lists 21,000 series titles available for distribution. Series are arranged by time formats: long, hour, half-hour comedy, half-hour, and short. Includes production data and distributor information.

0604 **DIRECTORY OF RELIGIOUS MEDIA**. Manassas, VA: National Religious Broadcasters, 1979–date, annual. Formerly DIRECTORY OF RELIGIOUS BROADCASTING. Directory of Christian broadcasting, publishing, and music industries. Includes radio and television stations, group owners, program producers, agencies, and suppliers. Available on diskette.

0605 **DWM: DIRECTORY OF WOMEN'S MEDIA**. New York: National Council for Research on Women, 1995 (17th ed.), 205 pp. Brief descriptions of over 1,600 print and electronic media, publishers, bookstores, libraries, distributors, and other media resources by, for, and about women. Published by the Women's Institute for Freedom of the Press between 1975 and 1989.

0606 Elving, Bruce F. **FM ATLAS: A GUIDE FOR TRAVELERS, HI-FI LISTENERS, MEDIA PEOPLE AND HOBBYISTS.** Esko, MN: FM Atlas Publishing, 1996 (17th ed.), 225 pp. Unique directory lists FM stations by state and includes SCA information and location of FM translators. Maps show location of FM stations in U.S., Canada, and Mexico. Published since early 1970s.

0607 **HUDSON'S WASHINGTON NEWS MEDIA CONTACTS DIRECTORY**. Rhinebeck, NY: Hudson's Directory, 1968–date, annual. Revisions issued three times yearly. Lists over 4,700 news outlets, including bureaus, newspapers, news services, radio, TV, magazines, newsletters, photographic services, syndicates, and freelance writers.

0608 **R&R PROGRAM SUPPLIER GUIDE**. Los Angeles: Radio & Records, 1987–date, annual. More than 1,800 listings of syndicated programs, radio networks, automated and satellite formats, production music libraries, jingle packages, and song catalogs. Listings include programming and technical information, description, and distributor information.

0609 **RADIO/TV REPORTS.** New York: RTV/Competitive Media Reporting, 1936–date. Broadcast monitoring service provides selected video clips, audio tapes and transcripts of TV, radio, and cable news shows. Available online through LEXIS/NEXIS with over 300 program hours daily of news summaries from leading network TV, radio, and cable news shows and local TV and radio stations in the top 20 markets. Competitive Media Reporting also monitors commercials and maintains commercial library, 1959–date.

5-B. Associations and Organizations

(Note: Organizations listed here focus on media content. See also: 4-D, Associations)

5-B-1. Print Media

0610 **Center for Investigative Reporting**. 568 Howard St., 5nd Fl., San Francisco 94105-3008. Voice: 415-543-1200. Fax: 415-543-8311; toll-free 800-733-0015. Internet: solar.rtd.utK.edu/ccsi/csusa/media/forjourn.html. An association of investigative journalists specializing in in-depth reporting of public issues. Produces television documentaries, newspaper, and magazine articles; provides consulting services to television news and other news organizations. Conducts an internship program, seminars, and workshops. Maintains a library and publishes reporting handbooks and a journal MUCKRAKER: JOURNAL OF THE CENTER FOR INVESTIGATIVE REPORTING (1992–date, quarterly).

0611 **Investigative Reporters and Editors (IRE)**. University of Missouri, 26A Walter Williams Hall, Columbia, MO 65211. Voice: 314-882-2042. Fax: 314-882-5431. Internet: www.ire.org; and www.nicar.org. An association of reporters, editors, and journalism educators and students with interests in investigative journalism. The IRE has a training arm, the National Institute for Computer-Assisted Reporting, offering national seminars to train reporters in using computer programs to analyze public records. Maintains an archive. Gives national awards to recognize investigative work in newspapers, broadcast journalism, books, and magazines. Publishes magazine, THE IRE JOURNAL (1978–date) and monthly newsletter, UPLINK (1990–date).

5-B-2. Electronic Media

0612 **Alliance for Community Media**. 666 11th St. NW, Ste. 806, Washington 20001. Voice: 202-393-2650. Fax: 202-393-2653. Electronic bulletin board: 217-359-9118. Annual budget under $500,000. Some 1,500 regional, state, and local access producers, community producers, public access organizations, public access professionals, cable television firms, cable regulators, and other organizations and individuals interested in making cable programming more responsive to the needs of individuals, local groups, and communities. Advocates at the federal level. Maintains referral services. Publishes bimonthly journal, COMMUNITY MEDIA REVIEW. Founded in 1976 as National Federation of Local Cable Programmers; name changed in 1992.

0613 **American Sportscasters Association**. 5 Beekman St., Ste 814, New York 10038. Voice: 212-227-8080. Fax: 212-571-0556. 500 members. Annual budget $200,000. Members are radio and television sportscasters. Sponsors awards program, Hall of Fame, and annual Hall of Fame Awards Dinner. Publishes member newsletter (bimonthly). Founded in 1980.

0614 **Cable in the Classroom**. 1900 N. Beauregard St., Ste. 108, Alexandria, VA 22311. Voice: 703-845-1400. Fax: 703-845-1409. Internet: www.ciconline.com. Public service initiative of local cable companies and national cable networks that facilitates cable television connections to primary and secondary schools. Negotiates copyright clearance on cable programming for use in classroom instruction. Provides teacher training workshops. Publishes CABLE IN THE CLASSROOM (monthly) listing upcoming programming by discipline. Founded in 1989.

0615 **Cable Television Public Affairs Association (CTPAA).** 1724 Massachusetts Ave., NW, Washington 20036. Voice: 202-775-1081. Fax: 202-955-1134. Public affairs professionals (500 members). Publishes CPR FACTS, a biweekly fax providing the latest information on successful PR projects. Also publishes the bimonthly THE POWER OF PUBLIC AFFAIRS providing specifics on creating and implementing effective and successful public affairs initiatives or projects. Provides a clearinghouse of PR materials. Sponsors annual 3-day conference (FORUM) and Beacon Awards which recognize excellence in public affairs. Annually publishes a case study handbook featuring the winners of Beacon awards. Cooperates with CATA (0525) to implement the Cable Industry Public Affairs Training Program, a project of the NCTA (0529). Founded in 1985.

0616 Not used.

0617 **The National Academy of Cable Programming**. 1724 Massachusetts Ave., NW, Washington 20036. Voice: 202-775-3611. Fax 202-775-3689. Internet: www.cableace.org. Industry organization for some 1,800 cable programming professionals. Promotes cable television programming excellence and innovation. Sponsors seminars, screenings, and local and national CableACE awards (formerly ACE Awards, 1979–date). Founded in 1985 by the National Cable Television Association (0529).

0618 **National Association of Farm Broadcasters (NAFB).** 26 Exchange St. East, Ste 307, St. Paul, MN 55101. Voice: 612-224-0508. Fax: 612-224-1956. 670 members. Annual budget $390,000. Seeks to encourage understanding among commercial farm broadcasting entities, farm organizations, governmental agencies, and other groups interested in reaching farm people. Works to improve and expand farm broadcasting. Members include on-air agricultural broadcasters and those working in related fields. Sponsors award programs and Farm Broadcasters Hall of Fame. Sponsors annual conference. Founded in 1944 as National Association of Radio Farm Directors; became National Association of Television–Radio Farm Directors in 1956 and assumed present name in 1964.

0619 **National Association of Radio Talk Show Hosts (NARTSH)**. 134 Saint Botolph St., Boston 02115-4819. Voice: 617-437-9757. Fax: 617-437-0797. Internet: NZTU49A@prodigy.com. 3,000 members. Nonprofit organization dedicated to preservation of free speech, education, and advancement of citizens in all aspects of talk broadcasting, maintenance of the town meeting ideals of talk radio, and promotion of talk radio as a dynamic source of information on key ideas. Members include talk show hosts and producers. Sponsors placement service, awards program, and annual conference. Publishes member newsletter (monthly). Founded in 1987.

0620 **National Association of Television Program Executives International (NATPE).** 2425 Olympic Blvd., Ste. 550E, Santa Monica, CA 90404. Voice: 310-453-4440. Fax: 310-453-5258. 2,300 members. Television programming association dedicated to the growth of the global television marketplace. Members include television station and network program directors and persons working in television programming and production. Publishes PROGRAMMER'S GUIDE (annual), STATION LISTING GUIDE (annual), and member newsletter (monthly). Sponsors annual conference and world's largest exhibition of television programming and software. Sponsors Iris Awards for excellence in locally produced television programming. Offers jobline and industry seminars. Founded in 1962.

0621 **National Black Programming Consortium**. 929 Harrison Ave., Ste. 101, Columbus, OH 43215. Voice: 614-299-5355. Fax: 614-299-4761. Internet: www.nbpc.com. Publishes newsletters TAKE ONE and TAKE TWO. Sponsors Prized Pieces International Film and Video Competition.

0622 **National Broadcast Association for Community Affairs (NBACA)**. 1200 19th St. NW, Ste 300, Washington 20036-2412. Voice: 202-857-1155. Fax: 202-223-4579. 285 members. Annual budget $140,000. Organization for electronic media professionals dedicated to strengthening community affairs programming and outreach. Members are managers of community affairs, public affairs, community relations, and editorials who work at stations, networks, group headquarters, and cable outlets. Seeks to establish and maintain good relations with all segments of community. Acts as resource and advocate. Offers seminars and workshops. Co-sponsors NBACA Community Service Awards. Publications include HOW TO ORGANIZE A COMMUNITY AFFAIRS/PUBLIC SERVICE PROJECT (n.d.) and CORPORATE-SPONSORED MEDIA CAMPAIGNS: NEW OPPORTUNITIES FOR PUBLIC HEALTH (1994). Publishes member newsletter (quarterly). Annual conference. Founded in 1974.

0623 **National Cable Television Cooperative, Inc.** 14809 W. 95th St., Lenexa, KS, 66215. Voice: 913-599-5900. Fax: 913-599-5903. e-mail: MEMP43A@PRODIGY.COM. Internet: www.cablevco-op.org. Cable industry's oldest and largest purchasing cooperative. Has as its major priority the negotiation of favorable contracts with basic and pay programmers. Intends to reduce the operating costs of membership that includes over 560 cable companies that provide basic cable television service to more than 5 million basic subscribers in over 2,800 systems spread across 49 states. Enters into a variety of master programming affiliation agreements and hardware group purchasing arrangements. Founded in 1984.

0624 **National Religious Broadcasters (NRB).** 7839 Ashton Ave., Manassas, VA 22110. Voice: 703-330-7000. Fax: 703-330-7100. Internet: www.nrb.com/nrb. 800 members. Annual budget $1.4 million. Organization devoted to safeguarding free and complete access to broadcast media for religious broadcasting. Supports rights of individuals, denominations, and other religious groups to purchase airtime and to use sustaining time on radio and television. Members include religious radio and television stations, program producers, and related organizations. Publishes RELIGIOUS BROADCASTING magazine (monthly), THE DIRECTORY OF RELIGIOUS MEDIA (annual), and member newsletter (bimonthly). Sponsors awards program and Hall of Fame. Provides regional chapters and college youth programs. Sponsors annual conference. Founded in 1944.

0625 **Radio-Television News Directors Association (RTNDA).** 1000 Connecticut Ave. NW, Ste. 615, Washington 20036-5302. Voice: 202-659-6510. Fax: 202-223-4007. Internet: rtnda@rtnda.org. 3600 members. Annual budget $1.9 million. Association serving electronic news profession. Members include news directors, electronic journalists, educators, and students. Monitors legislation and regulations affecting electronic news industry. Promotes electronic access to courtrooms, fights government efforts to control program content, and addresses ethical issues in the industry. Tracks trends in news profitability, salaries, staffing, and minority employment. Reports results in RTNDA COMMUNICATOR (monthly). Publishes CAMERAS IN THE COURTROOM (annual). Member services include faxed newsletter (RTNDA WEEKLY), JOB BULLETIN (biweekly), and jobline. Sponsors Edward R. Murrow Awards and the Paul White Award for achievements in electronic journalism. Sponsors annual conference. Maintains archives at University of Iowa in Iowa City. Founded in 1946 as the National Association of Radio News Directors; name changed in 1952.

5-C. Selected Secondary Resources

5-C-1. General Surveys

0626 Not used.

0627 Bogle, Donald. **BLACKS IN AMERICAN FILMS AND TELEVISION: AN ENCYCLOPEDIA**. New York: Simon & Schuster, 1988, 510 pp. Synopses of Black-oriented films and television programs with credits and critical commentary.

0628 Stedman, Raymond William. **THE SERIALS: SUSPENSE AND DRAMA BY INSTALLMENT**. Norman: University of Oklahoma Press, 1977, 574 pp. Historical study covering films, radio, and television. Appendices, bibliography, index.

5-C-2. Journalism and Newspapers

0629 Cook, Philip, Douglas Gomery and Lawrence Lichty, eds. **THE FUTURE OF NEWS: TELEVISION, NEWSPAPERS, WIRES, NEWSMAGAZINES.** Baltimore: Johns Hopkins University Press, 1992, 270 pp. Collection of 15 insightful papers including those arguing more TV may mean less news, the blurring of network vs. local news distinctions, and the rise of talk-show journalism. Useful context places television within other news media. Annotated bibliography, index.

0630 Cose, Ellis. **THE PRESS**. New York: William Morrow, 1989, 380 pp. Reviews work of editors at major national newspapers: *The Washington Post, Los Angeles Times, New York Times*, and the major group owners—Gannett and Knight-Ridder.

0631 Denton, Robert E., Jr., ed. **THE MEDIA AND THE PERSIAN GULF WAR**. New York: Praeger, 1993, 302 pp. Thirteen papers assess most aspects of press access to and reporting of the early 1991 war. Bibliographies, index.

0632 Fuller, Jack. **NEWS VALUES: IDEAS FOR AN INFORMATION AGE**. Chicago: University of Chicago Press, 1996, 251 pp. The publisher of the *Chicago Tribune* discusses underlying public values served by the press. Explores questions of credibility, matters of expression, profit margins, and the future of journalism.

0633 Hess, Stephen. **NEWSWORK.** Washington: Brookings, six vols. to date. Ongoing series of studies by a long-time observer and practitioner. These studies dissect the Washington news scene. The last volume collects previously issued essays. Notes, tables, statistics.

1 **THE WASHINGTON REPORTERS.** 1981, 174 pp.

2 **THE GOVERNMENT/PRESS CONNECTION.**1984, 160 pp.

3 **THE ULTIMATE INSIDERS: U.S. SENATORS IN THE NATIONAL MEDIA.** 1986, 151 pp.

4 **LIVE FROM CAPITOL HILL! STUDIES OF CONGRESS AND THE MEDIA.** 1991, 178 pp.

5 **INTERNATIONAL NEWS & FOREIGN CORRESPONDENTS.** 1996, 209 pp.

6 **NEWS & NEWSMAKING**. 1996, 148 pp.

0634 Koch, Tom. **JOURNALISM FOR THE 21st CENTURY: ONLINE INFORMATION, ELECTRONIC DATABASES, AND THE NEWS**. Westport, CT: Greenwood, 1991, 374 pp. Good analysis of the revolution that technology has caused in news research, gathering, and reporting. Notes, bibliography, appendix, index.

0635 Livingston, Steven. **THE TERRORISM SPECTACLE**. Boulder, CO: Westview, 1994, 220 pp. Discusses the relationship among foreign policy, media news reports, and terrorism. Notes, appendix, index.

0636 Paulos, John Allen. **A MATHEMATICIAN READS THE NEWSPAPER**. New York: Basic Books, 1995, 212 pp. A critique of numbers and statistics as used in a variety of journalistic reporting. Bibliography, index.

0637 Schudson, Michael. **THE POWER OF NEWS**. Cambridge, MA: Harvard University Press, 1995, 269 pp. Concepts of news, journalism, and information and society's need for interpretation of information.

0638 Smith, Hedrick, ed. **THE MEDIA AND THE GULF WAR: THE PRESS AND DEMOCRACY IN WARTIME.** Arlington, VA: Seven Locks, 1993, 438 pp. Documents and essays on the controversy over media access to and reporting of the military. Appendices.

0639 Weimann, Gabriel, and Conrad Winn. **THE THEATER OF TERROR: MASS MEDIA AND INTERNATIONAL TERRORISM**. White Plains, NY: Longman, 1994, 295 pp. Content analysis of two decades of terrorism as covered in major papers here and abroad. Tables, notes, index.

5-C-3. Political Communication

0640 Ansolabehere, Stephen, and Shanto Iyengar. **GOING NEGATIVE: HOW POLITICAL ADVERTISEMENTS SHRINK & POLARIZE THE ELECTORATE**. New York: Free Press, 1995, 243 pp. How negative advertising works to keep people home. Notes, index.

0641 Denton, Robert E., ed. **THE 1992 PRESIDENTIAL CAMPAIGN: A COMMUNICATION PERSPECTIVE**. Westport, CT: Praeger, 1994, 263 pp. All aspects of communication in the Bush–Clinton–Perot campaign. Bibliography, index.

0642 Diamond, Edwin, and Stephen Bates. **THE SPOT: THE RISE OF POLITICAL ADVERTISING ON TELEVISION**. Cambridge, MA: MIT Press, 1992 (3rd ed.), 418 pp. Now standard history first issued in 1984 that covers with good insight the 1952 through 1988 national campaigns. Photos, index.

0643 Graber, Doris A. **MASS MEDIA AND AMERICAN POLITICS** Washington: Congressional Quarterly, 1997 (5th ed.), 448 pp. Standard text treats media's role, influence, and coverage. Notes, bibliography, index.

0644 Kraus, Sidney., ed. **MASS COMMUNICATION AND POLITICAL INFORMATION PROCESSING**. Hillsdale, NJ: Erlbaum, 1990, 227 pp. Twelve research papers taking the term *politics* broadly. Index.

0645 **LET AMERICA DECIDE: THE REPORT OF THE TWENTIETH CENTURY FUND TASK FORCE ON PRESIDENTIAL DEBATES**. New York: Twentieth Century Fund, 1995, 187 pp. Useful survey of what has been done up to now and recommendations for future debates. Notes, index.

0646 Manheim, Jarol B. **ALL OF THE PEOPLE, ALL THE TIME: STRATEGIC COMMUNICATION AND AMERICAN POLITICS**. Armonk, NY: M.E. Sharpe, 1991, 255 pp. A book about modern political persuasion as practiced on and through the media rather than through the traditional political process. Notes, index.

0647 Nimmo, Dan, and James E. Combs. **MEDIATED POLITICAL REALITIES**. White Plains, NY: Longman, 1990, 242 pp. Basic text treatment of the interface between media and politics. Bibliography, index.

0648 Stempel, Guido H., and John W. Windhauser. **THE MEDIA IN THE 1984 AND 1988 PRESIDENTIAL CAMPAIGNS**. Westport, CT: Greenwood, 1991, 221 pp. Changes and trends in media use. Tables, bibliography, index.

5-C-4. Magazines

(Note: See 2-C-4 for extensive Greenwood Press series.)

5-C-5. Broadcasting

0649 Carroll, Raymond L., and Donald M. Davis. **ELECTRONIC MEDIA PROGRAMMING: STRATEGIES AND DECISION MAKING**. New York: McGraw-Hill, 1993, 532 pp. Multichapter sections on audience and program assessment, radio, television, and cable television including both local and national level program processes. Notes, illustrations, glossary, references, index.

0650 Eastman, Susan Tyler, ed. **BROADCAST/CABLE PROGRAMMING: STRATEGIES AND PRACTICES**. Belmont, CA: Wadsworth, 1997 (5th ed.), 588 pp. Includes such topics as the implications of compression technology on programming, public television's new process of program selection, and the role of the Fox network. The book's chapters are divided into five parts: programming resources and constraints, broadcast television, cable programming, commercial radio, and public broadcasting (radio and television) strategies. Glossary, bibliography, index.

0651 Erickson, Hal. **RELIGIOUS RADIO AND TELEVISION IN THE UNITED STATES, 1921–1991: THE PROGRAMS AND PERSONALITIES**. Jefferson, NC: McFarland, 1992, 264 pp. Alphabetically arranged with brief descriptions. Bibliography, index.

0652 Melton, J. Gordon et al. **PRIME-TIME RELIGION: AN ENCYCLOPEDIA OF RELIGIOUS BROADCASTING**. Phoeniz, AZ: Oryx Press, 1996, 368 pp. 416 pp. Over 400 entries covering people, programs, ministries, networks, and religious organizations.

0653 Vane, Edwin T., and Lynne S. Gross. **PROGRAMMING FOR TV, RADIO & CABLE**. Stoneham, MA: Focal Press, 1994, 258 pp. Broad textbook survey. Glossary, suggested readings, index.

5-C-6. Radio

i) "Old Time" Radio

0654 Buxton, Frank, and Bill Owen. **THE BIG BROADCAST: 1920–1950**. Metuchen, NJ: Scarecrow, 1997 (2nd ed.), 294 pp. Alphabetical listings of network and syndicated programs, with brief description and cast list. Bibliography, index.

0655 DeLong, Thomas A. **RADIO STARS: AN ILLUSTRATED BIOGRAPHICAL DICTIONARY OF 953 PERFORMERS, 1920 THROUGH 1960.** Jefferson, NC: McFarland, 1996. 306pp. Includes actors, singers, commentators, comedians, announcers, emcees, newscasters, preachers, and other artists who shaped and characterized the airwaves. Emphasizes performers' unique contributions to radio. Includes program credits.

0656 Doll, Bob. **SPARKS OUT OF THE PLOWED GROUND: THE HISTORY OF AMERICA'S SMALL TOWN RADIO STATIONS**. West Palm Beach, FL: Streamline Publishing, 1996, 322 pp. Informal account of the growth of radio from viewpoint of small market broadcaster.

0657 Dunning, John. **TUNE IN YESTERDAY: THE ULTIMATE ENCYCLOPEDIA OF OLD-TIME RADIO, 1925–1976**. Englewood Cliffs, NJ: Prentice-Hall, 1976, 703 pp. Annotated listing of network and syndicated drama, comedy, and variety programs. Index.

0658 Summers, Harrison B., ed. **A THIRTY-YEAR HISTORY OF PROGRAMS CARRIED ON NATIONAL RADIO NETWORKS IN THE UNITED STATES, 1926–1956.** New York: Arno, 1971, 228 pp. Originally published by Ohio State University Dept. of Speech, Columbus, 1958. Listings of programs carried during sample week, with sponsors, length, hour, rating.

0659 Swartz, Jon D., and Robert C. Reinehr. **HANDBOOK OF OLD-TIME RADIO: A COMPREHENSIVE GUIDE TO GOLDEN AGE RADIO LISTENING AND COLLECTING**. Metuchen, NJ: Scarecrow Press, 1993, 806 pp. Essays on old-time radio as a hobby and descriptions of better known programs broadcast between 1926 and 1962.

0660 Terrace, Vincent M. **RADIO'S GOLDEN YEARS: THE ENCYCLOPEDIA OF RADIO PROGRAMS 1930–1960**. San Diego: A.S. Barnes, 1981, 308 pp. Some 1,500 network and syndicated programs are briefly described.

ii) Contemporary Radio

0661 Halper, Donna L. **FULL-SERVICE RADIO: PROGRAMMING FOR THE COMMUNITY**. Stoneham, MA: Focal Press, 1991, 103 pp. Brief guide to practical aspects of "middle-of-the-road" stations. References, index.

0662 MacFarland, David T. **FUTURE RADIO PROGRAMMING STRATEGIES: CULTIVATING LISTENERSHIP IN THE DIGITAL AGE**. Mahwah, NJ: Erlbaum, 1997 (2nd ed.), 264 pp. One of the few serious studies of modern radio programming and strategy. Tables, notes, index.

0663 Norberg, Eric G. **RADIO PROGRAMMING: TACTICS AND STRATEGY**. Newton, MA: Focal Press, 1996, 191 pp. Lots of practical guidance and comment on the current commercial radio scene. Index.

5-C-7. Television

i) Television Journalism

0664 Campbell, Richard. **60 MINUTES AND THE NEWS: A MYTHOLOGY FOR MIDDLE AMERICA**. Urbana: University of Illinois Press, 1991, 279 pp. Argues there are at least four frames or approaches by which most of us see TV news: mystery, therapy, adventure, and arbitration. Notes, index.

0665 Cremer, Charles F. et al. **ENG: TELEVISION NEWS.** New York: McGraw-Hill, 1996 (3rd ed.), 441 pp. Combination of how-to and description of how electronic news gathering has changed the field. Photos, diagrams, glossary, bibliography, index

0666 Dayan, Daniel and Elihu Katz. **MEDIA EVENTS: THE LIVE BROADCASTING OF HISTORY**. Cambridge: Harvard University Press, 1992, 305 pp. How and why electronic media cover news and special events—and the impact of that (usually television) coverage. Notes, references, index.

0667 Dobkin, Bethami A. **TALES OF TERROR: TELEVISION NEWS AND THE CONSTRUCTION OF THE TERRORIST THREAT**. New York: Praeger, 1992, 133 pp. Content analysis of evening television news from 1981 to 1987 that details how television reacts to terrorist events and threats. Bibliography, index.

0668 Donahue, Hugh Carter. **THE BATTLE TO CONTROL BROADCAST NEWS: WHO OWNS THE FIRST AMENDMENT?** Cambridge, MA: MIT Press, 1989, 438 pp. Good overview of the major controversies in video journalism. Notes, index.

0669 Einstein, Daniel. **SPECIAL EDITION: A GUIDE TO NETWORK TELEVISION DOCUMENTARY SERIES AND SPECIAL NEWS REPORTS**. Metuchen, NJ: Scarecrow, 2 vols.: Describes television documentaries and special news programs over 35 years, with indexes.

1 **1955–1979.** 1987, 1051 pp. Covers 7,000 individual programs.

2 **1980–1989.** 1997, 870 pp. Adds 2,500 more programs.

0670 Goldberg, Robert, and Gerald Jay Goldberg. **ANCHORS: BROKAW, JENNINGS, RATHER AND THE EVENING NEWS**. New York: Birch Lane, 1990, 399 pp. Popular and useful survey of the rise, role, and decline of evening network TV newscasts. Photos, bibliography, index.

0671 Kellner, Douglas. **THE PERSIAN GULF TV WAR**. Boulder, CO: Westview, 1992, 460 pp. One of a small shelf of studies of the 1990–1991 conflict, this focuses on television. Photos, bibliography, index.

0672 Kimball, Penn. **DOWNSIZING THE NEWS: NETWORK CUTBACKS IN THE NATION'S CAPITAL**. Baltimore: Johns Hopkins University Press, 1994, 181 pp. The economic and other pressures squeezing the traditional television networks. Bibliography, index.

0673 Neuman, Johanna. **LIGHTS, CAMERA, WAR: IS MEDIA TECHNOLOGY DRIVING INTERNATIONAL POLITICS?** New York: St. Martin's Press, 1996, 327 pp. The foreign editor of *USA Today* argues that faster news reporting has impact on the political process. Photos, endnotes, index.

0674 Soley, Lawrence C. **THE NEWS SHAPERS: THE SOURCES WHO EXPLAIN THE NEWS**. New York: Praeger, 1992, 175 pp. Content analysis of network newscasts in 1987–1988 examines the fairly narrow sample of "experts" on whom networks rely to explain news events. References, appendix.

0675 Thaler, Paul. **THE WATCHFUL EYE: AMERICAN JUSTICE IN THE AGE OF THE TELEVISION TRIAL.** Westport, CT: Praeger, 1994, 239 pp. Case study of a New York murder trial enlightens this analysis of how televised trials impact news and the legal system. Notes, bibliography, index.

ii) Television Entertainment Directories

0676 Brooks, Tim, and Earle Marsh. **THE COMPLETE DIRECTORY OF PRIME-TIME NETWORK TV SHOWS, 1946–PRESENT**. New York: Ballantine, 1992 (5th ed.), 1,205 pp.

Annotated alphabetical listing over nearly five decades in what is perhaps the best of several available published listings. Index.

0677 Dintrone, Charles V. **TELEVISION PROGRAM MASTER INDEX: ACCESS TO CRITICAL AND HISTORICAL INFORMATION ON 1002 SHOWS IN 341 BOOKS**. Jefferson, NC: McFarland, 1996, 133 pp. Generally focused on network programs, excluding most syndicated or cable-only programs.

0678 Eagan, Daniel, ed. **HBO'S GUIDE TO MOVIES ON VIDEOCASSETTE AND CABLE TV**. New York: Harper Perennial, 1991 (2nd ed.), 857 pp. Over 7,000 entries for films available on tape. Intended to help viewers make informed decisions about television viewing. Each entry delineates title, release date, country of origin, rating, subject matter, run time, director, cast, and distributor. Also noted are production characteristics including color or B&W, closed captioning and subtitle information.

0679 Erickson, Hal. **SYNDICATED TELEVISION: THE FIRST FORTY YEARS, 1947–1987**. Jefferson, NC: McFarland, 1989, 424 pp. Brief program descriptions in chapters defined by decade and in sections by genre. Annotated bibliography, index.

0680 Gianakos, Larry James. **TELEVISION DRAMA SERIES PROGRAMMING: A COMPREHENSIVE CHRONICLE, 1947–1986.** Metuchen, NJ: Scarecrow, 1978–1992, 6 vols., 4,099 pp. A massive undertaking, this series (presumably to continue) lists every episode (and its cast) of every network dramatic series from the beginning. Brief program descriptions. Numerous appendices, index.

0681 Goldberg, Lee. **UNSOLD TELEVISION PILOTS 1955 THROUGH 1988**. Jefferson, NC: McFarland, 1990, 656 pp. Nearly 2,300 of them briefly described (arranged by year and network). Index.

0682 Marill, Alvin H. **MOVIES MADE FOR TELEVISION: THE TELEFEATURE AND THE MINI-SERIES 1964–1986**. New York: New York Zoetrope, 1987, 576 pp. Brief paragraphs and full credits for each.

0683 McNeil, Alex. **TOTAL TELEVISION: A COMPREHENSIVE GUIDE TO PROGRAMMING FROM 1948 TO THE PRESENT**. New York: Penguin Books, 1995 (4th ed.), 1,200 pp. Alphabetical listing of some 4,700 series with appendices on noteworthy specials, prime-time network schedules, Emmy and Peabody award winners, and top-rated series. Index of names.

0684 Parish, James Robert, and Vincent Terrace. **THE COMPLETE ACTORS' TELEVISION CREDITS, 1948–1988**. Metuchen, NJ: Scarecrow, 1989–1990 (2nd ed.), 2 vols., 1,007 pp. Covers the television work of some 1,587 actors and 1,739 actresses each of whom is listed with their television works.

0685 Shapiro, Mitchell E. **TELEVISION NETWORK...** Jefferson, NC:McFarland, 1989–1992, 3 vols. Offers detailed schedules in chart format and listings. Indexed.

1 **PRIME-TIME PROGRAMMING 1948–1988**, 1989, 743 pp.
2 **DAYTIME AND LATE-NIGHT PROGRAMMING 1959–1989**, 1990, 264 pp.
3 **WEEKEND PROGRAMMING 1959–1990**, 1992, 464 pp.

0686 Terrace, Vincent. **THE COMPLETE ENCYCLOPEDIA OF TELEVISION PROGRAMS 1947–1979.** South Brunswick, NJ: A.S. Barnes, 1979 (2nd ed.), 2 vols. Brief descriptions and major credits for each.

0687 _____. **ENCYCLOPEDIA OF TELEVISION SERIES, PILOTS AND SPECIALS.** New York: New York Zoetrope, 1986, three vols.

1 **1937–1973**. 480 pp.
2 **1974–1984.** 458 pp.
3 **THE INDEX: WHO'S WHO IN TELEVISION 1937–1984**. 662 pp. Detailed directory, covering some 8,000 programs and including casts and storylines, credits, network information, running times, and dates.

0688 _____. **TELEVISION CHARACTER AND STORY FACTS: OVER 110,000 DETAILS FROM 1,008 SHOWS, 1945–1992**. Jefferson, NC: McFarland, 1993, 539 pp. A narrative of the plots, storylines, and cast relationships associated with each of the included series and pilots.

0689 _____. **TELEVISION SPECIALS: 3,201 ENTERTAINMENT SPECTACULARS, 1939–1993**. Jefferson, NC: McFarland, 1995, 547 pp. Alphabetical listing of television specials showing cast and credits, dates, and running times. Name index.

iii) Television Entertainment Genre

(Note: In addition to the works cited there are many books about individual television series.)

0690 Adir, Karin. **THE GREAT CLOWNS OF AMERICAN TELEVISION**. Jefferson, NC: McFarland, 1988, 275 pp. Seventeen of them get a chapter each. Photos, notes, bibliography, index.

0691 Cassata, Mary, and Thomas Skill. **LIFE ON DAYTIME TELEVISION: TUNING-IN AMERICAN SERIAL DRAMA**. Norwood, NJ: Ablex, 1983, 214 pp. Twelve scholarly papers on most aspects of these programs. Bibliography, index.

0692 DeLong, Thomas A. **QUIZ CRAZE: AMERICA'S INFATUATION WITH GAME SHOWS.** New York: Praeger, 1991, 315 pp. Narrative history of their development. Appendix, notes, bibliography, index.

0693 Eisner, Joel, and David Krinsky. **TELEVISION'S COMEDY SERIES: AN EPISODE GUIDE TO 153 TV SITCOMS IN SYNDICATION**. Jefferson, NC: McFarland, 1984, 866 pp. Just that—after a description of the series, each episode is defined in a sentence or two. Index.

0694 Greenberg, Bradley S. **LIFE ON TELEVISION: CONTENT ANALYSIS OF U.S. TV DRAMA**. Norwood, NJ: Ablex, 1980, 220 pp. Focuses on four topics: pro- and antisocial behavior, portrayal of minorities, family structure, and sex roles. References, index.

0695 Klobas, Lauri E. **DISABILITY DRAMA IN TELEVISION AND FILM.** Jefferson, NC: McFarland, 1988, 477 pp. Unique resource discussing portrayal of a variety of disabilities in television drama.

0696 MacDonald, J. Fred. **WHO SHOT THE SHERIFF? THE RISE AND FALL OF THE TELEVISION WESTERN**. New York: Praeger, 1987, 159 pp. Analytical narrative on how the genre developed, prospered, and withered—and why. Tables, notes, bibliography, index. See also West, 0000.

0697 Marc, David, and Robert J. Thompson. **PRIME TIME, PRIME MOVERS: FROM *I LOVE LUCY* TO *L.A. LAW*—AMERICA'S GREATEST TV SHOWS AND THE PEOPLE WHO CREATED THEM**. Boston: Little, Brown, 1992, 336 pp. Long title sums it up—informal study of some 25 TV producers past and present and the programs they made, suggesting how the process works. Photos, index.

0698 Rose, Brian G., ed. **TV GENRES: A HANDBOOK AND REFERENCE GUIDE.** Westport, CT: Greenwood, 1985, 453 pp. Twenty chapters, each by a different expert, help explain many different program types. Bibliographic surveys, index.

0699 _____. **TELEVISION AND THE PERFORMING ARTS: A HANDBOOK AND REFERENCE GUIDE TO AMERICAN CULTURAL PROGRAMMING**. Westport, CT: Greenwood, 1986, 270 pp. Chapters on dance, classical music, opera, and theater on television. Index.

0700 Schemering, Christopher. **THE SOAP OPERA ENCYCLOPEDIA**. New York: Ballantine Books, 1985, 358 pp. Although dated, this remains a useful resource for programs to the mid-1980s.

0701 Schwartz, David, Steve Ryan, and Fred Wostbrock. **THE ENCYCLOPEDIA OF TV GAME SHOWS**. New York: New York Zoetrope, 1987, 587 pp. To that date, all are listed and annotated.

0702 Waldron, Vince. **CLASSIC SITCOMS: A CELEBRATION OF THE BEST PRIME-TIME COMEDY**. New York: MacMillan, 1987, 547 pp. An affectionate review of some of television's best efforts.

0703 West, Richard. **TELEVISION WESTERNS: MAJOR AND MINOR SERIES, 1946–1978**. Jefferson, NC: McFarland, 1987, 155 pp. Alphabetical program listing with descriptions and photos. Appendices, index. See also MacDonald, 0696.

0704 Woolery, George W. **ANIMATED TV SPECIALS: THE COMPLETE DIRECTORY TO THE FIRST TWENTY-FIVE YEARS, 1962–1987**. Metuchen, NJ: Scarecrow, 1989, 542 pp. Alphabetical directory, with photos and brief descriptions. Index.

iv) Children's Programming

0705 Davis, Jeffery. **CHILDREN'S TELEVISION, 1947–1990: OVER 200 SERIES, GAME AND VARIETY SHOWS, CARTOONS, EDUCATIONAL PROGRAMS AND SPECIALS**. Jefferson, NC: McFarland, 1995, 285 pp. Brief narratives on each program.

0706 Woolery, George W. **CHILDREN'S TELEVISION: THE FIRST THIRTY-FIVE YEARS, 1946–1981**. Metuchen, NJ: Scarecrow, 1983–1985 (2 vols.), 404 & 820 pp. First volume covers animated cartoons; the second deals with live, film, and taped series. Detailed description, cast, and credit lists. Chronology, indexes.

5-C-8. Cable and Newer Media

0707 The Annenberg Washington Program. **NEW VISIONS FOR VIDEO: USE OF CABLE, SATELLITE, BROADCAST, AND INTERACTIVE SYSTEMS FOR LITERACY AND LEARNING**. Washington: The Annenberg Washington Program, 1992, 88 pp. Three papers commissioned as discussion pieces for a workshop on video technologies focus on access, programming, and technology development. The workshop, co-sponsored by The Annenberg Washington Program and the Office of Technology Assessment (OTA), was part of the OTA Assessment of Technologies for Adult Literacy.

0708 Frantzich, Stephen, and John Sullivan. **THE C-SPAN REVOLUTION.** Norman: University of Oklahoma Press, 1996, 433 pp. First detailed study of the cable industry-supported public affairs network. Notes, index.

0709 Fuller, Linda K. **COMMUNITY TELEVISION IN THE UNITED STATES: A SOURCEBOOK ON PUBLIC, EDUCATIONAL, AND GOVERNMENTAL ACCESS**. Westport, CT: Greenwood Press, 1994, 280 pp. Overview and detailed information on community television, related organizations, and individuals. Discusses implications and predictions. Illustrations, appendices, glossary, bibliography, index.

0710 Goldberg, Kim. **THE BAREFOOT CHANNEL: COMMUNITY TELEVISION AS A TOOL FOR SOCIAL CHANGE**. Vancouver, CA: New Star Books, 1990, 176 pp. A narrative discussion of the history and potential of community television drawn from the author's three-year experience as community access TV channel coordinator.

0711 Gould, Dantia et. al. **THE PAY-PER-VIEW EXPLOSION**. York, ME: QV Publishing, Inc., 1991, 76 pp. Separate chapters discuss pay-per-view (PPV) genres from 1977 to 1991: sports, movies, music, marketing and promotion, technology. Summary of PPV market. Appendix provides directory information for satellite-delivered services, PPV movie sources, PPV sports distributors, and selected MSOs and PPV players. Tables, index.

0712 National Cable Television Association. **AMERICA'S STUDENTS: TRAVELERS ON CABLE'S INFORMATION HIGHWAY**. Washington: NCTA, 1993, 22 pp. This white paper provides statistics on cable television's contribution to education. Cites two key areas: educational resources and distance learning systems. After a brief overview, examples are cited in the following areas: interactive two-way educational networks, institutional networks, access channels, and statewide distance learning networks. The paper describes projects such as the TCI Education Project, X*PRESS X*CHANGE, and Mind Extension University. The appendix delineates education projects organized by cable television company within states.

6

Research and Audiences

Of the many bibliographies identified here, Shearer and Huxford's COMMUNICATION AND SOCIETY: A BIBLIOGRAPHY ON COMMUNICATIONS TECHNOLOGIES AND THEIR SOCIAL IMPACT (0732) perhaps best suggests the range of research efforts to understand the effects of communications technologies on audiences. Additionally, this chapter includes descriptions of the major scholarly and professional organizations that sponsor and publish research on all aspects of mass communications.

By far the most substantial research efforts have focused on television's effects on children. Schramm's THE EFFECTS OF TELEVISION ON CHILDREN AND ADOLESCENTS (0733) was a pioneering bibliographical effort of the 1960s. Each decade since then has seen other bibliographies on this subject. Signorelli's A SOURCEBOOK ON CHILDREN AND TELEVISION (0734) provides a useful synthesis of an enormous amount of research. The continuing timeliness of this topic is illustrated by its detailed coverage in any of several social sciences indexing and abstracting services, such as PSYCHOLOGICAL ABSTRACTS (0739).

6-A. Bibliographic Resources

6-A-1. Bibliographies

0713 Atkin, Charles K. et al. **TELEVISION AND SOCIAL BEHAVIOR: AN ANNOTATED BIBLIOGRAPHY OF RESEARCH FOCUSING ON TELEVISION'S IMPACT ON CHILDREN**. Rockville, MD: National Institute of Mental Health, 1971, 150 pp. Contains 300 annotated and 250 unannotated citations from a project related to the surgeon general's study of television and behavior. Author index.

0714 Austin, Bruce A. **THE FILM AUDIENCE: AN INTERNATIONAL BIBLIOGRAPHY OF RESEARCH**. Metuchen, NJ: Scarecrow Press, 1983, 177 pp. Some 1,200 annotated citations arranged by topic with title and author indexes.

0715 Comstock, George et al. **TELEVISION AND HUMAN BEHAVIOR**. Santa Monica, CA: Rand, 1975, 3 vols. To the time of its publication, this is a definitive treatment.

1 **A GUIDE TO THE PERTINENT SCIENTIFIC LITERATURE**, 345 pp. Some 2,300 items are listed in a master alphabetical bibliography followed by 11 specialized subject bibliographies. Author index.

2 **THE KEY STUDIES**, 251 pp. Examines 450 studies in considerable detail reviewing their findings and issues and trends in television research methodology. Author index.

3 **THE RESEARCH HORIZON, FUTURE AND PRESENT**, 120 pp. Describes studies then underway or projected. Appendices.

0716 Courtney, Alice E., and Thomas W. Whipple. **SEX STEREOTYPING IN ADVERTISING: AN ANNOTATED BIBLIOGRAPHY**. Cambridge, MA: Marketing Science Institute, 1980, 96 pp. Although dated, the entries are still of interest historically. The 253 sources, most of which are from the 1970s, are divided into eight broad subject classifications.

0717 Cutcliffe, Stephen H. et al. **TECHNOLOGY AND VALUES IN AMERICAN CIVILIZATION**. Detroit: Gale, 1980, 704 pp. American Studies Information Guide Series, 9. Classified annotated listing of literature addressing the "role of technology in American culture," both American attitudes toward technology as well as technology's influence and effects on the formation of values. Communications (pp. 313–331) includes radio and television. Author, title, subject indexes. Many cross references.

0718 Gordon, Thomas F., and Mary Ellen Verna, eds. **MASS COMMUNICATION EFFECTS AND PROCESSES: A COMPREHENSIVE BIBLIOGRAPHY, 1950–1975**. Beverly Hills, CA: Sage, 1978, 227 pp. About 2,700 items are listed (about 200 are annotated) in topical sections, with subject index and index of nonprimary authors. Begins with a brief survey of the quarter-century of literature listed.

0719 Hansen, Donald A., and J. Herschel Parsons, comps. **MASS COMMUNICATION: A RESEARCH BIBLIOGRAPHY**. Santa Barbara, CA: Glendessary Press, 1968, 144 pp. Some 3,000 subject-divided entries (not annotated) with author index.

0720 Hoban, C.F., and W.B. Van Ormer. **INSTRUCTIONAL FILM RESEARCH, 1918–1950**. Port Washington, NY: U.S. Naval Training Devices Center, 1951 (reprinted by Arno Press, 1971), 190 pp. Annotates and compares about 200 reports of pioneering research on the uses of motion pictures for training. Arranged in nine topical chapters assessing different aspects of the impact of instructional films. (See Reid and MacLennan, 0731, for later studies.)

0721 Langham, Josephine, and Janine Chrichley, comps. **RADIO RESEARCH: AN ANNOTATED BIBLIOGRAPHY 1975–1988**. Brookfield, VT: Avebury, 1989 (2nd ed.), 357 pp. Annotated entries for studies and reports on audience uses and perceptions of radio broadcasting. Sponsored by U.K.'s Independent Broadcasting Authority, and thus mostly British, but included here as there is little else available.

0722 Lent, John A. **WOMEN AND MASS COMMUNICATIONS: AN INTERNATIONAL ANNOTATED BIBLIOGRAPHY**. Westport, CT: Greenwood, 1991, 481 pp. First of its kind—covering all periods and countries with good author and subject indexes. Most of the more than 3,200 entries are annotated in topical and geographical arrangement. Indexed.

0723 McClusky, F. Dean. **THE A-V BIBLIOGRAPHY**. Dubuque, IA: Wm. C. Brown, 1950, 185 pp. Several hundred annotated entries arranged by level of educational use (primary, secondary); useful for finding early studies. Lacks overall index.

0724 **MEDIA RESEARCH INDEX 1950–1984: A LISTING OF MAJOR MEDIA RESEARCH STUDIES COMPILED BY NEWSWEEK**. New York: Newsweek, 1985, 25 pp. Useful short reference listing of corporate and industrial studies.

0725 Meringoff, Laurene, ed. **CHILDREN AND ADVERTISING: AN ANNOTATED BIBLIOGRAPHY**. New York: Children's Advertising Review Unit, Council of Better Business Bureaus, 1980, 87 pp. Several hundred items are described. Includes related references, bibliographies, relevant organizations, and a subject index.

0726 Meyer, Manfred, and Ursula Nissen. **EFFECTS AND FUNCTIONS OF TELEVISION, CHILDREN AND ADOLESCENTS: A BIBLIOGRAPHY OF SELECTED RESEARCH LITERATURE, 1970–1978.** Munich: K.G. Saur, 1979, 172 pp.

0727 Muller, Werner and Manfred Meyer, comps. **CHILDREN AND FAMILIES WATCHING TELEVISION: A BIBLIOGRAPHY OF RESEARCH ON VIEWING PROCESSES**. New York: Saur, 1985, 159 pp. First published in German. Classified listing of 450 international studies on children's reception processes, viewing situations, media education. Covers mainly 1975–1985. Keyword descriptions.

0728 Murray, John P. **TELEVISION & YOUTH: 25 YEARS OF RESEARCH & CONTROVERSY**. Boys Town, NE: Boys Town Center for the Study of Youth Development, 1980, 278 pp.

Multinational review of research on television between 1955 and 1980. Bibliographical essay assessing TV's impact on the young is followed by 3,000 citations classified into 13 subject headings. Some non-English sources.

0729 Ohliger, John, and David Gueulette. **MEDIA AND ADULT LEARNING: A BIBLIOGRAPHY WITH ABSTRACTS, ANNOTATIONS AND QUOTATIONS**. New York: Garland, 1975, 486 pp. About 1,600 citations are divided into 59 categories—but no overall index.

0730 Ramey, James W. **TELEVISION IN MEDICAL TRAINING AND RESEARCH: A SURVEY AND ANNOTATED BIBLIOGRAPHY**. Washington: GPO, 1965, 155 pp. Covers the two postwar decades with an overall essay followed by research bibliography divided by topic.

0731 Reid, J. Christopher, and Donald W. MacLennan. **RESEARCH IN INSTRUCTIONAL TELEVISION AND FILM**. Washington: GPO, 1967, 216 pp. An Office of Education study indexes and annotates about 330 studies done after 1950. (See Hoban and Van Ormer, 0720, for earlier material.)

0732 Shearer, Benjamin F., and Marilyn Huxford. **COMMUNICATION AND SOCIETY: A BIBLIOGRAPHY ON COMMUNICATIONS TECHNOLOGIES AND THEIR SOCIAL IMPACT**. Westport, CT: Greenwood, 1983, 242 pp. Arranges unannotated entries for 2,732 books and articles in chapters on development, influence, social impact, and politics. Useful author and subject indexes.

0733 Schramm, Wilbur. **THE EFFECTS OF TELEVISION ON CHILDREN AND ADOLESCENTS: AN ANNOTATED BIBLIOGRAPHY WITH AN INTRODUCTORY OVERVIEW OF RESEARCH RESULTS**. Paris: UNESCO *Reports and Papers on Mass Communication* No. 43, 1964, 54 pp. Title sums it up. Useful for early studies.

0734 Signorelli, Nancy, comp. **A SOURCEBOOK ON CHILDREN AND TELEVISION**. Westport, CT: Greenwood, 1991, 199 pp. Good subject-divided narrative review of the massive literature, with references. Indexed.

0735 _____, and George Gerbner, eds. **VIOLENCE AND TERROR IN THE MASS MEDIA: AN ANNOTATED BIBLIOGRAPHY**. Westport, CT: Greenwood, 1988, 233 pp. Over 700 items, many issued in the 1980s, are included in this subject-divided and indexed guide.

0736 Wolf, Michelle A., and Deanna Morris. **RESOURCES ON CHILDREN AND TELEVISION. FACTFILE #19**. Los Angeles: American Film Institute, 1989. Suggests both primary and secondary resources.

0737 Zureik, Elia, and Dianne Hartling. **SOCIAL CONTEXT OF THE NEW INFORMATION AND COMMUNICATION TECHNOLOGIES: A BIBLIOGRAPHY.** New York: Peter Lang, 1987, 310 pp. (*American University Studies: Series XV, Communications, 2*). Alphabetical listing of over 6,500 items on "social impact of information and communication technology," referenced by over 50 subject codes. Good coverage of U.S. and Canadian documents.

6-A-2. Abstracts, Indexes, Databases

See 0035. COMMUNICATION ABSTRACTS

0738 **CURRENT INDEX TO JOURNALS IN EDUCATION (CIJE)**. Phoenix, AZ: Oryx Press, 1969–date, monthly, with semiannual cumulations. Online version ERIC available from Ovid, Dialog, OCLC, and other services: covers 1966–date, updated monthly. CD-ROM version ERIC available from SilverPlatter, Knight-Ridder, Ovid, National Information Services Corporation (NISC), U.S. Department of Education, and other vendors: covers 1966–date, updated quarterly. Useful for coverage of scholarly and research literature on educational communication and information technology. Abstracts articles, with author and subject indexes, that are published in about 750 journals. Selectively indexes journals on mass media, with emphasis on media education, including AMERICAN JOURNAL OF DISTANCE EDUCATION and EC&TJ: EDUCATIONAL COMMUNICATION AND TECHNOLOGY JOURNAL. ERIC's complementary RESOURCES IN EDUCATION (RIE) (Washington: GPO, 1966–date) indexes other separately published ERIC documents, including all refereed papers presented at the annual meeting of the Association for Education in Journalism and Mass Communication (if the authors submit the papers to ERIC). Electronic versions cumulate CIJE and RIE.

See 0743. DISSERTATION ABSTRACTS INTERNATIONAL.

0739 **PSYCHOLOGICAL ABSTRACTS**. Lancaster, PA: American Psychological Association, 1927–date, monthly. Online version PSYCHINFO available from Dialog, OCLC, Ovid, and other services: covers 1967–date, updated monthly. CD-ROM version PSYCHLIT available from SilverPlatter: covers 1974–date, updated quarterly. The major index of psychology's research literature; also indexes core of mainstream mass communication journals, including COMMUNICATION EDUCATION, COMMUNICATION RESEARCH (1165), and JOURNAL OF COMMUNICATION (1173). Important indexing for scholarship and research on media content and impact of media on individuals, groups, and society. Detailed abstracts. Monthly issues include name and brief subject indexes; cumulative annual subject indexes are more detailed. Relevant subject headings include communications media, content analysis, and persuasive communications, as well as specific print and electronic media. Electronic versions offer superior access.

0740 **SOCIAL SCIENCE CITATION INDEX**. Philadelphia: Institute for Scientific Information, 1973–date, 3/year. Online version SOCIAL SCISEARCH available from Dialog and other services: covers 1972–date, updated weekly. CD-ROM version SOCIAL SCIENCES CITATION INDEX COMPACT DISC EDITION available from Institute for Scientific Information (ISI): covers 1986–date, updated quarterly. Interrelated source, citation, and "Permuterm" indexes analyze a wide range of scholarly and professional journals also covered by several of ISI's CURRENT CONTENTS series (0038). Particulary strong in marketing, management, and media uses and effects, covering journals like COMMUNICATION MONOGRAPHS, CRITICAL STUDIES IN MASS COMMUNICATION (1167), EDUCATIONAL COMMUNICATION AND TECHNOLOGY JOURNAL, INFORMATION AGE, JOURNAL OF ADVERTISING, JOURNAL OF ADVERTISING RESEARCH, JOURNAL OF BROADCASTING AND ELECTRONIC MEDIA (1209), and MEDIA, CULTURE, AND SOCIETY (1181). Availability of key word and subject field searching in electronic versions of indexes like HUMANITIES INDEX (0044) and PSYCHOLOGICAL ABSTRACTS (0739) marginalizes usefulness of ISI's "Permuterm" system. On the other hand, the importance of this resource cannot be overemphasized: It is essential for influence studies, identifying authors and works that have been cited in other research. Electronic versions greatly simplify use.

0741 **SOCIAL SCIENCES INDEX**. New York: H. W. Wilson, 1974–date, quarterly. Online version available from Wilsonline, OCLC, Ovid, and other services: covers 1983–date, updated twice weekly. CD-ROM version available from H. W. Wilson, Ovid, and SilverPlatter: covers 1983–date, updated monthly. For more information, see Wilson's homepage: www.hwwilson.com. Offers subject indexing of major scholarly journals in psychology, sociology, economics, political science, and education; useful for educational, psychological, political, and sociological research on applications, contents, and effects of new communication technologies. Indexes core mass communication journals, including COMMUNICATION RESEARCH (1165), JOURNAL OF BROADCASTING & ELECTRONIC MEDIA (1209), and POLITICAL COMMUNICATION. Features on advertising and political communication also appear frequently in indexed journals like AMERICAN DEMOGRAPHICS, PUBLIC OPINION QUARTERLY, and POLITICAL SCIENCE QUARTERLY. Formerly INTERNATIONAL INDEX (1906–1965) and SOCIAL SCIENCES AND HUMANITIES INDEX (1965–1974); older volumes important for historical research. Good source for identifying research on perennial media issues such as tobacco and alcoholic beverage advertising, sex role/racial stereotyping in the media, and television's influence on children.

0742 **SOCIOLOGICAL ABSTRACTS**. San Diego, CA: Sociological Abstracts, 1952–date, 5/year. Online version SOCIOFILE available from Ovid, Dialog, and OCLC: covers 1963–date, updated 6/year. CD-ROM version SOCIOFILE available from SilverPlatter: covers 1974–date, updated 3/year. Useful for analyses of scholarly research literature on media effects and the role of media in society and culture. Indexes major mass communication research journals, including COMMUNICATION MONOGRAPHS and JOURNAL OF BROADCASTING & ELECTRONIC MEDIA (1209). Category of "Mass Phenomena" includes subdivisions for communication and mass culture. Detailed subject indexing with cross references. Source list. Supplementary IRPS (International Review of Publications in Sociology) service lists. Abstracts books and book reviews; author and source indexes.

6-A-3. Theses and Dissertations

0743 **DISSERTATION ABSTRACTS INTERNATIONAL.** Ann Arbor, MI: University Microfilms, 1938–date, monthly. Online version available from Dialog, Ovid, OCLC, and other services: covers 1861–date, updated monthly. CD-ROM version available from University Microfilms International (UMI) and Ovid: covers 1861–date, updated quarterly. Identifies academic research in all aspects of mass communication. Monthly classified listing of doctoral dissertations, with abstracts of up to 350 words by the degree candidates, deposited for microfilming and sale by UMI. Section A (for humanities and social sciences) includes Communications and the Arts, with subdivisions for cinema, journalism, mass communications (which covers public relations); advertising included in section for marketing under business administration. Section B (sciences and engineering) includes subdivisions for acoustics, electrical engineering, and other technical fields. Separate author and key word indexes. Cumulated in COMPREHENSIVE DISSERTATION INDEX, 1861–1972 (Ann Arbor, MI: Xerox University Microfilms, 1973), with annual volumes (Ann Arbor, MI: Xerox University Microfilms, 1974–date), arranged by subject discipline with key-word and cumulative author indexes.

0744 Fielding, Raymond. **A BIBLIOGRAPHY OF THESES AND DISSERTATIONS ON THE SUBJECT OF FILM: 1916–1979**. Houston: University of Houston and University Film Association (Monograph No. 3), 1979, 70 pp. About 1,400 are listed alphabetically, with indexing.

0745 **JOURNALISM AND MASS COMMUNICATIONS ABSTRACTS**. Columbia, SC: Association for Education in Journalism and Mass Communication, 1963–date, annual. Indexes and abstracts dissertations and theses in journalism and mass communication from universities in U.S. and Canada, with abstracts written by the degree candidates. Indexes for authors, degree-granting institutions, and subjects.

0746 Kittross, John M. **A BIBLIOGRAPHY OF THESES AND DISSERTATIONS IN BROADCASTING: 1920–1973**. Washington: Broadcast Education Association, 1978, 200 pp. About 4,300 are listed alphabetically with subject indexes. While dated, this remains the most complete listing of early dissertations available.

6-A-4. Directories

0747 American Marketing Association, New York Chapter. **THE 1995–1996 GREENBOOK: INTERNATIONAL DIRECTORY OF MARKETING RESEARCH COMPANIES AND SERVICES**. New York: AMA, New York Chapter, annual (33rd ed.). 612 pp. Alphabetical listings provide standard directory information and description of services. Cross referenced by geographic area and principal personnel.

See 0922. GOVERNMENT RESEARCH DIRECTORY.

0748 **RESEARCH SERVICES DIRECTORY**. Detroit: Gale, 1981–date, irregular. Online version available on Dialog. 6th ed. for 1995 describes over 4,400 U.S. commercial firms and laboratories, including corporations, that conduct proprietary and nonproprietary research. Entries give brief data, including annual research budgets. Geographical, name, subject, and other indexes. Listings under advertising, electronic publishing, propaganda, public relations, radio communication, satellites, and video technology.

6-B. Research Organizations

6-B-1. Corporate Research

0749 **The Arbitron Company.** 142 West 57th St., New York, NY 10019. Voice: 212-887-1300. Fax: 212-887-1401. Offices in Chicago, Atlanta, Los Angeles, Dallas, Washington/Baltimore. Radio ratings and market research service. Uses written diaries to measure radio listenership in 12-week survey periods in over 260 markets. Publishes results in the RADIO MARKET REPORT, known as "The Book" (twice a year in 80 markets and annually in the others). Offers qualitative measurement in 97 markets through RetailDirect and Scarborough, services that measure radio listening, television viewing, and print readership and profile the shopping and purchasing behavior of audiences and readers. Provides personal computer applications. Publishes radio planning tools for subscribers including METRO MARKET GUIDE (mid-1980s–date, annual) a detailed market profile; RADIO USA (mid-1970s–date, quarterly), an overview of listening estimates for each market; RADIO MARKET SURVEY AREA GUIDE, (late 1970s–date, annual), RADIO COUNTY AND CITY DIRECTORY (1995–date, annual, formerly two publications: RADIO AND TELEVISION CITY BOOK and RADIO COUNTY DIRECTORY), which lists counties with corresponding Metro, TSA and DMA; RADIO METRO AND TELEVISION MARKET POPULATION ESTIMATES (1994–1995–date, semiannual, formerly two publications: RADIO METRO AND ADI MARKET POPULATION BOOK and UNIVERSE ESTIMATE SUMMARY BOOK), summary of total, Black and Hispanic population estimates for Arbitron Radio Metro Survey Areas and Television DMA Markets; HISPANIC RADIO MARKET REPORTS (1989–date, annual); BLACK RADIO MARKET REPORT TAPES (1989–date, annual); MARKET SURVEY SCHEDULE & POPULATION RANKINGS (early 1970s–date, annual); DESCRIPTION OF METHODOLOGY (1970s–date, variable; latest edition 1992), detailed description of methodology used in production of Arbitron Radio Market Reports; A GUIDE TO UNDERSTANDING AND USING RADIO AUDIENCE ESTIMATES (1986–date, variable; latest edition 1996); RADIO TODAY (1982–date, variable; latest edition 1995, title varies), a summary of America's radio listening habits. Publishes BEYOND THE RATINGS (BTR; 1978–date, quarterly), a client-service magazine. Published MEDIA TARGETING 2000: A NATIONAL STUDY OF CONSUMERS AND MEDIA (with Radio Advertising Bureau; 1995), a report on the media habits and consumer profiles of 116 consumer groups. Founded in 1949 as the American Research Bureau (ARB) to provide a syndicated TV rating service. Launched radio measurement in 1964. Name changed to Arbitron in 1973. Dropped television ratings service at end of 1993.

0750 **Bruskin/Goldring Research Inc.** Metroplex Corporate Center, 100 Metroplex Drive, Edison, NJ 08817. Voice: 908-572-7300. Fax: 908-572-7980. Market research firm commissioned by Television Bureau of Advertising to measure media preferences of U.S. adults with four major media and time spent with television, newspapers, radio, and magazines daily. Publishes results (1970–date) in periodically issued study most recently entitled MEDIA COMPARISONS STUDY (1995). Founded in 1958 as R. H. Bruskin Associates; became Bruskin Research in 1987 and Bruskin/Goldring Research in 1992.

0751 **Electronic Media Rating Council**. 200 West 57th St., Ste. 204, New York 10019. Voice: 212-765-0200. Fax: 212-765-1868. 37 members. Annual budget under $500,000. Independent industry association that seeks to maintain audience research confidence and credibility by securing valid, reliable, and effective audience measurement services. Accredits rating services and pursues relevant research issues. Members include advertising agencies, broadcasting and cable networks, media companies, and associations. Founded in 1964 as the Broadcast Rating Council; took present name in 1982.

0752 **International Demographics, Inc**. 3355 West Alabama, Ste. 500, Houston, TX 77098-1718. Voice: 713-626-0333. Fax: 713-626-0418. Consumer research firm whose primary product is THE MEDIA AUDIT, a multimedia, qualitative audience survey conducted in 70 markets throughout 33 states. Measures audience for local radio stations, local TV newscasts, cable TV networks, and daily newspapers. Founded in 1971.

0753 **Mediamark Research Inc**. 708 Third Ave., 8th Fl., New York 10017. Voice: 212-476-0271. Fax: 212-682-6284. Consumer research service producing marketing and media data for advertisers, ad agencies, and media companies. Provides data on product consumption and on media exposure to print, radio, television, cable, outdoor, and yellow pages. NATIONAL STUDY, Mediamarks's primary study (semiannual, 1979–date), surveys 20,000 adults and includes demographics, media usage, product consumption/purchase, activities, and lifestyles. Also publishes TEENMARK (annual, 1991–date), which surveys persons age 12–19; TWELVEPLUS (annual,1992–date), covering all persons 12+. Other studies include CABLEREPORT/CABLEPRO (1991–date, annual) and CUSTOM CABLE STUDY (1993–date, annual), measuring cable viewing; and UPFRONT STUDY (1991–date, annual), which measures new season TV program viewing. Software applications available to subscribers. Founded in 1979.

See 0512. National Association of Broadcasters.

0754 **Nielsen Media Research.** 299 Park Ave., New York 10171. Voice: 212-708-7500. Fax: 212-708-7795. A market research and television ratings service. Uses Nielsen People Meter, set-tuning meter, and paper diary methods to measure household and person audiences. NIELSEN TELEVISION INDEX (NTI) (1950–date) uses People Meter to measure daily and weekly tv viewing and national network program audiences. NIELSEN STATION INDEX (NSI; 1954–date) estimates local audiences in over 200 markets using diary measurement four times yearly during "sweep" months. Other services include NIELSEN HOMEVIDEO INDEX (NHI; 1980–date) measuring cable and VCR usage; NIELSEN SYNDICATION SERVICE (NSS; 1985–date); NIELSEN HISPANIC TELEVISION INDEX (NHTI) (1992–date); NIELSEN HISPANIC STATION INDEX (NHSI; 1992–date); and NIELSEN METERED MARKET SERVICE (1959–date) providing daily and weekly reports on audiences in 33 local markets. Also provides personal computer applications. Supplementary client reports include CABLE TV: A STATUS REPORT (1979–date, quarterly), reporting on the impact of cable on television broadcasting; VCR TRACKING REPORT (1984–date, annual) reporting trends of VCR usage; THE (NATIONAL) SPORTS REPORT (1984–date, quarterly), summarizing network and syndicated sports programming audiences; and NATIONAL CABLE SPORTS REPORT (1994–date, quarterly). Also publishes TELEVISON AUDIENCE (1960–date, annual), a compendium of audience data including trends on television ownership, population growth, households and persons viewing, and programming trends. Publications available to nonclients include NIELSEN REPORT ON TELEVISION (1956–1992, annual; various titles), a graphic report on trends in television including set ownership and station/channel growth as well as tv usage and program viewing patterns; WHAT TV RATINGS REALLY MEAN (1995); NIELSEN TUNES IN TO POLITICS: TRACING THE PRESIDENTIAL ELECTION YEARS 1960–1992 (1993); POCKET GUIDE TO TV TERMS (1994); U.S. TV HOUSEHOLD ESTIMATES (1954–date, annual; various titles). Founded in 1936 by Arthur C. Nielsen, Sr., as one of the first research companies to measure radio audiences (a service discontinued in 1964). Nielsen began television audience measurement in 1950.

0755 **Roper Starch Worldwide.** 205 East 42nd St., New York 10017. Voice: 212-599-0700. Fax: 212-867-7008. Marketing and media research firm. Tracks role of television in lives of Americans. Publishes report (1959–date, biennial) on public's attitude toward television, initiated and supported by Television Information Office (now defunct) until 1989. Most recent is AMERICA'S WATCHING: PUBLIC ATTITUDES TOWARD TELEVISION (1995) and was co-sponsored by Network Television Association (now defunct) and National Association of Broadcasters. Prior to 1971 studies were conducted by Roper Research Associates, (formerly Elmo Roper and Associates); became Roper Organization in 1971; current name ca 1994.

0756 **Scarborough Research Corporation.** 11 West 42nd St., New York 10036-8088. Voice: 212-789-3666. Fax: 212-789-3577. Market research firm. Provides demographic and media usage for 59 markets. Measures shopping and purchase behavior along with radio listening, television viewing, and print readership. Founded in 1975; affiliated with Birch in mid-1980s; became a joint venture between Arbitron (0749) and VNU in 1992.

0757 **Simmons Market Research Bureau.** 309 West 49th St., New York 10019. Voice: 212-373-8900. Fax: 212-373-8918. Offices in Los Angeles and Chicago. Market research firm. Measures lifestyles, brand preferences, leisure activities, and media usage of children, teenagers, adults, senior citizens, ethnic groups, computer professionals, and top management. Publications and services include SIMMONS STUDY OF MEDIA AND MARKETS (SMM; annual with semi-annual update, ca 1962–date), which measures product, service, and media usage of Americans 18+; THE KIDS STUDY, (biannual 1991–date), which measures product, brand, and media choices of children 6–14; SIMMONS TEENAGE RESEARCH STUDY (STARS; biannual 1988–date); THE HISPANIC STUDY (annual 1995–date), which measures media habits and preferences of Hispanics. Founded in 1962.

0758 **Statistical Research, Inc. (SRI).** 111 Prospect St., Westfield, NJ 07090. Phone: 908-654-4000. Fax: 908-654-6498. Internet: www.sriresearch.com. Designs and conducts professional research including media audience measurement. Conducts Radio's All Dimension Audience Research (RADAR; 1972–date, twice annually) which measures network radio audiences. Serves as consultant to Committee on Nationwide Television Audience Measurement (CONTAM), an industry group concerned with TV ratings, for whom it operates S.M.A.R.T. (Systems for Measuring and Reporting Television), an industrywide effort to modernize TV ratings. Prepares TELEVISION OWNERSHIP SURVEY (1981–date, annual) which includes ownership estimates of newer video technologies including cable, pay cable, and videocassette recorders for CONTAM as well as HOME TECHNOLOGY STUDY (1994–date, annual) which measures telephone and computer characteristics of the population. Founded in 1969.

6-B-2. University-Based Research

(See also: 6-A-3 for Theses and Dissertations; 7-C-1, Policy Research Organizations)

0759 **Bowling Green State University**. Center for Study of Popular Culture, Popular Culture Center, Bowling Green, OH 43402. Voice: 419-372-2981. Fax: 419-372-8095. Studies popular culture and folklore as portrayed in movies, radio, television, magazines, popular books, popular religions, nonintellectual history, and languages, including studies on relationship of popular culture in America with process of Americanization abroad. Publishes JOURNAL OF POPULAR CULTURE (1177); POPULAR MUSIC AND SOCIETY (quarterly); JOURNAL OF AMERICAN CULTURE (quarterly) and others. Maintains collection of popular fiction and popular music, including 100,000 books and 500,000 phonograph records. Founded in 1967.

0760 **Cleveland State University.** Communication Research Center, Department of Communication, 1860 E. 22nd St., Cleveland, OH 44115. Voice: 216-687-4636. Concerned with computer-assisted telephone interviewing of media audiences. Issues occasional CRC MONOGRAPHS.

0761 **Columbia University.** Alfred I. duPont Center for Broadcast Journalism, Graduate School of Journalism, 2950 Broadway, Rm. 701, New York 10027. Voice: 212-854-5047, Fax: 212-854-7837. Considers important issues of policy and practice in the field of television and radio news, administers annual duPont-Columbia awards in television and radio journalism, and holds forums on issues of importance to journalists especially in the electronic media. Holds annual conference and awards ceremony. Founded in 1942.

0762 **Florida State University.** Communication Research Center, College of Communication, 426 Diffenbaugh Bldg., R-42, Tallahassee, FL 32306-2064. Voice: 904-644-8742, Fax: 904-644-8642. e-mail: eforrest@mailer.fsu.edu. Studies communication processes, particularly studies on new communication technologies, interactive communication, communication policy issues, target audiences for political activities, marketing communications, and audiences for public service campaigns; analysis of television advertising, content of commercial and public broadcasting programs, and effects of mass media.

0763 **Fordham University**. McGannon Communication Research Center, Bronx, NY 10458. Voice: 718-817-4195. Fax: 718-817-4868. Studies communication policy and ethics, roles of media in the community, popular culture, and moral values. Specific projects have included studies of fiber optic technology and public policy, television hiring practices and the status of women and minorities, and ethical dilemmas of television professionals. Founded in 1986.

0764 **Harvard University.** Joan Shorenstein Center on the Press, Politics, and Public Policy, John F. Kennedy School of Government, 79 John F. Kennedy St., Cambridge, MA 01238. Voice: 617-495-8269. Fax: 617-495-8696. Dedicated to study of press and politics, graduate education, and training for leadership in public service and employment in press and politics. Supervises a graduate degree program in the public policy program. Twelve fellowships are granted annually to journalists and scholars to research and write about the intersection of press and politics. Publishes occasional reports of lectures and programs at the center. Founded in 1986.

0765 **Indiana State University.** Center for Communication Research. Reeve 424, Terre Haute, IN 47809. Voice: 812-237-3257. Fax: 812-237-4361. e-mail: cmmillar@ruby.indstate.edu. Researches communication issues, including apprehension and competence, personality and television viewing, film genres, communication ethics, crisis communication, and communication competence of managers. Founded in 1984.

0766 **Indiana University.** Bureau of Media Research, School of Journalism, Ernie Pyle Hall 212, Bloomington, IN 47405. Fax: 812-855-5678. e-mail: wilhoitc@journalism.indiana.edu. Focuses on process and effects of mass communication and journalism, including study of journalists and news organizations, evaluation of media performance, research on information seeking, and analysis of newspaper and television content. Founded in 1954.

0767 **Marquette University.** Center for Mass Media Research, College of Communication. 1131 W. Wisconsin Ave., Milwaukee, WI 53233. Voice: 414-288-6787, Fax: 414- 288-3099. e-mail: 6710griffinr@vms.csd.mu.edu Conducts social scientific research into the roles, processes, uses, and effects of mass communication among individuals and in society. Founded as Center for Study of the American Press in 1964.

0768 **Massachusetts Institute of Technology**. The Media Laboratory, 20 Ames St., Cambridge, MA 02139. Voice: 617-253-0338. Fax: 617-258-6264. With a staff of more than 200, the Media Lab studies new information technologies in electronic media, publishing, cinema, visual arts, and music, including computer music, image processing, computer graphics, human–machine interface, art and technology, electronic publishing, and information technology. Founded in 1985.

0769 **Michigan State University**. Communications Technology Laboratory. East Lansing, MI 48824. Voice: 517-353-3794. Fax: 517- 353-5498. Conducts research on virtual reality, multimedia, and other information technologies. Founded in 1984.

0770 **New York University**.

1 Center for War, Peace, and the News Media, 10 Washington Pl., 4th Fl., New York 10003. Voice: 212-998-7960, Fax: 212-995-4143. Studies news media coverage of U.S.–Soviet relations, nuclear issues, arms control, and other international security issues, including the environment. Issues DEADLINE (bimonthly journalism review), Occasional Papers, and Conference Proceedings. Founded in 1985.

2 News Study Group, Dept. of Journalism, 10 Washington Pl., New York 10003. Voice: 212-998-7978, Fax: 212-995-4148. Analyzes contemporary media, media criticism, and media coverage of significant political events and issues. Founded in 1972.

0771 **Ohio University.** Institute for Telecommunications Studies, Athens, OH 45701. Voice: 614-593-4870. Fax: 614-593-9184. Studies international social impact of mass communications, economic and management aspects of broadcasting and cable television industry, emerging technologies, computer applications, multimedia TV, and training. Founded as Broadcast Research Center in 1959.

0772 **Rutgers University.** Center for Environmental Communication, Cook College, P.O. Box 231, New Brunswick, NJ 08903-0231. Voice: 908-932-8795, Fax: 908-932-7815. Part of the Agricultural Experiment Station and the Edward J. Bloustein School of Planning and Public Policy and supported by federal and state governments, and foundations, the Center is concerned with improving communication of environmental issues, including understanding the public's response to risk, assessing communication approaches, environmental risk reporting, managing risk communication and documenting risk communication efforts. Issues research papers, reports, and books. Holds training workshops for industry governmental agencies. Founded as the Environmental Communication Research Program in 1987.

0773 **Stanford University.** Institute for Communication Research, Dept. of Communication, Stanford, CA 94305. Voice: 415-723-3696, Fax: 415-725-2472. Research areas include health communication, communication and children, social and economic impacts of new technologies, the information society, media and politics, and psychological processing of media. Founded in 1955.

0774 **Texas Tech University.** Institute for Communications Research, School of Mass Communication, P.O. Box 43082, Lubbock, TX 79409. Voice: 806-742-2315, Fax: 806-742-1085. Includes Advertising Research Center, Telecommunications Research Center, Speech Communications Research Center, and Journalism Research Center. Wide-ranging projects include public opinion and consumer surveys, communication experiments, economic and policy studies, television/radio production and testing, and studies on communication immunization and functions, and television personality and viewers' preference. Founded in 1972.

0775 **University of Colorado at Boulder.** Center for Mass Media Research, School of Journalism & Mass Communications, Boulder, CO 80309. Voice: 303-492-1357. Research on mass communications, including information campaigns and the evolution of media industries. Founded in 1988.

0776 **University of Connecticut.** Roper Center for Public Opinion Research, Inc., P.O. Box 440, Storrs, CT 06268. Voice: 203-486-4440, Fax: 203-486-6308. e-mail: testsfs@uconnvm.uconn.edu. Part of the university's Institute for Social Inquiry conducts public opinion research on social and political attitudes and behavior; also studies public affairs, public policy, and mass media. Maintains archive of public opinion information, which includes survey response data on computer tapes for over 10,000 surveys conducted in U.S. and 70 other countries from 1936 to present. Public Opinion Location Library (POLL) offered online directly and through Dialog and LEXIS/NEXIS. Offers customized searches. Founded in 1946.

0777 **University of Florida.**

1 Brechner Center for Freedom of Information, College of Journalism and Communications, 3208 Weimer Hall, Gainesville, FL 32611-2084. Voice: 904-392-2273, Fax: 904-392-3919. e-mail: schance@jou.ufl.edu. Studies mass media law, the First Amendment, and open records and meetings laws. Issues THE BRECHNER REPORT (monthly). Founded in 1977 as Florida Freedom of Information Clearinghouse.

2 Communication Research Center, College of Journalism and Communications, Gainesville, FL 32611. Voice: 904- 392-6660, Fax: 904-392-3919. Research projects in mass media development, international communication, political communication, organizational communication, risk commmunication, public opinion, and general media studies. Founded in 1962.

0778 **University of Georgia.** James M. Cox, Jr. Center for International Mass Communication Training and Research, Henry W. Grady College of Journalism and Mass Communication, Athens, GA 30602. Voice: 706-542-5023, Fax: 706-542-5036. Concerned with news flow in foreign national news agencies, comparative analysis of foreign broadcast news, theoretical considerations in international news and information flow, research in media change, and communications technology in developing nations, especially innovation in Eastern and Central Europe. Issues MONOGRAPH SERIES, HANDBOOK FOR THIRD WORLD JOURNALISTS, AN EASTERN EUROPEAN JOURNALISM PRIMER: BUILDING NEW NATIONS and a book series on press freedom in Eastern Europe. Founded in 1985.

0779 **University of Iowa.** Communication Research Laboratory, Department of Communication Studies, 105 Communication Studies Bldg., Iowa City, IA 52240. Voice: 319-335-0579, Fax: 319-335-2930. e-mail: blastd@blue.weeg.uiowa.edu. Includes research on experimental aspects of mass media and communication about interpersonal relationships. Founded in 1967.

0780 **University of Kansas**. William Allen White Foundation, 200 Stauffer-Flint Hall, Lawrence, KS 66045. Voice: 913-864-4755, Fax: 913-864-5318. Part of the School of Journalism, the Foundation is concerned with studies of newspaper commentary, including investigation of editorial content of given newspapers. It holds a collection of William Allen White first editions, magazine first issues, cartoon and comic strip originals, and various journalistic memorabilia. Sponsors annual professional development seminars. Offers the William Allen White Medallion to recognize one nationally known journalist annually. Founded in 1944.

0781 **University of Missouri—Columbia.** Center for Advanced Social Research, School of Journalism, PO Box 838, Columbia, MO 65205. Voice: 314-882-3396, Fax: 314-882-2890. Conducts national and international social, economic, and political field and telephone surveys. Specializes in mass communication, medical information and services, consumer and organizational research, and new technology in mass media. Founded in 1984.

0782 **University of Oregon.**

1 Division of Communication Research, School of Journalism & Communication, 310 Allen Hall, 1020 University St., Eugene, OR 97403-1275. Voice: 503-346-3744, E-mail: jlemert@oregon.uoregon.edu. Focuses on audience perceptions of news media and functions of mass communication in complex social systems, experimental studies of communication effects, investigations of communication dynamics or process, and opinion and attitude measurements, including source credibility. Specific projects have included studies of audience reaction to evening newspapers switching to morning publication, attitudes of those in journalism, political communication studies, mobilizing information in news of public controversies, the effects of televised presidential debates, and presidential campaign studies. Founded in 1962.

2 Communications Research Center, School of Journalism & Communication, Allen Hall, 1020 University St. Eugene, OR 97403-1275 Voice: 503-346-4175. Interests include both mass and interpersonal communications.

0783 **University of Tennessee, Knoxville.** Communications Research Center, College of Communications, Communications Bldg., Rm. 426 Knoxville, TN 37996. Voice: 615-974-6651. e-mail: hhoward@utkvx.utk.edu. Conducts broadcast station ascertainment surveys; broadcast, cable, and pay-TV economic studies (including studies of group ownership trends); newspaper readership studies, and broadcast programming and news analysis. Holds Communications Research Symposium annually in spring. Founded in 1973.

0784 **University of Wisconsin—Madison.**

1 Center for Environmental Communications and Education Studies, School of Journalism and Mass Communication, 5056 Vilas Communication Hall, 821 Univ. Ave., Madison, WI 53706. Voice: 608-263-3069, Fax: 608-262-1361. e-mail: dunwoody@facstaff.wisc.edu. Conducts experiments and surveys regarding risk communication, public perception of risk, and media coverage of science and technology. Conducts workshops for scientists on how best to present information for nonscientists.

2 Mass Communications Research Center, School of Journalism and Mass Communication, 5172 Vilas Communication Hall, Madison, WI 53706. Voice: (608) 262-3642. Studies mass media institutions, political communication, professionalization in the mass media, family communication, consumer and political socialization, attitude and behavior change, information-seeking and avoidance, general issues in communication research and its application, and methodological studies. Founed in 1959.

3 Wisconsin Center for Film and Theater Research, Department of Communication Arts, Vilas Communication Hall, 821 Univ. Ave., Madison, WI 53706. Voice: 608-262-9706, Fax: 608-

264-6472. Research interests include the performing arts in America, theater, cinema, radio, and television and their role in cultural history. Also serves as a national repository of primary source material. Founded in 1960 as Wisconsin Center for Theatre Research.

0785 **Western Michigan University.** Center for Communication Research, Communication Dept., 301 Sprau Tower, Kalamazoo, MI 49008. Voice: 616-387-3154, Fax: 616-387-3990. Wide-ranging scope includes studies in interpersonal, small group, health, organizational, and mass communication. Founded in 1958.

6-B-3 Other Organizations

See 0194. American Antiquarian Society.

0786 **American Association for the Advancement of Science**. 1333 H St., NW, Washington 20005. Voice: 202-326-6400. Fax 202-289-4021. Largest general scientific organization with some 135,000 individual and 300 societies as members. Annual budget of $44 million. Supports the Westinghouse Science Journalism Awards program for journalism and media coverage of science and its technological applications. Publishes SCIENCE (weekly). Founded in 1848.

0787 **Freedom Forum Media Studies Center**. 580 Madison Ave, New York 10022 Voice: 212-317-6500. Fax: 212-317-6572. Institute for the advanced study of mass communications and technological change. Supports original research and organizes national conferences, about major issues facing mass media and society and technological changes in the media industry. Publishes MEDIA STUDIES JOURNAL (1182) and occasional reports derived from forums, conferences and competitive fellowship program that supports scholars in residence at the Center. Maintains extensive library of print and electronic resources. Funded by the Freedom Forum Foundation, formerly the Gannett Foundation. Founded in 1985 as Gannett Foundation Media Studies Center; changed name in 1992.

0788 **Poynter Institute for Media Studies.** 801 Third Street South, St. Petersburg, FL 33701. Voice: 813-821-9494. Fax: 813-821-0583. Internet: www4.nando.net/prof/poynter/home.html. Educational institution offering professional seminars and stipends for university students, teachers and journalists working for newspapers and television in writing, graphics, and photography. Excellent library. Publishes annual POYNTER INSTITUTE CATALOG AND SCHEDULE OF SEMINARS describing programs. Established in 1975.

0789 **RAND Corporation,** 1700 Main St., P.O. Box 2183, Santa Monica, CA 90407-2138. Voice: 310-393-0411. Fax: 310-451-6915. Publishes analyses on numerous subjects. Bibliographic abstracts of RAND publications include COMMUNICATION SATELLITES, COMMUNICATION SYSTEMS and TELEVISION AND COMMUNICATION POLICY available free on request. Updated irregularly, these abstracts are organized by format: reports, notes, memoranda, and papers. Subject and author indexes. Founded in 1956.

6-C. Media Education

(See also: 6-A-3, Theses and Dissertations)

6-C-1. Associations

0790 **Accrediting Council on Education in Journalism and Mass Communication (ACEJMC).** School of Journalism, University of Kansas, Lawrence, KS. 66045. Voice: 913-864-3973. Fax: 913-864-5225. Annual budget of about $135,000. Officially recognized agency for accrediting university programs in professional journalism, of which there are about 100 at any one time (of some 400 total journalism programs). Publishes ACCREDITED JOURNALISM AND MASS COMMUNICATIONS EDUCATION (annual). Founded in 1929 as Joint Committee of Schools of Journalism; changed in 1945 to American Council on Education for Journalism and to current name in 1981.

0791 **Association for Education in Journalism and Mass Communication (AEJMC).** 1621 College St., University of South Carolina, Columbia, SC 29208-0251. Voice: 803-777-2005. Fax: 803-777-4728. Internet: aejmchq@univscvm.csd.scarolina.edu. Organization of 3,100 college and university educators and professional groups concerned with teaching and research in journalism and mass communication. Publications include JOURNALISM AND MASS COMMUNICATION QUARTERLY (1179), JOURNALISM AND MASS COMMUNICATION MONOGRAPHS (1178), JOURNALISM AND MASS COMMUNICATION EDUCATOR (quarterly), JOURNALISM AND MASS COMMUNICATION ABSTRACTS (0745), and JOURNALISM AND MASS COMMUNICATION DIRECTORY. Founded in 1912 as American Association of Teachers of Journalism; changed to Association for Education in Journalism in 1951 and to present name in 1982.

0792 **Broadcast Education Association (BEA).** 1771 N St. NW, Washington 20036-2891. Voice: 202-429-5355. Fax: 202-429-5343. Internet: www.usu.edu/~bea. 1000 members. Annual budget $300,000. Professional association for professors, industry professionals, and graduate students interested in teaching and research related to electronic media and multimedia enterprises. Works to promote understanding between university faculties who teach communications and media practitioners who employ their graduates. Administers over one dozen scholarships and awards. Publications include scholarly JOURNAL OF BROADCASTING & ELECTRONIC MEDIA (1209), membership magazine FEEDBACK (quarterly), and annual DIRECTORY. Sponsors annual convention immediately preceding National Association of Broadcasters Convention. Founded in 1955 as the Association of Professional Broadcast Education; name changed in 1973.

0793 **International Association for Media and Communication Research (IAMCR).** School of International Service, American University, 4400 Massachusetts Ave. NW, Washington 20016-8071. Voice: 202-885-1628. Fax: 202-885-2494. Has 2,300 members in 70 countries. Has consultative status A with UNESCO. International umbrella organization in mass communication research. Holds a general assembly and scientific conference biannually, a forum for researchers, practitioners, policy-makers in the communications field. Publishes membership directory, newsletter, and abstracts (R. Cheesman, IAMCR Secretary General, Communication Studies, Roskilde University, PO Box 260, DK-400, Denmark. Voice: 45-4675-7711. Fax: 45-4675-5313. e-mail: robin@ruc.dk.) Founded in 1957.

0794 **International Communications Association (ICA).** P.O. Box 9589, Austin, TX 78766. Voice: 512-454-8299. Fax: 512-454-4221. Major scholarly organization in field. Membership includes college and university faculty, professionals, and other researchers interested in all forms and functions of human communication in society. Divisions or councils include mass communications, resources (libraries), technology, law and policy, health, information systems, instruction and development, intercultural, interpersonal, philosophy, language and social interaction, organizational studies, political, popular, visual, public relations, feminism, and gay, lesbian, and bisexuality. Publishes JOURNAL OF COMMUNICATION (1173), COMMUNICATION YEARBOOK (annual), COMMUNICATION THEORY (quarterly), HUMAN COMMUNICATION RESEARCH (quarterly), quarterly ICA NEWSLETTER, and annual membership directory. Holds annual conferences. Founded in 1948.

0795 **Speech Communication Association (SCA).** 5105 Backlick Rd., Bldg. E, Annandale, VA 22003. Voice: 703-750-0533. Fax: 703-914-9471. Oldest U.S. association of communication scholars with budget of $1.4 million and 7,000 members (mainly speech teachers, college and university faculty, speech and theater professionals) interested in study and research on communication, particularly speech communication. Among its many divisions is one devoted to mass communication. Supports important scholarly publication program: publishes quarterly journals CRITICAL STUDIES IN MASS COMMUNICATION (1167), JOURNAL OF APPLIED COMMUNICATION RESEARCH, SPEECH COMMUNICATION, COMMUNICATION EDUCATION, COMMUNICATION MONOGRAPHS, SPEECH COMMUNICATION TEACHER, TEXT AND PERFORMANCE QUARTERLY (all quarterly), annual FREE SPEECH YEARBOOK, monthly membership newsletter SPECTRA, and SPEECH COMMUNICATION DIRECTORY. Sponsors annual conventions. Founded in 1914 as Speech Association of America; name changed in 1970.

6-C-2. Guides to Educational Programs

0796 Accrediting Council on Education in Journalism and Mass Communications. **ACCREDITED JOURNALISM AND MASS COMMUNICATIONS EDUCATION**. Lawrence, KS: ACEJMC, ca. 1978–date, annual. Useful guide to the 12 standards used to accredit programs with a professional orientation. Includes listing of the approximately 100 accredited programs in journalism and mass communication, listed by state.

0797 Bazalgette, Cary et al., eds. **NEW DIRECTIONS: MEDIA EDUCATION WORLDWIDE**. Bloomington: Indiana University Press, 1993, 256 pp. Two dozen articles assess the status in specific countries (mainly European), review teacher training, discuss research, and survey likely future directions. Notes, index.

0798 Becker, Lee B. and Gerald M. Kosicki. **ANNUAL SURVEY OF JOURNALISM & MASS COMMUNICATION...** Columbus: Ohio State University, annual, 2 vols:

1 **...ENROLLMENTS**. (1968-date). Numbers of students by gender, race, ethnic group.

2 **...GRADUATES**. (1964-date). What happens to graduates in the job market. (Published by the Newspaper Fund until 1967.)

0799 Becker, Lee B., and Joseph D. Graf. **MYTHS & TRENDS: WHAT THE REAL NUMBERS SAY ABOUT JOURNALISM EDUCATION**. Arlington, VA: The Freedom Forum, 1995, 21 pp. Descriptive information about the academic achievement of journalism students and entry-level salaries in their first jobs, recent decreased journalism education enrollments, starting salaries, and unemployment levels.

0800 Blanchard, Robert O., and William G. Christ. **MEDIA EDUCATION AND THE LIBERAL ARTS: A BLUEPRINT FOR THE NEW PROFESSIONALISM.** Hillsdale, NJ: Erlbaum, 1993, 187 pp. Thoughtful essay reviewing the relationship of universities and the proper place of professional training within them. References, index.

0801 Connelly, Theodore S. **CINCOM: COURSES IN COMMUNICATIONS**. San Francisco: Communications Library, 1988–date, biennial. Identifies higher education institutions offering communications courses. Over 1,200 entries encompass colleges, universities, academically sponsored courses and seminars, degree program specializations, and institutions. Doctoral programs classified by emphasis: CATV, data, telecommunications and telephony. Programs are listed both geographically and alphabetically. Includes international programs.

0802 **DIRECTORY OF MEDIA STUDIES CENTERS, MID-CAREER FELLOWSHIPS AND TRAINING PROGRAMS FOR JOURNALISTS**. Arlington, VA: Freedom Forum On-line Journalism Programs, 1995, 61 pp. A guide to fellowship and scholarship programs designed for journalists and based at universities. Includes international opportunities.

0803 Elmore, Garland C., ed. **THE COMMUNICATIONS DISCIPLINES IN HIGHER EDUCATION: A GUIDE TO ACADEMIC PROGRAMS IN THE UNITED STATES AND CANADA**. Annandale, VA: Association for Communication Administration, 1993 (2nd ed.), 489 pp. Directory of speech and media courses and degree programs, arranged by state and then school.

0804 Gaunt, Philip. **MAKING THE NEWSMAKERS: INTERNATIONAL HANDBOOK ON JOURNALISM TRAINING**. Westport, CT: Greenwood, 1992, 256 pp. Sponsored by UNESCO, this offers an introductory survey, then a region-by-region directory of what is available. Directory of training institutions, bibliography, index.

0805 Jones, Glenn R. **MAKE ALL AMERICA A SCHOOL: MIND EXTENSION UNIVERSITY, THE EDUCATION NETWORK**. Englewood, CO: Jones 21st Century, Inc., 1991 (2nd ed.), 79 pp. Defines Mind Extension University and distance education. Describes how they work. Epilogue, bibliography.

0806 Murray, Michael D., and Anthony J. Ferri, eds. **TEACHING MASS COMMUNICATION: A GUIDE TO BETTER INSTRUCTION**. Westport, CT: Praeger, 1992, 288 pp. Five articles on the introductory course, six more on applied coursework (reporting, production), and a final six on advanced courses (ethics, law, management, history, criticism). Emphasis is on print journalism. Readings, index.

0807 Sapolsky, Barry S., ed. **DIRECTORY OF [ELECTRONIC] MEDIA PROGRAMS IN NORTH AMERICAN UNIVERSITIES AND COLLEGES**. Washington: Broadcast Education Association, 1994, 125 pp. Occasional directory arranged by state and then by institution, providing in each case information on program and address, resources, faculty, students, and graduate funding.

0808 Sholle, David, and Stan Denski. **MEDIA EDUCATION AND THE (RE)PRODUCTION OF CULTURE**. Westport, CT: Bergin & Garvey, 1994, 184 pp. Argues that media education needs more of a critical approach. Bibliography, index.

0809 Sumner, David E. **GRADUATE PROGRAMS IN JOURNALISM AND MASS COMMUNICATIONS**. Ames: Iowa State University Press, 1996. 183 pp. Directory of master's and doctoral programs in general mass communication, print journalism, radio–television, film studies, advertising, public relations, and telecommunication. Includes list of graduate courses offered, strengths or unique features of each program, degree requirements, admission requirements, costs, and financial aid information.

6-C-3. Selected Fellowship and Continuing Education Programs

0810 **Frank Batten Fellowships for Journalists**. University of Virginia, P.O. Box 6550, Charlottesville, VA 22906-6550. Voice: 804-924-7281. Fax: 804-924-4859. Fellowships for journalists to prepare for leadership roles in the news media. Full tuition and partial stipend for living expenses to support full-time participation in an MBA program.

0811 **Congressional Fellowship Program**. American Political Science Association, 1527 New Hampshire Ave. N.W., Washington 20036. Voice: 202-483-2512. Fax: 202-483-2657. Structured 1-year fellowship program of three parts: an orientation seminar, successive internships as staff members for elected officials or committees in the House and Senate, weekly fellows seminars. Program includes home visit to legislators' districts and a spring visit to the Canadian Parliament. Open to journalists with a bachelor's degree and 2 to 10 years of professional experience in print or broadcast reporting. Compensation for the 10-month program covers a stipend for travel to Washington and to legislators' home districts and living expenses in DC.

0812 **The Freedom Forum Asian Studies Fellowships for Journalists**. University of Hawaii at Manoa, 2530 Dole St., Sakamaki Hall B101, Honolulu 96822-2383. Voice: 808-956-7733. Fax: 808-956-9600. A fellowship of one academic year to provide mid-career American journalists the opportunity to study an Asian region or country and complete an academic degree program. Compensation for the academic year plus a bonus for successful completion of academic studies.

0813 **Inter-American Press Association Scholarship Fund**. 2911 N.W. 39th St., Miami, FL 33142. Voice: 305-634-2465. Fax: 305-635-2272. A fellowship program for American and Canadian journalists or journalism school graduates, ages 21–35 years, with good language ability in Spanish or Portuguese. The program includes formal university courses and completing a major research project. The program is designed to foster a better understanding among the countries of the Western Hemisphere.

0814 **Kaiser Media Fellowships in Health**. The Henry J. Kaiser Family Foundation, 2400 Sand Hill Rd., Menlo Park, CA 94025. Voice: 415-854-9400. Fax: 415-854-4800. Twelve-month fellowships are designed to assist journalists in improving the reporting of health issues. Smaller grants are also given to journalists for projects focused on health policy or public health issues.

0815 **Kiplinger Mid-Career Program in Public Affairs Reporting**. Ohio State University, 242 West 18th Ave., Columbus, OH 43210. Voice: 614-292-2607; 614-292-9087. Fax: 614-292-3809. Funded by the Kiplinger Foundation, this 12-month university program assists journalists who want to improve their reporting of issues. For journalists with three years of full-time experience in reporting public affairs and with bachelor's degrees. Several fellowships are awarded each year.

0816 **John S. Knight Fellowships for Professional Journalists**. Stanford University, Department of Communication, Stanford, CA 94305-2050. Voice: 415-723-4937. Fax: 415-725-6154. This international fellowship program is designed to deepen journalists' understanding of major trends and issues through a seminar and a 9-month study program. Open to print and broadcast journalists. Twelve fellowships granted per year, U.S.; six, foreign. Established in 1966.

0817 **Knight Fellowship in Law for Journalists**. Yale Law School, P.O. Box 29815, New Haven, CT 06520-8215. Voice: 203-432-1681. Fax: 203-432-7362. Supports legal education for journalists to develop a systematic understanding of the law, including theory, policy and procedures. Supports a 1-year degree program leading to a master of studies in law. Open to applicants with professional accomplishment, promise, and academic ability. Requires 5 years of experience as reporters or free-lancers.

0818 **Michigan Journalism Fellows**. University of Michigan, Mike and Mary Wallace House, 620 Oxford Rd., Ann Arbor, MI 48104-2635. Voice: 313-998-7666. Fax: 313-998-7979. Funded by the Knight Foundation and other sources, this academic program for mid-career U.S. journalists offers access to all courses and facilities of the university. A dozen 8-month fellowships are awarded annually. Open to full-time print, photo, and broadcast journalists whose work appears in U.S. news organizations.

0819 **National Arts Journalism Program**. Northwestern University, NAJP-Medill School of Journalism, Northwestern University, 680 North Lake Shore Dr., Ste. 818, Chicago, IL 60611-4402. Voice: 312-503-0556. Fax: 312-503-1362. Funded by the Pew Charitable Trusts. Fellowship program for mid-career journalists in the arts and culture. Open to journalists with 5 years of full-time experience in the media or as affiliated free-lancers. Applicants are expected to have a significant body of work and a commitment to arts journalism. Participating universities include Northwestern, University of Georgia, Columbia University, and University of Southern California.

0820 **Nieman Fellowships for Journalists**. Harvard University, Walter Lippmann House, 1 Francis Ave., Cambridge, MA 02138. Voice: 617-495-2237. Fax: 617-495-8976. Awarded to support a university-wide program of noncredit study for an academic year to 12 U.S. and 10 to 12 foreign journalists. Full-time journalists working for at least 3 years in print and broadcasting media are eligible. Supports the NIEMAN REPORTS, a quarterly journal devoted to journalistic issues. Founded in 1938.

0821 **Prudential Fellowship Program for Children and the News**. Graduate School of Journalism, Columbia University, New York 10024. Voice: 212-854-3319. Fax: 212-854-7837. Designed for professional journalists with at least 5 years of experience in U.S. or Canada and with significant academic, social service, or policymaking experience in children's issues. Fellows are offered the opportunity of a self-directed study with faculty and colleagues from several graduate schools at Columbia, including Teachers College and the business and journalism schools.

0822 **Robert Bosch Foundation Fellowship.** CDS International, Inc., 330 7th Ave., 19th Fl., New York, NY 10001-5010. Voice: 212-760-1400. Fax: 212-268-1288. A 9-month program of internships in Germany for young practitioners and graduate students of journalism, public affairs, law, economics, political science or business administration. Compensation includes travel expenses, health insurance, and intensive language instruction. Fellows also attend seminars in Brussels, Paris, and Berlin. Program seeks to strengthen ties between Germany and the U.S.

0823 **Ted Scripps Fellowships in Environmental Journalism**. University of Michigan, 2020 Frieze Bldg, Ann Arbor, MI 48109 1285. Voice: 313-763-5943. Fax: 313-763-0451. Fellowships awarded to journalists who specialize in reporting on the environment. Intended to provide fellows (through university graduate coursework) with a comprehensive grounding in the scientific, political, and professional issues most vital to day-to-day work in the area. The program is open to print and broadcast journalists, including reporters, producers, photographers, graphic artists and editors, who work for U.S. commercial news organizations. Three years of full-time experience required. Previous experience in reporting environmental issues not required.

6-D. Selected Secondary Resources

6-D-1. Communication Theory

0824 De Fleur, Melvin L., and Sandra Ball-Rokeach. **THEORIES OF MASS COMMUNICATION**. New York: Longman, 1989 (5th ed.), 280 pp. Basic introduction combining history of print, film, and electronic media with essential theoretical concepts.

0825 Marchand, Philip. **MARSHALL McLUHAN: THE MEDIUM AND THE MESSENGER**. New York: Ticknor & Fields, 1989, 320 pp. Perhaps the best current evaluation of the long-time guru (1911–1980) and his seminal writings on communication theory. Notes, bibliography, index.

0826 McQuail, Denis. **MASS COMMUNICATION THEORY: AN INTRODUCTION**. Thousand Oaks, CA: Sage, 1994 (3rd ed.), 416 pp. Basic and comprehensive survey. Diagrams, references, index.

0827 _____, and Sven Windahl. **COMMUNICATION MODELS FOR THE STUDY OF MASS COMMUNICATION**. White Plains, NY: Longman, 1993 (2nd ed.), 229 pp. A diagram and a few pages of useful text on each of nearly 100 approaches. References, index.

0828 Schramm, Wilbur. **THE BEGINNINGS OF COMMUNICATION STUDY IN AMERICA: A PERSONAL MEMOIR.** Thousand Oaks, CA: Sage, 1997, 206 pp. The author's final book, completed by others, reviews the path-breaking work of Harold Lasswell, Paul Lazarsfeld, Kurt Lewin, and Carl Hovland

0829 Severin, Werner J., with James W. Tankard, Jr. **COMMUNICATION THEORIES**. White Plains, NY: Longman, 1992 (3rd ed.), 300 pp. Very broad overview of all types of communication theory.

6-D-2. General Audience Impact Surveys

0830 Anderson, James A., and Timothy P. Meyer. **MEDIATED COMMUNICATION: A SOCIAL ACTION PERSPECTIVE**. Newbury Park, CA: Sage, 1988, 366 pp. An integrated treatment of the massive theoretical and empirical literature of the past two decades—what we know, how we know it, and an organizing theory. Glossary, bibliography, index.

0831 Becker, Lee B., and Klaus Schoenbach, eds. **AUDIENCE RESPONSES TO MEDIA DIVERSIFICATION: COPING WITH PLENTY**. Hillsdale, NJ: Erlbaum, 1989, 376 pp. Papers on the impact of more channel choice and how it has affected audiences in several countries. Tables, references, index.

0832 Bogart, Leo. **COMMERCIAL CULTURE: THE MEDIA SYSTEM AND THE PUBLIC INTEREST**. New York: Oxford University Press, 1995, 384 pp. Explores the tension between the media system and public interest. Concludes: (a) media are excessively commercial; (b) content serves advertisers' rather than the public's purpose; (c) sensational, vulgar programming dominates; (d) sensationalism distorts perceptions and distracts public attention from social problems.

0833 Cissna, Kenneth N., ed. **APPLIED COMMUNICATION IN THE 21ST CENTURY**. Hillsdale, NJ: Erlbaum, 1995, 218 pp. A colloquium of scholars explore and debate the necessity and advantages of applied communication research. An excellent guide to the literature of applied communication research.

0834 Dennis, Everette E., and Ellen Wartella. **AMERICAN COMMUNICATION RESEARCH: THE REMEMBERED HISTORY**. Mahwah, NJ: Erlbaum, 1996, 210 pp. Anthology of edited lectures to Freedom Forum Media Studies Center in New York about (and some by) key research figures from the past. Notes, index.

0835 Gaunt, Philip, ed. **BEYOND AGENDAS: NEW DIRECTIONS OF COMMUNICATION RESEARCH**. Westport, CT: Greenwood, 1993, 248 pp. Summary of where the field is now and suggestions for new and varied research directions and applications. Tables, references, notes.

0836 Harris, Richard Jackson. **A COGNITIVE PSYCHOLOGY OF MASS COMMUNICATION**. Hillsdale, NJ: Erlbaum, 1989, 287 pp. A topically organized review of what we know about media impact—the psychology of such things as advertising, sports, news, politics, violence, sex, and prosocial uses of media. Notes, references, index.

0837 Klapper, Joseph T. **THE EFFECTS OF MASS COMMUNICATION.** New York: Free Press, 1960, 302 pp. Standard source for pre-1960 research on effectiveness and limitations of media in influencing their audiences. Notes, index.

0838 Lerner, Daniel, and Lyle M. Nelson, eds. **COMMUNICATION RESEARCH—A HALF-CENTURY APPRAISAL.** Honolulu: University of Hawaii Press, 1977, 348 pp. Key scholars assess what has been learned. Issued in honor of Wilbur Schramm and offering considerable detail on his life. Index.

0839 Lowery, Shearon, and Melvin De Fleur. **MILESTONES IN MASS COMMUNICATION RESEARCH.** New York: Longman, 1995 (3rd ed.), 415 pp. Detailed analysis of 15 specific research projects in light of current knowledge, making a useful record of developing methods and findings. Notes, references, index.

0840 Neuman, W. Russell. **THE FUTURE OF THE MASS AUDIENCE.** New York: Cambridge University Press, 1992, 202 pp. Conclusion of a 5-year study arguing that national mass media will continue to be important services despite growth of newer media. Notes, references, index.

0841 Schramm, Wilbur, and Donald F. Roberts, eds. **THE PROCESS AND EFFECTS OF MASS COMMUNICATION.** Urbana: University of Illinois Press, 1971 (2nd ed.), 997 pp. A standard anthology with several dozen readings arranged in sections on media and messages, audiences, attitudes and effects, social effects, public opinion and politics, innovation and change, and the technological future of mass communication. Notes, further reading, index.

6-D-3. Research Anthology Series

0842 **COMMUNICATION YEARBOOK.** Thousand Oaks, CA: Sage, 1976–date, annual. Collections of top research papers from International Communication Association, heavy on methods and theory. With vol. 11 in 1987 the content emphasis shifted to original research overviews. Especially valuable for state-of-the-art literature reviews on topics of both current and perennial interest, such as advertising and children, sex role, and racial stereotyping in the media.

0843 Dervin, Brenda et al. eds. **PROGRESS IN COMMUNICATION SCIENCES.** Norwood, NJ: Ablex, 1982–1993, 12 vols. Important series of original essays summarizing various areas of research. Notes, extensive references, index.

0844 **MASS COMMUNICATION REVIEW YEARBOOK.** Newbury Park, CA: Sage, 1980–87, 6 vols. Under various editors, each volume collected some 40 scholarly studies previously published in the U.S. and Europe. Notes.

6-D-4. Minorities/Women and Media

0845 Brown, Mary Ellen, ed. **TELEVISION AND WOMEN'S CULTURE.** Newbury Park, CA: Sage, 1990, 244 pp. Thirteen papers which concentrate mainly on the entertainment role of TV and portrayals of women. Notes, bibliography, index.

0846 Browne, Donald R. et al. **TELEVISION/RADIO NEWS AND MINORITIES.** Queenstown, MD: Aspen Institute, 1994, 177 pp. Covers the issue here and in other countries, including recruitment and training, enforcement, citizens' groups as broadcasters, languages and perceptions.

0847 Creedon, Pamela J., ed. **WOMEN IN MASS COMMUNICATION: CHALLENGING GENDER VALUES.** Newbury Park, CA: Sage, 1993 (2nd ed.), 398 pp. Twenty research papers evenly divided between academics and industry figures. Index.

0848 Dates, Jannette L., and William Barlow, eds. **SPLIT IMAGE: AFRICAN AMERICANS IN THE MASS MEDIA.** Washington: Howard University Press, 1993 (2nd ed.), 574 pp. Historical approach covering print, film, and broadcast media. Best overall coverage available to date. Photos, index, bibliographical references.

0849 Davis, Richard H., and James A. Davis. **TV'S IMAGE OF THE ELDERLY: A PRACTICAL GUIDE FOR CHANGE**. Lexington, MA: Lexington Books, 1986, 264 pp. Combination of what is televised and how to improve that image. Appendices, index.

0850 Dines, Gail, and Jean M. Humez, eds. **GENDER, RACE AND CLASS IN MEDIA: A TEXT-READER**. Newbury Park, CA: Sage, 1994, 648 pp. More than 60 papers on a cultural studies approach to issues such as advertising, romance novels and slasher films, pornography, TV by day, TV by night, and music videos and rap music. Glossary, bibliography, index.

0851 Hamamoto, Darrell Y. **MONITORED PERIL: ASIAN AMERICANS AND THE POLITICS OF TV REPRESENTATION**. Minneapolis: University of Minnesota Press, 1995, 311 pp. Explores cultural groups and television genre. Notes, bibliography, index.

0852 Hosley, David H., and Gayle Yamada. **HARD NEWS: WOMEN IN BROADCAST JOURNALISM**. Westport, CT: Greenwood, 1987, 198 pp. History of women's roles in radio and TV news. Notes, references, index.

0853 Keith, Michael C. **SIGNALS IN THE AIR: NATIVE BROADCASTING IN AMERICA**. Westport, CT: Praeger, 1995, 177 pp. Unique study of American Indian-owned and/or programmed stations. Appendix, notes, bibliography, index.

0854 MacDonald, J. Fred. **BLACKS AND WHITE TV: AFRICAN AMERICANS IN TELEVISION SINCE 1948**. Chicago: Nelson Hall, 1992 (2nd ed.), 345 pp. Thoughtful analysis of dramatically changing roles—in both kind and quantity. Photos, tables, notes, bibliography, index.

0855 Nelson, Jack A., ed. **THE DISABLED, THE MEDIA AND THE INFORMATION AGE**. Westport, CT: Greenwood, 1994, 249 pp. Fifteen chapters cover different disability groups and issues. Appendices, references, index.

0856 Riggins, Stephen Harold. **ETHNIC MINORITY MEDIA: AN INTERNATIONAL PERSPECTIVE**. Newbury Park, CA: Sage, 1992, 298 pp. Examples from the U.S. and abroad. References, index.

0857 United States Commission on Civil Rights. **WINDOW DRESSING ON THE SET**. Washington: GPO, 2 vols. Text and tables detail portrayal and employment patterns. Dated but still unique.

1 **WINDOW DRESSING ON THE SET: WOMEN AND MINORITIES IN TELEVISION.** 1977, 180 pp.

2 **UPDATE**. 1979, 97 pp.

0858 Veciana-Suarez, Ana. **HISPANIC MEDIA: IMPACT AND INFLUENCE**. Washington: The Media Institute, 1990, 82 pp. Detailed analysis of key Hispanic markets and media. Notes.

0859 Wilson, Clint C., and Félix Gutiérrez. **RACE, MULTICULTURALISM, AND THE MEDIA: FROM MASS TO CLASS COMMUNICATION**. Thousand Oaks, CA: Sage, 1995 (2nd ed.), 274 pp. Historical approach appraising changing roles of minorities in various media. Notes, index.

6-D-5. Newspapers and Magazines

0860 Abrahamson, David, ed. **THE AMERICAN MAGAZINE: RESEARCH PERSPECTIVES AND PROSPECTS**. Ames: Iowa State University Press, 1995, 240 pp. A collective report based on scholarly research about U.S. magazines. Reviews and annotates research about magazine typology, editors and editing practices, political content, regional publications, and literary magazines. Includes a unique section devoted to pedagogy about magazine journalism. Notes, index.

6-D-6. Broadcasting

0861 Beville, Hugh Malcolm. **AUDIENCE RATINGS: RADIO, TELEVISION, CABLE.** Hillsdale, NJ: Erlbaum, 1988 (2nd ed.), 380 pp. Detailed history and discussion of varied methods used by commercial ratings companies—in both radio and television—by a long-time expert. Best overview. Appendices, bibliography, index.

0862 Buzzard, Karen. **CHAINS OF GOLD: MARKETING THE RATINGS AND RATING THE MARKETS**. Metuchen, NJ: Scarecrow, 1990, 214 pp. Informal historical review of (primarily) Nielsen and Arbitron. Notes, index.

0863 Fletcher, James E., ed. **BROADCAST RESEARCH DEFINITIONS**. Washington: National Association of Broadcasters, 1988 (2nd ed.), 75 pp. Defines more than 650 technical and statistical broadcast research terms.

0864 Webster, James G., and Lawrence W. Lichty. **RATINGS ANALYSIS: THEORY AND PRACTICE.** Hillsdale, NJ: Erlbaum, 1991, 290 pp. The methods used to derive broadcast ratings, applications of the results, and modes of analysis. Glossary, appendices, bibliography, index.

i) Television.

0865 Ang, Ien. **DESPERATELY SEEKING THE AUDIENCE**. New York: Routledge, 1991, 203 pp. Review of what is known about television research methods and results. Notes, bibliography, index.

0866 Bellamy, Robert V., Jr., and James R. Walker. **TELEVISION AND THE REMOTE CONTROL: GRAZING ON A VAST WASTELAND**. New York: Guilford, 1996, 192 pp. Details the impact of the ubiquitous remote control device. References, index.

0867 Bianculli, David. **TELELITERACY: TAKING TELEVISION SERIOUSLY**. New York: Continuum, 1992, 315 pp. Argues against many of the anti-TV views prevalent among critics. Explores the medium's key roles. Bibliography, index.

0868 Bower, Robert T. **THE CHANGING TELEVISION AUDIENCE IN AMERICA**. New York: Columbia University Press, 1985, 172 pp. Comparative study of national survey results in 1960, 1970, and 1980. Charts, references, index.

0869 Bryant, Jennings, ed. **TELEVISION AND THE AMERICAN FAMILY**. Hillsdale, NJ: Erlbaum, 1990, 385 pp. Seventeen papers on uses by families, the portrayal of families on TV, effects of TV on families, mediating TV's impact, and public policy issues. References, index.

0870 Comstock, George, **THE EVOLUTION OF AMERICAN TELEVISION**. Newbury Park, CA: Sage, 1989, 210 pp. Not a history, but an overview of what is known of TV's impact and effects. Useful for its review of a now-massive literature. References, index.

0871 _____ et al. **TELEVISION AND HUMAN BEHAVIOR**. New York: Columbia University Press, 1978, 581 pp. The definitive assessment of research results to the time of publication. Tables, references, index.

0872 Condry, John. **THE PSYCHOLOGY OF TELEVISION**. Hillsdale, NJ: Erlbaum, 1989, 324 pp. Overview of research literature on psychological impacts of the medium including viewing behavior, attention, comprehension, influence on beliefs and judgments, and imitation. References, index.

0873 Fowles, Jib. **WHY VIEWERS WATCH: A REAPPRAISAL OF TELEVISION EFFECTS.** Newbury Park, CA: Sage, 1992 (2nd ed.), 280 pp. Argues the positive points of television viewing to undermine the anti-TV bias of so many critics. References, index.

0874 Houston, Aletha C. et al. **BIG WORLD, SMALL SCREEN: THE ROLE OF TELEVISION IN AMERICAN SOCIETY**. Lincoln: University of Nebraska Press, 1992, 195 pp. Important summary of scholarly findings on impacts of television as seen in multiyear project by an

American Psychological Association task force. Reviews in detail the research literature of the past decade. References, index.

0875 Jacobson, Ronald L. **TELEVISION RESEARCH: A DIRECTORY OF CONCEPTUAL CATEGORIES, TOPIC SUGGESTIONS AND SELECTED SOURCES.** Jefferson, NC: McFarland, 1995, 138 pp. Reference guide to studying television. Lists 29 television-related categories (such as audience, performance, sports) with brief conceptual overview, relevant research or lecture topic suggestions, and bibliography of selected print sources.

0876 Kubey, Robert, and Mihaly Csikszentmihalyi. **TELEVISION AND THE QUALITY OF LIFE: HOW VIEWING SHAPES EVERYDAY EXPERIENCE**. Hillsdale, NJ: Erlbaum, 1990, 287 pp. Well-received overview on research and its limits, the method of "experience sampling," and results from that research on viewing as cause, habit, and effect. Appendices, references, index.

0877 Selnow, Gary, and Richard R. Gilbert. **SOCIETY'S IMPACT ON TELEVISION: HOW THE VIEWING PUBLIC SHAPES TELEVISION PROGRAMMING**. Westport, CT: Greenwood, 1993, 225 pp. A different approach—ways in which elements of the audience affect programming. Mini case studies and examples throughout.

ii) Television and Children

0878 Adler, Richard et al., eds. **THE EFFECTS OF TELEVISION ADVERTISING ON CHILDREN: REVIEW AND RECOMMENDATIONS**. Lexington, MA: Lexington Books, 1980, 368 pp. Although dated, this is a valuable survey of research results to the time of publication. Bibliography, index.

0879 Liebert, Robert M., and Joyce Sprafkin. **THE EARLY WINDOW: EFFECTS OF TELEVISION ON CHILDREN AND YOUTH**. New York: Pergamon, 1988 (3rd ed.), 306 pp. Analyzes research literature—especially that from the 1972 report of the surgeon general's committee and its update a decade later. Notes, tables, index.

0880 Luke, Carmen. **CONSTRUCTING THE CHILD VIEWER: A HISTORY OF THE AMERICAN DISCOURSE ON TELEVISION AND CHILDREN, 1950–1980.** New York: Praeger, 1990, 331 pp. Useful historical review of the continuing debate over impact and effects. References, index.

0881 Manley, Casimir, and Carmen Luke. **CHILDREN AND TELEVISION: A CHALLENGE FOR EDUCATION**. New York: Praeger, 1987, 311 pp. Twelve original research and review articles stressing educational role for young children. Index.

0882 Van Evra, Judith. **TELEVISION AND CHILD DEVELOPMENT** Hillsdale, NJ: Erlbaum, 1990, 239 pp. Twelve chapters summarize what is known from research and theory of the tube's impact on growing up. Index.

6-D-7. Cable and Newer Media

0883 Dobrow, Julia R., ed. **SOCIAL AND CULTURAL ASPECTS OF VCR USE**. Hillsdale, NJ: Erlbaum, 1990, 219 pp. Eleven papers on how "watching TV" now means many different things because of VCR time shifting and other uses. Notes, index.

0884 Ganley, Gladys D. **THE EXPLODING POLITICAL POWER OF PERSONAL MEDIA**. Norwood, NJ: Ablex, 1992, 180 pp. Offers a number of case studies on use of VCRs, fax, computers, electronic news releases, and the like both here and abroad. Notes, index.

0885 Heeter, Carrie, and Bradley S. Greenberg. **CABLEVIEWING**. Norwood, NJ: Ablex, 1988, 311 pp. One of the few books on the topic of cable use and impact, this includes chapters on viewing choice, viewing styles, viewing time and channel type, program type selections, cable subscriber types, and manipulation of viewing through field experiments. Tables, notes, references, indexes.

0886 Levy, Mark R., ed. **THE VCR AGE: HOME VIDEO AND MASS COMMUNICATION.** Newbury Park, CA: Sage, 1989, 274 pp. One of the first research collections on impact of the VCR—14 papers on what greater choice and control do to viewing behavior and patterns.

0887 Walker, James R., and Robert V. Bellamy, Jr. **THE REMOTE CONTROL IN THE NEW AGE OF TELEVISION**. New York: Praeger, 1993, 288 pp. Sixteen research papers on history and development, individual use, uses and gratifications research, group viewing and use of remote devices, and the impact of such devices on media industries. Notes, references, index.

6-D-8. Educational and Public Media

0888 Chu, Godwin C., and Wilbur Schramm. **LEARNING FROM TELEVISION: WHAT THE RESEARCH SAYS**. Washington: National Association of Educational Broadcasters, 1968, 116 pp. Literature review in narrative form with a bibliography of studies. (A 1974 reprint edition adds an 11-page introduction as an update.)

0889 De Vaney, Ann, ed. **WATCHING CHANNEL ONE: THE CONVERGENCE OF STUDENTS, TECHNOLOGY, AND PRIVATE BUSINESS**. Albany: State University of New York Press, 1995. 244 pp. Sometimes critical study of the commercially supported news delivery system into thousands of the nation's high schools. Index.

0890 Frank, Ronald E., and Marshall G. Greenberg. **AUDIENCES FOR PUBLIC TELEVISION**. Beverly Hills, CA: Sage, 1982, 230 pp. Based on a large national survey, this volume describes 14 types of public TV viewers. Tables.

0891 Johnston, Jerome. **ELECTRONIC LEARNING FROM AUDIOTAPE TO VIDEODISC**. Hillsdale, NJ: Erlbaum, 1988. A broad synthesis of what the research shows.

0892 Kamil, Bobbi L. **DELIVERING THE FUTURE: CABLE AND EDUCATION PARTNERSHIPS FOR THE INFORMATION AGE**. Alexandria, VA: Cable in the Classroom, 1994, 232 pp. Reviews cable industry's support of education through many case studies. Illustrations.

0893 Schramm, Wilbur et al. **THE PEOPLE LOOK AT EDUCATIONAL TELEVISION**. Stanford, CA: Stanford University Press, 1963, 209 pp. The pioneering first national study, based on research in nine markets served at beginning of 1960s. Tables, appendices, bibliography, index.

0894 Zigerell, James. **THE USES OF TELEVISION IN AMERICAN HIGHER EDUCATION.** New York: Praeger, 1991, 185 pp. Telecourses, distance learning, evaluations of instructional efforts and case studies—an overview of national developments. Index.

6-D-9. Media Research Methods

0895 Adams, R.C. **SOCIAL SURVEY METHODS FOR MASS MEDIA RESEARCH**. Hillsdale, NJ: Erlbaum, 1989, 173 pp. Eight-chapter review including survey design, sampling, data collection, data processing, analysis of data, and survey reports. Tables, references, index.

0896 Anderson, James A. **COMMUNICATION RESEARCH: ISSUES AND METHODS**. New York: McGraw-Hill, 1987, 420 pp. Well-written broadscale overview of methods, ethics, and trends in research with many interesting case studies. Glossary, bibliography, index.

0897 Berger, Arthur Asa. **MEDIA ANALYSIS TECHNIQUES**. Newbury Park, CA: Sage Publications, 1991 (revised ed.), 143 pp. (vol. 10 of the Sage ComText Series). A guide to the application of critical research methodologies—semiology, semiotics, psychoanalytic, Marxist theory, and sociological criticism—useful in analyzing popular mass culture and media.

0898 Emmert, Philip, and Larry R. Barker, eds. **MEASUREMENT OF COMMUNICATION BEHAVIOR**. White Plains, NY: Longman, 1989, 390 pp. Fourteen chapters by as many experts on all types of communication measurement techniques. Glossary, references, index.

0899 Jensen, Klause Bruhn, and Nicholas W. Jankowski, eds. **A HANDBOOK OF QUALITATIVE METHODOLOGIES FOR MASS COMMUNICATION RESEARCH**. New York:

Routledge, 1991, 272 pp. Methods of studying media institutions, contents, audiences, and contexts. References, index.

0900 Rubin, Rebecca B. et al., eds. **COMMUNICATION RESEARCH MEASURES: A SOURCEBOOK**. New York: Guildford, 1994, 400 pp. Valuable reference guide to various quantitative texts and scales, all briefly described, with discussion of reliability and validity. References, index.

0901 Wimmer, Roger, and Joseph Dominick. **MASS MEDIA RESEARCH: AN INTRODUCTION**. Belmont, CA: Wadsworth, 1991 (3rd ed.). Stresses statistical applications to research questions.

7

Policy and Regulation

Here we detail resources that describe the process and organizations that implement U.S. communications policy. Included are the congressional, executive, independent agency, and judicial portions of the federal government, among them the National Telecommunications and Information Administration (0947) and Federal Communications Commission (0950). We have included descriptions of each of these federal legislative, regulatory, and judicial agencies because current information on a bill, regulation, or decision can often best be obtained by a phone call or faxed request.

A variety of indexes and full text sources, such as LEXIS-NEXIS (0912), and Thomas (0913) offer increasing access to these resources. Other chapter sections detail self-regulation and policy research resources. Selected secondary resources list general surveys, followed by media-specific sections.

A note of caution: although we provide contact address and telephone numbers for agencies current as of publication, these tend to change more often than do numbers in the private sector.

7-A. Bibliographic Resources

7-A-1. Bibliographies

0902 Bennett, James R. **CONTROL OF INFORMATION IN THE UNITED STATES: AN ANNOTATED BIBLIOGRAPHY**. Westport, CT: Meckler, 1987, 887 pp. Nearly 3,000 citations arranged by topic with author and subject indexes.

0903 _____. **CONTROL OF THE MEDIA IN THE UNITED STATES: AN ANNOTATED BIBLIOGRAPHY**. New York: Garland, 1992, 819 pp. Nearly 4,600 items are included in topical sections with author and subject indexes.

0904 Brightbill, George D. **COMMUNICATIONS AND THE UNITED STATES CONGRESS: A SELECTIVELY ANNOTATED BIBLIOGRAPHY OF COMMITTEE HEARINGS, 1870–1976**. Washington: Broadcast Education Association, 1978, 178 pp. More than 1,100 published hearings are listed, many dealing with telegraph, telephone, and later telecommunications concerns. Dated but historically valuable as the only guide of its kind.

0905 Gillmor, Donald M. et al. **MASS MEDIA LAW: A SELECTED BIBLIOGRAPHY**. Minneapolis, MN: Silha Center for the Study of Media Ethics and Law, School of Journalism and Mass Communication, University of Minnesota, 1987, 31 pp.

0906 McCoy, Ralph E. **FREEDOM OF THE PRESS:** Carbondale: Southern Illinois University Press, 1968–1994, 3 vols. Topically arranged listing of annotated entries with index.

1 **AN ANNOTATED BIBLIOGRAPHY**. 1968, ca. 500 pp. Some 8,000 citations to the mid-1960s.

2 **A BIBLIOCYCLOPEDIA: TEN YEAR SUPPLEMENT (1967–1977).** 1979, 557 pp. Over 6,600 entries. Index.

3 **AN ANNOTATED BIBLIOGRAPHY: SECOND SUPPLEMENT (1978–1992)**. 1994, 441 pp. Several thousand citations. Index.

0907 McKerns, Joseph P., ed. **NEWS MEDIA AND PUBLIC POLICY: AN ANNOTATED BIBLIOGRAPHY**. New York: Garland, 1985, 171 pp. Selective review of more than 700 studies, divided topically, with indexes.

0908 Swindler, William Finley. **A BIBLIOGRAPHY OF LAW ON JOURNALISM**. New York: Columbia University Press, 1947, 191 pp. Annotated guide to over 1,100 books and articles on U.S. and international press law in a subject arrangement covering censorship and control of speech and the press, privacy, copyright, and other topics. Author and subject indexes.

7-A-2. Abstracts, Indexes, Databases

0909 **CIS INDEX TO PUBLICATIONS OF THE UNITED STATES CONGRESS.** Washington: Congressional Information Service, 1970–date, monthly with annual cumulations. Online version available on Dialog (1970–date, updated monthly). CD-ROM version CONGRESSIONAL MASTERFILE 2 available from Congressional Information Service (1970–date, updated quarterly). Indexes Congressional committee hearings and prints; House and Senate reports, documents, and special publications; Senate executive reports; and Senate treaty documents. Separate abstract and index issues published monthly. Useful headings include government and the press, mass media, press, radio, and television. Index of subjects and names includes affiliations of witnesses at hearings. Other indices for document titles and names of committee and subcommittee chairs. Annual volume for legislative histories cumulates entries for hearings, debates, and reports related to laws enacted within that year. CIS also publishes CD-ROM CONGRESSIONAL MASTERFILE with retrospective files for the period 1879–1969 corresponding to CIS UNPUBLISHED U.S. SENATE COMMITTEE HEARINGS INDEX, 1823–1964 (1986), CIS U.S. CONGRESSIONAL COMMITTEE HEARINGS INDEX, 1833–1969 (1981), CIS U.S. CONGRESSIONAL COMMITTEE PRINTS INDEX, 1833–1969 (1980), and CIS U.S. SERIAL SET INDEX, 1789–1969 (1975); all are useful for historical research, particularly related to early communications patents. CIS offers the best access to U.S. legislative publications.

0910 **INDEX TO LEGAL PERIODICALS**. New York: H. W. Wilson, 1908–date, monthly with annual cumulations. Online version available from Wilsonline: covers August 1981–date, updated twice weekly. CD-ROM version available from H. W. Wilson: covers 1981–date, updated quarterly. For more information, see Wilson's homepage: www.hwwilson.com. Author and subject indexing of a broad range of legal periodicals published in the United States, Canada, Great Britain, Ireland, Australia, and New Zealand, as well as legal yearbooks and annual institutes and reviews, including CARDOZO ARTS & ENTERTAINMENT LAW JOURNAL (1253), HASTINGS COMMUNICATIONS AND ENTERTAINMENT LAW JOURNAL (1261), COMMUNICATIONS AND THE LAW (1256), COMPUTER/LAW JOURNAL, FEDERAL COMMUNICATIONS LAW JOURNAL (1260), HIGH TECHNOLOGY LAW JOURNAL, JOURNAL OF SPACE LAW, LOYOLA ENTERTAINMENT LAW JOURNAL (1263), and RUTGERS COMPUTER AND TECHNOLOGY LAW JOURNAL. Relevant subject headings include advertising, cable television, censorship, communications, freedom of the press, libel and slander, news media, obscenity, propaganda, radio and television, and videotapes. Listings for government agencies under United States. Also includes headings for names of individuals and organizations. Appendixed Table of Cases indexes articles by litigants; Table of Statutes references popular and official names of laws.

0911 **LEGAL TRAC** [CD-ROM]. Foster City, CA: Information Access, 1980–date, monthly. Online version LEGAL RESOURCE INDEX available from Dialog, LEXIS/NEXIS (0912), WESTLAW (0914), and other services: covers 1980–date, updated monthly. References to law reviews, case notes, biographies, professional news, legislative analyses, bibliographies, and reviews in over 800 legal publications.

0912 **LEXIS/NEXIS** [Online Service]. Dayton, OH: Reed Elsevier, 1973–date: coverage varies (newspaper, magazine coverage current 5 years); updating varies, dependent on publication, often same day or next day. Offers full-text coverage of hundreds of primary and secondary materials in U.S., foreign, national, and international law, business, medicine, and popular media. LEXIS and related services cover legal, legislative, and regulatory information. Foremost of LEXIS' libraries for communication research is FEDCOM (Federal Communications Library), including FCC decisions, reports, FCC DAILY DIGEST, FCC RECORD (well in advance of printed issues), federal case law related to communications, Title 47 of the U.S. CODE and Title 47 of the CODE OF FEDERAL REGULATIONS, and selected industry and policy publications such as COMMUNICATIONS DAILY and FEDERAL COMMUNICATIONS LAW JOURNAL (1260). Other useful LEXIS libraries are LEGIS (federal and state legislative documents and information, including CONGRESSIONAL RECORD) and GENFED (CODE OF FEDERAL REGULATIONS, among over 100 files). NEXIS and related services cover news, business, and trade information. Important NEXIS libraries for communication research are CMPCOM (Computers and Communications Library), covering trade and industry newsletters; ENTERT (Entertainment Library), containing industry newsletters, company profiles, and financial reports; and NEXIS (Nexis Library), including more than 650 domestic and foreign newspapers, newsletters, magazines, journals, wire services, and broadcast transcript services. Additional separate divisions useful for media industry information are COMPNY (Company Library), including investment bank market studies, SEC filings, and annual reports; and MARKET (Marketing Library), covering market research, consumer demographics, and product announcements and reviews. Also separate international libraries.

0913 **THOMAS** [Online System]. Washington: Library of Congress, January 1995–date, updating varies depending on legislative schedule (usually several times daily). Internet: thomas.loc.gov/. Name derives from Thomas Jefferson, founder of the Library of Congress. Tracks legislative activities and provides full-text searching of current bills, historical legislation, CONGRESSIONAL RECORD, committees, and the like, with links to other U.S government electronic sites and resources.

0914 **WESTLAW** [Online Service]. Eagan, MN: West Publishing, 1978–date: coverage and updating vary, depending on file. Similar to LEXIS/NEXIS (0912); provides comprehensive bibliographic and full-text access to U.S. statutory, regulatory, and case law. Includes WESTLAW COMMUNICATIONS LIBRARY file, which covers communications law, providing full texts of federal and state legislative, administrative, and judicial documents, as well as full texts of articles in law journals. Access to WESTLAW is typically limited to law libraries. Lacks strong coverage of popular media, trade newsletters featured in LEXIS/NEXIS.

7-A-3. Dictionaries

0915 Murray, John. **THE MEDIA LAW DICTIONARY.** Washington: University Press of America, 1979, 139 pp. Defines over 400 words and phrases commonly appearing in media law, many with references to pertinent cases and historical background. Intended for students, news handlers, and editorialists interested in First Amendment issues.

7-A-4. Directories

0916 **CARROLL'S FEDERAL DIRECTORY: EXECUTIVE, LEGISLATIVE, JUDICIAL.** Washington: Carroll Publishing, bimonthly. Voice: 202-333-8620. Fax: 202-337-7020. Entries give individual's name, job title, office address, and telephone number. Organized by agency with keyword and name indices.

0917 **CONGRESSIONAL QUARTERLY'S GUIDE TO CONGRESS.** Washington: Congressional Quarterly, 1991 (4th ed.), 836+ paged appendices. Standard guide to history, organization, and operations of Congress. Subject index identifies relevant sections on telecommunications.

0918 **CONGRESSIONAL STAFF DIRECTORY.** Mount Vernon, VA: Staff Directories, 1959–date, two editions annually. CD-ROM version STAFF DIRECTORIES ON CD-ROM available from Staff Directories; cumulates CONGRESSIONAL STAFF DIRECTORY, JUDICIAL STAFF DIRECTORY (0923), and FEDERAL STAFF DIRECTORY (0921): covers current editions, updated semiannually. Identifies members of Congress. Useful for committee assignments. Keyword subject and name indexes.

0919 **ENCYCLOPEDIA OF GOVERNMENTAL ADVISORY ORGANIZATIONS**. Detroit: Gale, 1973–date, irregular. 9th ed. (1994) for 1994/1995. Classified descriptions of 6,500 current and defunct federal committees, task forces, boards, panels, and other groups. Indexes for personnel, publications and reports, presidential administrations, federal departments and agencies, and keywords such as broadcasting, radio. Especially useful for historical research; tracks evolution of organizations.

0920 **FEDERAL REGULATORY DIRECTORY**. Washington: Congressional Quarterly, 1979–date, irregular (8th ed., 1996). Narrative descriptions of executive and independent departments and agencies covering history, personnel and offices (with addresses, telephone numbers), organizational structure, libraries and other information resources, with bibliographies. Useful for solid overviews of communications-related agencies.

0921 **FEDERAL STAFF DIRECTORY**. Mount Vernon, VA: Staff Directories, 1982–date, two editions annually. CD-ROM version STAFF DIRECTORIES ON CD-ROM available from Staff Directories. Guide to executive offices and agencies and independent agencies. Keyword subject and name indexes. Useful for current personnel and telephone information for FCC and other offices.

0922 **GOVERNMENT RESEARCH DIRECTORY**. Detroit: Gale, 1980–date, biennial. Formerly GOVERNMENT RESEARCH CENTERS DIRECTORY (1980–1982). 8th ed. for 1995–1996. Online version RESEARCH CENTERS AND SERVICES DIRECTORY available from Dialog (0748). Arranged by federal branches, departments, and agencies. Geographic, subject, and master index. Useful listings include radio communication, television.

0923 **JUDICIAL STAFF DIRECTORY**. Mount Vernon, VA: Staff Directories, 1986–date, annual. CD-ROM version STAFF DIRECTORIES ON CD-ROM available from Staff Directories. Guide to federal judiciary and staffs, with biographies. Keyword subject and name indexes.

0924 **OFFICIAL CONGRESSIONAL DIRECTORY.** Washington: GPO, 1809–date, annual. Includes Congressional members, offices, and committees; executive departments, agencies, judiciary, and diplomatic offices. Detailed contents; name index.

0925 **U.S. GOVERNMENT MANUAL**. Washington: GPO, 1935–date, annual. Variant titles. Electronic version available from GPO's Electronic Information Dissemination Services; e-mail: gpoaccess@gpo.gov. Official guide to U.S. government offices. Name, agency/subject indexes.

0926 **WASHINGTON INFORMATION DIRECTORY**. Washington: Congressional Quarterly, 1975–date, annual. Basic data for U.S. government offices as well as Washington trade, industry, press, media, and other interest groups and organizations. Relevant listings throughout, but especially in communications and the media, advocacy and public service (advertising, public relations), and education and culture (broadcasting, film, print media, and publishing). Perhaps the handiest one-volume guide to Washington and the national media.

7-B. U.S. Government

7-B-1. Bibliographic Resources

0927 **CONGRESS IN PRINT.** Washington: Congressional Quarterly, 1977–date, 48/year. Lists but does not annotate publications of CBO, OTA, and GAO as well as House and Senate committee hearings, reports, and committee prints.

0928 **GUIDE TO U.S. GOVERNMENT PUBLICATIONS**. McLean, VA: Documents Index, 1973–date, irregular. Earlier editions published as GUIDE TO U.S. GOVERNMENT SERIALS PUBLICATIONS. Offers complete bibliographic histories for some 35,000 U.S. government publications. Most useful for identifying early, pre-FCC serial publications on communications and other relevant topics, as well as examples of government's uses of mass media (e.g., films in agriculture, health-related publications). Arranged by government offices under SUDOC classes; see listings for FCC in "CC" class. Indexes for Agency Class Chronology, agencies, titles, and keywords in titles; useful keywords include advertising, film, marketing, radio, television.

0929 Low, Kathleen. **ELECTRONIC ACCESS TO GOVERNMENT AND GOVERNMENT INFORMATION: A SELECTIVE BIBLIOGRAPHY.** Monticello, IL: Vance Bibliographies, 1991, 7 pp. (Public Administration Series, P-3095). About 60 unannotated references on the "electronic city hall," televising federal and state legislatures and community information services.

0930 Maxwell, Bruce. **WASHINGTON ONLINE**. Washington: Congressional Quarterly, 1995, 2 vols.: HOW TO ACCESS THE GOVERNMENT'S ELECTRONIC BULLETIN BOARDS (1995, 340 pp.) and HOW TO ACCESS THE FEDERAL GOVERNMENT ON THE INTERNET (1995, 402 pp.). Usefully annotated guides to computer access to government information. Arranged by agency.

0931 **MONTHLY CATALOG OF UNITED STATES GOVERNMENT PUBLICATIONS**. Washington: GPO, 1895–date, monthly. Online version GPO MONTHLY CATALOG available from Dialog, OCLC, and other services: covers July 1976–date, updated monthly. CD-ROM versions (titles vary) available from SilverPlatter: covers 1976–date, updating varies (monthly on Information Access). Most comprehensive bibliography of literature produced by the U.S. government, though often lagging months behind date of publication. Arranges document entries by issuing department, office, or agency. Semiannual indexes of authors, titles, subjects, series/reports, contract numbers, stock numbers, and title keywords. Headings based on LIBRARY OF CONGRESS SUBJECT HEADINGS. Electronic versions offer access superior to print version.

7-B-2. Congressional Committees

Unless otherwise noted, addresses for Congress are RHOB: Rayburn House Office Bldg., Washington, DC 20515; and SHOB: Senate Hart Office Bldg., Washington, DC 20510. Senate homepage: http://www.senate.gov/. House homepage: http://www.house.gov/. Electronic mail addresses for individual Congressmen are listed in THOMAS (0913) for the Senate: http://www.senate.gov/senator/membmail.html; and for the House: gopher.house.gov. or www.house.gov.

0932 **House. Committee on Appropriations. Subcommittee on Commerce, Justice, State, and Judiciary**. H-309, The Capitol, Washington 20515. Voice: 202-225-3351. Appropriation of funds for FCC, Board of International Broadcasting, and U.S. Information Agency.

0933 **House. Committee on Commerce. Subcommittee on Telecommunications and Finance**. 2125 Rayburn House Office Bldg., Washington 20515. Voice: 202-225-2927. Primary House center for legislation related to interstate and foreign communications (broadcast, cable, radio, wire, microwave, satellite) plus FCC oversight.

0934 **House. Committee on Government Reform and Oversight. Subcommittee on Government Management, Information, and Technology**. B-373, Rayburn House Office Bldg., Washington 20515. Voice: 202-225-5147. Jurisdiction over FCC and USIA.

0935 **House. Committee on the Judiciary. Subcommittee on Commercial and Administrative Law.** B-353 Rayburn House Office Bldg., Washington 20515. Voice: 202-225-2825. Legislation related to anticompetitive practices and monopolies in communications, including cable and telephone industry practices.

0936 **House. Committee on the Judiciary. Subcommittee on Courts and Intellectual Property.** B-351A Rayburn House Office Bldg., Washington 20515. Voice: 202-225-5741. Legislation on copyrights, patents, and trademarks.

0937 **House. Committee on Science. Subcommittee on Basic Research.** B-374, Rayburn House Office Bldg., Washington 20515. Voice: 202-225-9662. Legislative jurisdiction over Office of Science and Technology Policy, National Science Foundation, and all sponsored scientific research in computer, communications, and information science.

0938 **House. Committee on Science. Subcommittee on Space and Aeronautics.** 2320 Rayburn House Office Bldg., Washington 20515. Voice: 202-225-7858. Jurisdictions include NASA and use of space, including space communications and related matters, and earth remote sensing policy.

0939 **House. Committee on Science. Subcommittee on Technology.** 2919 Rayburn House Office Bldg., Washington 20515. Voice: 202-225-8844. Jurisdiction over NIST and NTIS.

0940 **Senate. Committee on Appropriations. Subcommittee on Commerce, Justice, State, and Judiciary.** 146A The Capitol, Washington 20510. Voice: 202-224-7277. Appropriates funds for FCC, Board of International Broadcasting, NTIA, and U.S. Information Agency.

0941 **Senate. Committee on Commerce, Science, and Transportation. Subcommittee on Communications**. 227 Hart Senate Office Bldg., Washington 20510. Voice: 202-224-5184. Primary Senate center for legislation related to interstate and foreign communications (television, cable, local and long-distance telephone services, radio, international satellite communications). Oversees FCC and NTIA.

0942 **Senate. Committee on the Judiciary.** 224 Dirksen Senate Office Bldg., Washington 20510. Voice: 202-224-5225. Includes jurisdiction over copyright and patent policy.

0943 **Senate. Committee on the Judiciary. Subcommittee on Antitrust, Business Rights, and Competition.** 229 Hart Senate Office Bldg. 229, Washington 20510. Voice: 202-224-9494. Legislation related to competitive practices in communications, including cable and telephone industry practices.

0944 **Senate. Committee on the Judiciary. Subcommittee on Terrorism, Technology and Government Information**. 161 Dirksen Senate Office Bldg., Washington 20510. Voice: 202-224-6791. Jurisdiction over Freedom of Information Act.

7-B-3. Congressional Agencies

0945 **Congressional Budget Office**. Second and D Sts. SW, Washington 20515. Voice: 202-226-2700. Provides Congress with assessments of the economic impact of the federal budget.

0946 **General Accounting Office.** 700 4th St. NW., Washington 20548. Voice: 202-512-4800. Publications and reports: P.O. Box 6015, Gaithersburg MD 20884-6015. Voice: 202-512-6000. Fax: 301-258-4066. Internet: info@www.gao.gov. Investigative arm of Congress, independently audits government agencies. Examines all matters related to receipt and disbursement of public funds.

See 0190. **Library of Congress**. Relevant divisions include:

1 **Congressional Research Service**. Science Policy Research Division. Voice: 202-707-9547. Provides objective, nonpartisan research, analysis, and information to assist Congressional functions.

2 **Copyright Office**. Voice: 202-707-8350. Issues copyrights and publishes regularly updated information leaflets on all aspects of copyright process. PUBLICATIONS ON COPYRIGHT, *Circular 2,* is available by voice: 202-707-9100; fax: 202-512-2250.

7-B-4. Executive Branch Departments

0947 **Department of Commerce**. Herbert C. Hoover Bldg., 14th St. and Constitution Aves. NW, Washington 20230. Voice: 202-482-2000. Internet: www.doc.gov.

1 **International Trade Administration**. Under Secretary for International Trade. Voice: 202-482-3809. Promotes world trade and strengthening of U.S. international trade and investment position.

2 **National Institute of Standards and Technology** (NIST). 820 NIST Technology Services Bldg. Rte. I-270, Gaithersburg, MD 20899. Voice: 301-975-4500. Fax: 301-975-2183. Formerly National Bureau of Standards. Participates in standards development and promotes standards via publication, dissemination, and other information services. NIST also oversees National Information Standards Organization (NISO), which develops standards for publishing, libraries, information science.

3 **National Technical Information Service** (NTIS). 5285 Port Royal Rd., Springfield, VA 22161. Voice: 703-487-4808. Fax: 703-321-8547. Primary federal depository and distributor for research studies done for federal agencies. Supplies CCITT, ANSI, and other standards adopted by U.S. government agencies. Issues a variety of finding aids based on NTIS and other databases.

4 **National Telecommunications and Information Administration** (NTIA). Voice: 202-482-1551. Fax: 202-482-1635. Internet: www.ntia.doc.gov/. Develops telecommunication and information policy for executive branch. Develops and presents U.S. plans and policies in international organizations and coordinates U.S. telecommunications and information policy positions in consultation with FCC, Department of State, and other agencies. Manages federal use of radio spectrum. Government base for National Information Infrastructure (NII) programs. Conducts research on telecommunication. Provides information to federal and state agencies. Awards construction grants to noncommercial telecommunication services. Administers National Endowment for Children's Educational Television. Issues PUBLICATIONS ABSTRACTS (1979–date) through NTIS, an annual list of NTIA staff publications on results of research and engineering. NTIA includes these major units:

* Policy Coordination and Management. Voice: 202-482-1835
* Office of Policy Analysis and Development. Voice: 202-482-1880. Concerned with domestic policy development.
* Office of Spectrum Management. Voice: 202-482-1850.
* Interdepartment Radio Advisory Committee. (IRAC). Voice: 202-482-0599. Oldest federal telecommunications agency (created in 1922), this is a frequency spectrum coordination body for all federal users.
* Frequency Management Advisory Council. Voice: 202-482-1850.
* Office of International Affairs. Voice: 202-482-1304
* Information Infrastructure Task Force. Voice: 202-482-1840. Internet: www.iitf.doc.gov. Issued THE NATIONAL INFORMATION INFRASTRUCTURE: AGENDA FOR ACTION (1993) and many subsequent NII analyses.

0948 **Department of Justice**. 10th and Constitution Ave., Washington 20530. Locator: 202-514-2000. Internet: justice2.usdoj.gov.

1 **Antitrust Division**. Assistant Attorney General. 555 4th St. NW, Washington 20001. Voice: 202-514-5621. Investigates and litigates antitrust cases in communications. Participates in agency proceedings and rulemakings concerning communications; monitors and analyzes legislation.

2 **Regulatory Affairs**. Deputy Assistant Attorney General. Voice: 202-633-2404. Section on Communications and Finance. Voice: 202-272-4247.

0949 **Department of State**. 2201 C St. NW., Washington 20520. Locator: 202-647-4000.

1 **Bureau of Economic and Business Affairs**. Voice: 202-647-7971. Fax: 202-647-5713. Handles trade-related international communication issues. Includes functions and personnel of former Bureau of International Communications and Information Policy. Develops and manages international communication information policy. Liaison for other federal agencies and departments and the private sector in international communications issues.

2 **International Telecommunications Advisory Committee** (formerly U.S. National Committee for CCITT). Voice: 202-647-2592. Fax: 202-647-7407. Represents U.S. interests in ITU-T sector (formerly CCITT), advising and reporting back to State Department. Composed of study groups for telecommunication services and policy, switching, signaling, ISDN, telephone network operations, and data network and telematic terminals that reflect ITU-T activities. Membership includes organizations, product, and service providers.

3 **Office of Radio Spectrum Policy**. Voice: 202-647-2592.

7-B-5. Federal Communications Commission

0950 **Federal Communications Commission**, 1919 M. St. NW, Washington 20554. Public Service Division.Voice: 202-418-0200. Locator: 202-418-0500 (Public Affairs). Fax: 202-418-2809 (Public

Affairs). Internet: www.fcc.gov. [Note: FCC is scheduled to move to the Portals building complex in southwestern Washington in 1997–1998.] Agency holds primary responsibility for electronic communications authorization and regulation. Participates in development of technical standards and oversees operator compliance. Publishes, as formal legal record of all proceedings, FCC RECORD (1986–date, biweekly); formerly FCC REPORTS (1934–1986). Full text is available online on LEXIS/NEXIS (0912).

1 **INFORMATION SEEKERS GUIDE: HOW TO FIND INFORMATION AT THE FCC**. FCC Public Service Division, October 1996 (annually revised), 42 pp. Useful key to finding people, documents, and processes at the commission.

2 **FCC TELEPHONE DIRECTORY**. FCC Office of Managing Director, continually revised. Once issued four times a year, this loose-leaf directory is now revised continually, a section at a time. Most useful is the organizational listing (blue pages) which details FCC structure and key personnel.

3 **ANNUAL REPORT**. Washington: GPO, 1935–date, annual (editions for 1942–44 originally published only in limited mimeograph version; 1935–1955 issues reprinted by Arno Press in 3 vols., 1971). Annual report on FCC regulation of interstate and foreign communications. Includes FCC operating data: employees, funding, status of cases. Regulatory activities data: authorizations, licensing, permits, applications, denials, revocations, by class of operation; Field Operations Bureau statistics for applications, examinations, licensed operators, by type; private radio statistics for authorized stations, transmitters, authorization requests, by type; equipment authorization applications, acceptances, notifications, certifications, changes, by type. Data from reports by regulated companies and stations and FCC files. Indexed in STATISTICAL MASTERFILE (0109).

4 **Office of the Chairman**. Voice: 202-418-1000. Fax: 202-418-2801.

5 **Office of Engineering and Technology**. 2000 M St. NW, Washington 20554. Voice: 202-418-2470. Fax: 202-418-1944. Includes divisions on spectrum engineering, propagation analysis, engineering evaluation, equipment authorization, sampling and measurements, and technical standards.

6 **Office of Plans and Policy**. Voice: 202-418-2030. Fax: 202-418-2807. Think-tank and research arm (largely economic in approach) for the FCC.

7 **Office of Public Affairs**. Voice: 202-418-0500. Fax: 202-418-2809. Includes FCC Library (Room 639, Voice: 202-418-0450).

8 **Cable Services Bureau.** 2033 M St. NW, Washington 20554. Voice: 202-418-7200. Fax: 202-418-2376. The FCC had a cable bureau in the 1970s that disappeared with deregulation. This new version, set up in 1993, grew out of Congressional re-regulation of cable. Includes divisions on consumer protection, policy and rules, and technical services.

9 **International Bureau.** 2000 M St. NW, Washington 20554 Voice: 202-418-0437. Fax: 202-418-2818. Grew out of a smaller office to become a bureau in 1994 combining all FCC activities interacting with other countries and the ITU. Includes divisions on telecommunications (which centralizes all FCC satellite functions, domestic and international), and planning and negotiations (2025 M St. NW).

10 **Mass Media Bureau**. Voice: 202-418-2600. Fax: 202-418-2828. Centralizes all radio and television authorization and regulation in divisions on audio services, enforcement, (2025 M St. NW), policy and rules (2000 M St. NW), and video services (which includes MMDS services, 1919 M St. NW).

11 **Wireless Telecommunications Bureau,** 2025 M St. NW, Washington 20554. Voice: 202-418-0800. Fax: 202-418-0787. Formed out of the former Private Radio Bureau in 1994 to centralize all domestic wireless regulation (except satellite services), this includes divisions on auctions (of spectrum for selected services), commercial (mobile) radio, enforcement, policy, private (mobile) radio, operations (located in Gettysburg, PA), and licensing.

7-B-6. Federal Courts

(See LEXIS/NEXIS (0912) and Westlaw (0914) for electronic versions of federal and state court reporters.)

0951 **CONGRESSIONAL QUARTERLY'S GUIDE TO THE U.S. SUPREME COURT**. Washington: Congressional Quarterly, 1997 (4th ed.), 2 vols. Standard guide to history and practices of Supreme Court, with indexes of subjects, cases, lists of major decisions, and bibliographies.

0952 **The Supreme Court of the United States.** U.S. Supreme Court Building, 1 First St. NE, Washington 20543. Voice: 202-479-3211 (Public Information Office). Decides some cases appealed from lower federal courts. There are many ways to find texts of decisions:

1 **UNITED STATES REPORTS (U.S.).** Various private reporters and publishers prior to 1922; Washington: GPO, 1922–date, weekly when Court is in session. Official version of all Supreme Court decisions, this series now runs to nearly 500 volumes and should be found in any good law school library. First to appear during a session are slip opinions, followed by preliminary prints and then final bound volumes (3–4 per term). Although the official final authority on wording, volumes appear as much as 3 years late, making following private sources invaluable.

2 **SUPREME COURT REPORTER (S.Ct.).** Minneapolis: West Publishing Co., 1882–date, biweekly. Perhaps the best and most widely cited, although unofficial, source of Supreme Court decisions—best because it publishes decisions far faster than the official source. Decisions appear first in biweekly advance sheets, followed by interim volumes and then final volumes, usually three per term.

3 **UNITED STATES SUPREME COURT REPORTS: THE LAWYER'S EDITION.** Rochester, NY: The Lawyers' Cooperative Publishing Company, 1790–1955 First Series, 100 vols; 1956–date Second Series. Another commercial (unofficial) resource that includes summaries of lawyers' written briefs.

4 **UNITED STATES LAW WEEK.** Washington: Bureau of National Affairs, 1933–date, weekly. Publishes Supreme Court decisions within a week of their issue. These are cumulated in a loose-leaf service.

5 **UNITED STATES SUPREME COURT BULLETIN.** Chicago: Commerce Clearing House, 1980–date, weekly. Publishes Supreme Court decisions within a week or so of their issue, cumulating in a loose-leaf notebook.

6 **LANDMARK BRIEFS AND ARGUMENTS OF THE SUPREME COURT OF THE UNITED STATES.** Frederick, later Bethesda, MD: University Publications of America, 1978–date, irregular. Prints selected briefs and arguments of Supreme Court cases.

0953 **United States Court of Appeals for the District of Columbia Circuit.** U.S. Court House, Third and Constitution Ave., NW, Washington 20001. Voice: 202-535-3308. This is 1 of 13 such courts, important to telecommunications as the expert court dealing with most appeals from FCC decisions. Its decisions appear in the **FEDERAL REPORTER (F., F.2d, F.3d).** Minneapolis: West Publishing, 1880–1924 for First Series (300 volumes); 1925–1993 for Second Series (999 volumes); and 1993–date for Third Series. The best printed commercial resource for decisions of all the federal appeals courts. Note: prior to 1932, this series included decisions of U.S. District Courts.

0954 **United States District Court.** There are 89 federal district courts (1–4 per state). Sources for texts of decisions include:

1 **FEDERAL SUPPLEMENT (F.Supp.).** Minneapolis: West Publishing, 1923–date. The commercial resource for all federal district courts, although it includes only a small proportion of all cases decided (the judge writing the opinion makes the decision on whether to publish).

2 **FEDERAL RULES DECISIONS (F.R.D.).** Minneapolis: West Publishing, 1941–date. Includes those U.S. District Court decisions involving federal rules of civil procedure, and thus may include some communication-related decisions based on FCC rules.

7-C. Policy Organizations

7-C-1. Policy Research Organizations

(Note: see also: 6-B-2, University-based Research; 7-C-2, Public Interest Groups.)

0955 **Benton Foundation Communication Policy Project.** 1634 Eye St. NW, Washington 20006. Voice: 202-638-5770. Fax 202-638-5771. e-mail: benton@benton.org. Internet: cdinet.com/benton.

Nonprofit organization that promotes public interest values and noncommercial services for the National Information Infrastructure through research, policy analysis, print, video, and online publishing, and outreach to nonprofits and foundations. Works with and develops programs and resources for other nonprofit organizations. Publishes policy working papers, briefings, and bulletins by scholars and researchers.

0956 **Catholic University. Communications Law Institute**. Law School, Washington 20064. Voice: 202-319-5140. Publishes COMMLAW CONSPECTUS (1993–date, annual) and research studies.

0957 **City University of New York. Stanton Haskell Center for Public Policy & Telecommunications & Informations Systems**. New York 10036. Voice: 212-642-2984. Fax: 212-642-1959. Publishes working papers as well as major reports, e.g., BROADCAST OF TWO-WAY VIDEO IN DISTANCE EDUCATION (1993)

0958 **Columbia University. Columbia Institute for Tele-Information (CITI).** Graduate School of Business, New York 10027. Voice: 212-854-4222. Fax: 212-932-7816. Research program with many publications. Publishes annual report and a voluminous "Working Paper Series" (with over 600 titles to date), including C. Edwin Baker's MERGING PHONE AND CABLE (1994), Stanley M. Besen's RATE REGULATION, EFFECTIVE COMPETITION, AND THE CABLE ACT OF 1992 (1994), and Donald W. Hawthorne's REWIRING THE FIRST AMENDMENT: MEANING, CONTENT, AND PUBLIC BROADCASTING (1994), and many others.

0959 **Georgetown University Law Center. Institute for Public Representation.** 600 New Jersey Ave. NW, Washington 20001. Voice: 202-662-9535. Fax: 202-662-9681. Public interest law firm specializing in communications regulatory policy; helps citizens groups make input unto local and federal electronic media regulation. Publishes annual review of communications cases.

0960 **Harvard University. Harvard Program on Information Resources Policy.** 200 Aiken Hall, Cambridge, MA 02138. Voice: 617-495-4114. Internet: PIRP@DAS.HARVARD.EDU. Publishes research studies on communications and information, including Patricia Hirl Longstaff's INFORMATION THEORY AS A BASIS FOR RATIONAL REGULATION OF THE COMMUNICATIONS INDUSTRY (1994), Naoyuki Koike's CABLE TELEVISION AND TELEPHONE COMPANIES: TOWARD RESIDENTIAL BROADBAND COMMUNICATIONS SERVICES IN THE UNITED STATES AND JAPAN (1990).

0961 **Massachusetts Institute of Technology. Research Program on Communications Policy.** Cambridge, MA 02139. Voice: 617-253-4138. Fax: 617-253-7326. Internet: RPCP@FARNSWORTH.MIT.EDU. Telecommunications and information technology research program in MIT's Center for Technology, Policy, and Industrial Development. Focuses on technical, economic, and policy issues. Organizes Cambridge Roundtable discussion forum, hosts and participates in workshops and seminars. Publishes many studies and reports, including Ithiel de Sola Pool's CROSS OWNERSHIP POLICY IN A CHANGING MEDIA ENVIRONMENT (1993), Lisa Allen Vawter's DEREGULATION OF CABLE (1984), Charles L. Jackson's THE CHANGING BROADCAST SPECTRUM: SCA, LPTV, DBS, & MDS (1983).

0962 **New York Law School. Communications Media Center.** 57 Worth St., New York, 10013. Voice: 212-431-2160. Fax: 212-966-2053. Sponsors lectures, symposia, conferences, and academic programs, including Media Law Project, which publishes MEDIA LAW AND POLICY (1991–date, semiannual), formerly MEDIA LAW JOURNAL.

0963 **Syracuse University. Transactional Records Access Clearinghouse (TRAC).** 488 Newhouse II, Syracuse, NY 13244. Voice: 315-443-3563. Internet: tracinfo.syr.edu/. Nonprofit center organized to help journalists locate and analyze data about federal enforcement agencies and to provide training about researching federal agencies. Operates a Washington office: Suite 301, 666 Pennsylvania Ave. SE., Washington 20003.

0964 **University of Florida. Brechner Center for Freedom of Information**. Journalism Bldg., Gainesville, FL 32611. Voice: 904-392-2273. Fax: 904-392-3919. Research on telecommunications and media policy, especially First Amendment concerns. Publishes BRECHNER REPORT (1977–date).

0965 **University of Missouri. Freedom of Information Center.** 20 Walter Williams Hall, Columbia, MO 65211. Voice: 314-882-4856. Issues F.O.I CENTER REPORTS (monthly) that summarize topical issues about public's right to information. They are not indexed in the standard services. Excellent library offers reference and research services on a fee basis. Founded in 1958.

0966 **Vanderbilt University. The Freedom Forum First Amendment Center.** 1207 18th Ave., South, Nashville, TN 37212. Voice: 615-321-9588. Fax: 615-321-9599. Fosters public understanding of First Amendment rights through discussion and debate on free expression and freedom of information issues. Fellowship program supports research and writing of six residential scholars annually, whose projects are expected to promote public understanding of the First Amendment. Publishes scholarly reports and video recordings. Founded in 1992.

7-C-2. Public Interest Groups

0967 **Accuracy in Media**. 4455 Connecticut Ave. NW, Ste. 330, Washington, 20008. Voice: 202-364-4401. Fax: 202-364-4098. Internet: take.aim.org/aim.html. 28,000 members. Annual budget: $1.6 million. News media watchdog organization promoting fair, balanced, and accurate news coverage. Investigates complaints of media inaccuracies; publicizes cases, asks for corrections, and mobilizes public pressure to bring about remedial action; works for adoption by media of higher standards of reporting and editing. Publishes printed report twice monthly. Produces weekly column, 5-day-a-week radio commentary, and weekly television program dealing with media inaccuracies. Sponsors speakers bureau and conferences. Founded in 1969.

0968 **Alliance for Public Technology**. 901 15th St. NW, Washington, 20005. Voice: 202-408-1403. Fax: 202-408-1134. Internet: apt.org/apt.html. Public interest group with interest in affordable access to information and telecommunication services and technologies, especially for elderly, residential consumers, low-income groups, and disabled. Publishes newsletter APT NEWS (1991–date, bimonthly) and reports. Co-sponsored Telecommunity Conference (1993) and report BRINGING HOME THE ELECTRONIC HIGHWAY: PUBLIC TV AND UNIVERSAL ACCESS (1994), by Susan G. Hadden.

0969 **Center for Media Education**. 1511 K St. NW, Ste. 518, Washington, 20005. Voice: 202-628-2620. Fax: 202-628-2554. Internet: cme@cme.org. Nonprofit organization that has as its purpose the promotion of the democratic potential of the electronic media. Projects include Campaign for Kids' TV, aimed at improving the quality of children's television, and the Future of Media Project, dedicated to fostering a public interest vision for the new media and information superhighway. Organizes and educates consumer groups on issues of public policy and the media, serves as a clearinghouse for press, analyzes trends in electronic media, and monitors industry practices. Founded in 1991.

0970 **Center for Media in Public Affairs**. 2100 L St. NW, Ste. 300, Washington, 20037. Voice: 202-223-2942. Fax: 202-872-4014. Internet: www.proxima.com/cmpa. Nonpartisan research and educational organization that has as its purpose to analyze construction how news and entertainment media treat social and political issues. Primary research tool is content analysis. Conducts surveys to determine media's role in structuring national and international agenda. Publishes newsletter (bimonthly) and monographs. Founded in 1986.

0971 **Freedom of Information Clearinghouse**. 2000 P St. NW, P.O. Box 19367, Washington, 20036. Voice: 202-833-3000. Program of the Center for Study of Responsive Law. Monitors FOI issues and assists citizens, public interest groups and the media in getting information from the government. Founded in 1972.

0972 **Media Institute**. 1000 Potomac St. NW, Ste. 301, Washington, 20007. Voice: 202-298-7512. Fax: 202-337-7092. Internet: tmi@clark.net. Annual budget $750,000. Nonprofit research foundation specializing in communications policy issues. Advocates and encourages freedom of speech, a competitive communications industry, and excellence in journalism. Publishes books and reports, including ADVERTISING RIGHTS: THE NEGLECTED FREEDOM: TOWARD A NEW DOCTRINE OF COMMERCIAL SPEECH. Convenes conferences, sponsors lecture series and awards program. Founded in 1979.

0973 **Media Research Center**. 113 South West St., Alexandria, VA 22314. Voice: 703-683-9733. Fax: 703-683-9736. Internet: AJMRC@aol.com. Conservative research and education foundation that has as its mission to identify bias, to expose the liberal tilt in the news media, and to restore to the journalistic community balance and notion of fairness. Analyzes news and prime time entertainment programming and major print publications for evidence of bias in media. Records and archives programs for study; MRC Database consists of almost 90,000 hours of news and entertainment programming dating back to 1987. Publishes findings in newsletters, books, and reports. Publications include AND THAT'S THE WAY IT ISN'T: A REFERENCE GUIDE TO MEDIA BIAS and MEDIAWATCH (1990). Founded in 1987.

0974 **National Coalition on Television Violence**. P.O. Box 70956, Bethesda, MD 20813. Voice: 301-986-0362. Fax: 301-656-7031. 3,500 members. Annual budget $107,000. Membership organization whose primary goal is to reduce gratuitous violence on television by educating the public about the harm violence as entertainment does to society. Monitors prime-time and Saturday morning children's programming, compiles statistics on incidents of TV violence, supports efforts to develop regulatory and technological tools that give viewers control over programming coming into the home. Publishes member newsletter. Founded in 1980 and absorbed Council for Children's Television and Media in 1993.

0975 **National Council for Television and Families**. 10900 Wilshire Blvd., Ste. 700, Los Angeles, CA 90024. Voice: 310-443-2000. Fax: 310-208-5984. Annual budget $350,000. Nonprofit, nonadversarial, educational organization that communicates information to television executives, writers, and producers on issues impacting the family in the areas of education, health, environment, human relations, and public policy. Seeks to enhance quality of life for families and children by affecting the creation and uses of prime time entertainment. Sponsors conferences that bring together television's creative community and experts in issues affecting the family. Publishes member newsletter (monthly) and TELEVISION AND FAMILIES magazine (quarterly). Annual conference. Founded in 1977.

0976 **National Freedom of Information Coalition**. 400 S. Record St., 6th Floor, Dallas, TX 57202. Voice: 214-977-6658. Maintains a network of state freedom of information groups and academic centers to share resources and solutions to common FOI problems.

0977 **Reporters Committee for Freedom of the Press**. 1101 Wilson Blvd., No. 1901, Arlington, VA 22209. Voice 703-807-2100. Fax: 703-807-2109. Freedom of information hotline: 800-336-4243. e-mail: rcfp@capaccess.org. Membership includes reporters, editors, publishers, and lawyers working for print and broadcast organizations. The committee maintains a research fund for members involved in court cases and a library. Open to the public by appointment.

7-C-3 Legal Groups

(See also: 7-C-2, Public Interest Groups)

0978 **Federal Communications Bar Association**. 1722 Eye St. NW, Ste. 300, Washington, 20006. Voice: 202-736-8640; 202-833-2684. Fax: 202-736-8740. Internet: www.fcba.org/. 2600 members. Organization of attorneys and others involved in development, interpretation, and practice of communications law and policy. Promotes fairness and efficiency in development and application of communications law and policy. Monitors relevant legislative, agency and court developments. Holds monthly luncheons with speakers. Co-sponsors telecommunications seminars. Co-publishes FEDERAL COMMUNICATIONS LAW JOURNAL (1260); publishes member newsletter (monthly) and membership directory. Founded in 1936.

0979 **National Association of State Cable Agencies (NASCA).** Tower Bldg., 21st Fl., Governor Rockefeller Empire State Plaza, Albany, NY 12223. Voice: 518-474-4992. Fax: 518-486-5727. Meets irregularly to discuss regulatory strategy of state agencies that regulate cable. Founded in 1978 as Conference of State Cable Agencies; name changed in 1984.

7-D. Selected Secondary Resources

7-D-1. Surveys of Policy and Regulation

0980 Altschull, J. Herbert. **AGENTS OF POWER: THE MEDIA AND PUBLIC POLICY.** White Plains, NY: Longman, 1995 (2nd ed.), 461 pp. A provocative and careful historical-philosophical analysis of the performance and effect of the news media in the U.S. and internationally. Foremost is the question of who controls information disseminated through the mass media.

0981 Bagdikian, Ben H. **THE MEDIA MONOPOLY.** Boston: Becon Press,1992 (4th ed.), 288 pp. The author creates benchmarks that anticipate and predict the developing concentration of the media industry.

0982 **FREE SPEECH YEARBOOK.** Carbondale: Southern Illinois University Press, 1962–date, annual. A project of the Speech Communication Association, this useful annual reviews the year, offers a dozen or more scholarly assessments, and reviews important related books.

0983 Gillmor, Donald M. et al. **FUNDAMENTALS OF MASS COMMUNICATION LAW.** St. Paul, MN: West Publishing, 1996, 428 pp. Cohesive text treatment of freedom of expression, libel, privacy, journalist's privilege, obscenity and indecency, access to government, freedom of information, advertising law and regulation, ownership questions, and electronic media law. Glossary, notes, index.

0984 Hixson, Richard. **MASS MEDIA AND THE CONSTITUTION: AN ENCYCLOPEDIA OF SUPREME COURT DECISIONS.** New York: Garland, 1989, 529 pp. Covers 300 cases with summary, circumstances, opinion, referenced cases, and further reading citations. Notes, bibliography, index.

0985 Pember, Don R. **MASS MEDIA LAW.** Dubuque, IA: Brown & Benchmark, 1977–date, various editions and now annual, 650 pp. Effective with the 1996 edition, this will appear in annually revised versions, covering in text fashion all key areas of media regulation and law.

0986 Practising Law Institute. **COMMUNICATIONS LAW.** New York: PLI, 1973–date, annual (usually in 2 or 3 vols.). A short course handbook for lawyers, this includes cases, decisions, and articles from the previous year in media law.

0987 Regan, Priscilla M. **LEGISLATING PRIVACY: TECHNOLOGY, SOCIAL VALUES, AND PUBLIC POLICY.** Chapel Hill: University of North Carolina Press, 1995, 310 pp. Privacy as a philosophical and legal concept, privacy in American society, information and communication privacy, and Congress' role. Glossary, notes, index.

0988 Rosini, Neil J. **THE PRACTICAL GUIDE TO LIBEL LAW.** New York: Praeger, 1991, 229 pp. A three-step guide to staying out of trouble. Notes, table of cases, index.

0989 Strong, William S. **THE COPYRIGHT BOOK.** Cambridge: MIT Press, 1993 (4th ed.), 288 pp. The best brief overview of a complex area. Appendices, notes, index.

0990 Teeter, Dwight L. Jr., and Don R. Le Duc. **LAW OF MASS COMMUNICATIONS: FREEDOM AND CONTROL OF PRINT AND BROADCAST MEDIA.** Westbury, NY: Foundation, 1995 (8th ed.), 871 pp. Latest version of a specialized casebook that first appeared in 1969. Notes, table of cases, index.

0991 Van Alstyne, William W. **FIRST AMENDMENT: CASES AND MATERIALS.** Westbury, NY: Foundation Press, 1995 (2nd ed.), 1,187 pp. Valuable collection of lightly edited important case decisions across the spectrum of First Amendment issues. Notes, index.

7-D-2. Newspapers and Magazines

0992 Berdes, George R. **FRIENDLY ADVERSARIES: THE PRESS AND GOVERNMENT**. Milwaukee, WI: Center for the Study of the American Press, Marquette University, 1969, 187 pp. Collection of 13 interviews with veteran Washington reporters about press freedom and reponsibilities.

0993 Carpenter, Ted Galen. **THE CAPTIVE PRESS: FOREIGN POLICY CRISES AND THE FIRST AMENDMENT**. Washington: Cato Institute, 1995, 315 pp. Attempts to document the U.S. government's efforts to intimidate, co-opt, and censor the media and undermine the First Amendment. Covers wartime print and electronic press from American revolution to Haiti, Somalia, and Bosnia. Index.

0994 Dennis, Everette E., and Eli M. Noam. **THE COST OF LIBEL: ECONOMIC AND POLICY IMPLICATIONS**. New York: Columbia University Press, 1989, 293 pp. A volume in COLUMBIA STUDIES IN BUSINESS, GOVERNMENT, AND SOCIETY series. Ten essays by experts re-examine debate over libel law, with particular attention to 1964 landmark Supreme Court case, *New York Times v. Sullivan*, and others. Offers statistical evidence for the "chilling effect" of libel law law on the media. Index.

0995 Lawson, Linda. **TRUTH IN PUBLISHING: FEDERAL REGULATION OF THE PRESS'S BUSINESS PRACTICES, 1880-1920**. Carbondale: Southern Illinois University Press, 1993, 229 pp. Examines the press at the turn of the century "as a business susceptible to corporate abuses" that propelled subsequent government legislative and regulatory actions, including the Newpaper Publicity Act of 1912, required most publications to disclose hitherto private information about their ownership and to label as advertisements any reading notices designed to resemble news stories or editorials. Extensive bibliography; index.

7-D-3. Broadcasting

0996 Carter, T. Barton et al. **THE FIRST AMENDMENT AND THE FIFTH ESTATE: THE LAW OF ELECTRONIC MEDIA**. Westbury, NY: Foundation, 1996 (4th ed.), 959 pp. Basic casebook with extensive commentary and including the 1996 amendments. Notes, index.

0997 Ginsburg Douglas et al. **REGULATION OF THE ELECTRONIC MASS MEDIA: LAW AND POLICY FOR RADIO, TELEVISION, CABLE AND THE NEW VIDEO TECHNOLOGIES**. St. Paul, MN: West, 1991 (2nd ed.), 657 pp. Good casebook overview of important cases and current trends. Index.

0998 Huber, Peter W. et al. **THE TELECOMMUNICATIONS ACT OF 1996**. Boston: Little, Brown, 1996, 428 pp. One of the first analyses of the landmark changes in the Communications Act, including the Act itself and the congressional explanation of its provisions.

0999 Knauer, Leon T. et al. **TELECOMMUNICATIONS ACT HANDBOOK: A COMPLETE REFERENCE FOR BUSINESS**. Rockville, MD: Government Institutes, 1996, 620 pp. Analysis of the Telecommunications Act of 1996 from an historical and practical perspective. Explains how the Act will change each industry sector, including broadcast, cable, and wireless. Includes the text of the Act and the text of the Communications Act of 1934 as amended by the Telecommunications Act.

1000 Krattenmaker, Thomas G., and Lucas A. Powe, Jr. **REGULATING BROADCAST PROGRAMMING**. Cambridge, MA: MIT Press, 1994, 369 pp. Useful analysis arguing for further deregulation of broadcast content controls. References, indexes.

1001 Le Duc, Don R. **BEYOND BROADCASTING: PATTERNS IN POLICY AND LAW.** White Plains, NY: Longman, 1987, 216 pp. The changing context of broadcast regulation in era of cable and newer media. Notes, bibliography, index.

1002 Lipschultz, Jeremy H. **BROADCAST INDECENCY: FCC REGULATION AND THE FIRST AMENDMENT.** Newton, MA: Focal Press, 1996, 261 pp. One of the first book-length discussions of this controversial topic, this reviews the varied terms and findings of important cases. Appendices, references.

1003 National Association of Broadcasters. **NAB LEGAL GUIDE TO BROADCAST LAW AND REGULATION**. Washington: NAB, 1996 (5th ed.), 650 pp. Highly detailed desk guide to day-to-day programming and operational rules, including impact of 1996 Telecommunications Act. Extensive appendices of FCC forms, index.

1004 **PIKE & FISCHER'S DESK GUIDE TO COMMUNICATIONS LAW RESEARCH.** Bethesda, MD: Pike & Fischer, 1993, 396 pp. Guide to using PIKE & FISCHER RADIO REGULATION (1017) with sample searches, tables, indices, bibliography, and glossary. Includes description and directory of FCC departments.

1005 Powe, Lucas A., Jr. **AMERICAN BROADCASTING AND THE FIRST AMENDMENT**. Berkeley: University of California Press, 1987, 295 pp. Argues for more of a print free press model for broadcasting. Notes, index.

1006 Ray, William B. **FCC: THE UPS AND DOWNS OF RADIO-TV REGULATION.** Ames: Iowa State University Press, 1990, 193 pp. Sharply critical analysis of 1980s' deregulatory decisions and trends by a former long-time FCC official. Notes, bibliography, index.

1007 Smith, F. Leslie et al. **ELECTRONIC MEDIA AND GOVERNMENT: THE REGULATION OF WIRELESS AND WIRED MASS COMMUNICATION IN THE UNITED STATES**. White Plains, NY: Longman, 1995, 545 pp. Cohesive treatise (rather than casebook) treatment of the field. Notes, index.

7-D-4. Cable and Newer Media

1008 Brenner, Daniel L., and Monroe E. Price. **CABLE TELEVISION AND OTHER NONBROADCAST VIDEO: LAW AND POLICY**. New York: Clark Boardman, 1986–date (loose-leaf vol.), ca 750 pp. Directed toward practicing attorneys, this is a practical guide. Index.

1009 Brotman, Stuart N. (ed.). **TELEPHONE COMPANY AND CABLE TELEVISION COMPETITION: KEY TECHNICAL, ECONOMIC, LEGAL AND POLICY ISSUES**. Norwood, MA: Artech House, Inc., 1990, 509 pp. A compilation of previously published articles in the four areas listed in the subtitle: technical, economic, legal, and policy issues.

1010 Cohen, Frederick B. **PROTECTION AND SECURITY ON THE INFORMATION SUPERHIGHWAY**. New York: Wiley, 1995, 301 pp. Likely problems and protection ideas. Bibliography, glossary, index.

1011 Ferris, Charles D. et al. **CABLE TELEVISION LAW: A VIDEO COMMUNICATIONS PRACTICE GUIDE**. New York: Matthew Bender, 1983–date (three vols., updated twice yearly), ca 2,500 pp. Standard treatise on changing electronic media industry policy and regulation, including broadcasting. Appendices, indexes.

1012 Johnson, Leland L. **TOWARD COMPETITION IN CABLE TELEVISION**. Cambridge, MA: MIT Press, 1994, 215 pp. A long-time Rand economist sums up his years of research, arguing for further deregulation. References, index.

1013 Parsons, Patrick R. **CABLE TELEVISION AND THE FIRST AMENDMENT: THE POST-PREFERRED CASES**. University Park, PA: The National Cable Television Center and Museum, 1990, 25 pp. A discussion of arguments used in post-Preferred cases and proposal for rectifying the weaknesses of these arguments.

1014 Rose, Lance. **NETLAW: YOUR RIGHTS IN THE ONLINE WORLD**. Berkeley, CA: Osborne/McGraw-Hill, 1995, 372 pp. Includes such issues as copyright, privacy, security, as well as commercial law. Appendices, index.

7-D-5. Media Legal Reporters

1015 **ENTERTAINMENT LAW REPORTER.** Santa Monica, CA: Entertainment Law Reporter Publishing, 1979–date, monthly. News of legal developments in electronic media and entertainment; excerpts from key court decisions.

1016 **MEDIA LAW REPORTER.** Washington: Bureau of National Affairs, 1977–date, weekly. Reference service with full texts of federal and state court decisions and selected FCC and related rulings.

1017 **PIKE AND FISCHER RADIO REGULATION.** Bethesda, MD: Pike & Fischer, 1948–date, weekly. Multivolume. Comprehensive coverage of laws, regulations, and decisions governing federal communications law. Contains current rules, proposed rules, texts of cases, and case digests from the Federal Communications Commission, the federal court system, other federal regulatory bodies, and state courts. Extensive Finding Aids volumes. Second Series (RR 2d) began 1963. See also PIKE & FISCHER'S DESK GUIDE TO COMMUNICATIONS LAW RESEARCH (1004).

8

International

Chapter 8 differs from the rest of this book in that it moves beyond the domestic mass communications industry and details resources on international and foreign national organizations that help define the role of the United States in international communications. Here we identify resources that analyze U.S. media from international and comparative perspectives.

The International Telecommunication Union (ITU; 1064), the world's major international telecommunications organization, is also described here—including information about its 1994 restructuring, which in turn is reflected in U.S. agencies and offices. Additionally, Section 8-D includes resources and organizations in international and foreign national satellite communications. This chapter concludes with selected secondary resources on international communications and the role of U.S. media overseas.

8-A. Bibliographic Resources

8-A-1. Bibliographies

1018 Lasswell, Harold D. et al. **PROPAGANDA AND PROMOTIONAL ACTIVITIES: AN ANNOTATED BIBLIOGRAPHY**. Minneapolis: University of Minnesota Press, 1935 (reprinted by University of Chicago Press, 1969), 450 pp. Pioneering compilation includes several thousand citations divided topically. Most are annotated, covering material to 1934. See Smith et al. (1026, 1027) for continuation.

1019 Lent, John A. ed. **GLOBAL GUIDE TO MEDIA & COMMUNICATIONS**. New York: George Kurian, 1987, 145 pp. Twelve different bibliographies covering different parts of the world through 1984, including primarily English language titles, many of them annotated.

1020 Lichty, Lawrence W., comp. **WORLD AND INTERNATIONAL BROADCASTING: A BIBLIOGRAPHY**. Washington: Association for Professional Broadcasting Education, 1971, ca 600 pp. Unannotated but subject-divided citations—several thousand of them. Useful for locating older material. No index.

1021 Middleton, Karen P., and Meheroo Jussawalla. **THE ECONOMICS OF COMMUNICATION: A SELECTED BIBLIOGRAPHY WITH ABSTRACTS**. New York: Pergamon Press, in cooperation with the East–West Center, Hawaii, 1981, 249 pp. Intelligent record of the literature of a new field, that of the economics of the transmission of information (channels) and the economics of communication and development in rich and poor countries. Annotated entries, presented in topical sections, and indexed by author and subject.

1022 Mowlana, Hamid. **INTERNATIONAL FLOW OF NEWS: BIBLIOGRAPHY**. Paris: Unesco, 1986, 272 pp. Annotated guide to more than 400 items; topically arranged (including specific parts of the world), but not indexed.

1023 Nafziger, Ralph O. **INTERNATIONAL NEWS AND THE PRESS: COMMUNICATIONS, ORGANIZATIONS OF NEWS GATHERING, INTERNATIONAL AFFAIRS AND THE FOREIGN PRESS—AN ANNOTATED BIBLIOGRAPHY**. New York: H.W. Wilson, 1940 (reprinted by Arno Press, 1972), 193 pp. Subject-divided listing of prewar citations with useful annotations and author index.

1024 **THE NEW WORLD INFORMATION AND COMMUNICATION ORDER: A SELECTIVE BIBLIOGRAPHY**. New York: United Nations Dag Hammarskjold Library, 1984, 152 pp. Unannotated listing divided into topical sections, with the first half devoted to books and periodicals and the second to UN publications.

1025 Pisarek, Walery. **INTERNATIONAL BIBLIOGRAPHY OF MASS COMMUNICATION BIBLIOGRAPHIES**. Cracow, Poland: Bibliographic Section of the International Association of Mass Communication Research/Press Research Centre R.S.W. "Prasa" in Cracow, 1972, unpaged. "Draft version." Perhaps the only comprehensive (though certainly dated) listing of bibliographies in mass communications. Arranged by country.

1026 Smith, Bruce Lannes et al. **PROPAGANDA, COMMUNICATION, AND PUBLIC OPINION**. Princeton, NJ: Princeton University Press, 1946, 435 pp. Covers the 1934–1944 period with some 2,500 citations, nearly all annotated and divided by topic. Index. (For earlier material, see Lasswell et al., 1018.)

1027 _____, and Chitra M. Smith. **INTERNATIONAL COMMUNICATION AND POLITICAL OPINION: A GUIDE TO THE LITERATURE**. Princeton, NJ: Princeton University Press, 1956, 325 pp. Some 2,600 studies in the 1943–1955 period are annotated and indexed. (See previous entry)

1028 Ubbens, Wilbert. **JAHRESBIBLIOGRAPHIE MASSENKOMMUNIKATION.** Berlin: Wissenschaftsverlag Volker Speiss, 1982–date, annual. The most comprehensive international bibliography of mass communications research literature, including material in all languages, much of it in English. A unique resource.

1029 **UNESCO LIST OF DOCUMENTS AND PUBLICATIONS IN THE FIELD OF MASS COMMUNICATION**. Paris: UNESCO, 1976–date, irregular. These form the accessions listings of the main Paris headquarters library for the agency, using keywords instead of straight annotations. Indexed.

1030 Van Bol, Jean-Marie, and Abdelfattah Fakhfakh. **THE USE OF MASS MEDIA IN THE DEVELOPING COUNTRIES**. Brussels: International Center for African Social and Economic Documentation, 1971, 750 pp. Well-organized annotated coverage of some 2,500 citations in a variety of languages, provides invaluable record of early publications on this topic. Organized by subject and well-indexed.

8-A-2. Abstracts, Indexes, Databases

1031 **COMMUNICATION CONTENTS SISALLOT.** Tampere, Finland: University of Tampere and Nordicom, 1985–date, biannual. Reproduces tables of contents of more than 50 important communication journals from U.S., United Kingdom, France, Germany, Russia, Sweden, Norway, Denmark, Spain, Kenya, Singapore, Australia. A useful service for access to otherwise unindexed international journals.

1032 **INDICATOR CONTENTS**. Calgary, Alberta: International Federation of Communication Associations, 1992–date, 3/year. First issues reprinted tables of contents of nearly 100 major international communication research journals, with the intention of including at least another 100 in subsequent issues. Titles from Australia, Brazil, Canada, Croatia, Ecuador, Germany, Italy, Japan, Netherlands, Singapore, Sweden, U.K., and U.S.

1033 **INTERNATIONAL POLITICAL SCIENCE ABSTRACTS**. Oxford: Blackwell, 1951–date, quarterly. Comprehensive coverage of international political science literature in classified arrangement: relevant listings under mass media and television, among others.

1034 **MASS COM PERIODICAL LITERATURE INDEX**. Singapore: Documentation Unit, Asian Mass Communication Research & Information Centre, 1982–date, semiannual. Continues AMIC INDEX TO PERIODICALS (1972–1980) and MASS COM PERIODICAL LITERATURE

(1981). Classified listing of articles featured in Asian trade newsletters and major research journals (many covered nowhere else), including ASIAN COMMUNICATIONS, TELECOM ASIA, NEW BREEZE, MOBILE ASIA PACIFIC, ASIA PACIFIC TELECOMMUNICATIONS, NEW ERA OF TELECOMMUNICATIONS IN JAPAN. Relevant listings include cable, digital broadcasting, and HDTV. Coverage overlaps with AMIC's AMICNET online database, available by subscription, with document delivery services.

1035 **NORDICOM: BIBLIOGRAPHY OF NORDIC MASS COMMUNICATION LITERATURE; BIBLIOGRAFI OVER NORDISK MASSENKOMMUNICATIONS LITTERATUR.** Aarhus, Denmark: Nordic Documentation Center for Mass Communication Research, 1975–date, annual. Online version available from University of Aarhus via Internet. Comprehensive bibliography of mass communication research literature published in Denmark, Finland, Iceland, Norway, and Sweden. Vol. 1, Document List, includes numbered bibliographic citations. Non-English-language titles translated. Abstracts in language of publication. Vol. 2, Index, includes English-language keywords/subject headings. Relevant listings under cable television, communication policy, among others. Bibliography.

8-A-3. Directories and Yearbooks

1036 **ASIA PACIFIC TELEVISION: CABLE AND SATELLITE**. Shrub Oak, NY: Baskerville Communications Corp., 1995–date, annual. Analysis of developing cable and satellite market in the Asia-Pacific area. Summarizes and charts history and growth of cable and satellite in 13 countries. Profiles pan-regional cable and satellite channels and major satellites covering the region. Charts current and projected revenues, households.

1037 **BENN'S MEDIA**. Tonbridge, England: Benn Business Information Services, 1846–date, annual (multivolume). Title varies. Targeted to advertisers, this directory's first volume is useful for names of media in the United Kingdom and detailed information about the British publications. Vol. 2 covers Europe, and vol. 3 the world.

1038 **BIB WORLD GUIDE TO TELEVISION AND FILM**. Philadelphia: North American Publishing, 1990–date, annual. Entries for broadcast, cinema and home video organizations for 185 countries from A to Z. Statistics delineate currency, population, gross domestic product, cable connections, cable penetration, technical standards and regulatory organizations. Abbreviations, index of organizations, calendar of events and festivals, glossary, satellite section, interactive TV contacts, distributors lists, market reports, appendixes.

1039 **THE BUSINESS MEDIAMAP: THE YEARBOOK OF EUROPEAN BUSINESS MEDIA.** Woodbury, Devon, UK: CIT Publications, 1993–date, annual. Directory of companies concerned with business publishing including newspapers, magazines, television channels, media representatives, ad agencies, media buyers, business schools, regulatory and professional organizations, and exhibitions. Country profiles outline recent political and economic developments, status of business press, advertising expenditures, and other factors related to readership and revenue. Complements the MEDIAMAP which focuses on the consumer market.

1040 Central Intelligence Agency. **THE WORLD FACTBOOK.** Springfield, VA: NTIS, 1975–date, annual. Includes material on media in most countries of the world. Available online. Internet: www.odci.gov. Formerly NATIONAL BASIC INTELLIGENCE FACTBOOK.

1041 Drost, Harry, ed. **WORLD'S NEWS MEDIA: A COMPREHENSIVE REFERENCE GUIDE**. Essex, UK: Longman Group UK Limited, 1991, 604 pp. As ambitious as the older Kurian, WORLD PRESS ENCYCLOPEDIA (entry 1049), this guide surveys the world's news media, describing print and broadcast media in 198 countries and territories and covering the political background, regulation, media freedom, and ownership. Includes names of editors, addresses, fax and telex numbers for 4,000 newspapers, news agencies, broadcasting organizations, publishing groups, regulatory bodies, and press associations. Entries arranged alphabetically by country. Six essays describe the regional media (Americas, Asia-Pacific, Europe, Middle East, and North Africa, World Media).

1042 Electronic Industries Association. **INTERNATIONAL ELECTRONICS CONTACTS**. Washington: Electronic Industries Association, 1992, 67 pp. Directory of information sources in 70 countries.

1043 **EUROFILE: RADIO INDUSTRY DIRECTORY; YOUR COMPLETE GUIDE TO THE EUROPEAN RADIO BUSINESS AND RELATED INDUSTRIES.** Amsterdam: BPI Communications, 1988–date, annual. Title varies. Covers 22 European countries and includes listings for 600 public radio stations, 1,800 private radio stations, and 4,500 radio-related organizations. Station entries include contact names, music format, audience data, programming schedule. Additional listings include production services, consultants, research services, trade press, equipment, and related organizations. Arranged alphabetically by country.

1044 **EUROPA WORLD YEARBOOK**. London: Europa Publications, 1926–date, annual (2 vols.) Detailed information about 200 countries and territories, including the press, radio and television, plus international organizations.

1045 **EUROPEAN FM HANDBOOK**. Hyvinkaa, Finland: EFMH, 1988–date, annual. Directory of over 33,000 FM stations in Europe, Near East, Northern Africa, and Greenland. Gives frequencies, powers, transmitter sites, addresses, telephone and telefax numbers. Includes local stations, as well as national and regional stations. Some maps.

1046 **EUROPEAN TV PROGRAMMING.** Shrub Oak, NY: Baskerville Communications Corp., 1996 (2nd ed.), 184 pp. Programming developments on 26 European channels in Great Britain, Germany, France, Spain, and Italy.

1047 **INTERNATIONAL MULTIMEDIA YEARBOOK 1995–96**. Chicago: Fitzroy Dearborn Publishers, 1995–date, biennial. Directory of companies, 1,100 hardware and software products. First edition of 955 pp. included 55 articles and interviews, glossary, bibliography.

1048 Kagan World Media, Carmel, CA. and London. Issues the following:

1 **KAGAN'S EUROPEAN RADIO.** 1990–date, annual (there is also a monthly newsletter of the same title). Guide to the European radio market in 24 European countries. Describes recent radio programming and regulatory development in each country, followed by analysis of radio ad expenditures and audience figures. Includes projected radio revenues and directory information for related organizations.

2 **EUROPEAN CABLE/PAY TV DATABOOK**. 1992–date, annual. Profiles of cable operations in 21 countries. Includes analysis of current market and forecasts of cable and pay TV penetration and revenue, and projections of DBS and multichannel penetration. Contact lists include regulatory bodies, operators, and related associations.

3 **THE 1995 KAGAN DIRECTORY OF EUROPEAN MEDIA REGULATION**. 1992–date, annual (no 1996 edition). Analysis of legal scene concerning television, cable, video, film/cinema, radio, and telecommunications in 24 countries. Includes directory of regulatory contacts for each country.

4 **KAGAN'S ASIA PACIFIC TV.** 1994–date, annual. Analysis of the television market of Asia and Pacific Rim. Profiles 13 countries including advertising expenditures, programming requirements, cable and satellite developments, license fees, audience share, and industry contacts.

5 **KAGAN'S EUROPEAN TELEVISION CHANNELS: THE COMPREHENSIVE GUIDE TO 64 EURO TV CHANNELS.** 1992–date, annual. Analysis of Europe's major terrestrial and national satellite television services. Organizations are listed under country of origin and include financial analysis as well as programming data and historical overview. Title varies.

6 **KAGAN'S EUROPEAN TELEVISION COUNTRY PROFILES: COMPREHENSIVE GUIDE TO 27 EURO TV COUNTRIES**. 1992–date, annual. Detailed data including history, legislation, advertising revenues, license fees, viewing shares, programming schedules, channel penetration, and contacts for major associations and organizations. Title varies.

1049 Kurian, George Thomas, ed. **WORLD PRESS ENCYCLOPEDIA**. New York: Facts on File, 1982, 2 vols., 1202 pp. Now useful historically, this surveys the press in 180 countries and describes the history of the press, statistical information, and the political/social environment in which the press operates for each country. Country entries describe daily and nondaily newspapers, literacy rate, press law, censorship, newsprint usage, news agencies, electronic news media, professional education and training. Bibliographies for each country entry. The data range from the late 1970s into the early 1980s. Indexed. See Drost (1041) for more current information.

1050 **LATIN AMERICAN TELEVISION**. Shrub Oak, NY: Baskerville Communications Corp., 1996 (2nd ed.), 235 pp. Report on 17 countries in Latin America, providing forecasts to 2005 on television, cable, and satellite dish penetration as well as TV advertising expansion. Includes profiles of 24 networks or channels, satellite overview, and major contacts in each country.

1051 **THE LEO BURNETT WORLDWIDE ADVERTISING AND MEDIA FACT BOOK**. Chicago: Triumph Books, 1994, 498 pp. General and specific statistics related to advertising in 57 countries (including the U.S.), arranged by world region. Information on inflation in media prices, proportional spending on various media, media buying and buying services, top advertisers by company and by product. Very useful for specific comparative national details on mass media, like prime-time television and radio costs and cost per thousand; availability and hours of cable and satellite programming; proportion of homes with VCRs. Use with care; the U.S. regulations section has some errors.

1052 **THE MEDIAMAP [YEAR]: THE EUROPEAN MEDIA YEARBOOK**. Devon, UK: CIT Publications, 1990–date, annual. Guide to print and electronic media in 30 countries. Directory of print media, television channels, cable operators, radio stations, media representatives, and regulatory and professional organizations. Country profiles summarize recent political, economic, and regulatory developments which affect mass media as well as statistical data on media audiences. Company profiles outline financial highlights and recent activities. Updated by MEDIA MAP DATAFILE (monthly). Complements the BUSINESS MEDIAMAP (1039), which focuses on the business market.

1053 **PASSPORT TO WORLD BAND RADIO.** Penns Park, PA: International Broadcasting Services, 1984–date, annual. A directory of worldwide radio broadcasting with details by country, region, and time band as well as frequency, plus useful background articles. (Title was RADIO DATABASE INTERNATIONAL until 1988.)

1054 **TBI (TELEVISION BUSINESS INTERNATIONAL) YEARBOOK.** London: 21st Century Business Publications Ltd, 1992–date, annual. Divided into nine geographic regions, each with a descriptive overview of recent industry developments, followed by country-by-country breakdown of television services. Includes number of TV homes; TV ad spending; cable, satellite, and VCR penetration; viewing shares, total ad spending, description of historical development and current structure of television industry; terrestrial, cable, satellite, and pay TV services; regulatory organizations, and trade associations.

1055 **TRAVELER'S GUIDE TO WORLD RADIO**. New York: Billboard/Watson-Guptill, 1991–date, annual, 200 pp. Pocket guide to English-language services in more than 50 major international cities. Schedule charts.

1056 **TV INTERNATIONAL DIRECTORY 1997**. Shrub Oak, NY: Baskerville Communications Corp., 1996 (2nd ed.), 512 pp. Focuses on the global television program buying community. Key information includes program buyers, commissioning editors by genre, sources of programs, and program budgets of television channels outside the U.S.

1057 **WORLD RADIO–TV HANDBOOK**. New York: Billboard, 1947–date, annual. Country-by-country listings of (mainly shortwave) frequencies, hours of broadcast, and programs. The standard guide for international shortwave listeners.

8-A-4. Statistics

1058 BBC International Audience Research. **WORLD RADIO AND TELEVISION RECEIVERS**. London: BBC International Broadcasting Audience Research, 1985–date, annual. Tables of comparative data on the cover topic plus videocassette players, shortwave ownership.

1059 European Audiovisual Observatory. **STATISTICAL YEARBOOK: CINEMA, TELEVISION, VIDEO AND NEW MEDIA IN EUROPE**. Strasbourg, France: EAO, 1994–date, annual. Excellent resource with tabular and chart data for all of Europe (including the former Soviet Bloc nations), arranged by subject (basic data, household equipment, companies, film industry, video and new media, television, and advertising) and offering detailed comments on sources and validity of the data. Bibliography, acronyms.

1060 National Cable Television Association. **FACTS AT A GLANCE: INTERNATIONAL CABLE**. Washington: NCTA, 1991–date, irregular. Provides industry statistics for selected countries. Delineates U.S. interests in both systems and programming in these countries. Index, sources.

1061 UNESCO. **STATISTICS ON RADIO AND TELEVISION** (title varies). Paris: UNESCO, as follows:

1 **1950–1960**. "Statistical Reports and Studies," 1963, 87 pp.
2 **1960–1976.** "Statistical Reports and Studies No. 23," 1979, 124 pp.
3 **LATEST STATISTICS ON RADIO AND TELEVISION BROADCASTING**. "Statistical Reports and Studies No. 29," 1987, 130 pp. This three-part series offers comparative information on transmitters, receivers and programs in major regions. Tables, charts, notes.

8-A-5. Dictionaries

1062 Brown, Timothy G. **INTERNATIONAL COMMUNICATIONS GLOSSARY**. Washington: Media Institutes, 1984, 97 pp. Defines mass media terms in light of new world information order.

8-B. United Nations Organizations

8-B-1. International Telecommunication Union

1063 Codding, George A., Jr., and Anthony M. Rutkowski. **THE INTERNATIONAL TELECOMMUNICATION UNION IN A CHANGING WORLD**. Dedham, MA: Artech, 1982, 414 pp. The standard description of how the ITU functions and its major issue arenas for the 1980s—now badly dated, but still the most detailed study available. Annexes, glossary, bibliography, index.

1064 **International Telecommunication Union**. Place des Nations, CH-1211, Geneva 20, Switzerland. Voice 41-22-730-5111. Fax 41-22-733-7256. Internet: www@itu.ch. Maintains TIES online information service. Founded in 1865 as the International Telegraph Union, and broadened in the early 1900s to include telephone and wireless services, the ITU (a United Nations specialized agency since 1949) is the most important worldwide body in the field. In it reside (by both treaty and tradition) worldwide cooperation in allocation of radio frequencies and telecommunication technical standards. The first major reorganization of the ITU since 1947 took effect in mid-1994.

1 **Plenipotentiary Conference**. All members of the ITU; convenes every 4 years to determine policies, approve budget, adopt proposals for amendments to the ITU's governance agreements (the Constitution and the Convention), conclude agreements with other international organizations, and elect members to the Council, Secretary-General, Radio Regulation Board, and other offices.
2 **Secretary-General**. The chief administrative officer of the ITU, in charge of the General Secretariat of the ITU.
3 **Council**. Acts as ITU's governing body between plenipotentiary conferences (composed of 43 members). Exercises financial control over Secretary-General and sectors.

4 **Radiocommunication Sector**. (Until 1994, the CCIR.) Responsible for use of radio frequency spectrum. Sponsors conferences, studies, study groups. Oversees Radio Regulation Board (replaces International Frequency Registration Board) and Radiocommunication Bureau.

5 **Telecommunication Standardization Sector**. (Until 1994, the CCITT.) Responsible for recommending telecommunications standards worldwide. Studies technical, operating, and tariff issues; sponsors standardization conferences and study groups. Oversees Telecommunication Standardization Bureau.

6 **Telecommunication Development Sector**. Coordinates and provides technical assistance programs. Sponsors study groups. Operates Telecommunications Development Bureau.

7 Publications include: LIST OF PUBLICATIONS (1979–date, semiannual) with bibliographic and ordering information for ITU publications; LIST OF RECENT ACQUISITIONS/LISTE DES ACQUISITIONS RECENTES/LISTA DE ADQUISICIONES RECIENTES (ITU Central Library, 1972–date, quarterly) free on request; LIST OF ANNUALS/LISTE DES PUBLICATIONS ANNUELLES/LISTA DE PUBLICACIONES ANUALES (ITU Central Library, 1972–date, biennial) includes nearly 400 titles; free on request; LIST OF PERIODICALS/LISTE DES PERIODIQUES/LISTA DE REVISTAS (ITU Central Library, 1967–date, biennial) includes more than 1,000 titles; free on request; ITU GLOBAL DIRECTORY/REPERTOIRE GENERAL DE L'UIT/GUIA GENERAL DE LA UIT (6th ed.,1993, 372 pp.) is the "Official ITU desk reference of telecommunication officials and organizations" with contacts and electronic and postal addresses for membership. English, French, Spanish editions; also available on ITU's TIES online information service. Official organ was the monthly TELECOMMUNICATION JOURNAL, now continued by ITU NEWS (10/year). See also ITU's LIST OF PUBLICATIONS issued twice a year that details the many multivolume official documents growing out of international meetings on telegraph-telephone and on radio communication.

1065 Leive, David M. **INTERNATIONAL TELECOMMUNICATIONS AND INTERNATIONAL LAW: THE REGULATION OF THE RADIO SPECTRUM**. Leyden, The Netherlands: Sijthoff, 1970, 386 pp. Still useful historical study of ITU's developing role in spectrum allocation and management. Appendices, index.

1066 Smith, Delbert D. **INTERNATIONAL TELECOMMUNICATION CONTROL: INTERNATIONAL LAW AND THE ORDERING OF SATELLITE AND OTHER FORMS OF INTERNATIONAL BROADCASTING**. Leyden, The Netherlands: Sijthoff, 1969, 231 pp. Historical study of the ITU and its role in international broadcasting and satellite organizations. Charts, appendices, bibliography, index.

8-B-2. UNESCO

1067 Giffard, C. Anthony. **UNESCO AND THE MEDIA** New York: Longman, 1989, 288 pp. Details the controversy about the UN agency's media concerns and how these concerns led to the withdrawal of U.S. and U.K. membership. Notes, tables, index.

1068 MacBride, Sean et al. **MANY VOICES, ONE WORLD: COMMUNICATIONS AND SOCIETY TODAY AND TOMORROW**. Paris: UNESCO/New York: Unipub, 1980, 312 pp. Definitive UNESCO statement favorable to a new world information order. Data-studded controversial report was instrumental in the U.S. withdrawal four years later. UNESCO issued a shorter version in paperback in the mid-1980s. Appendices, index.

1069 Preston, William Jr. et al. **HOPE & FOLLY: THE UNITED STATES AND UNESCO 1945–1985**. Minneapolis: University of Minnesota Press, 367 pp. Critical discussion of changing American policy toward the U.N. body. Notes, bibliography, index.

1070 United Nations. **WORLD MEDIA HANDBOOK** New York: United Nations, 1995 (3rd ed.). Brief tabular listings by country of media (including for larger countries major owners/operators), cultural indicators. "Limited space allowed the inclusion per country of a maximum of 25 dailies, 30 periodicals, 8 news agencies, 15 radio and 15 television organizations, 10 media-related associations, and 20 communication educational institutions." Revision planned for every other year. Tables, sources.

1071 **United Nations Educational, Scientific, and Cultural Organization (UNESCO).** 7 Place de Fontenoy, 75700 Paris, France. Voice: 33-1-4568-1000. Fax: 31-1-4567-1690. Promotes world peace and security through mass communication and knowledge diffusion. Sponsors International Programme for the Development of Communication, which publishes IPDC NEWSLETTER. Maintains Culture and Communication Documentation Centre. Founded in 1947. Has also issued:

1 **WORLD COMMUNICATIONS: A 200-COUNTRY SURVEY OF PRESS, RADIO, TELEVISION, FILM.** 1975 (5th ed.), 533 pp. A standard one-volume reference first published in 1950, with updates in 1951, 1956, and 1964. Broken out by region of the world, and then specific countries. While badly dated, still useful. Index.

2 **WORLD COMMUNICATION REPORT.** 1989, 550 pp. Huge compilation of text, tables, charts, and reference sources/bibliography arranged by subject with much country-specific data. Good index.

3 **ANNOTATED BIBLIOGRAPHY OF UNESCO PUBLICATIONS AND DOCUMENTS DEALING WITH SPACE COMMUNICATION, 1953–1977.** 1977, 102 pp. Some 281 annotated items, with title index.

4 See 1029. LIST OF DOCUMENTS AND PUBLICATIONS IN THE FIELD OF MASS COMMUNICATIONS

8-B-3. WIPO

1072 **World Intellectual Property Organization (WIPO).** 34 Chemin des Colombettes, 1211 Geneva 20, Switzerland. Voice: 41-22-730-9111. Fax: 41-22-733-5428. Internet: 222.uspto.gov/wipo.html. Promotes intellectual property rights and protection. Operates library with collections covering copyright, industrial design, industrial property, patents, trademarks, and unfair competition.

8-C. Other Organizations

1073 **Center for Foreign Journalists.** 1616 H St. NW, Third Fl., Washington 20006. Voice: 202-737-3700. FAX 202-737-0530. e-mail: editor@cfj.org. Educational center for exchange of information among journalists. Offers referral services and fellowships for foreign journalists. Publishes handbooks in several languages. Publications include THE ENVIRONMENTAL SOURCEBOOK FOR JOURNALISTS, TEN PRACTICAL TIPS FOR BUSINESS AND ECONOMIC REPORTING IN DEVELOPING ECONOMIES, TEN PRACTICAL TIPS FOR ENVIRONMENTAL REPORTING, and Chris Sterling's A BRIEF OUTLINE OF AMERICAN ELECTRONIC MEDIA (1996). Founded in 1985.

1074 **Center for International Journalism.** University of Southern California, GFS 315, University Park, Los Angeles, CA 90089-1695. Voice: 213-740-8277. Fax: 213-740-8624. Offers financial support for working journalists to devote a year to studying political, social, and economic issues, with emphasis on Latin America, in particular, Mexico. Intended for aspiring foreign correspondents, reporters or gatekeepers, and editors covering international news and editorial writing. Nine months of classroom study at USC, followed by 9 months at El Colegio de Mexico in Mexico City.

1075 **Commission of the European Communities.** 200 rue de la Loi, B-1049 Brussels, Belgium. Voice: 2-295-1111. Fax: 2-236-4319. Organization of government-appointed representatives from European countries, including the European Economic Community. Purpose is to further European economic integration. Drafts proposals to advance the Economic Community in many areas, including broadcast programming and technology. Published TELEVISION WITHOUT FRONTIERS: GREEN PAPER ON THE ESTABLISHMENT OF THE COMMON MARKET FOR BROADCASTING, ESPECIALLY BY SATELLITE AND CABLE (1984), which urged establishment of a common regulatory framework for the flow of television transmissions between member states; PLURALISM

AND MEDIA CONCENTRATION IN THE INTERNAL MARKET: AN ASSESSMENT OF THE NEED FOR COMMUNITY ACTION: COMMISSION GREEN PAPER (1992), collection of laws and regulations about European media concentration; STRATEGY OPTIONS TO STRENTHEN THE EUROPEAN PROGRAMME INDUSTRY IN THE CONTEXT OF THE AUDIOVISUAL POLICY OF THE EUROPEAN UNION: GREEN PAPER (1994), which examines how the EU can compete in the television market. Founded in 1957.

1076 **1996 BRIEFING BOOK ON INTERNATIONAL ORGANIZATIONS IN GENEVA.** Geneva, Switzerland: American Mission, 1996, ca 250 pp. Valuable handbook to the many bodies based in the Swiss city, including brief history, current activities, key subparts, and contact addresses. Can also be obtained in updated fashion on the web: www.itu.ch/MISSIONS/US/.

1077 **University of Hawaii. The East-West Center**. 1601 East–West Road. Honolulu, HI 96848-1601. Voice: 808-944-7111. Fax: 808-944-7376 Internet: www.ewc.hawaii.edu. Regarded as a national and regional source of information and analysis about significant contemporary issues for the Asia-Pacific Region. Affiliates are scholars, government and business leaders, educators, journalists and other professionals from throughout the region. East–West Center Media Program sponsors fellowships, workshops, conferences, and other research, training and educational activities for professionals in the print and broadcast media. Sponsors Jefferson Fellowships (awarded annually since 1967) for journalists. Maintains vigorous and diverse publication program, publishing ASIA PACIFIC ISSUES PAPERS series.

8-D. International Satellites

8-D-1. General

1078 Baylin, Frank. **WORLD SATELLITE YEARLY**. Boulder, CO: Baylin Publications, 1993–date, annual. Major directory and text sections on technology, programming, companies, and satellites. Tables, maps.

1079 Demac, Donna A. ed. **TRACING NEW ORBITS: COOPERATION & COMPETITION IN GLOBAL SATELLITE DEVELOPMENT**. New York: Columbia University Press, 1986, 329 pp. Emergence of specialized and regional systems, national programs and perspectives, regulation of international satellite activity, and Soviet satellite systems. Bibliography, index.

1080 **INTERNATIONAL SATELLITE DIRECTORY: THE COMPLETE GUIDE TO THE SATELLITE COMMUNICATIONS INDUSTRY**. Sonoma, CA: Design Publishers, 1986–date, annual. Includes government regulators, global satellite operators, regional and domestic satellite operators, planned satellite systems, manufacturers of space, ground, and tvro equipment, mobile systems, network systems, programmers, service providers, uplink facilities, and programming schedules.

1081 International Telecommunication Union (see 1064). **REPORT BY THE ITU ON TELECOMMUNICATION AND THE PEACEFUL USES OF OUTER SPACE**. Geneva: ITU, 1962–date, annual. Best regular review of satellite developments in all involved countries. Photos, tables.

1082 Smith, Milton L. **INTERNATIONAL REGULATION OF SATELLITE COMMUNICATION.** Norwell, MA: Kluwer Academic, 1990, 245 pp. Details the organizations and their concerns and approaches, focusing on ITU Space WARC meetings. Notes, appendices, bibliography.

1083 **SATELLITE INDUSTRY DIRECTORY.** Potomac, MD: Phillips, 1979–date, annual. Directory of satellite operators, transponder brokers and resellers, product and equipment manufacturers and suppliers, business and support services, and regulatory and policy organizations. Includes product/service locator and glossary. Formerly THE WORLD SATELLITE DIRECTORY. Name changed in 1996.

1084 **SPACE ACTIVITIES OF THE UNITED NATIONS AND INTERNATIONAL ORGANIZATIONS.** New York: United Nations, 1992, 318 pp. Subtitle: "A review of the activities and resources of the United Nations, its specialized agencies and other international bodies relating to the peaceful uses of outer space." Covers ITU, International Maritime Organization, WIPO, as well as European Space Agency, INTELSAT, the now-defunct INTERSPUTNIK, INMARSAT, EUTELSAT, and Arab Satellite Communication Organization. Bibliography of UN documents related to outer space.

1085 White, Rita Lauria, and Harold M. White, Jr. **THE LAW AND REGULATION OF INTERNATIONAL SPACE COMMUNICATION**. Boston: Artech, 1988, 309 pp. Useful, although now dated, assessment. Bibliography, index.

1086 **WORLD SATELLITE ALMANAC: INCORPORATING THE SATELLITE SYSTEMS HANDBOOK AND THE WORLD SATELLITE ANNUAL**. Potomac, MD: Phillips, 1989–date, annual. Technical reference including satellite operators, transponder frequency plans, coverage maps, transponder brokers and resellers; technical and demographic information on 500 countries, territories, and islands.

8-D-2. INTELSAT

1087 Alper, Joel, and Joseph N. Pelton eds. **THE INTELSAT GLOBAL SATELLITE SYSTEM**. New York: American Institute of Aeronautics and Astronautics, 1984, 425 pp. Fifteen chapters that, although now dated, offer background on all aspects of the international consortium and the technology on which it is based. Acronyms and abbreviations.

1088 **International Telecommunications Satellite Organization** (INTELSAT). 3400 International Dr. NW, Washington, 20008-3098. Voice: 202-944-6800; 202-944-7500. Fax: 202-944-7890. Internet: www.intelsat.int:8080. 126 members. World's largest commercial satellite communications services provider. Owns and operates a satellite system that provides telephone and broadcasting service to users in more than 180 nations, territories, and dependencies on every continent. Establishes technical and operating standards for earth stations using its satellite network. Offers global connectivity. Member governments meet every 2 years. Library, not open to public. Founded in 1964. Publishes reports, bibliographies, INTELSAT ANNUAL REPORT (1965–date, annual), and INTELSAT NEWS (1985–date, quarterly).

1089 Pelton, Joseph N., and Marcellus S. Snow, eds. **ECONOMIC AND POLICY PROBLEMS IN SATELLITE COMMUNICATIONS**. New York: Praeger, 1977, 244 pp. Collects six scholarly papers on the INTELSAT organization's formative period. Appendix, index.

1090 Snow, Marcellus S. **THE INTERNATIONAL TELECOMMUNICATIONS SATELLITE ORGANIZATION: ECONOMIC AND INSTITUTIONAL CHALLENGES FACING AN INTERNATIONAL ORGANIZATION**. Baden-Baden, Germany: Nomos Verlags-gesellschaft, 1987. Detailed review of INTELSAT development, structure, and issues.

8-D-3. Direct Broadcast Satellites

1091 Fisher, David I. **PRIOR CONSENT TO INTERNATIONAL DIRECT SATELLITE BROADCASTING**. Norwell, MA: Kluwer Academic, 1990, 236 pp. The title topic has been a major matter of debate within the UN and UNESCO since the late 1960s. This traces the debate and its legal underpinnings. Bibliography, index.

1092 Luther, Sara Fletcher. **THE UNITED STATES AND THE DIRECT BROADCAST SATELLITE: THE POLITICS OF INTERNATIONAL BROADCASTING IN SPACE**. New York: Oxford University Press, 1988, 230 pp. American role and participation in the international legal debate. Notes, bibliography, index.

1093 Stewart, M. LeSueur. **TO SEE THE WORLD: THE GLOBAL DIMENSION IN INTERNATIONAL DIRECT TELEVISION BROADCASTING BY SATELLITE**. Norwell, MA: Kluwer Academic, 1991, 630 pp. Analysis of UN actions on IDTBS services with 400 pages of appendices reprinting key documents. Notes, appendices, index.

1094 Tondro, LaRene et al. **INTERNATIONAL DTH/DBS: GLOBAL BUSINESS DEVELOPMENTS, STRATEGIC DIRECTIONS AND MARKET PROSPECTS IN LATIN AMERICA, CANADA, EUROPE, JAPAN, CHINA AND ASIA-PACIFIC REGIONS.** Washington: National Association of Broadcasters, 1996, 157 pp. Focuses on the countries and regions which best represent direct-to-home and direct broadcast satellite technological advancements and the regulatory and social impacts of services unique to those areas.

8-E. U.S. International Agencies

8-E-1. USIA

(Note: In 1997, Congress made USIA a part of the Department of State.)

1095 Presidential Commission on Broadcasting to Cuba. **FINAL REPORT**. Washington: GPO, 1982, 211 pp. The document that led to creation of Radio Martí. Tables.

1096 U.S. Advisory Commission on Public Diplomacy. **REPORT** Washington U.S. Department of State, annual. Provides analysis and recommendations on USIA performance.

1097 **U.S. Information Agency**, 301 Fourth St. SW, Washington 20547. Voice: 202-619-4700. Has as its mission to understand, inform, and influence foreign commmunities in promotion of the national interest and to broaden the dialog between Americans, their institutions, and counterparts abroad. Conducts academic and cultural exchanges, international broadcasting, and informational programs. Known as U.S. Information Service overseas. Includes as one of its major functional elements the International Bureau of Broadcasting which is comprised of the Voice of America, the WORLDNET Television Service, Radio and TV Martí, (and as of 1995) Radio Free Europe and Radio Liberty.

1 **REVIEW OF OPERATIONS**. 1953–1976 (2/year, 44 issues; title varies). This was long the best way to follow the agency in text and tables. One final **REPORT TO CONGRESS 1978–79** appeared while USIA was briefly known (1978–1982) as the International Communication Agency. The report has not been published since.

2 **PROGRAM AND BUDGET IN BRIEF**. 1964–date, annual. Since 1980, this has been the only regular source of budget and supporting text material.

3 **GLOBAL AND REGIONAL THEMES.** annual. Details the message to be promoted by USIA print and broadcast media.

8-E-2. Secondary Resources on U.S. International Agencies

(Note: see also 8-G-6 on propaganda media)

1098 Alexandre, Laurien. **THE VOICE OF AMERICA: FROM DETENTE TO THE REAGAN DOCTRINE**. Norwood, NJ: Ablex, 1988, 199 pp. Sharply critical analysis of VOA. Notes, references, index.

1099 Elder, Robert E. **THE INFORMATION MACHINE: THE UNITED STATES INFORMATION AGENCY AND AMERICAN FOREIGN POLICY**. Syracuse, NY: Syracuse University Press, 1968, 356 pp. Analytic study of early USIA operations and how they affected U.S. foreign policy. Notes, index.

1100 Hansen, Allen C. **USIA: PUBLIC DIPLOMACY IN THE COMPUTER AGE**. New York: Praeger, 1984, 251 pp. Study of the agency's operations and impact. Bibliography, index.

1101 Henderson, John W. **THE UNITED STATES INFORMATION AGENCY**. New York: Praeger, 1969, 324 pp. Broadscale history and analysis of the operations of the agency. Charts, appendices, bibliography, index.

1102 Holt, Robert T. **RADIO FREE EUROPE**. Minneapolis: University of Minnesota Press, 1958, 249 pp. Scholarly study of the initial operation of the service, then theoretically private in control. Appendix, notes, index.

8-F. Media Trade

1103 Electronic Industries Association. **ELECTRONIC FOREIGN TRADE**. Washington (later Arlington, VA): EIA, 1982–date, monthly. Import and export figures for 300 products by unit sales and dollar volume; balance of trade by product group; rankings of markets and suppliers. Based largely on U.S. Commerce Department data. Indexed in STATISTICAL MASTERFILE (0109).

1104 Noam, Eli M., and Joel C. Millonzi, eds. **THE INTERNATIONAL MARKET IN FILM AND TELEVISION PROGRAMS**. Norwood, NJ: Ablex, 1993, 202 pp. Nine chapters by academic and industry experts. Tables, index.

1105 Wildman, Steven S., and Stephen E. Siwek. **INTERNATIONAL TRADE IN FILMS AND TELEVISION PROGRAMS**. Cambridge, MA.: Ballinger, 1988, 194 pp. One of the few books on this topic—a lot of specific data as well as overview. Tables, index.

8-G. Selected Secondary Sources

8-G-1 General Surveys

1106 Cooper, Thomas W., ed. **COMMUNICATION ETHICS AND GLOBAL CHANGE**. White Plains, NY: Longman, 1989, 385 pp. Nineteen papers on general theory, specific country case studies, with some comparisons and conclusions. Notes, bibliographies, index.

See 1041. Drost, THE WORLD'S NEWS MEDIA: A COMPREHENSIVE REFERENCE GUIDE.

1107 Fisher, Glen. **AMERICAN COMMUNICATION IN A GLOBAL SOCIETY**. Norwood, NJ: Ablex, 1987 (2nd ed.). Public and private concerns are reviewed.

1108 Fortner, Robert S. **INTERNATIONAL COMMUNICATION: HISTORY, CONFLICT, AND CONTROL OF THE GLOBAL METROPOLIS.** Belmont, CA: Wadsworth, 1993, 390 pp. Illustrated chapters discuss international communication in general, a theoretical perspective on the global metropolis, technical dimensions of international communication, the birth and early years of international communication (1835–1913), exploiting new possibilities (1914–1932), the triumph of international propaganda (1933–1945), developments since 1946, the periphery versus core (big and little countries and news flow questions), political and economic turmoil in the past 5 years, and the future of international communication. Appendices, references, glossary, index.

1109 Martin, L. John, and Ray Eldon Hiebert, eds. **CURRENT ISSUES IN INTERNATIONAL COMMUNICATION.** White Plains, NY: Longman, 1990, 390 pp. Collects about 60 articles on control systems, policies, flow of news, policies in specific countries, third world systems, and media in development. Tables, notes, index.

1110 Mowlana, Hamid. **GLOBAL INFORMATION AND WORLD COMMUNICATIONS: NEW FRONTIERS IN INTERNATIONAL RELATIONS**. New York: Longman, 1986, 248 pp. Combines findings from economics, political science, and other fields to propose a new framework of analysis. Bibliography, index.

1111 National Telecommunications and Information Administration. **GLOBALIZATION OF MASS MEDIA**. Washington: GPO, 1993, 325 pp. Discusses technologies, technical standards, corporate strategies, and national communication policies as contributing to fast-changing global media operations.

1112 Smith, Anthony. **THE AGE OF BEHEMOTHS: THE GLOBALIZATION OF MASS MEDIA FIRMS**. New York: Twentieth Century Fund, 1991, 83 pp. Expresses concern about trend to consolidation. Background reading, index.

1113 Stevenson, Robert L. **GLOBAL COMMUNICATION IN THE TWENTY-FIRST CENTURY**. White Plains, NY: Longman, 1994, 382 pp. Deals with media structures and issues along regional and topical lines. Index.

1114 Tunstall, Jeremy, and Michael Palmer. **MEDIA MOGULS**. New York: Routledge, 1991, 258 pp. Analysis of European media firms with chapters on Britain, France, Italy and Germany, as well as region-wide analyses. Notes, further reading, index.

8-G-2. Comparative/International Communications Law

1115 Barendt, Eric. **BROADCASTING LAW: A COMPARATIVE STUDY**. New York: Oxford University Press, 1993, 249 pp. Compares and contrasts practices in Britain, France, Germany, Italy and the U.S.; also studies European Community roles. Notes, selected bibliography, index.

1116 Hoffman-Riem, Wolfgang. **REGULATING MEDIA: THE LICENSING AND SUPERVISION OF BROADCASTING IN SIX COUNTRIES**. New York: Guilford, 1996, 424 pp. The U.S., Britain, Germany, France, Canada, and Australia are included, first in chapters by country, and then compared by topic across these nations. Notes, references, index.

1117 Lahav, Pnina, ed. **PRESS LAW IN MODERN DEMOCRACIES: A COMPARATIVE STUDY**. White Plains, NY: Longman, 1985, 366 pp. Compares and contrasts legal regime in the U.S., Britain, France, Germany, Sweden, Israel, and Japan. Index.

1118 Robillard, Serge. **TELEVISION IN EUROPE: REGULATORY BODIES—STATUS, FUNCTIONS AND POWERS IN 35 EUROPEAN COUNTRIES**. London: John Libbey, 1995, 310 pp. Arranged by nation with material in each case on legal framework, means of distribution, and regulatory bodies.

1119 Wincor, Richard. **COPYRIGHTS IN THE WORLD MARKETPLACE: SUCCESSFUL APPROACHES TO INTERNATIONAL MEDIA RIGHTS.** Englewood Cliffs, NJ: Prentice-Hall, 1990. Guide for attorneys, with useful details on how the process works—or should.

8-G-3. International Journalism

1120 Fenby, Jonathan. **THE INTERNATIONAL NEWS SERVICES**. New York: Schocken (Twentieth Century Fund), 1986, 250 pp. Best recent assessment of AP, UPI, Reuters, and Agence-France-Presse. Bibliography, index.

1121 Flournoy, Don M. **CNN WORLD REPORT: TED TURNER'S INTERNATIONAL NEWS COUP**. London: John Libbey, 1992. First book detailing the development of the international news service.

1122 Garnham, Nicholas. **CAPITALISM AND COMMUNICATION: GLOBAL CULTURE AND THE ECONOMICS OF INFORMATION**. Newbury Park, CA: Sage, 1990, 216 pp. Challenges the dominant information society theories, arguing that only Marxist political economy offers an adequate theoretical foundation for understanding communication processes. Tables, notes, index.

1123 Gaunt, Philip. **MAKING THE NEWSMAKERS: INTERNATIONAL HANDBOOK ON JOURNALISM TRAINING.** Westport, CT: Greenwood, 1992, 234 pp. In-depth survey of training needs, programs and facilities in 70 countries—apparently the first global assessment since a 1958 UNESCO report. Bibliography, index.

1124 Johnston, Carla Brooks. **WINNING THE GLOBAL TV NEWS GAME**. Newton, MA: Focal Press, 1995, 331 pp. The players and issues in different parts of the world—a useful handbook on news in the 1990s. Tables, notes, index.

1125 Merrill, John C., ed. **GLOBAL JOURNALISM: A SURVEY OF INTERNATIONAL COMMUNICATION**. New York: Longman, 1991 (2nd ed.), 401 pp. A regional approach comparing print and broadcast journalism around the world. Index, bibliography.

1126 O'Heffernan, Patrick. **MASS MEDIA AND AMERICAN FOREIGN POLICY: INSIDER PERSPECTIVES ON GLOBAL JOURNALISM AND THE FOREIGN POLICY PROCESS.** Norwood, NJ: Ablex, 1991. Various types of interaction between journalism and policymaking.

1127 Parker, Richard. **MIXED SIGNALS: THE PROSPECTS FOR GLOBAL TELEVISION NEWS**. New York: Twentieth Century Fund, 1995, 105 pp. Brief report on the economics and diplomacy involved in developing worldwide networks of news. Notes, index.

1128 **REPORTERS SANS FRONTIERES—FREEDOM OF THE PRESS THROUGHOUT THE WORLD.** London: John Libbey & Co., 1992–date, annual. Detailed, current, country-by-country analysis of the state of media freedom around the world, including official statistics and a narrative of a page or more on press freedom or lack of same. Arrangement is alphabetical.

1129 Van Dijk, Teun A. **NEWS ANALYSIS: CASE STUDIES OF INTERNATIONAL AND NATIONAL NEWS IN THE PRESS**. Hillsdale, NJ: Erlbaum, 1988, 325 pp. Structure of international news, with some case studies on how they were reported in various countries. Appendix, references, index.

1130 Wallis, Roger, and Stanley Baran. **THE KNOWN WORLD OF BROADCAST NEWS: INTERNATIONAL NEWS AND THE ELECTRONIC MEDIA.** New York: Routledge, 1990, 267 pp. Comparative study of how different countries/regions report news and see the world. Tables, references, index.

8-G-4. Broadcasting

1131 Avery, Robert K., ed. **PUBLIC SERVICE BROADCASTING IN A MULTICHANNEL ENVIRONMENT: THE HISTORY AND SURVIVAL OF AN IDEAL**. White Plains, NY: Longman, 1993, 211 pp. Anthology assessing the changing place of traditional public service radio–TV amidst technical, political, and economic change. Includes coverage of eight industrial nations. Index.

1132 Blumler, Jay G., and T.J. Nossiter. **BROADCASTING FINANCE IN TRANSITION: A COMPARATIVE HANDBOOK**. New York: Oxford University Press, 1991, 443 pp. A dozen countries (including the U.S.) are compared and contrasted. Tables, charts, notes, index.

1133 Head, Sydney W. **WORLD BROADCASTING SYSTEMS: A COMPARATIVE ANALYSIS.** Belmont, CA: Wadsworth, 1985, 457 pp. The most analytic comparative approach available; dated but still invaluable. Chapters on politics of ownership, access, laws and regulation, economics, facilities, programming, audience research, and transborder service—all with examples drawn worldwide. Maps, tables, glossary, citations, index.

1134 Hoffman-Riem, Wolfgang. **REGULATING MEDIA: THE LICENSING AND SUPERVISION OF BROADCASTING IN SIX COUNTRIES**. New York: Guilford Press, 1996, 424 pp. Compares and contrasts the U.S., Britain, Germany, France, Canada, and Australia. Notes, index.

1135 Johnston, Carla B. **INTERNATIONAL TELEVISION CO-PRODUCTION: FROM ACCESS TO SUCCESS**. Stoneham, MA: Focal, 1992, 110 pp. Discusses how the process works, legal and economic realities, acquisition and distribution.

1136 Lewis, Peter M., and Jerry Booth. **THE INVISIBLE MEDIUM: PUBLIC, COMMERCIAL AND COMMUNITY RADIO**. Washington: Howard University Press, 1990, 245 pp. One of the few studies of world radio broadcast systems, this includes material on U.S., British, Australian, Italian, French, and Third World systems.

1137 Lull, James, ed. **WORLD FAMILIES WATCH TELEVISION**. Newbury Park, CA: Sage, 1988. Countries included in these papers are Britain, Venezuela, Germany, India, U.S., China.

1138 Negrine, Ralph, and Stylianos Papathanassopoulos. **THE INTERNATIONALIZATION OF TELEVISION.** London: Pinter/New York: Columbia University Press, 1990, 191 pp. Broadscale assessment of recent trends: broadcast system restructuring in the 1980s and 1990s, television program exchange and national sovereignty, and the role of international agencies in Europe. Tables, index.

1139 Price, Monroe E. **TELEVISION, THE PUBLIC SPHERE, AND NATIONAL IDENTITY.** New York: Oxford University Press, 1995, 301 pp. Comparative analysis of the changing role of governmental regulation of television around the world. Notes, bibliography, index.

1140 Raboy, Marc, ed. **PUBLIC BROADCASTING FOR THE 21ST CENTURY.** Luton, England: University of Luton Press, 1996, 303 pp. Includes discussion of public service broadcasting in eight developed nations (including the U.S.) plus eight more chapters on specific nations and regions of developing countries. Papers are contributed by authorities in the countries discussed. Notes.

1141 Rosen, Philip T., ed. **INTERNATIONAL HANDBOOK OF BROADCASTING SYSTEMS.** Westport, CT: Greenwood, 1988. 309 pp. Information on 24 countries written by different experts to a common outline.

8-G-5. Cable and Newer Media

1142 Boyd, Douglas A. et al. **VIDEOCASSETTE RECORDERS IN THE THIRD WORLD.** White Plains, NY: Longman, 1989, 292 pp. Scholarly study on the adoption, use, and impact of VCRs in such countries. References, index.

1143 Ganley, Gladys, and Oswald H. Ganley. **GLOBAL POLITICAL FALLOUT: THE VCR'S FIRST DECADE, 1976–1985.** Norwood, NJ: Ablex, 1987,166 pp. Chapters on VCR penetration, black markets in VCRs, videocassette distribution patterns, what people are watching—and where, foreign government concerns on VCRs, global political acts involving VCRs. Notes, appendix, indexes.

1144 Koike, Naoyuki. **CABLE TELEVISION AND TELEPHONE COMPANIES: TOWARDS RESIDENTIAL BROADBAND COMMUNICATIONS SERVICES IN THE UNITED STATES AND JAPAN.** Cambridge, MA: Harvard University, 1990, 180 pp. Provides an overview of regulatory environment of cable television and telephone industries in United States and Japan. Figures, tables, acronyms.

1145 Negrine, Ralph M., ed. **CABLE TELEVISION AND THE FUTURE OF BROADCASTING.** New York: St. Martin's Press, 1985, 211 pp. Provides general surveys of developments in United States, Canada, the low countries, Great Britain, France, West Germany, Australia, and Japan. Tables, figures, glossary, index.

8-G-6. Propaganda Media

1146 **BBC SUMMARY OF WORLD BROADCASTS.** Reading, UK: British Broadcasting Corporation Monitoring Service, 1939–date, daily and weekly. Transcripts and summaries of broadcasts from 120 countries. Emphasizes information from countries for which other news sources are not readily available. Available on microform from Ann Arbor, MI: UMI, 1939–date. Available online through Data-Star, 1984–date; DataTimes, 1982–date; Dialog, 1984–date; FT Profile, 1984–date; LEXIS/NEXIS, 1979–date; and Westlaw, 1984–date.

1147 Frederick, Howard H. **CUBAN-AMERICAN RADIO WARS: IDEOLOGY IN INTERNATIONAL TELECOMMUNICATIONS.** Norwood, NJ: Ablex, 198x, 200 pp. Study of the content and purposes behind the two countries' propaganda warfare. Tables, bibliography, index.

1148 Jowett, Garth S., and Victoria O'Donnell. **PROPAGANDA AND PERSUASION.** Beverly Hills, CA: Sage, 1986, 246 pp. Broad survey of what it is, how it developed and current trends. Charts, photos, references, index.

1149 Martin, L. John. **INTERNATIONAL PROPAGANDA: ITS LEGAL AND DIPLOMATIC CONTROL.** Minneapolis: University of Minnesota Press, 1958, 284 pp. Definition, agencies, control by international agreement, control by municipal law, and control by diplomacy. Notes, index.

1150 Murty, B.S. **THE INTERNATIONAL LAW OF PROPAGANDA: THE IDEOLOGICAL INSTRUMENT AND WORLD PUBLIC ORDER.** Dordrecht, The Netherlands: Martinus Nijhoff, 1989, 310 pp. Reprints a 1968 Yale University Press study (entitled *Propaganda and World Public Order*) that characterizes world attempts to control propaganda and national legal claims. Index.

1151 Short, K.R.M., ed. **WESTERN BROADCASTING OVER THE IRON CURTAIN.** New York: St. Martin's Press, 1986, 274 pp. Thirteen chapters assess the past and present of such broadcasts. Bibliography, index.

1152 Soley, Lawrence C. **RADIO WARFARE: OSS AND CIA SUBVERSIVE PROPAGANDA** New York: Praeger, 1989, 250 pp. Historical treatment of OSS uses of radio in World War II and early CIA applications. Notes, bibliography, index.

1153 Soley, Lawrence C., and John S. Nichols. **CLANDESTINE RADIO BROADCASTING: A STUDY OF REVOLUTIONARY AND COUNTERREVOLUTIONARY ELECTRONIC COMMUNICATION.** New York: Praeger, 1986, 384 pp. Only study of its kind, with many case studies. Notes, references, index.

1154 Wasburn, Philo C. **BROADCASTING PROPAGANDA: INTERNATIONAL RADIO BROADCASTING AND THE CONSTRUCTION OF POLITICAL REALITY.** New York: Praeger, 1992, 179 pp. Combines history and theory to fill in the picture of a little-understood media service, including chapters on the rise of international radio broadcasting to 1945, the role of such services in international conflicts in the years since, the news and propaganda roles of international radio, a case study of international radio services toward the end of the Cold War, South Africa's use of international radio broadcasting, and a research agenda on broadcast propaganda. References, index.

9

Periodicals

by Harry Sova

This chapter offers a guide to some of the more important periodicals about print and electronic media. All were publishing when this book went to press. Because of their enormous number, newsletters, with one or two exceptions, are excluded. Each entry includes the title, ISSN, publisher, years published, frequency of appearance, and a brief annotation. The editors contributed part 9-A; the remainder is largely the work of Dr. Sova, whose COMMUNICATION SERIALS (1159) is an invaluable guide to the broader field of communications.

9-A. Guides to Periodicals

See 0025. ACCESS: THE SUPPLEMENTARY INDEX TO PERIODICALS.

See 0027. ARTICLE 1ST.

1155 Browne, Ray B., and Christopher D. Geist, eds. **POPULAR ABSTRACTS**. Bowling Green, OH: The Popular Press, 1978, 255 pp. Some 1,500 articles from JOURNAL OF POPULAR CULTURE (1967–1977), JOURNAL OF POPULAR FILM (1972–1977), and POPULAR MUSIC AND SOCIETY (1971–1975) are extensively annotated and indexed. Succeeded by short-lived ABSTRACTS OF POPULAR CULTURE (1976–1982).

See 0446. BUSINESS PERIODICALS INDEX.

See 0033. COMINDEX.

See 0035. COMMUNICATION ABSTRACTS.

See 0004, COMMUNICATION BOOKNOTES QUARTERLY.

See 1031. COMMUNICATION CONTENTS SISALLOT.

See 0036. CONTENTS 1ST.

See 0038. CURRENT CONTENTS.

See 0738. CURRENT INDEX TO JOURNALS IN EDUCATION.

1156 Dyer, Carolyn Stewart, and Shannon Heim, compilers. **IOWA GUIDE: SCHOLARLY JOURNALS IN MASS COMMUNICATION AND RELATED FIELDS**. Iowa City: University of Iowa Press, 1995 (6th ed.), 195 pp. Describes editorial focuses of journals and provides detailed practical information to assist authors with meeting manuscript preparation requirements.

See 0041. FILM LITERATURE INDEX.

See 0066. GALE DIRECTORY OF PUBLICATIONS AND BROADCAST MEDIA.

See 0043. GENERAL SCIENCE INDEX.

See 0044. HUMANITIES INDEX.

See 0449. INDEX OF ECONOMIC ARTICLES.

1157 **INDEX TO JOURNALS IN MASS COMMUNICATION**. Riverside, CA: Carpelan Publishing Co., 1988–date, annual. Author and subject indices to almost 50 journals in the research and legal areas, including several non-U.S. publications. Scholarly emphasis.

See 0910. INDEX TO LEGAL PERIODICALS.

See 1034. MASS COM PERIODICAL LITERATURE INDEX.

1158 Matlon, Ronald, and Sylvia P. Ortiz, eds. **INDEX TO JOURNALS IN COMMUNICATION STUDIES THROUGH 1990.** Annandale, VA: Speech Communication Association, 1992 (4th ed.), 2 vols. Cumulated every 5 years. Vol. 1 reproduces tables of contents of 19 major journals in communications, including CRITICAL STUDIES IN MASS COMMUNICATION, JOURNAL OF BROADCASTING & ELECTRONIC MEDIA, JOURNAL OF COMMUNICATION, and JOURNALISM AND MASS COMMUNICATIONS QUARTERLY. Reaching all the way back to the first issue of QUARTERLY JOURNAL OF SPEECH in 1914 makes "Matlon" particularly valuable for historical research, although its complex indexing in vol. 2 is rather intimidating and requires considerable digging. Includes indexes of contributors, subjects coded by subject matter (which covers all fields of communication), and subject keywords. CD-ROM version COMMSEARCH95 (0034) indexes and supplies full texts of selected SCA journals.

See 0008. Orenstein, FULLTEXT SOURCES ONLINE.

See 0048. PERIODICAL ABSTRACTS.

See 0049. READERS' GUIDE TO PERIODICAL LITERATURE.

See 0372. SCIENCE CITATION INDEX.

See 0740. SOCIAL SCIENCE CITATION INDEX.

See 0741. SOCIAL SCIENCES INDEX.

See 0742. SOCIOLOGICAL ABSTRACTS.

1159 Sova, Harry and Patricia Sova. **COMMUNICATION SERIALS 1992–93: AN INTERNATIONAL GUIDE TO PERIODICALS IN COMMUNICATION AND THE PERFORMING ARTS**. Virginia Beach, VA: Sovacom, 1992. A self-published labor of love, this is an invaluable extensively annotated guide to some 3,000 different titles in 38 subject areas with multiple indexes.

1160 Slide, Anthony. **INTERNATIONAL FILM, RADIO, AND TELEVISION JOURNALS**. Westport, CT: Greenwood, 1985, 428 pp. Includes detailed discussion of some 200 titles that "have research value, no matter the area of their expertise and regardless of whether they are trade papers, fan magazines, academic journals, or popular reading matter." Gives information on their publication history, content, contributors, editorial policies, special issues and features, and bibliographies of works about them. Briefly identifies an additional 100 titles. Appendices, index.

See 0050. TOPICATOR...

1161 Uhlan, Miriam and Doris B. Katz. **GUIDE TO SPECIAL ISSUES AND INDEXES OF PERIODICALS**. Washington: Special Libraries Association, 1994 (4th ed.).

See 0011. ULRICH'S INTERNATIONAL PERIODICALS DIRECTORY.

9-B. General

1162 **AMERICAN JOURNALISM** (0882–1127), Athens, GA: University of Georgia, Grady School of Journalism, 1983–date, quarterly. Published by American Journalism Historians Association. Provides an historical forum for review of U.S. journalism.

1163 **AMERICAN JOURNALISM REVIEW** (1067–8654), Adelphi, MD: College of Journalism of the University of Maryland at College Park, 1977–date, 10 issues per year. Evaluative coverage of broadcast and print journalism. Formerly WASHINGTON JOURNALISM REVIEW.

1164 **COLUMBIA JOURNALISM REVIEW** (0010–194X), New York: Columbia University Graduate School of Journalism, 1961–date, bimonthly. Authoritative periodical for journalism ethics. Deals with broadcast and print journalism in the United States. Articles cover salient controversies, such as the ongoing struggle among government, the public, and the news media.

1165 **COMMUNICATION RESEARCH** (0093–6502), Thousand Oaks, CA: Sage Publications, 1974–date, quarterly. Scholarly research articles designed to advance theoretical understanding of the human communication process, including, but not limited to, the international, organizational, political, legal, and family arenas.

1166 **COMMUNICATION RESEARCH TRENDS** (0144–4646), St. Louis, MO: Saint Louis University, 1980–date, quarterly. Issued by Centre for the Study of Communication and Culture. Serves as a clearinghouse for current communication research from a variety of international scholars, with one theme per issue. Formerly CENTRE FOR THE STUDY OF COMMUNICATION AND CULTURE NEWSLETTER.

1167 **CRITICAL STUDIES IN MASS COMMUNICATION** (0739–3180), Annandale, VA: Speech Communication Association, 1984–date, quarterly. Standard in the academic communication community for considered analysis, commentary and research dealing with the evolution, organization, control, economics, administration, and technological innovations of mass communication systems

1168 **DAILY VARIETY** (0011–5509), New York: Cahners Publishing, 1933–date, daily. Entertainment news and gossip about the film, broadcasting, recording, and theatrical industries.

1169 **THE FINANCIAL MANAGER FOR THE MEDIA PROFESSIONAL** (no ISSN). Des Plaines, IA: Broadcast Cable Financial Management Association and Broadcast Cable Credit Association, 1971–date, bimonthly. Practical articles for financial, credit, MIS, and human resources professionals in the media industry. Many changes in title.

1170 **FORBES MEDIACRITIC: THE BEST AND WORST OF AMERICA'S JOURNALISM** (1067–4926), New York: Forbes Publishing, Inc., 1992–date, quarterly. Critiques and reviews journalistic media. Formerly MEDIAGUIDE (to 1992).

1171 **HISTORICAL JOURNAL OF FILM, RADIO AND TELEVISION** (0143–9685), Abingdon, England: Carfax Publishing, 1980–date, quarterly. Scholarly articles, book reviews, and archival reports about media within the political and social history of the 20th century. Also reviews films, television, and radio programs of historical and educational importance. Published in association with the International Association for Media and History.

1172 **INSIDE MEDIA** (1046–5316), Stamford, CT: Cowles Business Media, 1980–date, semimonthly. Explores advertising and marketing through various media, reporting on advertising strategies, case studies, unique publication opportunities for advertisers. Formerly INSIDE PRINT (to 1989) and MAGAZINE AGE (to 1986).

1173 **JOURNAL OF COMMUNICATION** (0021–9916), Cary, NC: Oxford University Press, 1951–date, quarterly. Scholarly studies of communication theory, practice and policy; explores relationship between communication and human relations. Emphasizes research and applications. Issues are theme-oriented. Largely media focused since 1974.

1174 **JOURNAL OF COMMUNICATION INQUIRY** (0196–8599), Iowa City, IA: Center for Communication Study, University of Iowa, 1976–date, semiannual. Includes scholarly studies that emphasize "interdisciplinary inquiry into communication and mass communication phenomena within cultural and historical perspectives."

1175 **JOURNAL OF MEDIA ECONOMICS** (0899–7764), Mahwah, NJ: Erlbaum, 1988–date, quarterly. This scholarly research journal explores economic issues integral to mass media industries including newspaper, magazine, film, radio, television, and cable.

1176 **JOURNAL OF MEDIATED COMMUNICATION** (0888–1596), Aliquippa, PA: Edwards Co. Inc., 1984–date, quarterly. Concerned with information, applications and trends of computer usage in the journalism and mass communication fields. Formerly NEWS COMPUTING JOURNAL.

1177 **JOURNAL OF POPULAR CULTURE** (0022–3840), Bowling Green, OH: Popular Culture Association, Bowling Green State University, 1967–date, quarterly. Examines the cultural norms and eccentricities of U.S. culture including most media.

1178 **JOURNALISM AND MASS COMMUNICATION MONOGRAPHS** (1077–6966), Columbia, SC: Association for Education in Journalism and Mass Communication, 1966–date, bimonthly. Each issue is devoted to a single scholarly research study. Formerly JOURNALISM MONOGRAPHS (to 1995).

1179 **JOURNALISM AND MASS COMMUNICATION QUARTERLY** (1077–6990), Columbia, SC: Association for Education in Journalism and Mass Communication, 1924–date, quarterly. Scholarly research and commentary in journalism and mass communication. Articles present a variety of research methodologies and perspectives. Formerly JOURNALISM QUARTERLY (to 1995) and JOURNALISM BULLETIN (to 1928).

1180 **MASS COMM REVIEW** (0193–7707), Columbia, SC: University of South Carolina, Association for Education in Journalism and Mass Communication, 1973–date, 3/year. A scholarly treatment focused on the interaction between medium and consumer, the media regulator and the regulated medium.

1181 **MEDIA, CULTURE, AND SOCIETY** (0163–4437), London: Sage Publications, 1979–date, quarterly. Scholarly research and discussion across the whole field of cultural practice. The main focus has been on mass media, but there is a newer, additional focus on the concept of the information society. Seeks to relate academic work to contemporary cultural practice, particularly to mass media and communication policy.

1182 **MEDIA STUDIES JOURNAL** (1057–7416), New York: Media Studies Center, 1987–date, quarterly. Each issue is devoted to a specific topic and includes pieces by scholars, industry personnel, and commentators interested in mass media and technological change. Formerly GANNETT CENTER JOURNAL (to 1991).

1183 **MEDIAWEEK** (1055–176X), New York: Adweek, 1966–date, weekly. Furnishes detailed news, interviews, and commentaries on media buying and market positioning for advertising and in-house agencies, with special emphasis on media planning and purchasing. Formerly MARKETING & MEDIA DECISIONS (to 1990) and MEDIA DECISIONS (to 1979).

1184 **VARIETY** (0042–2738), New York: Cahners Publishing Co., 1905–date, weekly. Standard trade publication for the entertainment industry, including film, television, theater. News and reviews.

9-C. Specific Media

9-C-1. Newspapers

1185 **BULLETIN OF THE AMERICAN SOCIETY OF NEWSPAPER EDITORS** (0003–1178), Reston, VA: American Society of Newspaper Editors, 1923–date, 9/year. Newspaper industry news and events. Issues usually focus on specific topic and include diverse articles, often with a critical bite.

1186 **DESIGN** (1050–9224), Washington: Society of Newspaper Design, 1980–date, quarterly. Goal is to improve newspapers through enhanced design. For art and design directors, publishers, and editors. Features design makeovers and their effect on readability, circulation, and advertising.

1187 **EDITOR & PUBLISHER** (0013–094x), New York: Editor & Publisher, 1901–date, weekly. Written from management perspective and known for in-depth coverage of business and regulation of the U.S. newspaper industry.

1188 **JOURNALISM HISTORY** (0094–7679), Las Vegas: University of Nevada, Greenspun School of Communication, 1974–date, quarterly. Includes several scholarly articles per issue, focusing mainly on print journalism, plus reviews and listings of historical work in other venues.

1189 **NEWSINC** (1043–7452), Wilton, CT: Simba Information Inc., 1989–date, monthly. Geared to the business side of newspapers. Written for and about top newspaper executives. Features people and strategies that make newspapers successful.

1190 **NEWSPAPER RESEARCH JOURNAL** (0739–5329), Columbia, SC: Association for Education in Journalism and Mass Communication, 1979–date, quarterly. Features articles on current issues and technologies impacting modern newspapers as well as more traditional research on newspaper coverage of historical topics, such as disasters, elections, and crime.

1191 **PRESSTIME** (0194–3243), Reston, VA: Newspaper Association of America, 1979–date, monthly. Trade news magazine resulting from a merger of several ANPA newsletters. Discusses employee relations, new technology, circulation, government regulation, costs of operation, and other areas of concern for newspaper publishing management.

1192 **PUBLISHERS' AUXILIARY** (0048–5942), Arlington, VA: National Newspaper Association, 1865–date, biweekly. Management related topics concerning the newspaper industry, especially weekly and community papers. Topics include advertising, circulation, labor, reporting, and new technology.

9-C-2. Magazines

1193 **FOLIO: THE MAGAZINE FOR MAGAZINE MANAGEMENT** (0046–4333), Stamford, CT: Cowles Business Media, 1972–date, 21 per year. Wide-ranging array of topics authored by magazine professionals with practical information on the management of magazine publication. Formerly (to 1988) PUBLISHING NEWS.

1194 **MAGAZINE & BOOKSELLER: MASS MARKET RETAILERS' AND PUBLISHERS' GUIDE** (0744–3102), New York: North American Publishing Co., 1946–date, 8/year. Beginning as NEWSDEALER, and later BESTSELLERS, this serves the retailer and distributor of magazines, newspapers, and paperback books.

1195 **MAGAZINE DESIGN & PRODUCTION** (0882–049x), Prairie Village, KS: South Wind Publishing, 1985–date, monthly. Designed for press management; covers design, clients, new technology, circulation. Features thematic issues.

9-C-3. Broadcasting

1196 **AUDIO** (0004–752X), New York: Hachette Filipacchi, 1917–date, monthly. For the audio professional or consumer with technical knowledge and appreciation of quality audio electronic products. Focuses on technical aspects. Earlier titles included RADIO (1921–1947) and AUDIO ENGINEERING (1947–1954).

1197 **BILLBOARD** (0006–2510), New York: BPI Communications, 1894–date, weekly. News, personality profiles, playlists, and business indicators critical to the audio and video recording industry. Known for weekly top music and video playlists.

1198 **BROADCAST ENGINEERING** (0007–1994), Overland Park, KS: Intertec Publishing, 1959–date, monthly. Provides a professional, technical forum for problem solving concerning current technology and the development of a professional engineering staff. Case studies. Assumes technical background.

1199 **BROADCASTING & CABLE** (0007–2028), Washington: Cahners Publishing, 1931–date, weekly. Standard trade publication covers news and current issues in broadcasting and cable television. Emphasizes programming, marketing, corporate changes, regulation, emerging technologies and international developments. Continues BROADCASTING and earlier titles. BROADCASTING INDEX (1972–1981, annual).

1200 **COMMUNICATOR** (0003–7153), Washington: RTNDA (Radio-Television News Directors Association), 1946–date, monthly. Promotes broadcast journalism and journalists through features, news articles, and op-ed pieces. Often referred to as RTNDA COMMUNICATOR.

1201 **CURRENT** (0739–991X). Washington: Current Publishing, 1982–date, biweekly. Newspaper focusing on public radio and television organizations and stations, programming, funding, and policies.

1202 **Db: THE SOUND ENGINEERING MAGAZINE** (0011–7145), Commack, NY: Sagamore Publishing, 1967–date, bimonthly. Technical news coverage designed for the engineering community, with practical advice, new applications, and discussions about the state of the recording industry. Assumes knowledge of electronics.

1203 **ELECTRONIC MEDIA** (0745–0311), Chicago: Crain Communications, 1982–date, weekly. Coverage includes problems, status, and potential of electronic media, technical innovations, advertising concepts, methods of management, program development and legal actions.

1204 **EMMY** (0164–3495), Burbank, CA: Academy of Television Arts and Sciences, 1979–date, bimonthly. Focus is the U.S. television industry, targeting both the industry and the television viewer. Articles cover programs, personalities, directors, and the audience.

1205 **FILM & VIDEO: THE PRODUCTION MAGAZINE** (1041–1933), Los Angeles: Optic Music, 1984–date, monthly. Focuses on production for teleproductions, motion pictures, music videos, commercials, special effects, facilities, and audio. Designed for industry professionals, especially crew and producer/directors.

1206 **IBE: INTERNATIONAL BROADCAST ENGINEER** (0020–6229), Eton Berks, England: Argus Business Media, 1958–date, 7/year. An independent journal devoted to the design, manufacture and operation of professional television and radio broadcast, and video equipment. Assumes some electronic engineering knowledge.

1207 **IEEE TRANSACTIONS ON BROADCASTING** (0018–9316), New York: Broadcast Technology Society, 1955–date, quarterly. Provides fast publication of original and significant contributions relevant to all aspects of broadcast technology.

1208 **IMAGE TECHNOLOGY: TECHNOLOGY OF MOTION PICTURE FILM, SOUND, TELEVISION, AUDIO, VISUAL** (0950–2114), London: British Kinematograph Sound and Television Society, 1936–date, 10/year. Covers the technical side of film and television as the official publication of the Society. Formerly BKSTS JOURNAL, earlier BRITISH KINEMATOGRAPHY: SOUND AND TELEVISION, and initially BRITISH KINEMATOGRAPHY, which focused on motion picture production.

1209 **JOURNAL OF BROADCASTING & ELECTRONIC MEDIA** (0883–8151), Washington: Broadcast Education Association, 1956–date, quarterly. Research journal that provides a forum for serious discussion of pedagogical and industry issues. Explores electronic media with a growing emphasis on international topics and quantitative research. AUTHOR AND TOPIC INDEX TO VOLUME 1 THROUGH 25 (WINTER 1956/57 THROUGH FALL 1981), 1982, 107 pp. covers first 25 years of BEA's journal. Has since been indexed on disc; inquire of publisher for latest index available. Formerly JOURNAL OF BROADCASTING (to 1985).

1210 **JOURNAL OF RADIO STUDIES** (no ISSN), Garden City, NY: Department of Communications, Nassau Community College, 1992–date, irregular. This independent scholarly publication is the first national research forum dedicated exclusively to radio studies. It offers interdisciplinary historical and contemporary studies. With Vol. 5 (1998), published twice yearly by BEA (0792)

1211 **KIDSNET MEDIA GUIDE** (1064–1114) Washington, DC: KIDSNET, 1985–date, monthly. Guide to children's television and radio programs, arranged by network and cable channel. Listings summarize programs and indicate grade level, curriculum area, and support materials available.

1212 **MIX MAGAZINE: PROFESSIONAL RECORDING, SOUND & MUSIC PRODUCTION** (0164–9957), Emeryville, CA: Cardinal Business Media, 1977–date, monthly. The art and technique of studio recording for all media. Emphasis on products for the consumer market. Of special note is a directory providing vendor and studio lists.

1213 **POST MAGAZINE** (0891–5628), Port Washington, NY: Post Pro Publishing, 1986–date, monthly. Published for the postproduction video facility, providing advice on post house management, technology, media trends, client relationships and case stories of successful postproductions. Technological concepts explained from engineering and management viewpoints. PRODUCERS QUARTERLY has appeared as a supplement since 1989.

1214 **QUARTERLY REVIEW OF FILM AND VIDEO** (1050–9208), Cooper Station, NY: Harwood Academic Publishers, 1976–date, quarterly. Offers scholarly research and review essays exploring historical, theoretical, and critical issues relevant to film and television/video studies. Formerly QUARTERLY REVIEW OF FILM STUDIES (to 1989).

1215 **R & R** (0277–4860), Los Angeles: Radio & Records, 1971–date, weekly. Trade newspaper concerned with radio business and music. Features playlists and news about radio broadcasting and record production and promotion.

1216 **RADIO INK: RADIO'S PREMIER MANAGEMENT & MARKETING MAGAZINE** (1064–587X), West Palm Beach, FL: Streamline Publishing, 1985–date, 25/year. Covers all aspects of commercial radio station operation. Former titles include PULSE OF BROADCASTING, PULSE OF RADIO (to 1992).

1217 **THE RADIO WORLD MAGAZINE** (1078–2184), Falls Church, VA: IMAS Publishing, 1977–date, biweekly. Reports on technical, production, and regulatory developments affecting radio. Emphasizes equipment and applications for radio production and recording. Includes product guide and equipment exchange.

1218 **RELIGIOUS BROADCASTING** (0034–4079), Manassas, VA: National Religious Broadcasters, 1969–date, monthly. For Christian religious station operators, managers and programmers.

1219 **SMPTE JOURNAL** (0036–1682), White Plains, NY: Society of Motion Picture and Television Engineers, 1916–date, monthly. Follows progress of motion picture and television engineering and developments in allied fields. Includes technological, engineering, and scientific developments. Has schematics, charts, and graphic illustrations. Often publishes historical material.

1220 **STUDIO SOUND** (0144–5944), London: Miller Freeman Entertainment, 1959–date, monthly. Showcases studio recording facilities, trends, technology, and the profit side of the art and technique of studio sound. Addresses issues of a technological or business nature, and discusses the status of studio recording in both Britain and the United States. Formerly STUDIO SOUND AND BROADCAST ENGINEERING (to 1995). Many earlier titles.

1221 **TELEVISION BROADCAST** (0898–767X), New York: Miller Freeman PSN Inc., 1978–date, monthly. Reports new, interesting, or unique applications of television technology at the station and the teleproduction environment. Some coverage of technical regulations.

1222 **TELEVISION DIGEST WITH CONSUMER ELECTRONICS** (0497–1515), Washington, DC: Warren Publishing, Inc., 1945–date, weekly. Two-part newsletter about the broadcast television and cable industry. First section covers regulatory, legislative, and business developments; second section reports on consumer electronic sales and marketing.

1223 **TELEVISION INDEX, INC.** (0739–5531), Long Island City, NY: Television Index, Inc., 1949–date, weekly. Provides commercial network series history and production credits.

1224 **TELEVISION NEWS INDEX AND ABSTRACTS** (0085–7157), Nashville, TN: Freedom Forum Television News Archive, Vanderbilt University, 1972–date, monthly. Detailed content listing of network evening newscasts and related programs with subject, person, and place indexing.

1225 **TELEVISION QUARTERLY** (0040–2796), New York: The National Academy of Television Arts and Sciences, 1962–date, quarterly. Offers a serious look at television, with study of and commentary on issues current in U.S. television. Contributors are often broadcast executives or others involved in the industry.

1226 **TV GUIDE** (0039–8543), Radnor, PA: Murdoch Magazines, 1953–date, weekly. Examines relationship of television, including cable television, to society including its impact, importance, entertainment, and informational qualities. Published in nearly 100 regional editions providing local network and cable program listings with national editorial material in front. See also TV GUIDE INDEX...., 4 vols. (no longer published), with indexing based on the New York Metropolitan edition:

1 TV GUIDE 25 YEAR INDEX: BY AUTHOR AND SUBJECT: APRIL 3, 1953–DECEMBER 31, 1977, 506 pp.

2 TV GUIDE INDEX: 1978–1982 CUMULATIVE SUPPLEMENT: BY AUTHOR AND SUBJECT, JANUARY 7, 1978–DECEMBER 25, 1981. 1983, 176 pp.

3 TV GUIDE INDEX: 1983–87 CUMULATIVE SUPPLEMENT: BY AUTHOR AND SUBJECT: JANUARY 1, 1983–DECEMBER 26, 1987. 1988, 299 pp.

4 TV GUIDE INDEX: 1988 SUPPLEMENT: BY AUTHOR AND SUBJECT: JANUARY 2, 1988–DECEMBER 31, 1988. (News America Publications), 1989, 81 pp.

1227 **TV TECHNOLOGY** (0887–1701), Falls Church, VA: IMAS Publishing Inc., 1983–date, semi-monthly. For radio/television production and engineering staffs. Provides technical information with a warm editorial style. Each issue has three main sections: Engineering, Production, and Buyers Guide.

1228 **VIDEO SYSTEMS** (0361–0942), Overland Park, KS: Intertec Publishing, 1975–date, monthly. Initially focused on technology, technique, and programming in the industrial (corporate) television area, but now deals with independent production field, providing news of video production. Features production techniques of top production houses.

9-C-4. Cable and Newer Media

1229 **ADVANCED IMAGING** (1042–0711), Melville, NY: PTN Publishing, 1988–date, monthly. Covers imaging science, including designs, equipment, and techniques. Helpful for corporate media personnel in studying materials and processes of communication media.

1230 **AV VIDEO: PRODUCTION AND PRESENTATION TECHNOLOGY** (0747–1335), White Plains, NY: Knowledge Industry Publications, 1978–date, monthly. Covers all aspects of the audio–video industry including computer graphics with considerable how-to information.

1231 **CABLE WORLD: THE NEWS MAGAZINE FOR VIDEO, VOICE AND DATA** (1042–7228), Stamford, CT: Cowles Business Media, 1989–date, weekly. Covers marketing, technology, and programming developments in cable.

1232 **CABLEVISION** (1361–8374), New York: Chilton Co./ABC Media, 1975–date, biweekly. Trade journal covers regulation, technology, city–cable relationships and general audience trends. Considerable coverage of the potential of cable television.

1233 **CED: COMMUNICATIONS ENGINEERING & DESIGN** (0191–5428), New York: ABC, Inc., 1975–date, monthly. Covers cable television communications hardware and other broadband technologies. Assumes technical knowledge of electronic media operation.

1234 **CONVERGENCE** (1080–7454), New York: Capital Cities Media, 1993–date, monthly. Focus is on merging of media systems worldwide, with emphasis on the impact of technological, cultural, and regulatory developments on the consumer. Includes philosophical and management discussions.

1235 **CONVERGENCE: THE JOURNAL OF RESEARCH INTO NEW MEDIA TECHNOLOGIES** (1354–8565), Luton, England: University of Luton/John Libbey Media, 1995–date, twice a year. Debates and research concerned with convergence of media systems.

1236 **DIGITAL VIDEO MAGAZINE** (1075–251X), Bedford, NH: TechMedia Publishing, 1993–date, monthly. Focuses on convergence between computers and video technologies, including computer enhancement, animation and graphics.

1237 **INTERACTIVE AGE** (1080–4927), Manhasset, NY: CMP Publications, 1994–date, biweekly. This newspaper for electronic commerce provides news coverage of www activities, regulatory and corporate developments, with emphasis on technology.

1238 **MULTICHANNEL NEWS** (0276–8593), New York: Chilton Publishing, 1980–date, weekly. Trade newspaper on all aspects of newer electronic media including programming, production, regulation, economics, and audience surveys.

1239 **MULTIMEDIA PRODUCER** (1079–4689), White Plains, NY: Knowledge Industry Publications, 1995–date, monthly. Explores interactive multimedia in CD-ROM, WWW, kiosk and VOD (video on demand), as well as more traditional forms of mass communication. Highlights new technologies and applies these to the marketplace from a media management perspective.

1240 **MULTIMEDIA WORLD** (1073–4759), San Francisco: PC World Communications, 1993–date, monthly. Convergence of electronic media and computers with articles on content, applications, and technology.

1241 **NEW MEDIA: THE MAGAZINE FOR CREATORS OF THE DIGITAL FUTURE** (1060–7188) San Mateo, CA: HyperMedia Communications, 1990–date, 10/year. Focuses on the interface between computers and video media, including Internet.

1242 **ON DEMAND** (1076–0334), Stamford, CT: Cowles Business Media, 1994–date, monthly. Emerging from the parent publication, CABLE WORLD, this explores video on demand opportunities and constraints. Includes a listing of PPV motion pictures and their economic status on VOD systems.

1243 **PRIVATE CABLE & WIRELESS CABLE: COVERING ALTERNATIVE VIDEO DELIVERY SYSTEMS** (1080–9570), Rosenberg, TX: National Satellite Publishing, 1981–date, monthly. MMDS systems, PPV, and private cable system business and technology.

1244 **SATELLITE BUSINESS NEWS** (1043-0865), Washington: Satellite Business News, 1990–date, biweekly. Covers satellite tv industry.

1245 **SATELLITE COMMUNICATIONS** (0147–7439), Overland Park, KS: Intertec Publishing, 1977–date, monthly. Covers programming, legal challenges, promotions, technological developments, and trade news. Of special note is an international viewpoint applied to events and trends in the satellite communication field.

1246 **T.H.E. JOURNAL** (0192–592x), Tustin, CA: Information Synergy, 1974–date, monthly. Focuses on technological horizons in education, addressing the application of technology to various classroom and pedagogical uses. Useful case studies.

1247 **VIA SATELLITE** (1041–0643), Potomac, MD: Phillips Business Information, 1986–date, monthly. Technical and business aspects of satellite communication with many features on media applications of satellite delivery.

1248 **VIDEO AND MULTIMEDIA PRODUCER** (ISSN pending), White Plains, NY: Knowledge Industry Publications, 1978–date, monthly. Industry news, business operations, new products, and features.

1249 **VIDEO BUSINESS** (0279–571x), New York: Chilton Publishers, 1981–date, weekly. For retailers and distributors of home videos, reports on the status of the videocassette sale and rental industry. Covers store operations, industry trends, and changing consumer tastes.

1250 **WIRED** (1059–1028), San Francisco: Wired Ventures, 1993–date, monthly. Designed for industry professionals. Concentrates on the effect of the merging of computing, communications and the media from business to politics, education to entertainment. News and information about emerging interactive media.

1251 **WIRELESS BROADCASTING: COVERING DOMESTIC & INTERNATIONAL WIRELESS CABLE & COMMUNICATIONS**. Sugar Land, TX: Windbreaker Publications, 1992–date, monthly. News and features on both business and technology.

9–D. Policy and Law

(Note: for legal reporters, see 7-D-7.)

1252 **ACCESS REPORTS/FREEDOM OF INFORMATION** (0145–3939), Lynchburg, VA: Access Reports, Inc., 1975–date, biweekly. Latest developments in the freedom of information field, especially freedom of obtaining access to government materials and information. Emphasis on legal aspects of the Freedom of Information Act.

1253 **CARDOZO ARTS & ENTERTAINMENT LAW JOURNAL** (0736–7694), New York: Benjamin N. Cardozo School of Law, Yeshiva University, 1981–date, semi-annual. Law review on all aspects of media, arts, and entertainment law and regulation. Reflects decisions handed down in major court tests.

1254 **CENSORSHIP NEWS** (0749–6001), New York: National Coalition Against Censorship, 1975–date, quarterly. Late-breaking news and updates about censorship of ideas and media.

1255 **COMMUNICATION LAW AND POLICY** (1081–1680), Mahwah, NJ: Erlbaum, 1996–date, quarterly. Journal of the law division of the AEJMC (0790), this law review includes scholarly assessments of media and telecommunications questions.

1256 **COMMUNICATIONS AND THE LAW** (0162–9093), Littleton, CO: Fred B. Rothman Co., 1979–date, quarterly. Expanding technologies, censorship, public opinion formation by government and related issues are the focus of this publication.

1257 **COMMUNICATIONS LAWYER** (0737–7622), Chicago: American Bar Association, 1983–date, quarterly. Aimed at attorneys who devote a major portion of their practice to print and electronic media, satellites, telecommunications (common carrier), entertainment, intellectual property law, and related areas.

1258 **ENTERTAINMENT AND SPORTS LAWYER** (0732–1880), Chicago: American Bar Association, 1982–date, quarterly. For lawyers who deal with entertainment, sports, intellectual property law, and related areas. Scholarly, current, and practical information.

1259 **EXTRA!** (0895–2310), New York: FAIR (Fairness & Accuracy in Reporting), 1987–date, eight issues per year. Focuses on the increasing concentration of the U.S. media in fewer and fewer corporate hands. Seeks to correct bias and imbalance in media.

1260 **FEDERAL COMMUNICATIONS LAW JOURNAL** (0163–7606), Bloomington, IN: Indiana University School of Law, 1937–date, three issues per year. Issued with the Federal Communications Bar Association, this law review offers several detailed articles on media or telecommunications law, plus briefer notes. Formerly FEDERAL COMMUNICATIONS BAR JOURNAL.

1261 **HASTINGS COMMUNICATIONS AND ENTERTAINMENT LAW JOURNAL** (1061–6578), San Francisco: University of California, Hastings College of the Law, 1977–date, quarterly. Includes a wide scope of media and telecommunications legal issues, including First Amendment, defamation, obscenity, television, cable television, satellite communications, intellectual property, entertainment, and sports. Formerly COMM/ENT: HASTINGS JOURNAL OF COMMUNICATIONS AND ENTERTAINMENT LAW (to 1994) and originally, COMM/ENT.

1262 **JOURNAL OF MASS MEDIA ETHICS** (0890–0523), Mahwah, NJ: Erlbaum, 1985–date, quarterly. Scholarly articles and essays concerning media ethics and morality among academic and professional groups, especially focused on journalism ethics in broadcast and print media.

1263 **LOYOLA ENTERTAINMENT LAW JOURNAL** (0740–9370), Los Angeles: Loyola of Los Angeles School of Law, 1981–date, quarterly. Provides a continuing dialogue between the legal community and the entertainment industry, with coverage of trends, issues, and recent litigation in the fields of performing arts, mass communication, and sports. Formerly ENTERTAINMENT LAW JOURNAL (to 1982).

1264 **MEDIA ETHICS** (no ISSN), Boston, MA: Emerson College, 1988–date, 2/year. A cooperative publication of five institutions offering expressions of opinion, case studies and comments, philosophical investigations and discourses, news items, professional codes, policies and procedures affecting or practiced by media professionals, and the academic study of such phenomena. Formerly MEDIA ETHICS UPDATE (to 1992).

1265 **NEWS MEDIA & THE LAW** (0149–0737), Arlington, VA: Reporters Committee for Freedom of the Press, 1973–date, quarterly. Details legal decisions concerning news media and the law, and scholarly comment on same within the United States. Emphasis is on recent court actions and their potential impact on the news-gathering process.

9-E. International

(Excludes country-specific titles.)

1266 **ABU TECHNICAL REVIEW** (0126–6209), Kuala Lumpur, Malaysia: Asia-Pacific Broadcasting Union, 1969–date, bimonthly. A forum for news and discussion about technological developments in broadcast technology for the membership. Assumes a knowledgeable readership.

1267 **ASIAN JOURNAL OF COMMUNICATION** (0129–2986), Singapore: Asian Mass Communication Research and Information Centre (AMIC), 1990–date, semi-annual. This joint effort of AMIC and the Department of Mass Communication, National University of Singapore, is a research publication seeking to advance the understanding of the process of communication in the Asia-Pacific region.

1268 **BROADCASTING & CABLE INTERNATIONAL** (1064–6124), Washington: Cahners Publishing, 1983–date, monthly. Trade coverage of international electronic media, with emphasis on people within programming, sales, and management. Addresses regulation, advertising, programming and technology. Formerly BROADCASTING ABROAD (to 1993).

1269 **BULLETIN OF THE EUROPEAN INSTITUTE FOR THE MEDIA** (1021–5719, English edition), Dusseldorf: European Institute for the Media, 1984–date, quarterly. Features issues impacting European media, including copyright, transborder broadcasting, television programming quotas, and EU media regulation. Country-by-country reports on latest media developments. Also published in French and German editions. Formerly MEDIA BULLETIN.

1270 **COMBROAD** (0951–0826), London: Commonwealth Broadcasting Association, 1966–date, quarterly. Technical, policy, and program developments in member countries of the British Commonwealth, especially in Africa.

1271 Journals published by the European Broadcasting Union (Case Postale 67, CH-1218, Grand-Saconnex (GE), Switzerland) have been considerably modified from former long-running bi-monthlies to two quarterlies:

1 **DIFFUSION** (1021-3465), 1992–date, quarterly. Covers range of topics on radio-television broadcasting including role in society, programs, regulation, economics, audience research, and statistics. Replaces EBU REVIEW—PART B (1968–71) and EBU REVIEW—PROGRAMMES, ADMINISTRATION, LAW (1972–90).

2 **EBU TECHNICAL REVIEW** (1019-6587), 1950–date, quarterly since 1992. Covers all technical and professional engineering aspects of radio and television. Replaces BULLETIN DE DOCUMENTATION ET E'INFORMATION DE I'UER (1950–57), EBU REVIEW—PART A (1968–1971), EBU REVIEW-TECHNICAL (1972–1991).

1271a **EUROPEAN JOURNAL OF COMMUNICATION** (0267–3231), London: Sage Publications, 1986–date, quarterly. Scholarly journal of communication theory and research in Europe.

1272 **GAZETTE: INTERNATIONAL JOURNAL FOR MASS COMMUNICATION STUDIES** (0016–5492), Dordrecht, Netherlands: Kluwer Academic, 1955–date, bimonthly. Scholarly forum for research including international exchange of ideas in public relations, politics, government information services, media economics, and advertising.

1273 **INDEX ON CENSORSHIP** (0306–4220), London: Writers & Scholars International, 1972–date, 10/year. Overview of the relative freedom of the press vis-à-vis world governments, with special emphasis on press freedom within those nations where political struggles are more active.

1274 **INTERMEDIA** (0309–118X), London: International Institute of Communications, 1973–date, bimonthly. Useful combination of reports on research on all media worldwide, focusing on administration and regulation, research trends, applications of technology. Formerly IBI NEWSLETTER.

1275 **INTERNATIONAL BROADCASTING** (0957–4425), London: EMAP Media, 1978–date, monthly. News and features for engineers and managers of radio and television stations on all aspects of sound and television broadcast engineering worldwide from management to support services, from operational concepts to equipment design. Formerly INTERNATIONAL BROADCASTING SYSTEMS AND OPERATION and BROADCASTING SYSTEMS AND OPERATIONS.

1276 **INTERNATIONAL CABLE: COVERING THE GLOBAL BUSINESS OF MULTI-CHANNEL DELIVERY SYSTEMS** (no ISSN), Denver: CT Publications, 1989–date, monthly. News and features focusing on business and programming aspects. Features on media in different countries and cities.

1277 **IPI REPORT** (0019–0314), Vienna: International Press Institute, 1952–date, bimonthly. Concerned with freedom of information, print and broadcast journalists, press freedom. Includes the "World Press Freedom Review," a nation-by-nation scorecard of press freedom.

1278 **MEDIA ASIA** (0129–6612), Singapore: Asian Mass Communications Research and Information Centre, 1974–date, quarterly. News of ongoing research, workshops, and other issues of mass communication in Asian cultures.

1279 **MEDIA INTERNATIONAL** (0266–8688), Sutton, England: Reed Business Publishing Group, 1973–date, monthly. Provides in-depth coverage on international advertising campaigns and mass media, especially about trends in cost, production, and response. Each issue provides an assessment of a particular nation's or region's communication media.

1280 **MOVIE-TV MARKETING** (0047–8288) Tokyo: Movie-TV Marketing, 1953–date, monthly. An international publication for the promotion and exhibition of motion picture and television products. Formerly MOVIE MARKETING (to 1966) and FAR EAST FILM NEWS (to 1962).

1281 **MOVING PICTURES INTERNATIONAL** (0959–6992), London: Moving Pictures International, 1990–date, monthly. International review of events, trends, new product releases, and the economic box office status of motion pictures, broadcast and cable television, and associated video services. Articles address the business side of entertainment.

1282 **POLITICAL COMMUNICATION: AN INTERNATIONAL JOURNAL** (0195–7473), Bristol, PA: Taylor & Francis, 1980–date, quarterly. An examination in an objective and scholarly fashion of what is happening in international channels of communication and persuasion. Formerly (to 1992) POLITICAL COMMUNICATION AND PERSUASION.

1283 **TBI: TELEVISION BUSINESS INTERNATIONAL** (0953–6841), London: FT Media & Telecoms, 1979–date, monthly. Covers international electronic entertainment business. Reports on developments in broadcasting, program production and distribution, finance, advertising, regulatory, and new technology issues.

1284 **TV WORLD** (0142-7466), London: Emap Media, 1978–date, monthly. Programming production and distribution news and features about television worldwide.

1285 **VIDEO AGE INTERNATIONAL: THE BUSINESS JOURNAL OF FILM, TV BROADCASTING, CABLE, PAY TV, PPV, HOME VIDEO, DBS, PRODUCTION** (0278–5013), New York: TV Trade Media Inc., 1981–date, 10/year. Concerns the independent production field, providing news of video production world wide. Shows production techniques of top production houses. Focused initially on industrial (corporate) television.

1286 **WORLD BROADCAST NEWS** (1050–012X), Overland Park, KS: Intertec Publishing, 1978–date, 11/year. International magazine of broadcast technology provides information on emerging technical equipment, comparing existing world facilities and serving as an advertising vehicle to reach international broadcast executives. Formerly BME'S WORLD BROADCAST NEWS.

10

Audiovisual Resources

by Louise Benjamin

This chapter provides a selective listing of AV material (films, tapes, audio recordings) pertaining to mass communications. Most entries are videotapes that may be rented or purchased. Generally excluded are tapes on specific individuals or programs—of which there are many—as well as most older recordings. Unless otherwise noted, all electronic media are VHS cassette format. Entries also indicate running time and identify distributors by acronym. Some items are from Britain or Australia, but most originate in the U.S. Appendix provides information for commercial and educational distributors. NOTE: Video titles in this chapter (Sec. 10-B on) are NOT indexed.

10-A. Reference Sources

(See also: 2-B-1 for recorded historical archives and chapter 5 for published filmographies and guides to radio and television programs.)

1287 Calkins, Carolyn et al. **FILMS ABOUT MOTION PICTURES AND TELEVISION**. Frederick, MD: University Publications of America, 1981, 54 pp. Describes about 250 films and videocassettes. Useful for older material. Bibliography; subject index.

1288 **EDUCATIONAL FILM/VIDEO LOCATOR.** New York: R. R. Bowker Co. 1987-date, annual. Most up-to-date list of locator services in the United States. Lists all available sources for educational film and video.

1289 Emmens, Carol A. **FAMOUS PEOPLE ON FILM**. Metuchen, NJ: Scarecrow Press, 1977, 355 pp. Identifies films (with brief description and distributor information) about filmmakers, inventors, journalists, and other media and related individuals. Subject index.

1290 Frewin, Anthony, comp. **THE ASSASSINATION OF JOHN F. KENNEDY: AN ANNOTATED FILM, TV, AND VIDEOGRAPHY, 1963-1992**. Westport, CT: Greenwood, 1993, 170 pp. Covers more than 230 specific resources organized by medium. Indexes.

1291 Gebauer, Dorothea, comp., **BIBLIOGRAPHY OF NATIONAL FILMOGRAPHIES**. Brussels: FIAF, 1985, 80 pp. Compiled with the assistance of the Cataloging Commission of the International Federation of Film Archives. Detailed descriptions of current and retrospective guides and catalogs of films arranged alphabetically by country. Provides coverage of retrospective, historically important, or otherwise dated U.S. filmographies.

1292 Hitchens, Howard B., and Vidge Hitchens. **AMERICA ON FILM AND TAPE: A TOPICAL CATALOG OF AUDIOVISUAL RESOURCES FOR THE STUDY OF UNITED STATES HISTORY, SOCIETY, AND CULTURE**. Westport, CT: Greenwood Press, 1985, 392 pp. Subject-arranged listing includes brief descriptions and distribution information for films and audiorecordings on newspaper journalism, television, and films. List of distributors and title index.

1293 Library of Congress. **AUDIOVISUAL MATERIALS**. Washington: Library of Congress, 1979–date, quarterly with annual cumulations (published only in microfiche after 1983). Describes motion pictures, filmstrips, sets of transparencies and slides, and video recordings cataloged by the

Library of Congress. It continues the Library of Congress' MOTION PICTURES AND FILMSTRIPS (1958-1973) and FILMS AND OTHER MATERIALS FOR PROJECTION (1974-1979).

1294 Pitts, Michael. R. **RADIO SOUNDTRACKS: A REFERENCE GUIDE**. Metuchen, NJ: Scarecrow, 1986 (2nd ed.), 337 pp. Most complete reference available, this describes radio programs available as tape recordings, radio specials on tape, radio programs available only on LP records, performer appearances recorded on LPs, and compilation record albums based on radio material. Appendix of sources, index.

1295 Pratt, Douglas. **THE LASER VIDEO DISC COMPANION: A GUIDE TO THE BEST (AND WORST) LASER VIDEO DISCS**. New York: New York Zoetrope, 1988, 447 pp. Reviews U.S. and foreign discs released from 1984-1987. Not indexed.

1296 **VIDEO SOURCE BOOK**. Syosset, NY: National Video Clearinghouse, 1979–date, annual. Lists programs recorded on videotape and videodisc, with title, subject, and distributor indexes.

1297 **WORDS ON TAPE**. Westport, CT: Meckler, 1984–date, annual. Lists audio cassettes published in U.S. and Canada, with author, title, and subject indexes.

10-B. History

10-B-1. General

1298 **THE DEVELOPMENT OF MASS COMMUNICATION.** 1989, 26 min. Tracing development from telegraphy to modern satellite technology, this program explores early days of radio broadcasting, development of television, and beginnings of national networks. Dist: Insight Media.

1299 **GIRDLE AROUND THE EARTH.** 1966, 16mm b/w film, 20 min. Invention and development of telegraph, telephone, and radio. Discoveries of Bell, Edison, Marconi, Fleming, de Forest, and others. Geared to high school level but one of the few films covering these subjects. Dist: ASU, IU, SYU, UC/B.

10-B-2. Broadcasting

1300 **THE GREAT RADIO COMEDIANS.** 1972, 16mm, 88 min. Review of radio's best comedians of the 1930s and 1940s. Contemporary interviews, old stills, audio and film clips cover the careers of Burns and Allen, Edgar Bergen, Bob Hope, Jack Benny, Fred Allen, and Fibber McGee and Molly. Dist: Contemporary Films/McGraw-Hill.

1301 **IS EVERYBODY LISTENING?** 1947, 16mm, 20 min. Newsreel from *March of Time* series that appraises overall content of radio during its peak pretelevision era. Dist: Time-Life Films.

1302 **RADIO.** 1961, 16mm film, 29 min. Traces radio as it developed program formats in the 1930s including concerts, drama, and on-the-spot reporting. Emphasizes radio as a unifying force in society. Dist: IU.

1303 **A VAST WASTELAND.** 1961, Audio tape, 42 min. Recording of then-FCC chairman Newton Minow's speech to the 1961 Convention of the National Association of Broadcasters. Dist: Pacifica.

1304 **WHISPER IN THE AIR: THE MARCONI STORY.** 1994, 58 min. Profiles Guglielmo Marconi and development of wireless telegraphy. Dist: Insight Media.

10-B-3. Broadcast Journalism

1305 **EDWARD R. MURROW SERIES.** 1992, Four tapes, length not given. Includes best of *Person to Person* and *See It Now* series plus *The McCarthy Years* and *Harvest of Shame.* Dist: Viewfinders, Inc.

1306 **HUNGER IN AMERICA.** 1968, 16mm, 51 min. One of the most sharply focused CBS documentaries, this blends personal interviews with narrated sequences. Dist: Carousel Films and IU, Kent, PSU, SYU, UC/B, UI, MI, MN.

1307 **MEDIA IN POLITICS.** 1990, 90 min. Three-part program illustrates media concepts employed successfully on behalf of countless candidates before and after they took office. Dist: Films for the Humanities.

1308 **PENSIONS: THE BROKEN PROMISE.** 1972, 16mm film, 39 min. Classic NBC documentary of private pension plans and the Social Security system. Dist: IU, Kent, PSU, SYU, UC/B, UI, MI, MN.

1309 **REBUTTAL TO *THE SELLING OF THE PENTAGON.*** 1971, 16mm, 22 min. The Defense Secretary Melvin Laird and VP Spiro Agnew respond to program listed immediately below. Dist: Carousel Films and UC/B, MI, USF.

1310 **THE SELLING OF THE PENTAGON.** 1971, 16mm, 52 min. Classic CBS documentary on Pentagon use of media to influence public opinion. Dist: Carousel Films and BU, Iowa, PST, SYU, UC/B, UW/M.

1311 **TELEVISION AND THE PRESIDENCY.** 1984, 98 min. Examines role of television in political campaigns from the whistle stop in the 1950s to Reagan presidency. Dist: Insight Media.

10-C. Technology

10-C-1. General

1312 **COMMUNICATION TECHNIQUES.** 1995, 23 min. Discusses development of sophisticated communication tools such as photocopiers, cellular telephones, and computer systems. Explains how they work and their potential uses. Dist: Films for the Humanities.

1313 **COMMUNICATIONS: THE WIRED WORLD.** 1971, 16mm, 22 min. From the *Toward the Year 2000* series, this examines what were then considered future communications and information storage and retrieval systems. Dist: SYU, UC/B.

1314 **GLOBAL COMMUNICATION.** 1995, 23 min. Highways of optic fibers, copper wires, coaxial cables, and satellites on which images, sound, and computer data are transmitted around the world. Dist: Films for the Humanities.

1315 **TELECOMMUNICATIONS.** 1995, 26 min. Demonstrates radio electromagnetic waves and geostationary satellite links in the world communications network. Dist: Films for the Humanities.

1316 **TOOLS OF THE AV TRADE.** 1993, Four 15-min. tapes. Describes basic tools of audiovisual technology, explaining what each does and how: (1) The Cinematograph, explains cinema antecedents with excerpts from films of Lumiere and Melies; (2) Daguerre and the Photo Camera, shows photographic technological innovations; (3) Mr. Edison and His Phonograph; and (4) The Development of Television up to Satellite Transmission and HDTV. Dist: Films for the Humanities.

10-C-2. Radio and Recording

1317 **HOW A RADIO STATION WORKS.** 1989, 26 min. Behind the scenes of radio stations that feature different formats—adult contemporary, all news, rock, and easy listening—and responsibilities of disk jockeys, announcers, and program directors. Dist: Insight Media.

1318 **RADIO AND RADAR.** 1961, 16mm, 12 min. Shows how radio waves are produced and how they travel, various bands of radio waves, difference between AM and FM, and patterns of reception. Dist: IU, OSU.

1319 **THE RADIO STUDIO.** 1990, 31 min. Introduces radio studio hardware: console, microphones, telephone talkback, turntables and CDS, cart players, tape recorders, cassette decks, and DAT recorders. Teaches procedures for cueing, labeling, cleaning, and caring for machines. Dist: Insight Media.

1320 **RADIO TALKBACK.** 1990, 35 min. Explores approaches to live call-in shows plus phone operation, delay systems, and call-dumping. Dist: Insight Media.

1321 **SOUND AND VISION: AM AND FM SOUND.** 1990, 28 min. First part of a Michael Faraday lecture on sound and vision, covering pitch and loudness, telephone sound, microphones, band widths, AM and FM, short wave and long wave, digital sound, and other aspects of sound wave nature and transmission. See 1330. Dist: Films for the Humanities.

10-C-3. Television and Video

1322 **THE DEVELOPMENT OF TELEVISION.** 1993, 15 min. Program traces TV from pioneers Nipkow, Baird, and Zworykin to satellite transmission and HDTV. Dist: Films for the Humanities.

1323 **ELECTRONIC EFFECTS.** 1990, 37 min. Principles and applications of chromakey and digital video effects. Examples of complex sequences from BBC productions and how they were made. Dist: Films for the Humanities.

1324 **THE ELECTRONIC RAINBOW.** 1977, 16mm, 20 min. Traces invention of television equipment, receivers, and programming from 1940s to 1970. Animation illustrates TV transmission and reception. Dist: BU, IU, Kent, PST, PUR, MI.

1325 **THE HOLD UP: AN EDITING EXERCISE.** 1991, 20 min. Film critic Roger Ebert examines rushes to final cut of a bank robbery scene illuminating basic editing techniques and concluding with two versions showing differing approaches in assembling a sequence. Dist: Insight Media.

1326 **HOW DOES TELEVISION WORK?** 1970, 16mm, 10 min. Principles of transmitting and receiving a television picture. Dist: BU.

1327 **AN INTRODUCTION TO THE STUDIO.** 1990, 17 min. BBC survey of work in a television studio. Covers the production team and the studio crew, equipment available in a modern broadcast studio, and basic shots and camera moves that a studio pedestal can make. Dist: Films for the Humanities.

1328 **THE NEW AGE OF DIGITAL VIDEO COMPRESSION.** 1994, 71 min. Examines this technology using simple language, analogies, and animated graphics. Applications demonstrated include television delivery over wire and desktop video conferencing. Dist: Shelburne Films.

1329 **RECORDING AND REPRODUCTION TECHNIQUES.** 1995, 23 min. Three technologies used to record and reproduce sounds and images are assessed: computer graphics, laser discs, and holography. Dist: Films for the Humanities.

1330 **SOUND AND VISION: TELEVISION.** 1990, 28 min. Second half of Faraday lecture (see 1321) covers illusion of movement, how images are transmitted, differences between film and video formats, color transmission, visual effects and use of color blue (chromakey), wave forms as digital signals, HDTV, and fiber optics. Dist: Films for the Humanities.

1331 **VISUAL EFFECTS FOR TV: THE BATTLEFIELD.** 1990, 30 min. Describes 3-day technical build-up to a re-enactment of the Battle of Waterloo for a final sequence running only a few minutes. Dist: Films for the Humanities.

10-C-4. Satellites and Newer Services

1332 **A BASIC INTRODUCTION TO SATELLITES FOR BEGINNERS.** 1990, 14 min. Fundamentals of geostationary orbits, satellites, and receiving dishes, plus how satellite television works and what kind of equipment is needed. Dist: Shelburne Films.

1333 **THE ERA OF DIRECT BROADCAST SATELLITES.** 1993, 56 min. Explores DBS services in England, Japan, and Australia. Dist: Shelburne Films.

1334 **EXPLORING VIRTUAL REALITY.** 1995, 23 min. Technology of virtual reality and use of computers to simulate or reproduce sounds. Dist: Films for the Humanities.

1335 **INFORMATION SUPERHIGHWAY: UNDERSTANDING AND USING THE INTERNET.** 1994, 30 min. Step-by-step guide to the Internet, including service providers , modems, and software with graphical interfaces. Basics of e-mail, telnet, file transfer protocol, Gopher, the World Wide Web, Archie, Veronica, and WAIS are explored. Dist: Insight Media.

1336 **INFORMATION TECHNOLOGY AND THE FUTURE.** 1995, Three 52-min. tapes: (1) Selling the Future—the electronic, technological, and conceptual worlds; (2) Welcome to the Jungle—how new technologies will transform how we live and work, including Internet; and (3) The Virtual Wasteland—asks whether this new technological world isn't in fact a virtual wasteland. Dist: Films for the Humanities.

1337 **THE INTERNET SHOW.** 1994, 66 min. PBS explanation of Internet and how to use it. Dist: Viewfinders.

1338 **LEARN TO USE THE INTERNET.** 1995, 45 min. Explains what the Internet is and how it can be accessed, and how to send e-mail, use the World Wide Web, and download information. Package contains a video and a CD-ROM, as well as free trial service on Prodigy, America On-Line, and ImagiNation. Dist: Insight Media.

1339 **NEWER ALTERNATIVE MEDIA.** 1994, 20 min. Examines a broad array of alternative media: billboards and transit signs to in-store advertising and direct-response television. Differentiates between narrowcast and broadcast advertising techniques, showing the current trend towards the unconventional, including interactive television. Dist: Insight Media.

1340 **WHAT IS MULTIMEDIA?** 1993, 20 min. Multimedia brings together graphics, animation, audio, video, and text to create a new kind of experience. Covers basic ingredients including hardware, software, scripting, interactivity and robotics. Dist: First Light Video.

1341 **THE WORLD AT 12 GIGAHERTZ.** 1995, 60 min. Overview of Ku-band satellite uses and technology, showing advantages this frequency band offers. Applications and technical comparison with C-band. Dist: Shelburne Films.

10-D. Industry and Economics

10-D-1. Print Media

1342 **BEHIND THE SCENES OF THE TRADE PUBLICATION INDUSTRY.** 1989, 30 min. Compares mass circulation and controlled circulation magazines, responsibilities of the reporter, photographer, art director, and graphic designer. Dist: Insight Media.

1343 **EXPLORING NEWSPAPER PUBLISHING.** 1995, 27 min. Profiles careers in newspapers by interviewing a reporter, an editor, a photographer, a graphic artist, an advertising manager, a distribution manger, and production staff members. Each describes his or her responsibilities and explains what type of education is needed. Dist: Insight Media.

1344 **THE MAKING OF A MAGAZINE.** 1989, 35 min. Development of the magazine industry in the United States, operations at a city and a regional magazine. Role of publisher, editor, art director, photographer, and layout director, promotions, targeted advertising, and circulation. Dist: Insight Media.

1345 **THE MAKING OF A NEWSPAPER.** 1988, 28 min. Producing a daily metropolitan newspaper; how news is collected, written, typeset, and printed, and how computers and satellites are utilized. Daily operations of advertising, composition and layout, platemaking, printing, and distribution departments. Dist: Insight Media.

1346 **NEWSPAPER ADVERTISING.** 1989, 22 min. Explains pros and cons of newspaper advertising and its various formats. Discusses shoppers, zoned editions, supplements, and preprints and examines the functions of institutional advertising and retail advertising. Differentiates between single-item, assortment, theme, and omnibus formats. Dist: Insight Media.

1347 **NEWSPAPER WARS.** 1989, 26 min. Changing role of newspapers in society, what it means for the public when papers no longer have to compete for readers, and how the quality of information affects the way we govern ourselves. Dist: Films for the Humanities.

1348 **PRINT MEDIA.** 1994, 20 min. Examines pros and cons of advertising in daily, weekly, and free newspapers and consumer, business, trade, and industrial magazines. When to use special editions and total market coverage programs. Defines terms and teaches how to compute CPM for print media. Dist: Insight Media.

1349 **THE WORLD OF MAGAZINES.** 1990, 30 min. Introduction to magazine publishing: history and structure of the business, trends in magazine publishing, and how magazines have changed over the years. Dist: Insight Media.

1350 **WRITING POSITIONS IN A NEWSPAPER.** 1990, 28 min. Offers tips on entering the newspaper profession, including profiles of a wide range of careers: reporting, editing, advertising, copyrighting, layout and design, plate making, and printing. Dist: Insight Media.

10-D-2. Broadcasting

1351 **60-SECOND SPOT.** 1974, 16mm, 25 min. Classic portrayal of how a big-budget television commercial is made. Film follows the production of a 7-Up ad from storyboard concept through preproduction planning and casting to filming on location. Dist: BU, IU, UC/B, UI, MN, UWY, UWa.

1352 **BEST TV COMMERCIALS: THE CLIO AWARDS,** Various years, 16mm (more recently available on videotape), 45 min. Winners in different categories plus the best foreign commercials. Some present Clio winners by categories, others by year. Dist: Clio Awards.

1353 **BROADCAST MEDIA.** 1994, 16 min. Advertising on broadcast television, cable television, and radio, and use of rating systems for television media buyers. Dist: Insight Media.

1354 **CLASSIC TELEVISION COMMERCIALS.** 1958, 3/4" or 1/2" cas., 120 min. Unusual collection from the C. N. Diamant Memorial library of 1948-1957 commercials arranged by product category. Dist: Brooklyn College.

1355 **MAKING TELEVISION: INSIDE CBS.** 1986, 3/4" or 1/2" cas., 45 min. CBS tape features interviews with Gene Jankowski and other top executives in the Broadcast Group. Programming, news, and sports are discussed in three separate segments. Dist: CBS.

1356 **SECRETS OF EFFECTIVE RADIO ADVERTISING.** 1990, 75 min. Three-part program offers a guide to radio messages that work and why. Dist: Films for the Humanities.

1357 **THE TECHNIQUE OF TELEVISION COMMERCIALS.** 1986, 23 min. Surveying 14 categories of television commercials, this explores how television advertisements differ. Features examples of each type including demonstration, testimonial, slice-of-life, customer interview, and product comparison, highlighting what makes each effective. Dist: Insight Media.

1358 **WORLD'S FUNNIEST COMMERCIALS.** 1989, 30 min. Some 41 funny television commercials including "Where's the Beef?" and "A Russian Fashion Show." Dist: Viewfinders.

10-D-3. Cable and Newer Services

1359 **CABLE: DELIVERING ON PROMISE.** 1986, 3/4" cas., 10 min. Growth of cable audiences and how advertisers can use cable to target their messages. Dist: Cabletelevision.

1360 **CABLE: SPECIAL FOR YOU.** 1984, 3/4" or 1/2" cas., 11 min. Cable industry growth, history, technological development, and programming. Dist: National Cable TV Assn.

10-E. Content

10-E-1. Print Media

1361 **CIVIC JOURNALISM.** 1995, 33 min. Two time-tested efforts that combine public participation with old-fashioned reporting: (1) journalists in Charlotte, NC, work to "Take Back Our Neighborhoods" from drug dealers and other troublemakers; and (2) a statewide "We the People" effort in

Wisconsin engages citizens in issues of health care, elections, and the state budget. The video is accompanied by a study guide with questions for classroom discussion. Dist: Commonwealth Film Labs.

10-E-2. Broadcast Entertainment

1362 **THE RADIO INTERVIEW.** 1990, 20 min. Top interviewers discuss how to conduct a radio interview: how to prepare questions, how to get the subject to relax, and how to deal with subjects who dominate the interview or evade questions. Dist: Insight Media.

1363 **REVIEWING TELEVISION.** 1991, 20 min. Television reviewer for the London *Evening Standard* describes how she goes about writing, the problems posed by different genres, and restrictions placed on her writing by the nature of her audience. Her review of a comedy show demonstrates the process of writing a review. Dist: Films for the Humanities.

1364 **SCRIPT TO SCREEN.** 1990, 39 min. Producing a sitcom is shown to be highly complex, involving hundreds of people, from production and design staff to gofers, and consuming hundreds of work hours for each half-hour episode. Dist: Films for the Humanities.

1365 **TALK, TALK, TALK: OPINION OR FACT?** 1995, 28 min. Examines the conditioning of information in our society and its impact upon forming public attitudes, the role of the media in polling, and the significance of the public's voice in shaping individual opinions. Among those featured are talk radio hosts. Dist: Films for the Humanities.

1366 **TALK, TALK, TALK: THE RISE OF THE TELEVISION TALK SHOW.** 1995, 28 min. Television talk shows and the public's fascination with them. Features Phil Donahue and Vicki Abt, a sociologist at Penn State University. Dist: Films for the Humanities.

1367 **TELEVISION: THE ENCHANTED MIRROR.** 1981, 16mm or 3/4" cas., 29 min. Interviews with TV directors, writers, a network executive, a behavioral scientist, an advertiser, and viewers explore television's role in creation of images and moral values. Dist: UW/M.

1368 **WHAT IS SITCOM?** 1993, 19 min. Defines sitcom form and essential ingredients of a good sitcom. Discusses writing, story structure, comic development, and the production process. Dist: First Light Video.

1369 **WRITING FOR TELEVISION.** 1988, 48 min. Four veteran TV writers discuss components of a successful television script: telling a story with pictures, creating a character, generating dialogue, collaborating and role playing, rewriting, adapting a novel, and developing a mini-series. Dist: Insight Media.

1370 **WRITING FOR RADIO.** 1988, 44 min. Radio writers talk about their craft, emphasizing radio's potential as a medium of the imagination. Covers characteristics of a good radio writer, working within limitations of time slots and budget, developing plot, and using music and sound effects. Dist: Insight Media.

10-E-3. Broadcast Journalism

1371 **BROADCAST NEWS: HOW IT WORKS.** 1989, 26 min. Provides a definition of news and examines basic aspects of a news story including significance, timeliness, proximity, conflict, and prominence. Discusses how a daily news program is produced and modern technologies that aid in news gathering, including satellite and microwave transmission. Dist: Insight Media.

1372 **CAREERS IN BROADCAST NEWS.** 1989, 30 min. Educational requirements for a career in broadcast news, types of jobs available, responsibilities of the producer, news director, editor, videographer, field producer, and anchor. Dist: Insight Media.

1373 **CRIME, VIOLENCE, AND TV NEWS.** 1993, 83 min. This *Nightline* special report probes how television covers crime and violence and explores accusations of bias and sensationalism. Dist: Insight Media.

1374 **THE DUPONT-COLUMBIA AWARDS.** 1994, four 30-min. tapes. Series of programs reviews the best TV journalism produced over previous decade. Produced by the Columbia University Graduate School of Journalism (0761), narrated by Peter Jennings: (1) Covering the World— Reports Without Borders; (2) Health and Medicine—On the Cutting Edge; (3) Investigative Reporting—the Righteous Lens; and (4) Ten Years of Social Struggles. Dist: Films for the Humanities.

1375 **ETHICAL CONSIDERATIONS IN JOURNALISM.** 1989, 23 min. Investigates some ethical issues a journalist faces when writing and reporting, presenting the recommendations of the Radio-Television News Directors Association and the Society of Professional Journalists. Dist: Insight Media.

1376 **EXPLORING BROADCAST TELEVISION.** 1995, 27 min. A behind-the-scenes look at a news broadcast, plus career opportunities in broadcast television. Producers, directors, news anchors, lighting directors, engineers, and sales managers explain what their jobs entail and discuss educational requirements. The video also explores how news is obtained, how stories are written and edited, how lighting and sound are used, how graphics are produced, and how weather information is obtained. Dist: Insight Media.

1377 **IMAGES OF CONFLICT: LEARNING FROM THE MEDIA COVERAGE OF THE GULF WAR.** 1992, 12 min. Learning curriculum resource with video, *Lines in the Sand.* Dist: Center for Media and Values.

1378 **INSIDE CBS NEWS.** 1990, 29 min. Mike Wallace, Dan Rather, Connie Chung, Leslie Stahl, Harry Smith, and Paula Zahn join Phil Donahue to take a behind-the-scenes look at TV journalism. Dist: Films for the Humanities.

1379 **INSIDE TELEVISION NEWS: ETHICS.** 1990, 10 min. Investigates conflict between right to privacy and the public's right to know, as well as conflict between breaking a story and importance of covering it thoroughly. Dist: Insight Media.

1380 **INSIDE TELEVISION NEWS: THE POWER OF TV NEWS.** 1990, 10 min. How news coverage is molded by tragedies and other dramatic stories, often at the expense of the airing of substantive issues. Dist: Insight Media.

1381 **INSIDE TELEVISION NEWS: WHAT IS NEWS?** 1989, 14 min. Defines parameters of what constitutes news, differentiates between broadcast and print news, discusses how opinion is distinguished from fact, and considers differences between local and national news orientations. Dist: Insight Media.

1382 **INTERVIEW TECHNIQUES.** 1992, 25 min. From putting the interviewee at ease to getting enough material to edit, this program demonstrates techniques needed to conduct a successful television news interview. Dist: Insight Media.

1383 **THE MAKING OF THE TELEVISION NEWS.** 1990, 40 min. Behind-the-scenes view of how television news is produced, following events on one day to show the complex process by which teams of reporters and cameramen relay news to the BBC Television Centre in London. Shows how newscasters and producers decide which stores to use and how to present them. Dist: Films for the Humanities.

1384 **NEWSROOM DECISION MAKERS.** 1991, three 40-min. tapes. Television news producers from small, medium, and large stations discuss their responsibilities, explaining their roles in determining the line-up, look and feel, and pacing of a program. Dist: Insight Media.

1385 **NEWSWOMEN.** 1987, 28 min. Jane Pauley, Maria Shriver, Leslie Stahl, Connie Chung, Joan Lunden, Rita Flynn, and Mary Alice Williams talk about their jobs. Dist: Films for the Humanities.

1386 **ONLY THE NEWS THAT FITS.** 1989, 28 min. Shorter version of *The World is Watching* *(see 1393)* with Peter Jennings. Dist: First Run/Icarus Films.

1387 **RADIO NEWS.** 1990, 38 min. Five seasoned journalists detail the production of radio news programs, discussing news sources, item selection and scripting, preparation for broadcast, presentation, telephone interviews, and filed reports. Dist: Insight Media.

1388 **REPORTING.** 1991, 20 min. Ideas about reporting, basic training, and some of the editorial constraints on writing. Dist: Films for the Humanities.

1389 **THE TELEVISION NEWSROOM: NEWS GATHERING.** 1991, 12 min. Shows interlocking roles performed by assignment editors, producers, news directors, reporters, writers, and photographers. Filmed at WHDH in Boston, the program illustrates how decisions are made regarding what stories to cover and how much time to allot to each. Dist: Insight Media.

1390 **THE TELEVISION NEWSROOM: NEWS PRODUCTION.** 1991, 10 min. How a director, technical director, floor manager, and assistant director work with tape editors, camera operators, audio mixers, and engineers to bring an evening newscast to the right length. Shows creation of graphics, production of a live remote, use of robot cameras, and color keying on the set. Dist: Insight Media.

1391 **TRIALS BY TELEVISION.** 1993, 60 min. Produced for Arts & Entertainment Network, this discusses legal cases that have been complicated by too much media attention. Dist: Viewfinders, Inc.

1392 **WAR REPORTERS.** Year not given, 52 min. British documentary covering the fears and ethical dilemmas that confront the war correspondent daily, the need to keep a record, the discredit that the coverage of World War I brought to journalism, the trauma of photography in Vietnam, the difficulty of convincing news organizations of the need to analyze, and reporting in Vietnam and Cambodia. Dist: Films for the Humanities.

1393 **THE WORLD IS WATCHING.** 1988, 59 min. Follows Peter Jennings and ABC News in gathering and reporting news on Central America. Analyzes how broadcast networks work (see 1386). Dist: First Run/Icarus Films.

10-E-4. Politics and Media

1394 **THE CLASSICS OF POLITICAL TV ADVERTISING.** 1986, 60 min. History and impact of political advertising on television from its inception in the 1950s to the present. Shows 75 of the most effective and innovative political ads in tracing evolution of profile spots, testimonials, and negative record spots. Dist: Insight Media.

1395 **THE GREAT HEALTH CARE DEBATE: THE ROLE OF THE MEDIA.** 1994, 60 min. Examines role of media and special interest groups in demise of national health care reform. More than $100 million was spent on public relations, advertising, lobbying, and lawyering, and nearly 100 public relations and lobbying firms worked to influence the outcome. These facts raise tough questions about how democracy works. Dist: Films for the Humanities.

1396 **GOVERNMENT AND THE MEDIA.** 1989, 30 min. Explores media and politics; how media both influence public opinion and reflect it: case studies of media's role in the Iranian hostage situation and the building of a shopping mall on the Manassas Civil War battlefield. Dist: Insight Media.

1397 **THE LIVING ROOM CAMPAIGN.** 1993, length not given. Produced for the Arts and Entertainment Network on the campaign commercials that won the White House from 1952-1988. Dist: Viewfinders.

1398 **THE MEDIA AND PRESIDENTIAL POLITICS.** 1988, 12 min. Going behind the scenes during one day of the 1988 presidential campaign, this program examines the media's role in influencing the outcome of an election. It considers what message the candidates tried to convey on that day, how the message was portrayed in the media, and what message voters actually received. Dist: Insight Media.

1399 **POLITICAL SPOTS.** 1982, 16 mm film, 30 min. Shows media spots from around the country representing both major parties and several levels of government. Accompanies two media consultants into their editing rooms as they explain the process of making vote-winning TV commercials. Dist: Time-Life Films.

1400 **POLITICS, PRIVACY AND THE PRESS.** 1990, 60 min. What conduct of public officials is relevant to the public's right to know? Panelists—including *Washington Post* publisher Katharine

Graham, TV reporters Peter Jennings and Mike Wallace, and politician-turned-broadcaster Geraldine Ferraro—debate. Dist: Insight Media.

1401 **A PUBLIC VOICE.** 1991, 58 min. Reveals ways in which the press and political leaders typically approach issues such as race, abortion, and international crises. Dist: Kettering.

1402 **THE POWER AND ROLE OF THE PRESS.** 1994, 56 min. Australian documentary questioning the power and role of journalists today, the inconsistent and fragmented system of ethics, accountability governing journalism and the market forces, tricks, pressures, and traps that are part of everyday news gathering and packaging. Exposing the pitfalls of checkbook journalism, it shows how even ethical journalists can become part of a media frenzy and points to the need for greater journalistic accountability. Dist: Films for the Humanities.

1403 **THE 30-SECOND PRESIDENT.** 1984, 55 min. Role of advertising in politics featuring an interview with the late Rosser Reeves, an advertising executive who worked on early political television advertising for Dwight D. Eisenhower. Bill Moyers also talks with media whiz Tony Schwartz about how electoral politics have changed with increased use of television advertising. *A Walk Through The 20th Century With Bill* Moyers Series. Dist: PBS Video.

10-E-5. Stereotyping

1404 **COLOR ADJUSTMENT.** 1991, 87 min. Analyzes past and present stereotyping of African-Americans in film and television. Dist: California Newsreel.

1405 **HOLLYWOOD'S FAVORITE HEAVY: BUSINESSMEN ON PRIME TIME TV.** 1987, 58 min. Interviews stars, producers and executives for behind-the-scenes look at how prime-time TV images are created, suggesting that programs create stereotypes of business people, Blacks, Hispanics, women, and police officers. Dist: HFH Film Library.

1406 **SEXUAL STEREOTYPES IN MEDIA: SUPERMAN AND THE BRIDE.** 1993, 20 min. Demonstrates how pervasive images are of man as Superman and woman as his slavish bride in film and TV, in the fiction on which the films are based, even in so-called documentaries. Dist: Films for the Humanities.

1407 **WOMEN SEEN ON TELEVISION.** 1991, 11 min. Aimed at stimulating discussion on media perpetuation of gender stereotypes, this presents condensed broadcast footage from two consecutive days to show how women are portrayed, how men dominate airtime and how women often appear either as sex objects or in matronly roles. Dist: Insight Media.

1408 **YELLOW TALE BLUES.** 1990 30 min. Documentary on ethnic stereotypes with clips from Hollywood movies that reveal nearly a century of disparaging representations of Asians. Dist: Insight Media.

10-F. Research and Audiences

10-F-1. Media Research

1409 **CAN YOU BELIEVE TV RATINGS?** 1992, 60 min. Examines the tricky business of finding out who's watching what and when. From the WGBH collection. Dist: Films for the Humanities.

1410 **GOOD-BYE GUESSWORK: HOW RESEARCH GUIDES TODAY'S ADVERTISERS.** 1995, 27 min. Demonstrates research techniques used to solve three marketing/advertising situations. Participants include Campbell Soup, Maidenform, and AT&T and their respective agencies. Dist: Advertising Educational Foundation.

10-F-2. Media Impact

1411 **ARE WE SCARING OURSELVES TO DEATH?** 1994, 50 min. ABC-TV news explores society's fears about crime and disease and questions whether the media's reporting of these issues exacerbates people's fears. Dist: Insight Media.

1412 **BEYOND BLAME: CHALLENGING VIOLENCE IN THE MEDIA.** 1994, 5 tapes). Provides a new approach for community education to change responses to media violence. Described as the first comprehensive package of multimedia resources for use throughout a community. Dist: Center for Media Literacy.

1413 **CHILDREN AND TELEVISION.** 1986, no length given. Bob Keeshan (Captain Kangaroo) details effects of television on children and offers suggestions for positive use. Dist: Cokesbury.

1414 **CREATING CRITICAL TV VIEWERS.** 1993, six 15-min. segments. Part of the *TV Alert* package: A Wake-Up Guide for Television Literacy with activities to help classes and groups analyze key issues of TV including: news, commercials, stereotyping, violence, sexuality, and who controls the remote control. Features a step-by-step leader's guide with lesson plans. Dist: Center for Media Literacy.

1415 **THE FUNCTIONS OF MASS COMMUNICATIONS.** 1989, 26 min. Examines how media select and interpret news events and serve as forum for new ideas, media involvement in entertainment, transmission of culture, and enforcement of societal norms. Dist: Insight Media.

1416 **THE GLITTER: SEX, DRUGS, AND THE MEDIA.** 1995, 23 min. Fast-paced documentary explores powerful effects of media on people's behavior. Advertising experts explain how they use imagery, distortion, and repetition to sell products. Dist: Insight Media.

1417 **HAROLD INNIS: PATTERNS IN COMMUNICATION.** 1993, 52 min. Profiles Canadian theoretician who criticized monopolization of communication technologies throughout history, from ancient to contemporary civilizations. Featuring interviews with his colleagues and family, as well as with commentators, the video explores the thematic continuity of his economic work and later research in communications. Dist: Insight Media.

1418 **THE IMPACT OF TABLOID TV.** 1995, 26 min. Guests addressing concerns about such programs on this specially adapted *Phil Donahue* show include Dan Rather, the general manger of a Minneapolis station that pioneered family-sensitive news, the editor-in-chief of a Santa Fe newspaper devoted entirely to good news, and the *Washington Post* media critic. Dist: Films for the Humanities.

1419 **THE IMPACT OF TELEVISION.** 1980, 16mm, 20 min. Without making a value judgment, this discusses influence of television on the lives of Americans. Dist: Encyclopedia Britannica.

1420 **THE KILLING SCREENS.** 1995, 37 min. Dr. George Gerbner suggests new ways of thinking about the negative effects of mass media on society. Dist: Media Education Foundation.

1421 **PRIME TIME VIOLENCE.** 1994, 50 min. Produced for the Arts and Entertainment Network, this asks the question, does violence on television cause violence in the home and on the streets? Dist: Viewfinders.

1422 **PSYCHOLOGY OF ADVERTISING.** 1991, two parts in 39 min. Examines psychological principles that underlie effective advertising campaigns. Part 1 (22 min.) focuses on print advertising, looking at critical advertising assumptions, social trends, consumer life cycles, and social trends. Part 2 (17 min.) explains how to design an advertisement to fit a target market and shows how to use survey results, comparative ads, and testimonials in an advertising program. Dist: Insight Media.

1423 **PSYCHO-SELL: ADVERTISING AND PERSUASION.** 1992, 25 min. Explores scientific techniques advertisers use to influence buying decisions. Describes how the opening two seconds of a TV ad are carefully designed to capture the attention of even the most disinterested viewer. Dist: Learning Seed.

1424 **MASS MEDIA.** 1991, 26 min. Analyzes mass media influence on individuals and society. Discusses how media reflect and influence culture, aid in setting a national agenda, establish cultural norms. Also covers effects of biased reporting and limitations of mass media. Dist: Insight Media.

1425 **THE PUBLIC MIND WITH BILL MOYERS.** 1994, four 60-min. programs. Series explores image and reality in America—how public opinion is formed through mingling of fact and fiction in a society saturated with images. Examines impact of a mass culture whose basic information comes from image-making, the media, public opinion polls, public relations, and propaganda. Dist: Films for the Humanities.

1426 **TEACH THE CHILDREN.** 1992, 56 min. Chronicles continuing tension between public service and TV as commercial enterprise. Explores values television communicates and role models it provides. Commentary by critics, scholars, and network executives, Includes user's guide with reports on recent research and legislation, a policy history, an action guide and resource list. Dist: Insight Media.

1427 **TELEVISION AND HUMAN BEHAVIOR.** 1992, 26 min. Explores the early warning signals of television addiction, the four types of TV viewers, televiolence, TV as a distorted mirror. Dist: The Learning Seed.

1428 **THE USES OF MEDIA.** 1989, 26 min. Impact of television on the way we see ourselves, exploring the subliminal messages television communicates and how they influence viewers. The program profiles Tony Schwartz, advertising and political media producer, and shows how he uses media to influence people. Dist: Films for the Humanities.

1429 **VIOLENCE AND SEX ON TV.** 1994, 28 min. Explores effects of watching TV violence on young people. Asks whether TV has altered their view of reality and whether there should be government restrictions. Dist: Films for the Humanities.

1430 **THE VIOLENCE FACTOR.** 1984, 58 min. Scientific studies and Congressional hearings explore relationships between real life violence and television, including both positive and negative effects and suggestions for improvement. Dist: Insight Media.

10-G. Regulation

1431 **COPYRIGHT.** 1986, Two 20-min. segments. Using dramatic vignettes, program poses 40 common questions about copyright laws, relating to video, film, computer software, print materials, and music. An attorney answers questions and explains the laws. Dist: Insight Media.

1432 **THE COST OF FREE SPEECH.** 1989, 26 min. Raises question of whether media have the right to be wrong sometimes, how much freedom of the press is too much, and whether and when freedom of the press can become the freedom to do harm. Dist: Films for the Humanities.

1433 **THE THEORIES OF THE PRESS.** 1991, 25 min. Covers five categories of world press systems—authoritarian, libertarian, totalitarian, socially responsible, and developmental—their intent and development, who owns and controls media, and who may use it. Dist: Insight Media.

1434 **LEGAL CONSIDERATIONS OF BROADCAST NEWS.** 1989, 23 min. Legal requirements with which broadcast stations must comply when covering the news. Defines legal terms and presents cases that have set precedents including libel, privacy, freedom of information, equal time for politicians, the Fairness Doctrine, and obscenity on television. Dist: Insight Media.

1435 **NATIONAL SECURITY AND FREEDOM OF THE PRESS.** 1984, 60 min. Examines whether the public has a right to know about issues of national security. James Schlesinger and Griffin Bell debate topic. Dist: Insight Media.

1436 **PUBLIC TRUST OR PRIVATE PROPERTY.** 1988, 56 min. Three in-depth case studies: (1) the merger mania sweeping television resulting in the sale of all three networks, (2) the 1963 WLBT case in Jackson, Mississippi, and (3) the Fairness Doctrine explained through the 1984 case of a station which ran ads favoring nuclear power plant construction. Dist: Insight Media.

10-H. International

1437 **CONSUMING HUNGER.** 1988, three 30-min. tapes. Three videos on how television covered world hunger. Dist: Maryknoll.

1438 **DISTRESS SIGNALS: AN INVESTIGATION OF GLOBAL TELEVISION.** 1991, no length given. Looks at how American television programs dominate airwaves around the world. Dist: National Film Board of Canada.

1439 **GLOBAL TELEVISION.** 1979, 3/4" cas., 29 min. From the *Fast Forward* series, this offers excerpts from news broadcasts for one single day from 20 different counties. Shows influence of varying technical standards and politics on the television medium. Dist: Ontario Educ. Comms. Auth.

1440 **WHOSE WORLD VIEW?** 1989, 20 min. Examines impact of North American culture on people and cultures of the Caribbean. Dist: Intermedia, National Council of Churches.

Appendix: Audiovisual Sources

A. Distributors

Advertising Educational Foundation, 666 Third Ave., New York 10017. 212-986-8060.

Brooklyn College, Dept. of Radio and Television, 304 Whitehead Hall, Brooklyn, NY 11210. 718-951-5555.

Cabletelevision Advertising Bureau, 767 Third Ave., New York 10017. 212-751-7770.

California Newsreel, 149 Ninth St. #420, San Francisco 94603. 415-621-6196.

Carousel Films, Inc., 1501 Broadway, New York 10036. 212-683-1660

CBS, Office of Communications, 51 W. 52nd St., New York 10019. 212-975-4321.

Center for Media and Values, 1962 S. Shenandoah St., Los Angeles 90034. 310-559-2944.

Center for Media Literacy, 1962 S. Shenandoah St., Los Angeles 90034. 800-226-9494.

Clio Awards, Film Coordinator, 336 E. 59th St., New York 10022. 212-593-1900.

Cokesbury, 201 8th Ave., Nashville, TN 37202. 615-749-6113.

Commonwealth Film Labs. 1500 Brook Rd. Richmond, VA 23220. 800-345-9556.

Contemporary Films/McGraw-Hill, 1221 Ave. of the Americas, New York 10020. 212-512-2342.

Encyclopedia Britannica Educ. Corp., 425 N. Michigan Ave., Chicago, IL 60611. 312-347-7000.

Films for the Humanities and Sciences, P.O. Box 2053, Princeton, NJ 08543. 800-257-5126; Fax 609-275-3767.

First Light Video Publishing, 8536 Venice Blvd., Los Angeles 90034. 800-777-1576.

First Run/Icarus Films, 153 Waverly Pl., New York 10014. 800- 876-1710.

HFH Film Library, 445 West Main St., Wyckoff, NJ 07481.

Insight Media, 2162 Broadway, New York 10024-6642. 800-233-9910; Fax 212-799-5309.

Intermedia, National Council of Churches, 475 Riverside Dr., Rm 670, New York 10115. 212-870-2376.

Kettering Foundation, 200 Commons Rd., Dayton, OH 45459-2799. 513-434-7300.

Learning Seed, 330 Telser Rd., Lake Zurich, IL, 60047. 800-634-4941.

Maryknoll World Productions, Media Relations, PO Box 308, Maryknoll, NY 10545. 800-227-8523.

Media Education Foundation, 26 Center St., Northampton, MA, 01060. 800-659-6882.

National Cable TV Assn., 1724 Massachusetts Ave., Washington 20036. 202-775-3550.

National Film Board of Canada, P.O. Box 1600, Station A, Montreal, QC H3C 3H5,. 416-973-9096.

Ontario Educational Communications Authority, P.O. Box 200, Station Q, Toronto, Ontario M4T 2T1. 416-463-6886.

Pacifica Foundation Tape Library, Pacifica Archives, 3729 Cahuenga Blvd. W., North Hollywood, CA 91604. 818-506-1077.

PBS Video, 1320 Braddock Pl., Alexandria, VA 22314. 800-344-3337.

Shelburne Films, 54545 S.R. 681, Reedsville, OH 45772. 614-378-6297; Fax 614-378-6191.

Time-Life Films, Time-Life Building, 1271 Ave. of the Americas, New York 10020.

Viewfinders, Inc.—Uncommon Video!!, P.O. Box 1665, Evanston, IL 60204-1655. 800-342-3342; Fax 847-869-1710.

B. Educational Distributors

(Listed alphabetically by code used in video listings.)

(ASU) Arizona State University, Audio-Visual Center, Tempe AZ 85281. 602-965-9011.

(BU) Boston University, Krasker Memorial Film/Video Library, 565 Commonwealth Ave., Boston 02215. 617-353-3272.

(Iowa) University of Iowa, Media Library, C-5 Seashore Hall, Iowa City, IA 52242. 319-353-5885.

(IU) Indiana University, Audio Visual Center, Bloomington, IN 47405-5901. 812-855-2103; 800-552-8620 (except IN); 800-942-0481 (IN only); Fax: 812-855-8404.

(Kent) Kent State University, Audio Visual Services, 330 University Library, Kent, OH 44242. 216-672-3456; 800-338-5718.

(MI) University of Michigan, Film and Video Library, 400 Fourth St, Ann Arbor, MI 48103. 313-764-5360; 800-999-0424.

(MN) University of Minnesota, University Film and Video, 1313 5th St, SE, Suite 108, Minneapolis, MN 55414. 612-627-4270; 800- 847-8251 (outside MN); 800-542-0013 (MN only).

(PST) The Pennsylvania State University, Audio Visual Services, Special Services Building, University Park, PA 16802. 814-865-6314, 800-826-0132; Fax: 814-863-2574.

(PSU) Portland State University, Continuing Education, Film and Video Library, 1633 S.W. Park, P.O. Box 1383, Portland, OR 97207. 503-725-4890; 800-547-8887 ext 4890 (except OR); 800-452-4909 ext 4890 (OR only).

(PUR) Purdue University, Film Library, Stewart Center, West Lafayette, IN 47907. 317-494-6742.

(SYU) Syracuse University, Film Rental Center, 1455 E. Colvin St., Syracuse, NY 13210. 315-479-6631; 800-223-2409 (except NY); 800- 345-6797 (NY only).

(UC/B) University of California at Berkeley, Extension Media Center, 2176 Shattuck Ave., Berkeley, CA 94704. 415-642-0460.

(UI) University of Illinois, University Film Center, 1325 South Oak St., Champaign, IL 61820. 217-333-1360; 800-367-3458.

(USF) University of South Florida, Film and Video Library, 4202 Fowler Ave., Tampa, FL 33620. 813-974-2874.

(UWa) University of Washington, Seattle Educational Media Services, 35D Kane Hall DG-10, Seattle, WA 98195. 206-543-9909.

(UW/M) University of Wisconsin-Madison, Bureau of Audio Visual Instruction, 1327 University Avenue, P.O. Box 2093, Madison, WI 53701-2983. 608-262-3902; 800-362-6888 (WI only); Fax: 608-262-7568.

(UWy) University of Wyoming, Audio Visual Services, Box 3273 University Station, Room 14 Knight Hall, Laramie, WY 82701. 307- 766-3184.

Appendix A: Library Guide for Mass Communication Subjects

Introduction

This guide is intended to aid in library shelf searches on most aspects of mass communications. Almost any library of significance has a guide or other materials on how to best utilize that particular library—and this appendix is intended to supplement such published material.

Although there are many schemes for organizing libraries, this guide covers the two most common systems used in academic and public libraries. Indeed, many libraries use both as they decided some years ago to switch from Dewey Decimal to Library of Congress but lacked funds and manpower to totally reclassify existing collections (this guide had its inception from the difficulties of using such a library). The two systems detailed here are:

> DEWEY DECIMAL SYSTEM (DDC): First compiled by Melvil Dewey as the earliest of "modern" systems of library organization, the Dewey system appeared in 1876 and is now in its 20th edition (1990) or revision. It consists of 10 classes each covering an area of knowledge. Most relevant to this book are 000–099 (general works), 300s (social science), 600s (technology), 700s (the arts), and 900s (history). It is still thought one of the best means of organizing a small-to-medium-sized library because it can expand with the collection, although it lacks the flexibility for a truly large collection. Citations in the Dewey system consist of numbers, often carried to two or three decimal places as human knowledge has expanded.
>
> LIBRARY OF CONGRESS SYSTEM (LC): As the largest library in the country and one of the biggest in the world, the Library of Congress needed a completely expandable classification scheme and so several people over many years devised the letter–number scheme now in use. It is a complicated and detailed system and is constantly under revision. Citations in the LC scheme always begin with one or two letters and then numbers (often up to four digits or more).

Most government documents are filed by a classification scheme established by the issuing agency (state, U.S. government, League of Nations, United Nations) and are ordered by agency rather than subject. Each library handles documents differently; some file them separately, others intermix them in the stacks using the overall library classification scheme. The same holds true for periodicals—some libraries file them in a single place by title; others separate them throughout the library by subject. Most libraries maintain reference collections, a cross-section of the full collection filed on a noncirculating basis, and the only copy of a mass communications reference may be there.

This guide is based on the published detailed descriptions of both Dewey and LC (the latter supplements amounting to over 50 volumes) rather than on books on the shelf because each library takes a certain amount of liberty with the schemes. Misclassification in mass communications is common, so check related categories.

Using This Guide

To be useful this guide incorporates a subject division that tends to overcompartmentalize what is increasingly an integrated whole. Cable and newer media usually appear in the sections labeled broadcasting (or television) on these lists. On the following pages are sections that roughly parallel the first eight chapters of this book:

1. General Reference—Bibliographies
2. History
3. Technology
4. Industry and Economics
5. Content
6. Research and Audiences
7. Policy and Regulation
8. International

The listing appears in two columns, with classification for the Dewey System on the left, and the newer and usually more complicated LC system on the right. Following each classification is a brief notation very roughly explaining what will be found there. General references come first, followed by print media and then electronic media. As much as possible, given the vagaries of both systems, similar material appears in both columns on the same line. Please understand, however, that these brief lists are suggestive rather than exhaustive.

1. General Reference—Bibliographies

LC is more complicated than Dewey in that the former has many classifications whereas the latter crowds all bibliographies under a single main number.

Dewey	**LC**
016.001 5 (communications)	Z 5630 (communications)
016.659 (same, all aspects)	
016.301 (advertising)	Z 7164.C81 (advertising)
016.070-79 (periodicals)	Z 6940-72 (journalism)
016.384 (broadcasting business)	Z 7711 (television in general)
016.632 (technical aspects)	Z 6455.R2 (broadcast law)
016.791 (broadcasting entertainment)	(broadcasting in general)
016.371-74 (broadcasting in education)	Z 5814 (broadcasting in education)

2. History

Historical references are both technical and general—and are thus often found in two places under either classification scheme.

Dewey	**LC**
655.1 (printing history)	Z 4-8 (printing history)
070.1 (periodicals in general)	PN 4801-4829 (periodicals in general)
070.9 (specific histories)	PN 4832 (magazines)
	PN 4855-4900 (U.S. periodicals)
384.5 (radio business history)	TK 5711-5739 (wireless telegraphy history)
621.384 (radio technical history)	TK 6545-6548 (radio technical history)
791.44 (radio entertainment history)	HE 8660-8678 (wireless industry history)
	HE 8690-8698 (radio broadcasting history)
	PN 1991.2 (radio programs)
384.55 (television business history)	TK 6600-6635 (television technical history)
621.388 (television technical history)	HE 8690-8698 (television broadcasting history)
791.45 (television entertainment history)	PN 1992.2 (television programs)
940.488 (propaganda in WWI)	D 619.3 (propaganda in WWI)
	D 639.P6-7 (Public opinion and propaganda)
940.548 (propaganda in WWII)	D 753.3 (propaganda in WWII)
	D 910.6-7 (same)

3. Technology

Although this overlaps somewhat with history, the intent here is to stress current state of the art. Check here and under history for full coverage.

Dewey	**LC**
655.2-3 (methods of printing)	Z 124-242 (printing)
655.7 (specific types, methods)	Z 250-276 (all aspects of printing)
534 (sound)	QC 221-146 (sound)
535 (optics)	QC 350-495 (optics)

384.5-384.54 (radio)	TK 5700-5865 (wireless telegraphy)
621.384 (radio technology)	TK 6540-6575 (radio technology)
690.523, 725.23 (antenna towers)	
384.55 (general television)	TK 6600-6653 (television technology)
621.388 (television technology)	TR 882 (television cameras)

4. Industry and Economics

Included are management, finance, advertising, industry organization, operations, personnel, and related topics.

Dewey	LC
659.1 (advertising)	HF 5801-5866 (advertising) HF 6178-81 (advertising agencies)
070.2-3 (periodicals)	HF 5871-6141 (newspapers and magazines) PN 4709-28 (periodical reference) PN 4826-99 (U.S. periodicals)
384.5 (radio industry)	HD 9999.R15 (radio industry) HE 8688-98 (radio broadcasting)
659.14 (radio advertising)	HF 6146.R3 (radio advertising)
384.55 (television industry)	HD 999.T37 (television industry) HE 8690-98 (television broadcasting)
659.143 (television advertising)	HE 6146.T42 (television advertising)

5. Content

Most aspects of journalism, entertainment, and educational content are included here.

Dewey	LC
070.4 (periodical content)	PN 4709-4731, 4751-4771 (general and reference sources for periodicals) PN 4825-4853 (same) PN 4877-4899 (specific titles in U.S. by area)
371.805 (school newspapers)	LH 1-3 (school and college papers and magazines) LB 1044.N4 (newspapers as teaching aids)
782.86-7 (broadcast music)	ML 176.5, 1527.5 (broadcast music) ML 52.8 (radio operas) ML 68 (radio and music; general) MT (music instruction by radio)
808.822 (broadcast drama anthologies, scripts)	PN 6072 (broadcasting scripts) PN 6120.R2 (radio plays)
374.26 (radio in adult education)	LB 1044.5 (radio in education) LC 6751-6779 (extension courses, instruction by radio)
070.46 (broadcast journalism)	PN 4784 (broadcast journalism)
254.3 (broadcast religion)	BV 656.3 (broadcast religion) BV 4301 (radio sermons)

789.91 (recordings content)
371.335 8 (television in education)
374.27 (television in adult education)

ML 155.5-157 (recordings content)
LB 1044.7 (television in education)
LC 6751-6779 (extension courses, television instruction)

6. Research and Audiences

Includes information about audiences and the influences of media on audiences (and vice versa).

Dewey

001.5 (general and theoretical works on communications)

301.183 (social psychology of audiences)
301.343 (cultural effects of media)
070.1 (periodical audiences, impact)

070.33 (circulation studies)

384.5 (broadcasting audiences)
791.44-45 (roles of broadcasting)

LC

P 85-92 (general works on human communication)
HM 251-299 (social psychology in general)

PN 4756-71 (relationship of periodicals to society)

HE 8694, 8697.A6 (radio audiences)
PN 1991.6 (radio's influence)
HQ 784 (broadcasting and children)
PN 1992.6 (television's influence)

7. Policy and Regulation

Includes all aspects of law, regulation, policy, and industry responsibility. Many of the classifications listed below will be found in law libraries.

Dewey

323.4 (freedom of speech)
016.243, 277, 364 (press law and defamation)
177.3 (press law)

340 & 655.6 (copyright)
338.8 and 658.04 (monopoly and anti-trust)
070.11 (press ethics)
659.193 4 (advertising law)
384 (general electronic media law)

LC

HE 8697.L5 (freedom of the press)
KF 4774-4775 (press law)
KF 2760 (press law)
PN 4731-4751 (press regulation and control)
Z 551-656 (copyright)
KF 1631-1663 (monopoly and anti-trust)
KF 5386 (business ethics)
HF 5817-19, 5833 (general advertising law)
KF 2761-64 (general electronic media law)
KF 2765 (FRC and FCC)
KF 2801-28 (radio broadcasting law)
KF 2840-49 (television law)
TK 215-255 (electronic media legislation)

8. International

References concern foreign (domestic media within a single country) and international (media reaching across the borders of more than one country) communications.

072-079 (periodicals by country)

PN 4701-05 (foreign periodicals)
PN 4714, 4736 (world news agencies)
PN 4748 (press law, by country)
PN 4793 (foreign media training and research)
PN 4830 (general foreign journalism)
PN 4900-5639 (media by country)

384.5 (radio by country)

HE 8665 (wireless in specific countries)
HE 8668-70 (international radio law)
HE 8692-93, 8699 (broadcasting abroad)
PN 1991.3 (foreign radio entertainment)

384.55 (television by country)

PN 1992.3 (foreign television entertainment)

301.152 3 (propaganda, general)
327.14 (propaganda and international relations)

HM 263 (propaganda, general)
JF 1525.P8 (government publicity and propaganda)
JK 468.R3 (government use of radio)
KF 2765.2 (wartime propaganda controls)

016.301 (propaganda bibliographies)

Z 7204.S67 (propaganda bibliographies)

Appendix B: Library of Congress Subject Headings for Mass Communication

Based on LIBRARY OF CONGRESS SUBJECT HEADINGS (Washington: Library of Congress, Cataloging Distribution Service, 1994), 4 vols., containing "subject headings created by catalogers and used at the Library of Congress since 1898" (p. iii). Users should also consult the "Introduction" (pp. vii–xvii) for additional guidance regarding subject headings for personal names, corporate bodies, jurisdictions, and other kinds of headings.

Advertising, Magazine
Advertising, Newspaper
African-Americans and mass media
African-Americans in mass media
African-Americans in television
African-Americans in the newspaper industry
Aged in mass media
Aged in television
Aggressiveness (psychology) in television
Alcoholism in mass media
Animals in mass media
Animals in television
Armed Forces and mass media
Art in television
Asian Americans and mass media
Asian Americans in television
Automobiles in mass media
AIDS (disease) in mass media
Black mass media
Black English in mass media
Black newspapers
Blacks and mass media
Blacks in mass media
Blacks in television
Broadcast advertising
Broadcast journalism
Broadcasters
Broadcasting
Broadcasting archives
Broadcasting policy
Broadcasting studios
Businessmen in television
Cable television
Cable television advertising
Canards (journalism)
Characters and characteristics in mass media
Children's mass media
Cities and towns in television
City planning and the press
Closed caption television
Collective bargaining—Effect of mass media on
Color television
Comedy programs
Copy-reading
Copyright—Newspaper articles
Copyright of periodicals
Crime in mass media
Crime in television
Criminal investigation in mass media
Dance in motion pictures, television
Death in mass media
Deviant behavior in mass media
Digital television
Direct broadcast satellite television
Documentary mass media
Drinking in television
Drugs and mass media
Editorials
Education in mass media
Electronic journals
Electronic news gathering
Electronic newsletters
Ethnic mass media
Family in mass media
Family in the press
Fantasy in mass media

Feature stories
Free circulation newspapers and periodicals
Gay newspapers
Gossip in mass media
Grazing (television)
Handicapped in television
Healers in mass media
Health in mass media
Heroes in mass media
High definition television
Hispanic Americans and mass media
Hispanic Americans in television
Home video systems
Homosexuality in television
Horror in mass media
Intelligence levels in mass media
Interactive television
Interviewing in journalism
Journalism
Journalism and education
Journalism and literature
Journalism and motion pictures
Journalism teachers
Journalism, Aeronautical
Journalism, Agricultural
Journalism, Anarchist
Journalism, Automotive
Journalism, College
Journalism, Commercial
Journalism, High school
Journalism, Labor
Journalism, Legal
Journalism, Pictorial
Journalism, Religious
Journalistic ethics
Journalists
Journalists as artists
Journalists in government
Journalists' spouses
Local government and the press
Local mass media
Magazine covers
Magazine design
Magazine format television programs
Magazine illustration
Maps in journalism
Mass media
Mass media and architecture
Mass media and art
Mass media and business
Mass media and children
Mass media and criminal justice
Mass media and culture
Mass media and educators
Mass media and ethnic relations
Mass media and language
Mass media and literature
Mass media and minorities
Mass media and music
Mass media and public opinion
Mass media and race relations
Mass media and sex
Mass media and social service
Mass media and sports
Mass media and technology
Mass media and teenagers
Mass media and the aged
Mass media and the arts
Mass media and the environment
Mass media and the family
Mass media and war
Mass media and women
Mass media and young adults
Mass media and youth
Mass media criticism
Mass media in agricultural extension work
Mass media in birth control
Mass media in community development
Mass media in counseling
Mass media in education
Mass media in health education
Mass media in literature
Mass media in religion
Mass media policy
Mass media surveys
Media literacy
Medicine in television
Melodrama in television
Men in mass media
Men in television
Men's magazines
Men's mass media
Mental illness in mass media
Mexican Americans and television
Minorities in broadcasting
Minorities in television
Monsters in mass media
Motion pictures and television
Murder in mass media
National characteristics in mass media
News agencies
Newsletters

Newspaper agents
Newspaper and periodical wholesalers
Newspaper buildings
Newspaper carriers
Newspaper cooperatives
Newspaper court reporting
Newspaper editors
Newspaper employees
Newspaper layout and typography
Newspaper libraries
Newspaper ownership
Newspaper presses
Newspaper publishing
Newspaper reading
Newspaper vendors
Newspapers
Newspapers—Circulation
Newspapers and children
Newspapers in education
Newspapers in literature
Newsprint
Newsprint industry
Nonverbal communication in television
Nuclear energy in television
Nuclear warfare in television
Nurses in television
Occupations in television
Offset printing of newspapers
Oppression (psychology) in mass media
Organizational behavior in television
Periodical editors
Periodical vendors
Periodicals
Periodicals, Publishing of
Photojournalism
Phototypesetting of newspapers
Physicians in television
Police and mass media
Police in mass media
Postal service—Second-class matter
Press
Press and propaganda
Press conferences
Press councils
Press law
Prison periodicals
Public access television
Public broadcasting
Race relations and the press
Radio
Radio actors and actresses
Radio adaptations
Radio addresses, debates
Radio advertising
Radio and baseball
Radio and children
Radio and literature
Radio and music
Radio and television towers
Radio and the arts
Radio announcing
Radio art
Radio audiences
Radio broadcasters
Radio broadcasting
Radio broadcasting of sports
Radio broadcasting policy
Radio comedies
Radio criticism
Radio engineers
Radio frequency
Radio frequency allocation
Radio frequency identification systems
Radio frequency modulation
Radio frequency modulation, Narrow-band
Radio in adult education
Radio in agriculture
Radio in community development
Radio in consumer education
Radio in education
Radio in espionage
Radio in health education
Radio in medicine
Radio in parapsychology
Radio in politics
Radio in propaganda
Radio in publicity
Radio in religion
Radio in rural development
Radio journalism
Radio journalists
Radio music
Radio plays
Radio producers and directors
Radio programming consultants
Radio programs
Radio programs for children
Radio programs for the blind
Radio programs, Musical
Radio programs, Public service
Radio public speaking
Radio scripts

Radio stations
Radio stations, African-American
Radio stations, Amateur
Radio supplies industry
Radio writers
Rape in mass media
Realism in television
Religious broadcasting
Reporters and reporting
Satellite master antenna television
Scholarly periodicals
Science news
Sensationalism in journalism
Sensationalism in television
Serial publications
Sex differences in mass media
Sex in mass media
Sex in television
Sex-oriented periodicals
Sex role in mass media
Sex role in television
Sexism in mass media
Social classes in mass media
Social problems in mass media
Sports journalism
Stereoscopic television
Stereotype (psychology) in mass media
Student newspapers and periodicals
Subscription television
Syndicates (journalism)
Tabloid newspapers
Television
Television actors and actresses
Television adaptations
Television advertising
Television advertising and children
Television advertising directors
Television and baseball
Television and children
Television and family
Television and history
Television and music
Television and politics
Television and reading
Television and sports
Television and teenagers
Television and the aged
Television and the arts
Television and women
Television and youth
Television announcing
Television archives
Television authorship
Television bandwidth compression
Television broadcasting
Television broadcasting of animated films
Television broadcasting of films
Television broadcasting of music
Television broadcasting of news
Television broadcasting of sports
Television broadcasting policy
Television camera operators
Television camera tubes
Television cameras
Television comedies
Television comedy writers
Television commercial films
Television criticism
Television dance parties
Television display systems
Television feature stories
Television film
Television film recording
Television frequency allocation
Television graphics
Television in adult education
Television in agriculture
Television in community development
Television in consumer education
Television in education
Television in medicine
Television in police work
Television in politics
Television in propaganda
Television in publicity
Television in religion
Television in rural development
Television in science
Television in social service
Television interactive toys
Television journalists
Television mini-series
Television music
Television news anchors
Television personalities
Television picture tubes
Television pilot programs
Television plays
Television producers and directors
Television program genres
Television program locations
Television programs

Television programs for children
Television programs for women
Television programs, Public service
Television projection
Television public speaking
Television relay systems
Television scripts
Television serials
Television specials
Television stage management
Television stations
Television supplies industry
Television transformers
Television viewers
Television weathercasters
Television weathercasting
Television writers
Teenagers in mass media
Terrorism and mass media
Terrorism in mass media
Terrorism in television
Trade unions and mass media
Underground newspapers
Villains in mass media
Violence in mass media
Violence in television
War in mass media
Weather broadcasting
West (U.S.) in mass media
Whites in television
Women and journalism
Women in mass media
Women in television
Women in the broadcasting industry
Women in the mass media industry
Women's mass media
Women's periodicals
Working class in television
Youth in mass media
Youth in television
Youths' periodicals
Zapping (Television)

Index by Author of Main Entries

(Note: Only main entries from chapters 1-9 and 10-A are included. Cross references and the video titles in chapter 10 are NOT included. Titles (in full CAPS) are given only for those works lacking specific authors. Please note that to save space, this index incorporates substantial abbreviation of standard words, although not with proper names)